MW00338430

THE SEED OF PROMISE:

THE SUFFERINGS AND GLORY OF THE MESSIAH

ESSAYS IN HONOR OF

 T. DESMOND ALEXANDER

GLOSSAHOUSE FESTSCHRIFT SERIES 3

GFS 3

THE SEED OF PROMISE:

THE SUFFERINGS AND GLORY OF THE MESSIAH

ESSAYS IN HONOR OF

T. DESMOND ALEXANDER

EDITORS

Paul R. Williamson   Rita F. Cefalu

GH

GlossaHouse
Wilmore, KY
www.glossahouse.com

The Seed of Promise: The Sufferings and Glory of the Messiah
Essays in Honor of T. Desmond Alexander

GlossaHouse, LLC
110 Callis Circle
Wilmore, KY 40309
www.GlossaHouse.com

The Seed of Promise: The Sufferings and Glory of the Messiah
Essays in Honor of T. Desmond Alexander
Edited by Paul R. Williamson and Rita F. Cefalu

> xxv, 396 pp. 25.4 cm. — (GlossaHouse Festschrift Series; Ref.)
> Includes bibliographical references.

> ISBN: 978-1-942697978 (paperback)
>   978-1-942697985 (hardback)
> Library of Congress Control Number: 2020934866

1. Bible. Old Testament—Criticism, interpretation, etc. 2. Bible. New Testament—Criticism, interpretation, etc. 3. Alexander, T. Desmond (Thomas Desmond). I. Title. II. The Seed of Promise: The Sufferings and Glory of the Messiah. III. GlossaHouse Festschrift Series, Volume 3. IV. Williamson, Paul R. V. Cefalu, Rita F. VI. Alexander, T. Desmond (Thomas Desmond).

The fonts used to create this work are available from: www.linguistsoftware.com/lgku.htm
Cover design by T. Michael W. Halcomb and Fredrick J. Long. Cover image has been adapted from the painting of Caravaggio, "Madonna and Child with St. Anne" (c. 1605-1606) in the public domain.
Text layout and interior book design by Paul R. Williamson, Rita F. Cefalu, and Fredrick J. Long
Author Index prepared by Paul R. Williamson
Subject index prepared by Andrew J. Coutras and Fredrick J. Long

GLOSSAHOUSE FESTSCHRIFT SERIES

The purpose and goal of the GlossaHouse Festschrift Series is to facilitate the creation and publication of innovative, affordable, and accessible scholarly resources—whether print or digital—that advance research in the areas of both ancient and modern texts and languages.

SERIES EDITORS

FREDRICK J. LONG   T. MICHAEL W. HALCOMB   CARL S. SWEATMAN

VOLUME EDITOR

FREDRICK J. LONG

CONTENTS

T. DESMOND ALEXANDER, AN APPRECIATION

Thomas Desmond Alexander (Desi to everybody!) was born (21 January 1955) and grew up in Clough, County Antrim, Northern Ireland. He attended Ballymena Academy from 1966–1973, then went to Queen's University, Belfast (QUB). He graduated with a BA (1st class Honors) in Semitic Studies in 1977. At that time the department was blessed by having not one but two conservative evangelical teachers of the highest standard: David F. Payne and Gordon J. Wenham (I use the word "blessed" advisedly—I studied under them too at the same time). Desi went on to do his PhD in the department, completing in 1983 with a thesis entitled "A Literary Analysis of the Abraham Narrative in Genesis." He was a Lecturer in QUB's Department of Semitic Studies from 1980 until 1999 when the department was closed (most small departments of Queen's were axed at that time). Desi moved into a role within the Presbyterian Church in Ireland, as Director of Christian Training, remaining in that role until 2009. The role had eventually involved some teaching for Union Theological College (the college of the Presbyterian Church in Ireland), and in 2009 Desi was appointed Senior Lecturer in Biblical Studies. He has remained in this position as well as the additional role of Director of Post Graduate Studies until the present time. For many years Union Theological College was a recognized college of the Institute of Theology of Queen's University, so, in addition to students for the ministry of the Presbyterian Church, it had a much larger number of students who were completing a module of theology as part of a Queen's University Arts degree. Desi has also served as Senior Adviser of Studies for the Institute of Theology.

Desi's impressive scholarly contribution includes all of the following:

1. Mentoring research students from all over the world and facilitating the dissemination of such research to an international audience.

2. Working on the copious task of producing a new Bible translation—the ESV—which has become widely used and respected.

3. Editing and writing material for two massive Study Bible projects, thus reaching a wide, non-specialist audience with the fruits of modern conservative scholarship. The notes in both the ESV and NIV Study Bibles are extensive; there is no comparison with my old Oxford Annotated Bible of 1962!

4. Editing theological dictionaries and authoring numerous articles for these and several other such collaborative projects.

5. Publishing influential articles in peer-reviewed academic journals—mostly in his area of expertise, the Pentateuch.

6. Writing exegetical commentaries on biblical books. His most significant one to date is his Apollos volume on Exodus—at over 700 pages, one of the more comprehensive commentaries on this key OT book. This volume reflects the following hallmarks of Desi's work:

    • A detailed interaction with extensive secondary literature. Desi does not shy away from interaction with the standard critical interpretation of the day, and he does so with clarity and winsomeness of spirit.[1]

    • A robust defense of the historical accuracy of the text, eschewing and critiquing the more speculative and skeptical approaches of most OT critics.

    • A consistent respect for the claims of the text (e.g., taking the statements "God spoke" seriously, in contrast to views which water these down by understanding them to describe how Israel's idea of God gradually developed over centuries).

    • A penetrating exposition of the book's relevance for the Christian today, within a framework of whole-Bible biblical theology. Indeed, this entire commentary, not just one section or sections of it, draws out

---

[1] E.g., *From Paradise to Promised Land* begins with 109 pages of discussion on pentateuchal criticism from Astruc to the present!

the relevance of Exodus for our own and every age: because it also reveals a God who passionately longs to draw people into a close and exclusive relationship with himself.

7. Being instrumental in the resurgence of Biblical Theology. By 1970 Biblical Theology, as both a movement and a subject in theological colleges, was in trouble. In the prevailing scholarship it appeared that there *was* no biblical theology—no consistent theology of the whole Bible—just the different theologies of different circles, books, and periods. Moreover, one of Biblical Theology's traditional emphases, word-study, had been dealt a severe blow by James Barr (especially in *The Semantics of Biblical Language*). However, since 1970, Biblical Theology has seen a resurgence among evangelicals, particularly those holding to a high view of Scripture, the belief in the underlying unity of Scripture, its historical accuracy, and a genuine respect for the integrity of the canonical text. Numerous studies have been conducted along these lines showing the important themes that run through the Bible—from Genesis to Revelation, demonstrating that there is a coherent story-line that enables us to read Scripture as an overarching metanarrative. Desi has been in the thick of this ongoing resurgence.

The fruit of this study has led him to an interesting and important conclusion; namely, that the glorious future God has in store for his people will be in the same space-time universe that we currently inhabit—on a radically healed earth, rather than life in a completely different dimension or order of existence.

In addition to Desi's scholarly contribution to the field of Biblical Theology, he has served as UK Chairman of the Tyndale Fellowship for Biblical and Theological Research (2009 to present) and on the editorial board of the *Tyndale Bulletin* and the *Journal for the Evangelical Study of the Old Testament*, while at the same time carrying a full teaching load for Union Theological College, research supervision for Queen's University Belfast, and external examining for other tertiary institutions. He has also served the church well in organizing and teaching courses for both ministers and lay church members. Desi has always been a warm, friendly and approachable teacher, carefully prepared, and able to deliver courses of the highest quality. Moreover, he has supervised numerous research students—I am particularly aware of a number of such students from far-reaching corners of the globe who have sought him out because of his scholarly ability and commitment to the work of the Gospel. I can speak from personal experience of the help he has been to such students!

Desi's contribution has not just been in the field of academics. As a committed churchman, he has served in a variety of demanding and time-consuming roles in his local congregation of Fitzroy Presbyterian Church (i.e., Elder, Sunday School Superintendent), within the structures of the denomination (e.g., decades serving on the Doctrine Committee of the Presbyterian Church in Ireland), and in para-church organizations (e.g., The Scripture Gift Mission, and Southern Theological Seminaries that seek to promote grassroots theological education in Southern Argentina).

Lastly, but certainly not leastly, Desi is first and foremost a committed Christian and family man. None of the above accomplishments could have been done apart from the enabling power of Christ, and the faithful and loving commitments of Desi's wife, Anne, and their two children Jane and David (who are now grown and married!).

I know I speak for the editors and contributors when I say that we hope that the studies which make up this volume will please him and in some small way impress on him how highly we regard him.

IAN HART, THD
Formerly, Trinity Theological College, Singapore (Emeritus)
Belfast

PREFACE

Both editors of this volume have studied under the supervision of Dr. T. Desmond (Desi) Alexander. As many know, the student-supervisor relationship is key to a successful outcome in the doctoral studies process. However, with Desi it has always been more than that. We can both attest to the enormous influence he has had in shaping our spiritual formation as biblical theologians. At least one of us can still hear his thoughtful editorial comments in our head while engaged in the process of writing, and for this, and many other things, we are eternally grateful.

First and foremost, Desi is a deeply devoted follower of Jesus Christ, a dedicated family man, and churchman. People who come in contact with him are immediately drawn to his Christ-like humility and genuine servant's heart. Although a biblical theologian of the highest caliber, Desi shies away from being in the limelight. He is not driven by ambition to make himself known, but rather, to bring all glory and honor to God alone. His scholarly body of work testifies to this, as do all who know him personally, some of whom have contributed to this present volume.

In speaking about Desi's scholarly work, we are reminded of a series of lectures given by J. Gresham Machen in 1932 to the Bible league in London on the importance of Christian scholarship in the service of the Gospel. In his first lecture, Machen dealt with the subject of evangelism, highlighting the importance of the proclamation of the full Gospel message in bringing people to the Christian faith. He pointed out that faith in Christ requires the knowledge of Christ, a knowledge which is found only in the Bible. This is one of the reasons why Christian biblical scholarship is so important. He writes, it is important "in order that we may tell the story of Jesus and his love straight and full and plain.... Ignorance is obscure; but scholarship brings order out of confusion, places things in their logical relationships, and makes the message shine forth clear." With respect to the apologetic task, Machen observed that "God has raised up, in the time of need, not only evangelists to appeal to the multitudes, but also

Christian scholars to meet the intellectual attack," and prays that the same may be true in our age "in God's good time and in his way. Sad indeed are the substitutes for the gospel of Christ."

Now, almost a century later, God continues to raise up new generations of Christian scholars, who, building on the shoulders of others, are committed to bring order out of confusion in addressing the intellectual challenges of their time. Desi's work in the area of biblical theology is one example of this; while engaging the critical scholarship of the present, at the same time he produces useful resources for the church. At the scholarly level, Desi has a subtle and gentlemanly way of undermining the critical perspective by using their own arguments and examples against them, and this he does with scholarly acumen and cogent reasoning. A good example of this is the first half of his book, *From Paradise to Promised Land*. On the practical level, Desi is passionate about helping people engage the Bible for all its worth. He wants us to understand how to read Scripture as a whole, so that we might better understand its *message* as *the* Word of God to *us*. One of his greatest contributions to this end is his canonical development of themes that connect the Old and New Testaments together. The tracing of biblical themes across the testaments enables readers to see the big picture, or what is often termed, the "biblical metanarrative." His popular-level books, such as *From Eden to the New Jerusalem* and *The City of God and the Goal of Creation*, exemplify this kind of thematic study, which has enriched and will continue to enrich the church for generations to come.

In honor of Desi's extensive contributions to biblical scholarship and the church, we wish to humbly present this volume to him in the year of his 65th birthday as a token of our deepest respect and appreciation. All of our contributors have expressed similar sentiments, some of which appear within the frame of their personal essays. We acknowledge and regret the fact that we were unable to include everyone who in some way has been assisted or influenced by Desi. The restraints of this volume would not allow for such an enterprise. Nevertheless, we trust that you will understand and join with us in this tribute to our colleague and friend.

This volume is structured (fittingly) around the biblical theological theme of the seed promise of Genesis 3:15 (the Protoevangelium), with its subtheme focused on the sufferings and glory of the Messiah. Accordingly, we have asked biblical scholars (both OT and NT), who have in some capacity benefited from Desi's scholarship and are known for their work in particular book(s) of the Bible and/or the discipline of biblical theology, to investigate these particular themes in light of their respective book(s). While all except the first chapter was written specifically for this volume, not every contribution coheres [or agrees] with the overarching biblical-theological emphases reflected in the book's title. Nevertheless, each contributor has given careful thought to the latter, and has sought to address it in some manner in the essay they have graciously worked at in the midst of very busy schedules. This Festschrift represents the fruit of their labors, for which we, as editors, are deeply appreciative, and is offered with gratitude to the glory of God and in honor of his faithful servant, Dr. Desi Alexander.

RITA F. CEFALU, PHD
Writer and Lecturer in Biblical and Theological Studies
San Diego (CA), USA

PAUL R. WILLIAMSON, PHD
Lecturer in Old Testament at Moore College
Sydney, Australia

PUBLICATIONS OF T. DESMOND ALEXANDER

Books Authored

From Paradise to the Promised Land: An Introduction to the Main Themes of the Pentateuch. Carlisle: Paternoster, 1995; Grand Rapids: Baker, 1998.

Abraham in the Negev: A Source-critical Investigation of Genesis 20:1–22:19. Carlisle: Paternoster, 1997.

Pentateuchal Criticism Today: A Guidebook for Beginners. Leicester: Religious and Theological Students Fellowship, 1998.

The Servant King: The Bible's Portrait of the Messiah. Leicester: Inter-Varsity Press, 1998; Vancouver: Regent College Publishing, 2003. (Translations in Danish, Khmer and Polish)

From Paradise to the Promised Land: An Introduction to the Pentateuch. Revised edition. Carlisle: Paternoster, 2002; Grand Rapids: Baker, 2002. (Translations in Chinese, Korean and Portuguese)

From Eden to the New Jerusalem. Nottingham: Inter-Varsity Press, 2008; Grand Rapids: Kregel, 2009. (Translations in Chinese and Korean)

Discovering Jesus: Four Gospels, One Person. Wheaton, IL: Crossway; Nottingham: Inter-Varsity Press, 2010.

From Paradise to the Promised Land: An Introduction to the Pentateuch. 3rd ed. Grand Rapids: Baker, 2012. (Chinese translation in preparation).

Exodus, Teach the Text. Grand Rapids: Baker, 2016.

Exodus, Apollos OT Commentary; Nottingham: Apollos, 2017. (Chinese translation in preparation)

The City of God and the Goal of Creation. Wheaton, IL: Crossway: 2018.

Books Co-authored

Obadiah, Jonah and Micah. Co-authored with D. W. Baker and B. K. Waltke. Tyndale Old Testament Commentaries; Leicester: Inter-Varsity Press, 1988. (Translations currently available in Chinese; Japanese; Portuguese; in preparation: Bulgarian)

Salvation to the Ends of the Earth: A Biblical Theology of Mission. 2nd ed. NSBT 53. Co-authored with A. Köstenberger. London: Apollos; Downers Grove, IL: InterVarsity Press, 2020.

Books Edited

The New Dictionary of Biblical Theology. Co-edited with B. S. Rosner. Leicester: Inter-Varsity Press, 2000. (Translations currently available in French, Korean and Portuguese; in preparation: Arabic, Chinese, Italian.)

Dictionary of the Old Testament: Pentateuch. Co-edited with D. W. Baker. Downers Grove, IL: InterVarsity Press, 2003. (Translation in Spanish and Korean.)

Heaven on Earth: The Temple in Biblical Theology. Co-edited with S. Gathercole. Carlisle: Paternoster; 2004.

Selected Chapters in Books and Journal Articles

"Genesis 22 and the Covenant of Circumcision," *JSOT* 25 (1983): 17–22.

"Jonah and Genre," *TynBul* 36 (1985): 35–59.

"Lot's Hospitality: A Clue to His Righteousness," *JBL* 104 (1985): 289–91.

"The Old Testament View of Life After Death," *Them* 11:2 (1986): 41–46.

"The Psalms and the Afterlife," *IBS* 9 (1987): 2–17.

"From Adam to Judah: the Significance of the Family Tree in Genesis," *EvQ* 61 (1989): 5–19.

"Justice and the Old Testament Laws," *Christian Arena* 42:3 (1989): 2–5.

"The Wife/Sister Incidents of Genesis: Oral Variants?" *IBS* 11 (1989): 2–22.

"The Hagar Traditions in Genesis xvi and xxi." Pages 131–48 in *Studies in the Pentateuch*. Edited by J. A. Emerton. VTSup 41. Leiden: Brill, 1990.

"Jonah – God's Missionary to Nineveh?: *Asian Challenge* 21 (1991): 12–13.

"Are the Wife/sister Incidents of Genesis Literary Compositional Variants?" *VT* 42 (1992): 145–53.

"Abraham Re-assessed Theologically: The Abraham Narrative and the New Testament Understanding of Justification by Faith." Pages 7–28 in *He Swore an Oath: Biblical Themes from Genesis 12–50*. Edited by R. S. Hess, P. E. Satterthwaite and G. J. Wenham. Cambridge: Tyndale House, 1993; 2nd ed. Carlisle: Paternoster; Grand Rapids: Baker, 1994.

"Genealogies, Seed and the Compositional Unity of Genesis," *TynBul* 44 (1993): 255–70.

"Exodus." Pages 92–120 in *New Bible Commentary: 21st Century Edition*. Edited by D. A. Carson, R. T. France, J. A. Motyer, and G. J. Wenham. Leicester: Inter-Varsity Press, 1994.

"Messianic Ideology in the Book of Genesis." Pages 19–39 in *The Lord's Anointed: Interpretation of Old Testament Messianic Texts*. Edited by P. E. Satterthwaite, R. S. Hess and G. J. Wenham. Carlisle: Paternoster; Grand Rapids: Baker, 1995, 19–39.

"The Passover Sacrifice." Pages 1–24 in *Sacrifice in the Bible*. Edited by R. T. Beckwith and M. Selman. Carlisle: Paternoster; Grand Rapids: Baker, 1995, 1–24.

Introductory articles on the books of "Job," "Psalms," "Proverbs," "Ecclesiastes" and "Lamentations." Pages 533–34, 571–72, 666–67, 701–702, 863 in *The NIV Thematic Study Bible*. Edited by Alister McGrath. London: Hodder and Stoughton, 1996.

Articles on 32 Hebrew words. Pages *1*: 475–76, 487, 484, 823, 834–36, 1133–34; 2:18–19, 287, 311–12, 323–24, 358, 592–93, 840, 857, 870–71, 1058; *3*:14–15, 226, 438–40, 446, 507–508, 577, 609, 825, 865–68, 1003, 1120, 1206, 1207; *4*:255–56, 287–88 in *New International Dictionary of Old Testament Theology and Exegesis*. Five volumes. Edited by W. VanGemeren. Grand Rapids: Zondervan, 1997.

"Further Observations on the Term 'Seed' in Genesis," *TynBul* 48 (1997): 363–67.

"A Religious Book in a Secular University." Pages 93–100 in *Making the Old Testament Live: From Curriculum to Classroom*. Edited by R. S. Hess and G. J. Wenham. Grand Rapids: Eerdmans, 1998.

"Royal Expectations in Genesis to Kings: Their Importance for Biblical Theology," *TynBul* 49 (1998): 191–212.

"The Composition of the Sinai Narrative in Exodus xix 1–xxiv 11," *VT* 49 (1999): 2–20.

Articles on "Genesis to Kings," "Abraham," "Seed." Pages 115–20, 367–72, 769–73 in *New Dictionary of Biblical Theology*. Edited by T. Desmond Alexander and Brian S. Rosner. Leicester: Inter-Varsity Press, 2000.

"Beyond Borders: The Wider Dimension of Land." Pages 35–50 in *The Land of Promise: Biblical, Theological and Contemporary Perspectives*. Edited by P. Johnston and P. Walker. Leicester: Apollos, 2000.

"The Old Testament view of life after death." Pages 120–33 in *Solid Ground: 25 Years of Evangelical Theology*. Edited by C. R. Trueman, T. J. Gray, C. L. Blomberg. Leicester: Apollos, 2000 (reprinted from *Them* 11.2 [1986]: 41–46).

"The Future of Christian Training: Some Personal Reflections." Pages 143–50 in *Seek the Welfare of the City*. Edited by M. Halteman and A. Thomson. Belfast: Centre for Contemporary Christianity in Ireland, 2002.

Articles on "Authorship of Pentateuch," "Book of the Covenant," "Promises, Divine."
Pages 61–72, 94–101, 655–62 in *Dictionary of the Old Testament: Pentateuch*.
Edited by T. Desmond Alexander and David W. Baker. Downers Grove, IL:
InterVarsity Press, 2003.

"Epilogue." Pages 267–78 in *Heaven on Earth*. Edited by T. Desmond Alexander and
Simon Gathercole. Carlisle: Paternoster, 2004.

"Dead Sea Scrolls." Pages 205–7 in *New Dictionary of Christian Apologetics*. Edited
by C. Campbell-Jack and G. J. McGrath. Leicester: Inter-Varsity Press, 2006.

"Old Testament Story." Pages 19–27 in *IVP Introduction to the Bible: Story, Themes
and Interpretation*. Edited by P. Johnston. Nottingham: Inter-Varsity Press,
2006.

"Pentateuch." Pages 49–67 in *IVP Introduction to the Bible: Story, Themes and
Interpretation*. Edited by P. Johnston. Nottingham: Inter-Varsity Press, 2006.

"The Regal Dimension of the תלדות־יעקב: Recovering the Literary Context of Genesis
37–50." Pages 196–212 in *Reading the Law: Studies in Honour of Gordon J.
Wenham*. Edited by J. G. McConville and K. Möller. Library of Hebrew
Bible/Old Testament Studies, 461; Edinburgh: T&T Clark, 2007.

"[Notes on] Genesis." Pages 1495–1580 in *English Standard Version Study Bible*.
Edited by W. Grudem et al. Wheaton, Illinois: Crossway, 2008.

Articles on "The Five Books," "The Tabernacle," and "The Calendar of Israel's
Worship." Pages 73–76, 132–37 in *The Eerdmans Companion to the Bible*.
Edited by G. D. Fee, R. L. Hubbard et al. Grand Rapids: Eerdmans, 2011.

"Biblical Theology." Pages 728–38 in *The Routledge Companion to Modern Christian
Thought*. Edited by J. Beilby and C. Meister. London: Routledge, 2013.

"Introduction to the Pentateuch." Pages 3–4 in *NIV Proclamation Bible: Correctly
Handling the Word of Truth*. Edited by Lee Gatiss. London: Hodder &
Stoughton, 2013.

Articles on "Introduction to the Old Testament," "Introduction to the Pentateuch," "[Notes on] Genesis 11:27–50:26," "Introduction to The Wisdom and Lyrical Books," "[Notes on] Jonah," "Law," "Temple," "The Kingdom of God," "The City of God." Pages 3–7, 10–16, 45–112, 896–900, 1795–99, 2649–53, 2662–63, 2666–67 in *NIV Zondervan Study Bible*. Edited by D. A. Carson et al. Grand Rapids: Zondervan, 2015.

"Pentateuch." Pages 677–84 in *T&T Clark Companion to Atonement*. Edited by A. J. Johnston. London: Bloomsbury T&T Clark, 2017.

CONTRIBUTORS

David A. Baker, Professor of Old Testament and Semitic Languages, Ashland Theological Seminary, Ashland (OH), USA.

Rita F. Cefalu, Writer and Lecturer in Biblical and Theological Studies, San Diego (CA), USA.

Sarah Dalrymple, Biblical Studies Tutor (Old Testament), Irish Baptist College, Northern Ireland.

Stephen G. Dempster, Professor of Religious Studies, Crandall University, Moncton (New Brunswick), Canada.

Graeme Goldsworthy, Retired; formerly Lecturer in Old Testament and Biblical Theology, Moore College, Sydney, Australia.

James A. Hamilton Jr., Professor of Biblical Theology, Southern Baptist Theological Seminary, Louisville (KY), USA.

Ian Hart, Emeritus lecturer, Trinity Theological College, Singapore.

Philip S. Johnston, Senior Tutor at Hughes Hall and Affiliated Lecturer in Old Testament, University of Cambridge, England.

Andreas J. Köstenberger, Research Professor of New Testament and Biblical Theology and Director of the Center for Biblical Studies at Midwestern Baptist Theological Seminary, Kansas City (MO), USA.

J. Gordon McConville, Professor of Old Testament Theology, University of Gloucestershire, England.

James McKeown, Adjunct Lecturer in Old Testament and Hebrew at Union Theological College, Belfast; Formerly Vice-Principal, Belfast Bible College, Northern Ireland.

J. Gary Millar, Principal, Queensland Theological College, Brisbane, Australia.

Stephen Motyer, Retired, formerly Lecturer in New Testament, London School of Theology, England.

Dane C. Ortlund, Chief Publishing Officer and Bible Publisher, Crossway Publishing, Wheaton (IL), USA.

John N. Oswalt, Distinguished Professor of Old Testament, Asbury Theological Seminary, Wilmore (KY), USA.

Anthony R. Petterson, Lecturer in Old Testament, Morling Theological College, Sydney, Australia.

Brian S. Rosner, Principal, Ridley College, Melbourne, Australia.

Paul R. Williamson, Lecturer in Old Testament, Moore College, Sydney, Australia.

ABBREVIATIONS

The abbreviations used throughout this work follow the standard forms, established by and found in the SBL Handbook of Style, 2nd edition (2014). Those employed but not appearing in the Handbook are listed here (according to abbreviation):

BETS   *Bulletin of the Evangelical Theological Society*

BTCP   Biblical Theology for Christian Proclamation

BTNT   Biblical Theology of the New Testament Series

DOT:HB   *Dictionary of the Old Testament: Historical Books*. Edited by B. T. Arnold and H. G. M. Williamson. Downers Grove, IL: InterVarsity Press, 2005.

DOT:P   *Dictionary of the Old Testament: Pentateuch*. Edited by T. Desmond Alexander and David W. Baker. Downers Grove, IL: InterVarsity Press, 2003.

DOT:Pr   *Dictionary of the Old Testament: Prophets*. Edited by M. J. Boda and J. G. McConville. Downers Grove, IL: InterVarsity Press, 2012.

DOT:WPW   *Dictionary of the Old Testament: Wisdom, Poetry and Writings*. Edited by T. Longman III and P. Enns. Downers Grove, IL: InterVarsity Press, 2008.

EHLL   *Encyclopedia of Hebrew Language and Linguistics,* 4 volumes. Edited by Geoffrey Khan et al. Leiden: Brill, 2013.

IBS   *Irish Biblical Studies*

IVPNTC   IVP New Testament Commentary Series

JPS   Jewish Publication Society

NDBT   *New Dictionary of Biblical Theology*. Edited by T. Desmond Alexander and Brian S. Rosner. Leicester: Inter-Varsity Press; Downers Grove, IL: InterVarsity Press, 2000.

NIV   New International Version (2011, unless indicated otherwise)

NIVAC   New International Version Application Commentary

OEBT	*Oxford Encyclopedia of the Bible and Theology*. Edited by S. E. Balentine. New York: OUP, 2015.
PilNTC	Pillar New Testament Commentary
SBJT	*Southern Baptist Journal of Theology*
SGBC	The Story of God Bible Commentary
SSBT	Short Studies in Biblical Theology
THOTC	Two Horizons Old Testament Commentary
TSF	Theological Students Fellowship
ZECOT	Zondervan Exegetical Commentary on the Old Testament

THE SEED OF PROMISE:

SUFFERINGS AND GLORY OF THE MESSIAH

ESSAYS IN HONOR OF

 T. DESMOND ALEXANDER

THE SKULL CRUSHING SEED OF THE WOMAN: INNER-BIBLICAL INTERPRETATION OF GENESIS 3:15

—James M. Hamilton Jr.

1. Introduction[1]

The use of the OT in the NT has been much discussed, with some concluding that, to put it simply, the authors of the NT wrongly interpreted the OT.[2] This being the case, their exegesis cannot be legitimately imitated today. Those who come to this conclusion are sometimes mystified as to how the authors of the NT could possibly see a reference to the Messiah in texts the NT applies to him, at points even arguing that particular applications of OT texts to Jesus in the NT do not actually refer to him at all.[3] Another argument against the imitation of apostolic use of the OT is that their

---

[1] I am so thankful to have this opportunity to honor T. Desmond Alexander. His writings, particularly the "seed" essays and *From Paradise to the Promised Land*, influenced me profoundly at an early stage. In fact, when I first began to explore biblical theology, Tom Schreiner recommended that I read Desi's work. Doing so was formative, as can be seen from this essay and virtually everything I have written. I am thankful to have fellowshipped with Desi in person at meetings of the Tyndale Fellowship and have been blessed by his pastoral concern for my wife and children. What a privilege to serve the Lord in common cause. I also wish to thank the editor of *The Southern Baptist Journal of Theology* (*SBJT*), Dr. Stephen Wellum, for granting permission for this essay, which originally appeared in *SBJT* 10.2 (2006): 30–54, to appear here.

[2] Extensive bibliography could be cited. See esp. Greg Beale, "Did Jesus and His Followers Preach the Right Doctrine from the Wrong Texts?," *Them* 14 (1989), 89–96, and the volume of collected essays he edited in *The Right Doctrine from the Wrong Texts?* (Grand Rapids: Baker, 1994).

[3] Commenting on Peter's citation of Deut 18:15–19 in Acts 3:22–23, Daniel Block writes, "New Testament scholars generally adduce Peter's citation as evidence for a messianic interpretation of Deut. 18:15, but this interpretation of Peter's citation is less certain than it appears." Block continues to parry the thrust of Acts, writing, "We should be equally cautious about finding a reference to a prophetic messiah in Stephen's citation of Deut. 18:15 in Acts 7:37." Perhaps recognizing the implausibility of his position, Block asks, "Even if Peter and/or Stephen viewed Jesus as a messianic prophet 'like Moses,' are we thereby authorized to read their use of Deut. 18:15 back into the original context?" Block then counters the rise of Messianism in the intertestamental period and the common

hermeneutical methods are not valid today.[4] This means that while an understanding of the hermeneutical milieu can help us make sense of what the authors of the NT were doing, it does not validate their method for us. Others would agree with Moisés Silva's objection to this conclusion: "If we refuse to pattern our exegesis after that of the apostles, we are in practice denying the authoritative character of their scriptural interpretation—and to do so is to strike at the very heart of the Christian faith."[5]

It seems to me that certain presuppositional starting points have the potential to ameliorate every intellectual difficulty with the way that the NT interprets the OT, regardless of the hermeneutical tools employed. I have in mind one thing in particular, namely, the hypothesis that from start to finish, the OT is a messianic document, written from a messianic perspective, to sustain a messianic hope.[6] Adopting this

---

suggestion that Deut 34:10–12 points to an expectation for a unique prophet like Moses ("My Servant David: Ancient Israel's Vision of the Messiah," in *Israel's Messiah in the Bible and the Dead Sea Scrolls*, ed. Richard S. Hess and M. Daniel Carroll R. [Grand Rapids: Baker, 2003], 29, 30, 31). Both respondents to Block's essay, J. Daniel Hays and M. Daniel Carroll R., effectively refute Block's attempt to reinvent the meaning of Deut 18 in Acts 3 and 7 (ibid., 61–62, 74–75).

[4] See Richard N. Longenecker, *Biblical Exegesis in the Apostolic Period*, 2nd ed. (Grand Rapids: Eerdmans, 1999), xxxviii: "I do not, however, think it my business to try to reproduce the exegetical procedures and practices of the New Testament writers, particularly when they engage in what I define as 'midrash,' 'pesher,' or 'allegorical' exegesis." Longenecker also interacts with Richard B. Hays' argument that apostolic exegesis should be imitated (xxxiv–xxxix).

[5] Moisés Silva, "The New Testament Use of the Old Testament: Text Form and Authority," in *Scripture and Truth*, ed. D. A. Carson and John D. Woodbridge (Grand Rapids: Zondervan, 1983), 164.

[6] Two caveats here. First, I wish to make plain the inductive steps that led to this hypothesis. We inductively observe that there is much messianic speculation in Second Temple Judaism (both in the NT and the intertestamental lit.). We add to this the observation that this speculation is anchored in the OT. We then set aside the possibility that ancient people were stupid, which seems to be an implicit assumption of a good deal of modern scholarship, and we seek a hypothesis that explains the data. Since the authors of these texts are presumably seeking to be persuasive to their contemporaries (see, e.g., John 20:31), it seems to me unlikely that their contemporaries would grant the imposition of new meanings onto these texts. One hypothesis that explains the fact that "Early Christians, rabbinic sources, and the sectarians at Qumran cite the same biblical texts in their portrayals of the royal messiah" (J. J. M. Roberts, "The Old Testament's Contribution to Messianic Expectations," in *The Messiah*, ed. J. H. Charlesworth [Minneapolis: Fortress, 1992], 41 n.2) is that the OT is a messianic document, written from a messianic perspective, to sustain a messianic hope. This would mean that these disparate groups are not *imposing* a messianic interpretation on these texts but rightly interpreting them. This is not the only available hypothesis, but it seems to me to be the most convincing. I agree with John Sailhamer, who writes, "I believe the messianic thrust of the OT was the *whole* reason the books of the Hebrew

perspective might go a long way toward explaining why the NT seems to regard the whole of the OT as pointing to and being fulfilled in the one it presents as the Messiah, Jesus of Nazareth. Further, it might be in line with texts such as Luke 24:27, 44–45, which could indicate that Jesus read the OT in precisely this way (cf. also Matt 5:17 and John 5:46).[7] If Jesus and the authors of the NT did read the OT in this way, they were apparently not alone. Craig Evans notes, "The saying of Rabbi Yohanan, though uttered in the post-NT era, probably reflects what was assumed by many in the first century: 'Every prophet prophesied only for the days of the Messiah' (*b. Ber.* 34b)."[8]

The only way to verify such a hypothesis is to test it against the data. The evidence is, of course, disputed. I am not suggesting that we should look for "Jesus under every rock" or in every detail of the description of the temple, a straw man which

---

Bible were written. In other words, the Hebrew Bible was not written as the national literature of Israel. It probably also was not written to the nation of Israel as such. It was rather written, in my opinion, as the expression of the deep-seated messianic hope of a small group of faithful prophets and their followers" ("The Messiah and the Hebrew Bible," *JETS* 44 [2001]: 23). The variations in messianic expectation show that the developing portrait of the coming Messiah was not crystal clear, but the pervasive expectation supports the hypothesis.

My second caveat is that though I am calling this "messianic," I do recognize that this term seems not to receive a technical meaning until the Second Temple period. But as Rose has written, "It is a matter of confusing language and thought … to conclude on this basis that one can speak of messianic expectations properly only after a particular word was used to refer to the person at the center of these expectations" (W. H. Rose, "Messiah," in *DOT:P*, 566). Cf. also John J. Collins, *The Scepter and the Star*, ABRL (New York: Doubleday, 1995), 11–12. For an essay that is almost entirely at odds with the claims of the present study, see J. H. Charlesworth, "From Messianology to Christology: Problems and Prospects," in *The Messiah*, ed. J. H. Charlesworth (Minneapolis: Fortress, 1992), 3–35.

[7] See E. Earle Ellis, "Jesus' Use of the Old Testament and the Genesis of New Testament Theology," *BBR* 3 (1993): 59–75. See too Roy A. Rosenberg, "The Slain Messiah in the Old Testament," *ZAW* 99 (1987): 259–61. Cf. also Collins, *Scepter and the Star*, 20, 22–28; and Maurice Casey, "Christology and the Legitimating Use of the Old Testament in the New Testament," in *The Old Testament in the New Testament*, ed. Steve Moyise, JSNTSup 189 (Sheffield: Sheffield Academic, 2000), 63–64.

[8] Craig Evans, "The Old Testament in the New," in *The Face of New Testament Studies*, ed. Scot McKnight and Grant R. Osborne (Grand Rapids: Baker, 2004), 136. Evans describes this kind of interpretation as typological resignification that reinterprets Scripture in light of what God has accomplished/fulfilled in the Messiah (cf. ibid., 137). But if the OT was indeed *written from a messianic perspective*, that is, if the perspective attributed to Jesus and Rabbi Yohanan (and Peter, Acts 3:24) is the correct one, then no *resignification* and *reinterpretation* has taken place. Rather, the NT can be understood as claiming that the original messianic meaning of the OT texts has been fulfilled in Jesus.

at times seems to be the only thing conceivable to certain "OT only"[9] interpreters when they hear the kind of suggestion I am making. We need not abandon the discipline of looking carefully at what the texts actually say to see the OT as a messianic document.[10] Nor is the objection that there is proportionally very little about the messiah in the OT necessarily devastating to this proposal, for it is always possible that a certain feature is not everywhere named in the text because it is everywhere assumed.[11] Still, such suggestions are greatly strengthened by evidence.

A full-scale demonstration of the hypothesis is beyond the scope of this chapter, so this study will examine one foundational element of the theory. If, for instance, we were to argue that the Messianism of the OT is introduced in Gen 3:15, such an assertion would be more plausible if the influence of this text could be shown through the rest of the OT and into the New. Here I will put on these lenses—lenses that assume that the OT is a messianic document, written from a messianic perspective, to sustain a messianic hope—and point to the ways that Gen 3:15 is interpreted in the Old and New Testaments.[12]

---

[9] Cf. Daniel Hays' response to Block, "Sometimes he seems to be pushing for an 'Old Testament only' concept of Messianism, one in which it is not valid to use New Testament or even intertestamental interpretation of Old Testament texts" ("If He Looks Like a Prophet and Talks Like a Prophet, Then He Must Be … A Response to Daniel I. Block," in *Israel's Messiah*, 59).

[10] I have tried to partially flesh out what I have in mind in my essay, "The Messianic Music of the Song of Songs: A Non-Allegorical Interpretation," *WTJ* 68 (2006): 331–45. Cf. also Nicholas Perrin, "Messianism in the Narrative Frame of Ecclesiastes?," *RB* 108 (2001): 37–60.

[11] As Walther Eichrodt argued regarding the concept of the covenant in the OT (*Theology of the Old Testament*, 2 vols., trans. J. A. Baker, OTL [Philadelphia: Westminster, 1961, 1967], 1:13–14). E. P. Sanders argued the same for extrabiblical Jewish lit. (*Paul and Palestinian Judaism* [Minneapolis: Fortress, 1977], 420–21).

[12] There is extrabiblical evidence for what I am arguing, but space considerations permit only pointing to it in the footnotes. Further, this is a study in inner-*biblical* interpretation in the service of biblical theology, and I agree with Scobie and others that biblical theology is to be based on the canon of Scripture. I am in general methodological agreement with recent arguments for "canonical biblical theology." For several expositions of this method, see B. S. Childs, *Biblical Theology: Old and New Testaments* (Minneapolis: Fortress, 1992), 70–79, 91–94; Stephen G. Dempster, *Dominion and Dynasty: A Theology of the Hebrew Bible*, NSBT 15 (Downers Grove, IL: InterVarsity, 2003), 15–43; Paul R. House, *Old Testament Theology* (Downers Grove, IL: InterVarsity, 1998), 54–57; John H. Sailhamer, *Introduction to Old Testament Theology* (Grand Rapids: Zondervan, 1993), 197–252; and Charles H. H. Scobie, *The Ways of Our God: An Approach to Biblical Theology* (Grand Rapids:

2. The Context of Genesis 3:15

God's first act of judgment in the Bible is accompanied by his first promise of salvation, and the salvation will come through the judgment. As the serpent is cursed, he is told that he will proceed on his belly and that he will eat dust (Gen 3:14). Further, enmity is placed between himself and the woman, and between his seed and the seed of the woman. This enmity will issue in the seed of the woman crushing the head of the serpent (3:15). This salvation from the serpent's sneaky ways (3:1) is a salvation that comes through judgment. Obviously, judgment falls on the serpent as his head is crushed, but there is also judgment on the seed of the woman as the serpent crushes his heel. There is judgment for the woman, too, for the bearing of the saving seed will be painful (3:16a); and, the relations between male and female, which are necessary for the seed to be born, will be strained (3:16b). Judgment falls on the man as well, as the ground from whose fruit the seed will be fed is cursed, and in painful, sweaty toil he will labor until he eventually returns to the dust (3:17–19).

In the short span of Gen 3:14–19, the God of the Bible is shown to be both just and merciful. The scene puts God on display as one who upholds righteousness and yet offers hope to guilty human rebels. He is a God of justice and so renders just condemnation for the transgressors. Yet he is also a God of mercy, and so he makes

---

Eerdmans, 2003), 49–76. I recognize that there are variations among these authors, but they all agree on working with the final form of the canon rather than with a critically reconstructed account of what happened. I am going to deal with the canonical form of the OT text, and I am going to study the texts on the basis of the story that the text tells. I will not engage the reconstructed story told by critical scholarship. There are many ways to justify this kind of decision, but I will simply quote the following judicious words: "We are Old Testament scholars, then, who … operate out of the context of Christian theism; and it is we who are writing this book, not some other people possessing a different set of core beliefs and convictions…. We have no interest in simultaneously being metaphysical theists and methodological non-theists…. Indeed, if we were never able to read books with profit unless we shared the presuppositions of their authors, we should read very few books with profit at all" (Iain Provan, V. Phillips Long, and Tremper Longman III, *A Biblical History of Israel* [Louisville: Westminster John Knox, 2003], 102–3, the section whence these words come is attributed in the preface to Provan). See too V. Philips Long, "Renewing Conversations: Doing Scholarship in an Age of Skepticism, Accommodation, and Specialization," *BBR* 13 (2003): 234 n.30: "what we do write should be compatible with our core convictions."

plain that his image bearers will triumph over the wicked snake.[13]

My aim in the present study is to highlight the theme of the head crushing seed of the woman in the Bible.[14] Even if at many points my interpretation of the data is disputed, this study will nevertheless contribute a catalog of the intertextual use of the theme of the smashing of the skulls of the enemies of God.[15]

In order to understand the Bible's presentation of the victory of the seed of the woman over the seed of the serpent, we must first discuss the tension between the one and the many in the Bible. Is the seed of the woman to be understood as a particular

---

[13] Thus, this passage fits with the thesis of my essay, "The Center of Biblical Theology: The Glory of God in Salvation through Judgment?," *TynBul* 57 (2006): 57–84. As a side note, though I think that the OT is a messianic document, written from a messianic perspective, to sustain a messianic hope, I do not think that Messianism/Christology is the center of biblical theology. Rather, I see the center of biblical theology as the manifestation of the glory of God in salvation through judgment. The Messiah is, of course, central to the manifestation of the glory of God in salvation through judgment. If it did not make the phrase too long, I might argue that the center of biblical theology is the glory of God in salvation through judgment *accomplished by the Messiah*. But this is too cumbersome, and certain texts show that the glory of God is primary, central, and ultimate (e.g., Num 14:21; Ps 19:1; Isa 6:4; John 17:1; Rom 11:33–36; 1 Cor 15:24, 28; Eph 1:6, 12, 14; Phil 2:11; Col 3:17; Heb 1:3; 1 Pet 4:11; Jude 1:25). Many of these texts give God glory *through* Jesus Christ.

[14] My attention was drawn to this theme by the allusions made to it in two short articles: Thomas R. Schreiner, "Editorial: Foundations for Faith," *SBJT* 5.3 (2001): 2–3, and Walter Wifall, "Gen 3:15—A Protevangelium?," *CBQ* 36 (1974): 361–65. I wish to thank my friend Jason S. DeRouchie for alerting me to Wifall's piece.

[15] There are different ways to account for the existence of the interpretations of Gen 3:15 in the rest of the Bible that I will argue for here. For instance, T. Desmond Alexander argues that the whole of Genesis–Kings was brought together at one time ("Authorship of the Pentateuch," in *DOT:P*, 70), so he could explain these phenomena as the work of the redactor of this literary unit. John Sailhamer might attribute such things to the "canonicler" (*Introduction to the Old Testament Theology*, 240). As another type of example, Lyle Eslinger has criticized Michael Fishbane for the fact that "Fishbane's categorical analysis is already premised on the diachronic assumptions of historical-critical literary history" ("Inner-Biblical Exegesis and Inner-Biblical Allusion: The Question of Category," *VT* 42 [1992]: 52). Eslinger proposes "a self-consciously literary analysis of the textual interconnections in biblical literature. In it, we continue to use the indications of sequence that historical-critical scholarship has (improperly) relied on, but in full awareness of this reliance and without the conceit that we use a 'scientific' historical framework independent of it" (56). Eslinger seems to be saying that historical-critical conclusions are unscientific and unreliable but should be assumed anyway. If this can be suggested, there should be no objection to my decision to take the biblical texts at face value, bypassing the tortuous tangles of the purported redactional histories of the texts. I have my opinions on these matters, but they are not the issue here. I am in agreement with Scobie's repeated assertion that biblical theology "focuses on the final form of the text" (*Ways of Our God*, 49, 130, 144, 166, *et passim*).

person, or is it to be understood as a group of people? I will suggest that the texts indicate that the answer is "yes" to both questions. The seed of the woman can be *both* a particular descendant *and* the group of descendants who hope for the victory of their seed. Having pointed to evidence for this conclusion, I will note the conflict between the seed of the woman and the seed of the serpent in the Bible in broad terms, before narrowing in on the use of the imagery arising from Gen 3:15 in the rest of the Bible. Perhaps one reason Gen 3:15 is generally excluded from discussions of the use of the OT in the OT or in the NT is that scholars have explored "intertextuality" mainly on the basis of verbal connections. Meanwhile imagery—such as a crushed head or an enemy underfoot, which, as will be seen below, can be communicated in a variety of ways—has not received as much attention.[16]

3. The Collective-Singular Seed

The noun זֶרַע (seed) never occurs in the plural in the Old Testament.[17] Accordingly, the singular term can be used "collectively," that is, the singular form is used for both an individual seed and a group of seeds.[18] In the case of humans, it can refer to a single *descendant* or to multiple *descendants*. Jack Collins, however, has demonstrated through a syntactical analysis that "when *zera'* [seed] denotes a specific descendant, it appears with singular verb inflections, adjectives, and pronouns."[19] This leads Collins to conclude that "on the syntactical level, the singular pronoun *hû'* [he] in

---

[16] I use the term "intertextuality" here as an "'umbrella' term for the complex interactions that exist between 'texts,'" as recommended by Steve Moyise, "Intertextuality and the Study of the Old Testament in the New Testament," in *Old Testament in the New*, 41. The failure to attend to imagery, it seems to me, explains the absence of Gen 3:15 from Ian Paul's discussion of the OT in Rev 12 ("The Use of the Old Testament in Revelation 12," in *Old Testament in the New*, 256–76). For Paul's list of possible allusions, which underlines verbal correspondences, see 275–76. Paul cites Gen 3:13, but the crucial enmity between the seeds is announced in Gen 3:15, and this enmity explains why the dragon is interested in the male child (Rev 12:13) as well as the rest of the woman's seed (12:17). See further below.

[17] A. Even-Shoshan, ed., *A New Concordance of the Old Testament* (Jerusalem: Kiryat Sefer, 1997), 340–42.

[18] For discussion of this aspect of Hebrew grammar, see GKC § 123b; Joüon § 135b.

[19] Jack Collins, "A Syntactical Note (Genesis 3:15): Is the Woman's Seed Singular or Plural?," *TynBul* 48 (1997): 144.

Genesis 3:15 is quite consistent with the pattern where a singular individual is in view."[20]

T. Desmond Alexander builds on the data presented by Collins, to suggest that these conclusions are also relevant for interpreting Gen 22:17–18a and 24:60.[21] Genesis 22:17–18a will serve to illustrate the point being pursued here. It is clear that the first use of the term seed in 22:17 has a collective referent, for the text reads, "I will make your seed to be many, like the stars of the heavens or as the sand which is upon the lip of the sea."[22] Because of a singular pronominal suffix in the next statement (אֹיְבָיו, *his* enemies, not *their* enemies), the referent of the next two uses of the term seed could be a singular descendant. In this case, we might render 22:17b–18a as follows: "and your seed (one descendant, not all of them this time) will possess the gate of his enemies. And they will be blessed by your seed (one descendant, not all of them)—all the nations of the earth." I agree with Alexander's argument that the text switches from a collective referent to a singular one,[23] and I introduce this consideration here to point up this flexibility between the individual "seed" and the collective "holy seed" (cf. Isa 6:13) found in the OT.[24]

This ambiguity between the one and the many is witnessed in the variation between the singular and plural forms of second person address in Deuteronomy: "the

---

[20] Collins, "A Syntactical Note," 145. See also Max Wilcox, "The Promise of the 'Seed' in the New Testament and the Targumim," *JSNT* 5 (1979): 13–14, where he notes that Targums Onkelos, Neofiti, and Pseudo-Jonathan seem to interpret Gen 3:15 in a messianic way. Contra John Goldingay, *Old Testament Theology: Israel's Gospel*, vol. 1 (Downers Grove, IL: InterVarsity, 2003), 141 n.14: "the passage offers no pointer to the 'offspring' being singular rather than collective."

[21] T. Desmond Alexander, "Further Observations on the Term 'Seed' in Genesis," *TynBul* 48 (1997): 363–67.

[22] Unless otherwise indicated, translations of biblical texts are my own.

[23] Alexander ("The Term 'Seed' in Genesis," 365–66) argues for this understanding of the passage from the syntax of the passage (the clause "does not begin with a *vav*-consecutive; rather it is introduced by the imperfect verb יִרַשׁ preceded by a non-converting *vav*"), the allusion to this text in Ps 72:17, and the fact that "the entire book of Genesis is especially interested in highlighting the existence of a unique line of male descendants which will eventually give rise to a royal dynasty." For this last point, see T. Desmond Alexander, "From Adam to Judah: The Significance of the Family Tree in Genesis," *EvQ* 61 (1989): 5–19.

[24] Wifall sees this dynamic in the reference to David's seed in 2 Sam 7:12: "the term 'seed' has a 'collective' meaning, it is also applied 'individually' to each of the sons of David who assume his throne" ("Gen 3:15—A Protevangelium?," 363).

singular emphasizes Israel as a unity ... the plural is an arresting variation, focusing (paradoxically perhaps) on the responsibility of each individual to keep the covenant."[25] This interplay could also be what opens the door to the possibility of one person standing in place of the nation, as when Moses offers himself for the people (Exod 32:30–33), or when we read of a servant who at places appears to be the nation (Isa 41:8; 44:1) and at others an individual (42:1; 52:13).[26] As Dempster states, "An oscillation between a group and an individual within the group as its representative is certainly common in the Tanakh."[27]

The possibility of an individual or a collective whole being in view can also be seen in the way that Paul interprets OT seed texts. On one occasion, Paul emphasizes the singularity of the seed: "It does not say, 'and to seeds,' as to many, but as to one, 'and to your seed,' which is Messiah" (Gal 3:16). On another occasion, Paul can take the seed text of Gen 3:15 and apply it collectively to the people of God: "Now the God of peace will soon crush Satan under your feet" (Rom 16:20).[28] Though some might not be willing to credit the "Hebrew of Hebrews" with respect for OT context and an ability to recognize a tension between the collective and the singular in these seed texts, it seems at least plausible that Paul has recognized the dynamic to which I am pointing.[29] Namely, that the OT bears witness to an ambiguity between an individual and a group. Another example of this dynamic in the NT is the way that Jesus is presented as "recapitulating Israel's history" in the early chapters of the Gospel

---

[25] J. G. McConville, *Deuteronomy*, ApOTC (Leicester, England: Apollos/Downers Grove, IL: InterVarsity, 2002), 38.

[26] See also the interplay between the individual and the nation in Num 23:9; 24:17.

[27] Dempster, *Dominion and Dynasty*, 69 n.26.

[28] Similarly Wilcox, "The Promise of the 'Seed' in the New Testament and the Targumim," 2–3.

[29] See also Pss. Sol. 18:3, ἡ ἀγάπη σου ἐπὶ σπέρμα Αβρααμ υἱοὺς Ισραηλ—"your love is upon the *seed* of Abraham, the *sons* of Israel" (my trans.). R. B. Wright renders this, "your love is for the descendants of Abraham, an Israelite" (*OTP* 2:669, see discussion in his note b, where he writes: "Lit. 'of a son of Israel,'" misrepresenting the plural υἱοὺς as a singular. He then refers to the syntax as "awkward," but this is apparently because he does not see the dynamic between the collective and the singular in the word *seed*, as witnessed in his consistent translation of it as "descendants." A more fitting translation, which would capture the collective-singular, would be something like "offspring," which like "seed" can refer to one or to many).

according to Matthew. A poignant example is Hos 11:1, which in its OT context referred to the nation, but Matthew claims it is fulfilled in Jesus (Matt 2:15).[30]

4. Conflict Between the Seeds

Almost immediately after the judgment is announced that there will be enmity between the seed of the woman and the seed of the serpent (Gen 3), the text recounts that one who pleased God, Abel, was slain by one who did not please God and then rejected a divine warning, Cain (Gen 4:1–16).[31] The escalation of hostility seen in Cain's descendants (see esp. 4:23–24) points to his line as representing those whose actions mirror the one who "was a murderer from the beginning" (John 8:44).[32] The point here is not that Cain's line has been physically sired by Satan; rather, the Bible commonly describes people figuratively as children of those whose characteristics they emulate.[33]

---

[30] Cf. the comments of W. D. Davies and Dale C. Allison, *A Critical and Exegetical Commentary on the Gospel according to Saint Matthew*, 3 vols., ICC (London; New York: T&T Clark, 1988–97), 1:263, 352. See too C. H. Dodd, *According to the Scriptures* (London: Nisbet & Co., 1952), 103, where he refers to "this far-reaching identification of Christ, as Son of Man, as Servant, as the righteous Sufferer, with the people of God in all its vicissitudes…"

[31] Cf. T. Desmond Alexander, "Messianic Ideology in the Book of Genesis," in *The Lord's Anointed*, ed. P. E. Satterthwaite, R. S. Hess, and G. J. Wenham (Carlisle: Paternoster/Grand Rapids: Baker, 1995), 24; Schreiner, "Foundations for Faith," 2.

[32] This statement in John's Gospel could be meant to indicate that Jesus interpreted Satan as the force of wickedness driving Cain's murder as recounted in Gen 4. Cf. J. H. Bernard, *A Critical and Exegetical Commentary on the Gospel according to St. John*, 2 vols., ICC (Edinburgh: T&T Clark, 1928), 314, who also notes that this could be "a reference to the Jewish doctrine that death was a consequence of the Fall, which was due to the devil's prompting." He cites Wis 2:24. The reference to Gen 4, in view of 1 John 3:8–12, seems more likely. So also R. E. Brown, *The Gospel according to John*, 2 vols., AB (New York: Doubleday, 1966, 1970), 358.

[33] For some of the expressions, see זֶרַע מְרֵעִים "seed of wicked ones" in Isa 1:4; 14:20 (cf. 57:3–4). בְּנֵי־בְלִיַּעַל "sons of worthlessness" in Deut 13:13 (MT 13:14); Judg 19:22; 20:13; 1 Sam 2:12; 1 Kgs 21:10, 13; 2 Chr 13:7. Righteous men could be in view when we read of בְּנֵי־הָאֱלֹהִים "sons of God" in Gen 6:2, 4, but it is more likely that as in Job 1:6 and 2:1 the reference is to angels. Nevertheless, the statement in 2 Sam 7:14 that David's heir would be a "son" to God could have been interpreted not as a reference to the divinity but to the character of the coming King. We also read of בֶּן־חַיִל "son of valor" in 1 Sam 14:52 and 2 Sam 17:10. This manner of speaking is not limited to the OT. For example, Matthew shows Jesus telling the Pharisees that when they make a convert they make him "twice as much a son of hell as yourselves" (Matt 23:15), and in Ephesians we read of the "sons of disobedience" (Eph 2:2). See also the designations "sons of light" and "sons of darkness" in the Qumran scrolls,

The conflict between Isaac and Ishmael can also be seen as enmity between the respective seed—one the seed of the promise and the other of a failure to believe (Gen 21:9–10, 12; Rom 9:7).[34] Egypt's attempt to destroy the male children of Israel also continues this battle between the lines of descent (Exod 1:16, 22). Both the collective singularity of Israel and their place as the chosen seed can be seen in the statement in Exod 4:23, "And I say to you, send my son that he may serve me, but if you refuse to send him, behold, I am about to kill your son, your firstborn." The conflict between the seeds continues throughout the OT, and seems to be one of the main points of the book of Esther, where the genocidal enemy of the people of God, Haman, is an Agagite (Esth 3:1), which in the book's canonical context calls to mind the statement in Num 24:7, "and his king shall be higher than Agag," as well as Saul's failure to kill Agag (1 Sam 15). As Dempster writes, "Esther's opposition to Haman continues the major theme running through the narrative, that of the woman against the beast: Eve versus the serpent..."[35]

From the statements to be discussed below, which I am suggesting reflect the influence of Gen 3:15, it seems that the authors of the Bible regard the enemies of the people of God as those whose heads, like the head of the serpent (the father of lies), will be crushed. Those who are understood as opposing the purposes of God and his people appear to be regarded as the seed of the serpent.[36] This would inform the

---

especially since the "sons of darkness" are equated with the "army of Belial" (1Q33 [1QM] 1:1; cf. also 1Q28 [1QS] 1:9–10). The subjection of the evil seed is also seen in 1Q33 [1QM] 1:14–15, "God's great hand will subdue [Belial, and all] the angels of his dominion and all the men of [his lot.]." Unless otherwise noted, all Qumran texts cited herein are from Florentino García Martínez and Eibert J. C. Tigchelaar, eds. *The Dead Sea Scrolls: Study Edition*, 2 vols. (Grand Rapids: Eerdmans, 1997, 1998).

[34] The emphasis on the important line of descent is also attested to in Heb 11:11, though translations usually obscure it. The text is almost universally translated, "Sarah received power to conceive" (ESV, NAB, NASU, NET, NIV, NJB, RSV). This is one more reason to reject "dynamic equivalence," because the text "woodenly" reads, "barren Sarah received power for the foundation of the seed." In view of the Bible's interest in the "holy seed," the statement that "Sarah received power for the foundation of the seed" carries more freight than "Sarah received ability to conceive." This common rendering of the text obscures all connection to the Bible's "seed" theme. KJV and NKJV include the word "seed," and the HCSB has "offspring."

[35] Dempster, *Dominion and Dynasty*, 223.

[36] This seed conflict might help us to understand the holy wars of total destruction in

depiction of John the Baptist denouncing the Pharisees and Sadducees as a "brood of vipers" (Matt 3:7; Luke 3:7). Can such an identification be a mere coincidence of language? Jesus is shown repeating this denunciation of the Pharisees in Matthew's Gospel (12:34; 23:33),[37] and John shows him telling those who seek to kill him (John 8:40) that they do the deeds of their father (8:41), the devil (8:44).[38]

5. Salvation through Judgment: The Skull Crushing Seed

Perhaps the word-study fallacy has closed many ears to the echoes of Gen 3:15 that run through the Bible.[39] Even though nearly everyone is aware of the potential pitfall, it remains true that often in the modern academy discussions of "messianic hope in the OT" give too much space and weight to word studies of the term "anointed" and/or limit themselves to examination of the ideas surrounding the promises to David. Whereas older and/or more conservative discussions began their treatments of messianic hope with Gen 3:15,[40] modern self-consciously academic approaches

---

Deuteronomy and Joshua. Though Tremper Longman does not develop the notion at length, he does cite Gen 3:15 at the end of his essay in *Show Them No Mercy: Four Views on God and Canaanite Genocide* (Grand Rapids: Zondervan, 2003).

[37] Cf. David R. Bauer, *The Structure of Matthew's Gospel*, JSNTSup 31 (Sheffield: Almond, 1989), 69: "If the opponents of Jesus are children of Satan, they are also understood by Matthew to form a unity of evil."

[38] The concern with "seed" is not limited to the Old and New Testaments. See, for example, the comments on the seed of Lot in Jub. 16:9; the blessing on Jacob's seed in Jub. 22:10–30; and the cursing of the seed of Canaan in Jub. 22:20–21.

[39] Cf. J. Daniel Hays, "If He Looks Like a Prophet," 59–60, esp. 59 n.1. See too R. E. Clements, "The Messianic Hope in the Old Testament," *JSOT* 43 (1989): 6: "The changing attitudes to the subject of the messianic expectation in the Old Testament have been strongly reflective of changing methods in studying it."

[40] R. A. Martin ("The Earliest Messianic Interpretation of Genesis 3:15," *JBL* 84 [1965]: 427) concludes, "If the above explanation is correct, the LXX becomes thereby the earliest evidence of an individual messianic interpretation of Gen 3 15, to be dated in the 3rd or 2nd century B.C." See also Justin's *Dialogue with Trypho* in ANF 1:250; Irenaeus, *Against Heresies* in ANF 1:548 [5.21]. The *Westminster Confession of Faith*, 7.3, in reference to the "second" "covenant of grace," refers to Gen 3:15 in a footnote. In covenant theology, the *protoevangelium* of Gen 3:15 is understood as the first outworking of the "eternal covenant of redemption" between the members of the Godhead. Thus, Fred Malone writes, "I believe … [t]hat God did reveal historically the 'promise of grace' in Genesis 3:15, commonly called the Covenant of Grace" (*The Baptism of Disciples Alone: A Covenantal Argument for Credobaptism Versus Paedobaptism* [Cape Coral, FL: Founders, 2003], xxxiii). Dispensationalists also

sometimes mention this text and its influence only in passing, if at all.[41] Further, until recently, there has been a widespread tendency to ignore a text's canonical context and minimalize what one book or author may add to another.[42]

In fact, there are a number of thematic images that, taking the biblical text in its final, canonical form, are introduced in Gen 3:14–15 as God pronounces the curse on the serpent. The enmity between the respective seed has been noted above. The serpent will have his head damaged, and the seed of the woman will have his heel damaged. In many biblical texts this is interpreted to mean that the seed of the woman will trample on the seed of the serpent. It is true that the term שׁוּף (bruise, cover) is not used to designate the defeat of the evil seed other than in Gen 3:15,[43] but the use of several terms for crushing/shattering/breaking seems to indicate that the biblical authors understood the damage in view to be a smashing of the serpent's skull.[44] Often

---

include this text in their treatments of messianic hope, see Craig A. Blaising and Darrell L. Bock, *Progressive Dispensationalism* (Wheaton, IL: Bridgepoint, 1993). While Bock's comments are very cautious (81, but see 99), Blaising's words are robust (216).

[41] The issues raised by Gen 3:15 are not considered by Marinus de Jonge, "Messiah," in *ABD* 4:777–88, nor does the text even appear in the index of Donald Juel's *Messianic Exegesis: Christological Interpretation of the Old Testament in Early Christianity* (Philadelphia: Fortress, 1988). Block does not mention Gen 3:15 until the last paragraph of his essay, "My Servant David: Ancient Israel's Vision of the Messiah," in *Israel's Messiah in the Bible and the Dead Sea Scrolls*, 56. It is amazing to me that Sigmund Mowinckel, to name one prominent exponent of the position, can summarily dismiss the possibility of Gen 3:15 being a messianic text in one paragraph (*He that Cometh*, trans. G. W. Anderson [Nashville: Abingdon, 1954], 11). See the far more plausible, thought provoking discussion in Dempster, *Dominion and Dynasty*, 68–72.

[42] Alexander writes, "By atomising the received text into short sections and interpreting these as self-contained units, we may fail to appreciate adequately the impact of the larger literary context upon our understanding of these smaller units" ("Messianic Ideology," 32).

[43] Apparently the LXX translator did not know what to do with this term, rendering it with future forms of τηρέω, I keep/watch over (!), and this is matched by the verb נטר in the Targum, which also means "keep/watch." Unless otherwise noted, all references to Targumic material in this essay are to the text provided by *BibleWorks10*, whose Targum material is derived from the Hebrew Union College CAL (Comprehensive Aramaic Lexicon) project.

[44] The fact that the judgment is visited upon the serpent's head could also have given rise to the idea of the wicked having their evil deeds "returned upon their own heads," as in Judg 9:57; 1 Kgs 2:32–33, 37, 44; 8:32; 2 Chr 6:23; Neh 4:4 (MT 3:36); Esth 9:25; Ps 7:16 (MT 17); 140:9 (MT 10); Ezek 9:10; 11:21; 16:43; 17:19; 22:31; Joel 3: 4, 7 (MT 4:4, 7); Obad 15. Related to this, not a few of the wicked in the OT have their heads conquered, that is, cut off, see Judg 7:25; 1 Sam 5:4; 31:9; 2 Sam 4:7; 16:9 (threatened); 20:21–22; 2 Kgs 10:6–7; 1 Chr 10:9–10.

we read of the enemies of the people of God being "broken," or, more specifically, of their craniums being crushed. Bad guys get broken heads in the Bible. In some texts it is specifically stated that the ones shattered are serpents. The serpent was told he would eat dust (Gen 3:14), and in several places the rebellious eat or lick dust. At points, a number of these images are used together, but the enmity between the seeds and some aspect of the curse is present in them all.[45] We now turn to a discussion of each of these thematic images that, it seems to me, reflect the biblical authors' interpretation and application of the primeval curse on the serpent. I will discuss the use of these images in the OT first, grouping them as they appear in the Law, the Prophets, and the Writings. Possible allusions to Gen 3:15 in the NT will then be briefly discussed.

6. Broken Heads

6.1. In the Law

Several messianic themes are sounded in the Balaam oracles,[46] but most

---

[45] Wifall suggests that these images are common in ancient Near Eastern art and literature ("Gen 3:15—A Protevangelium?," 363–64). It is possible that the imagery in the texts I will discuss simply derives from a common milieu, but I find the view I am arguing more persuasive than that explanation. According to the Bible's presentation of human history, these images in the ancient Near Eastern could find their ultimate source in what is narrated in Gen 3, for the Bible provides an account of the descent of all the earth's nations from Adam and Eve in Gen 5, 10, and 11. I should note also that the images I am discussing do not exhaust the possible influence(s) of Gen 3:15 in the Bible. For instance, I do not discuss Gen 49:17, which seems to have given rise to a Jewish tradition that the antichrist would come from Dan (cf. T. Dan 5:6–7). I owe this reference to G. K. Beale, *The Book of Revelation*, NIGTC (Grand Rapids: Eerdmans, 1999), 420 n.133.

[46] In my view, the seed promise of Gen 3 gave rise to the hope for one who would restore an edenic state (cf. Gen 3:17 with 5:29). Genesis then carefully traces a line of male descent to Abraham in the genealogies of chapters 5 and 11 (see Alexander, "From Adam to Judah"). The promises to Abraham in Gen 12:1–3 and elsewhere (esp. the royal promises in Gen 17:6, 16; 49:9–11) are then layered onto the earlier ones, beginning from Gen 3:15. If this is not clear from Genesis itself, the Balaam oracles bring these statements together. Thus, we find numerous comments about blessing and cursing (Num 22:6, 12, 17; 23:8, 11, 25; 24:9–10), an individual who seems to represent the nation (23:9), indications that a great king will arise in Israel (23:21; 24:7, 17, 19), citations of the blessing of Judah in Gen 49:9–11 (23:24; 24:9), overtones of a return to Eden (24:8; cf. Gen 2:8) and smashing of enemies (Num 24:8), even the crushing of their heads (24:17). See John Sailhamer, "Creation, Genesis 1–11, and the Canon," *BBR* 10 (2000): 89–106. The imagery of Gen 49 and Num 24 is also present in 1Q28b (1QSb) 5:24–29, and Gen 3:15, refracted through 2 Sam 22:43 (see note 65 below), might also be reflected in the trampling of the nations (1Q28b [1QSb] 5:27).

prominent for the present is what appears to be the interpretation of Gen 3:15 in Num 24:17.[47] There is enmity between Israel and Moab, and fearing Israel's numbers (22:3) Balak king of Moab summons Balaam to curse Israel. As Balaam's oracles are recounted, the text indicates that a male Israelite will arise whose coming is associated with the arrival of a star and the rising of a scepter, pointing to his royal status. The Targum on this text seems to interpret the star as "the King" (מַלְכָּא) and the scepter as "the Messiah" (מְשִׁיחָא). This individual will "crush the forehead of Moab" (Num 24:17).[48] The words used in Numbers are not the words used in Genesis,[49] but the image of the crushed head of an enemy is clearly invoked.[50]

6.2. In the Former Prophets

The story of Jael "crushing the head" of Sisera is told in Judg 4 and then celebrated in song in Judg 5. The terminology of Judg 5:26 might allude to Num 24:17, as the verb מחץ (crush, shatter, smite through) is used with several synonymous terms[51] to describe this gruesome deed. Once again, the collective seed of the woman through Abraham, Israel, is at enmity with another seed, the Canaanites. Interestingly, the text

---

[47] The overtones of Gen 3:15 in Num 24 may have influenced the Greek translation of Num 24:7, "A *man* shall come forth *from his seed*, and he shall rule many nations. And his King shall be higher than Gog" (emphasis added). Cf. the MT, "Water shall flow from his buckets, and his seed shall be on many waters. His King shall be higher than Agag." See Craig Evans' discussion of this text's relevance for understanding the use of Hos 11:1 in Matt 2:13–15 ("The Old Testament in the New," 136).

[48] This text is cited in the War Scroll in connection with the felling of the "hordes of Belial" (1Q33 [1QM] 11:6–8). See also 4Q175 (*4Q Testimonia*) 1:12–13, 19. Dempster takes Num 24:17 as I do (*Dominion and Dynasty*, 116).

[49] Genesis 3:15 has a form of שׁוּף for "bruise" and רֹאשׁ (Gen. 3:15 BHS) for "head," whereas the phrase in Num 24:17 reads, "and he will *crush* (וּמָחַץ) the *corners* of Moab (פַּאֲתֵי מוֹאָב), and break down (וְקַרְקַר) all the sons of Sheth." As will be seen below, the verb מחץ is used in a number of texts that seem to be alluding to Gen 3:15, and "corners" (פֵּאָה) seems to be used here for "corners of the head" (cf. Lev 13:41) as reflected in most English translations (e.g., ESV, HCSB, NASU, NET, NJB, RSV). For another text that describes justice upon the head of Moab with the same language, see Jer 48:45.

[50] Cf. B. S. Rosner, "Biblical Theology," in *NDBT*, 6: "Concepts rather than words are a surer footing on which to base thematic study such as that involved in biblical-theological synthesis." So also Schreiner, "Foundations for Faith," 3. See too Sir 36:10, "Crush the heads of the rulers of the enemy…"

[51] Judges 5:26 reads, "she struck (הלם) Sisera; she crushed (מחק 1x in OT) his head; she shattered (מחץ) and pierced (חלף, only time with this meaning in the OT) his temple (רַקָּה)."

argues that Israel has been subjugated to Jabin king of Canaan because Israel did what was evil in the sight of Yahweh (Judg 4:1–2). As in Gen 3, one of the causes of enmity between the respective seed is the rebellion of those who are supposed to be loyal to Yahweh. Yahweh has judged his rebels, and now one of their seed will deliver them from Yahweh's judgment by crushing the head of Jabin's general, Sisera (cf. Judg 4, esp. 4:21, where Jael drives a tent peg through Sisera's temple as he sleeps).[52] The theme of the salvation of the seed of the woman through judgment—judgment that the seed experiences and renders—is sounded here as the seed of the woman crushes the head of the enemy seed.

In some cases, those who have their heads crushed are physically descended from Abraham, but by their actions they show themselves to be at enmity with those who are faithful to Yahweh. Like Cain, who was physically a seed of the woman but showed himself to be the seed of the serpent by killing his brother, Abimelech shows the lineage of his ethical character by killing 70 of his brothers (Judg 9:1–5; cf. also 9:34–49, where he slaughters his subjects [9:6]). Judgment falls on the seed of the serpent (Abimelech), however, when a woman throws a millstone on Abimelech's head (רֹאשׁ) and his skull (גֻּלְגָּלְתּ)[53] is crushed (רצץ)[54] (9:53).

It is surely no coincidence that when the seed of the woman named David lets fly his stone, the uncircumcised Philistine seed of the serpent who defied the armies of the living God gets struck (נכה) on the forehead (מֵצַח). The stone sinks into his forehead (וַתִּטְבַּע הָאֶבֶן בְּמִצְחוֹ), and with a crushed head the Philistine falls dead (1 Sam 17:49). The collective seed of the woman are delivered from the seed of the serpent by the judgment administered through the singular seed of the woman.[55]

---

[52] Similarly, Dempster, *Dominion and Dynasty*, 132.

[53] This term occurs in other texts that could reflect judgment on the seed of the serpent; see its use in 2 Kgs 9:35 and 1 Chr 10:10. See also note 88 below.

[54] This term is also used in relevant texts which will be noted below, Isa 42:3–4 and Ps 74:14.

[55] Cf. Dempster, *Dominion and Dynasty*, 140: "The seed of the woman has arrived, and in David's first action as king he is a warrior, an anointed one who conquers and beheads a monstrous giant, whose speech echoes the serpent's voice."

6.3. In the Latter Prophets

When we come to the latter prophets, we find that Isaiah employs the imagery of Gen 3:15 as he addresses the sinful nation as the "seed of wicked ones" (זֶרַע מְרֵעִים), and then asks why they should continue to be struck when the whole head is sick (Isa 1:4–5). Here it seems that Isaiah is depicting the divine discipline upon the nation of Israel in terms of their heads being struck, seed of the serpent that they have become.

It is possible that Isaiah returns to imagery from Gen 3:15 in the exchange with Ahaz in chapter 7, using the term "head" (רֹאשׁ) four times in two verses in reference to Ahab's enemies as he describes them being "shattered" (חתת) (Isa 7:8–9). In this context, Isaiah is challenging Ahaz to be firm in faith (7:9). If this head-shattering language is alluding to Gen 3:15, then we might conclude that Isaiah is not calling for an abstract, undefined "faith," but for trust in the specific promises Yahweh has given to his people beginning from Gen 3:15.[56] Messianic overtones are perhaps made more likely in this text because it is set between the reference to the "holy seed" in 6:13 and the "Immanuel" prophecy in 7:14. Further, with the messianic tenor of chapters 9 and 11, Isa 7–12 is sometimes referred to as the "book of Immanuel."

Imagery from Gen 3:15 again shows up in the prophecy of Isaiah, and again it seems to be ironically directed against Israelites. Isaiah 28:3 states, "The majestic crown of the drunks of Ephraim will be trampled by feet." Heads trampled by feet as God's judgment falls. This seems to assume a well-known image: a heel damaged from stomping on a serpent's head.

Moving to Jeremiah, in the very chapter that describes the righteous Davidic branch who will reign as king and execute justice and righteousness (Jer 23:5, the Targum uses the noun משיח twice in this verse), we also read "Behold the storm of Yahweh: rage goes forth, and a tempest excites itself; upon the head (ראשׁ, sg.) of the wicked ones (pl.) it shall dance." This chapter is an oracle against shepherds who

---

[56] As noted above, the term רצץ is used in several head-crushing texts (Judg 9:53; Isa 42:3–4; Ps 74:14). In Isa 7, the king of Syria is several times named as "Rezin" (רְצִין) (7:1, 4, 8). E. J. Young writes, "Lindblom suggests that the king was tendentiously called Resin, 'pleasure,' suggesting the root *rātzatz*, 'crush'" (*The Book of Isaiah* [Grand Rapids: Eerdmans, 1965], 1:274 n.19).

scatter the people (23:1), false prophets who do not speak from Yahweh (23:9–22, esp. 16). The remedy to these shepherds who do not care for the sheep appears to be the good shepherd, the Davidic branch (23:5). Significantly, in Jer 23:19 the punishment visited upon the wicked shepherds is described in imagery that reflects Gen 3:15. Thus, Jer 23 seems to weave together the threads of promise having to do with a Davidic ruler (23:5) who will save the people and restore them to their land (23:6–8), with a simultaneous divine justice that is visited upon the head of the wicked (23:19). If the verb in 23:19 is translated "dance,"[57] then the raging storm on the head of the wicked is depicted as being wrought by dancing *feet*, perhaps alluding to the crushed heel of Gen 3:15. If this is the case, the justice visited upon the head of the wicked is rendered by the heel of the storm of Yahweh.

The likelihood of this interpretation would seem to be strengthened if there are indeed numerous allusions to Gen 3:15 peppered through the OT (the point this study is hoping to establish). For this reason, it is important that a very similar collocation of Davidic and head-crushing themes recurs in Jeremiah in the restoration prophecies of chapter 30 (cf. 30:3). After Yahweh has broken the foreign yokes from the necks of his people (30:8), he declares through Jeremiah that "they shall serve Yahweh their God and David their King, whom I will raise up for them" (30:9). Toward the end of the same chapter, we read, "And it shall come about that the majestic one of him [Targum: "their king"] shall come from him, and the one who rules him [Targum: "their Messiah"] will go forth from his midst…. Behold the storm of Yahweh: rage goes forth; a tempest excites itself; upon the head (ראש, sg.) of the wicked ones (pl.) it shall dance" (30:21a, 23).[58] Like Jer 23, in chapter 30 we find interwoven promises of a Davidic ruler (30:9, 21) and justice visited upon the head of the wicked (30:23). Once again, the justice visited upon the head of the wicked is rendered by the heel of the storm of Yahweh. These texts in Jeremiah seem to promise the triumph of the future

---

[57] The verb is חול, and BDB lists "whirl, dance, writhe" as possible glosses (296). They list Jer 30:23 under the meaning "whirl" (297). *HALOT* lists the use of the verb in Jer 30:23 under "dance … to whirl" (297). For a similar use of the verb, see 2 Sam 3:29.

[58] Jeremiah 23:19 and 30:23 are identical except for a single conjunctive waw in 23:19 which begins the phrase "and a tempest excites itself."

Davidic ruler, and the judgment visited when he reigns is described in imagery
reminiscent of Gen 3:15. Both Jer 23:19 and 30:23 are followed by the intriguing
statement, "In the latter days you will understand this" (23:20; 30:24).[59]

Another image of head-crushing is found in Hab 3:13. In a description of the
coming of Yahweh in wrath and mercy (Hab 3:2), Yahweh threshes the nations in
anger (3:12). Habakkuk then moves from just wrath to merciful salvation in 3:13, as
Yahweh is addressed with the words, "You went out for the salvation of your people,
for the salvation of your anointed [or, Messiah]; you crush (מחץ)[60] the head from the
house of the wicked, laying bare from tail to neck. Selah." Ralph Smith provides a
helpful comment: "'Your Anointed' probably refers to the Davidic king in Jerusalem.
'From tail to neck' (v 13) appears to be a reference to the enemy in the form of a
dragon."[61] The serpentine quality of the enemy in Hab 3:13 is heightened by the
possible allusion to the description of the snake in Gen 3:1. The snake is described as
"crafty" with the term עָרוּם in Gen 3:1. In Hab 3:13 the word ערה (lay bare, make
naked) is used to describe the "laying bare" of this creature (cf. also Gen 2:25, where
the man and woman are both "bare," i.e., naked, and the term is עֲרוֹם).

Just as Yahweh promises a crushed head to the serpent in Gen 3:15, Yahweh
is described crushing the head of the wicked in Hab 3:13. If it is correct to see dragon
imagery in Hab 3:13,[62] this text brings together the Messiah and divine justice in the
form of a serpent with a crushed head. Further, in this text Yahweh's head-crushing
justice is side by side with the salvation of his people.

---

[59] The only difference between the two statements is the addition of the term בִּינָה
("understanding," which results in the addition of the word "clearly" in several translations) at the end
of Jer 23:20.

[60] We have seen the term for "crush" (מחץ) in several other head-crushing texts: Num 24:8, 17;
Judg 5:26; and we will see it in several more: 2 Sam 22:39; Job 26:12; Ps 68:21, 23; 110:6. These will
be discussed below.

[61] Ralph L. Smith, Micah–Malachi, WBC 32 (Waco, TX: Word, 1984), 116.

[62] In my translation I follow Smith (Micah-Malachi, 113–14, 116, citing W. F. Albright, "The
Psalm of Habakkuk," in Studies in Old Testament Prophecy, ed. H. H. Rowley [Edinburgh: T&T Clark,
1950], 1–18) in translating יְסוֹד as "tail" to bring out the dragon imagery. BDB offers "foundation, base,
bottom" as possible glosses (414), and HALOT suggests "foundation wall, base" (417).

6.4. In the Writings

Psalm 68 sings the triumph of God over his enemies for the benefit of his people. In verses 20–21 (MT 21–22) judgment and salvation are placed side by side, and we read, "The God for us is a God of deliverances, and to Yahweh our LORD belong escapes from death. But God will crush (מחץ) the head (ראש, sg.) of his enemies (pl.), the hairy crown of the one who walks in his guilt." Yahweh then says he will bring back his enemies from Bashan and the sea (68:22, MT 23), "that your feet (sg.) may stomp (מחץ) in blood..." (68:23, MT 24). Thus, Ps 68 describes the enemies of God having their heads crushed by Yahweh (68:21, MT 22), but it also indicates that Yahweh will deliver up his enemies so that his people will stomp in the blood of their foes (68:23, MT 24).[63] This is reminiscent of the way that the OT often speaks of Yahweh giving a nation to the Israelites in battle—Yahweh determines that Israel will prevail, but Israel actually goes out and physically defeats the enemy (e.g., Deut 2:30–37; 2 Sam 8:1–14). In Ps 68, the victory is described with the imagery of Gen 3:15, with the seed of the serpent receiving a crushed head from the feet of the seed of the woman.

Several images from Gen 3:15 seem to be brought together in Ps 110. The statement in 110:6 that is sometimes translated, "he will shatter chiefs" (cf. ESV, NASU, NIV, NKJV, RSV), could just as well be translated, "he will crush (מחץ) the head (ראש, sg.) on the broad land" (cf. JPS, NAB, NJB, NLT, NRSV). This is a Davidic Psalm (110:1), and the use of the verb מחץ (crush, shatter) and the term ראש in a number of head-crushing contexts in the OT (cf. Num 24:8, 17; Judg 5:26; 2 Sam 22:39; Job 26:12; Ps 68:22, 24; Hab 3:13) would seem to color the use of these terms in Ps 110. The statement that the enemies will be made a footstool for the feet of the Davidic king (110:1) seems to draw on the connection between the damaged heel and head in Gen 3:15.[64] The reference to the scepter being sent forth (110:2) calls to mind

---

[63] Cf. also 68:30 (MT 31), where the text might be translated "Trample underfoot those who lust after tribute" (ESV) or "Trampling under foot the pieces of silver" (NASU). The other option is to take the hitpael of רפס differently, as it is in the only other occurrence of this verb in the hitpael in the OT, Prov 6:3, and with the NET read, "They humble themselves and offer gold and silver as tribute." See the discussion in *HALOT*, 1279–80.

[64] Dempster, *Dominion and Dynasty*, 200; Wifall ("Gen 3:15—A Protevangelium?," 363)

texts such as Gen 49:10, Num 24:17, and Ps 2:9 (though a different term is used for "scepter" in those texts).[65] And finally, the Lord will also do some shattering in 110:5 (מחץ again). Yahweh smashes, the Messiah smashes, and the enemies are under the feet. Genesis 3:15 is not directly quoted, but it is not far away.[66]

7. Broken Enemies

The texts looked at in the previous section connected the judgment of Yahweh to the head of the enemy, with some having Davidic/messianic overtones. The texts to be considered in this section designate shattered enemies, but they do not limit the smashing to the skull. This constitutes a loosening of the image of the crushed head of the seed of the serpent in Gen 3:15, but it still seems related.

7.1. In the Law

In the song of triumph celebrating Yahweh's deliverance of Israel from Egypt, we read that Yahweh's right hand "shatters (רעץ) the enemy" (Exod 15:6). Several statements from Num 24 have been discussed above, and that context also contains the words: "and as for their bones, he will break (גרם) them, and his arrows will crush (מחץ) them" (Num 24:8).

7.2. In the Former Prophets

The books of Samuel may be bookended by interpretations of Gen 3:15. The first half of the *inclusio* may be seen in 1 Sam 2:10, where the conclusion of Hannah's prayer reads in part, "Yahweh will shatter (חתת) the ones who contend with him; upon them he will thunder in the heavens. Yahweh will judge the ends of the earth, and he will give strength to his King. And he will exalt the horn of his Anointed." The second

---

notes this text and Ps 8:6 in this regard (with Schreiner, "Foundations for Faith," 3).

[65] Rosner's words ("Biblical Theology," in *NDBT*, 6) are relevant here as well (see note 48 above). These concepts—all things under the feet of the Messianic King (see also Ps 8) and him ruling with a scepter—could have grounded statements such as the one a demon is depicted making to Solomon in *T. Sol.* 18:3, "But you, King, are not able to harm us or to lock us up; but since *God gave you authority over all the spirits of the air, the earth, and (the regions) beneath the earth,* we also have taken our place before you like the other spirits" (*OTP* 1:977, emphasis added).

[66] Schreiner, "Foundations for Faith," 3.

half of the *inclusio* comes in David's song of deliverance in 2 Sam 22, which ends with statements about Yahweh's anointed (messianic) king and the seed of David (2 Sam 22:51). As he extols the capability Yahweh gave to him (22:40), David describes what he did to his enemies: "I grind them as the dust of the earth. As clay of the streets I crushed (דקק) them; I stamped (רקע) them" (22:43; cf. Ps 18:42, MT 43).[67] Since they are likened to the clay of the streets, it seems that David crushed his enemies with his feet (cf. the NET, "I crush them and stomp on them"). Dust, crushing, and feet are all mentioned in the curse on the enemy of the seed of the woman found in Gen 3:14–15. 1 Samuel 2 and 2 Sam 22 would seem to be linking David with the seed of the woman, and describing his victories in terms reminiscent of the curse on the seed of the serpent.

7.3. In the Latter Prophets

The imagery of Gen 3:15 appears again in Isa 14:25, where Yahweh declares that he will "break (שבר) Assyria" and "trample (בוס) them." Because they have broken the covenant, Jeremiah proclaims what Yahweh will do to "the kings who sit on David's throne, the priests, the prophets, and all who dwell in Jerusalem" (13:13), "'I will dash them to pieces (נפץ), a man against his brother, fathers and sons together,' declares Yahweh, 'I will not spare, and I will not show pity, and I will not show compassion while destroying them'" (13:14). Jeremiah 23:29 describes Yahweh's word in terms of a hammer that shatters (פצץ) rock. Jeremiah 48:4 states that Moab is broken (שבר). In Jer 51:20–23, Babylon is called Yahweh's weapon, his war club, and nine times the verb "dash in pieces" (נפץ in the piel) is repeated as all the things that will be smashed are enumerated.

7.4. In the Writings

The conflict between the seed of the woman and the seed of the serpent appears again in Ps 2:1–3. Yahweh responds to the plotting of the nations with the decree that he has installed his king on Zion (2:4–6), and then the king tells of how Yahweh

---

[67] As noted above (note 44), the language of 2 Sam 22:43 might also be reflected in 1Q28b (1QSb) 5:27, where the text reads, "May you trample the nations as clay of the streets" (... תנכח כפ]ר (ותרמוס עמ]ים כטיט חוצות). The verb in 2 Sam 22:43 is not רמס (note that the Qumran text is uncertain here as the brackets designate), but the phrase "as clay of the streets" (כְּטִיט־חוּצוֹת) is identical.

proclaimed to him, as in 2 Sam 7:14, that he would be Yahweh's son (Ps 2:7). Further, the king, son of Yahweh, will break his enemies (רעע)[68] with an iron rod and dash them to pieces (נפץ in the piel) like pottery (2:9). If the thesis of this essay is on the mark, Psalm 2 connects the smashing of Gen 3:15 to the sonship of 2 Sam 7.

Psalm 72 appears to be a prayer of David for the prosperity of Solomon's reign as the latter ascends the throne (72:1, 20). Verse 17 echoes Gen 12:3, and there are at least two places where Gen 3:14–15 might be invoked. Verse 4 concludes with the words, "and may he crush (דכא) the oppressor." Then verse 9 ends with the wish, "and as for his enemies, may they lick (לחך) the dust."[69] The licking of the dust calls to mind the fact that the serpent was told that he would eat dust (Gen 3:14).[70]

Psalm 89:20 speaks of the anointing of David, and then verse 29 refers to the establishment of his seed forever. Between these two statements are the words, "And I will crush (כתת)[71] his adversaries before him, and the ones who hate him I will strike (נגף)" (89:23, MT 24). In Ps 89 the promises of 2 Sam 7 seem to be aligned with Gen 3:15.[72]

If I am correct in what I am arguing, the gruesome statement in Ps 137:9, though perhaps not softened, is at least given a context. Apparently in exile (137:1), the psalmist concludes with a frightful blessing: "Happy is the one who seizes your children that he might dash them in pieces (נפץ in the piel) against the rock" (137:9). There is no mitigating this brutality, but if the statement reflects the age old conflict between the seed of the woman and the seed of the serpent, and if the psalmist is here longing for God's judgment to fall on the seed of the serpent, then vicious as this text may be, it righteously expresses a desire for God to save his people by triumphing over their enemies (note, too that Ps 137:9 employs the same verb, "dash," as seen in Ps 2:9). The Babylonian children in this text are the seed of the serpent, and the dashing of them against the rock expresses the crushing of the serpent and the realization of

---

[68] *HALOT*, 1270: "II רעע . . . . 1. a. to smash, shatter."

[69] Cf. Schreiner ("Foundations for Faith," 2) and Wifall ("Gen 3:15—A Protevangelium?," 363).

[70] See the discussion of licking/eating dust below.

[71] This term is also used in 1Q33 (1QM) 18:2–3: "the Kittim shall be crushed (כתת) ... when the hand of the God of Israel is raised against the whole horde of Belial."

[72] So also Wifall, "Gen 3:15—A Protevangelium?," 363.

the hopes of the seed of the woman. Since the verbs for grasping and smashing here are singular, and given the Davidic tinge to the Psalter, perhaps the individual who accomplishes this triumph is the Davidic Messiah.[73]

Daniel 2:34–35 describes the smashing of a statue that represents the kingdoms of the earth by a small stone that becomes a great mountain (cf. 3:26–45). The shattering of the earthly kingdoms brings in the Kingdom of God. Job 34:22–25 depicts God breaking (רעע) and crushing (דכא) those whom he judges. This is a common image in biblical texts, and in the final form of the canon, Gen 3:15 prepares the reader for such statements.[74]

8. Trampled Underfoot

As noted above, the damage done to the head of the serpent and the damage done to the heel of the seed of the woman in Gen 3:15 both seem to be interpreted in later biblical texts as resulting from the stomping of the serpent. The seed of the woman tramples on the head of the serpent, crushing the serpent's head and incurring damage to his own heel.[75] This reality lends significance to references to the enemies of the people of God being "trodden down" or "placed underfoot."

When Joshua leads Israel to victory, their triumph over their enemies is celebrated by the placement of their feet on the necks of the defeated kings (Josh 10:24). The seed of the serpent is under the foot of the seed of the woman. Similarly,

---

[73] It might be observed that Israel's king is viewed as their deliverer (cf. 2 Sam 25:28), and the OT is not reticent to cast the savior of Israel in bloody terms (1 Sam 18:27; Isa 63:1–6). Another pointer in this direction is Bruce Waltke's argument that all of the Psalms should be read with reference to Israel's hoped for king, "A Canonical Process Approach to the Psalms," in *Tradition and Testament* (Chicago: Moody, 1981), 3–18. In support of this, see "*Midr. Ps.* 24:3 (on Ps. 24:1): 'Our Masters taught: In the Book of Psalms, all the Psalms which David composed apply either to himself or to all of Israel.' The midrash goes on to say that in some instances the Davidic psalm may have application for the 'Age to Come' (the messianic age)" (Evans, "The Old Testament in the New," 136).

[74] There is also a reference to enemies being crushed/shattered in the 12th of the *Shemoneh Esreh*, the Eighteen Benedictions (Babylonian version). In 1 Maccabees, four times Judas is depicted speaking of his enemies being "crushed" (συντρίβω) (3:22; 4:10, 30; 7:42). Further, "the most popular explanation" of Judas' nickname is "that 'Maccabeus' derives from the word 'hammer' (Heb *mqbt*)" (Uriel Rapaport and Paul L. Redditt, "Maccabeus," in *ABD*, 4:454).

[75] See the above discussions of the following texts: 2 Sam 22:43/Ps 18:42 (MT 43); Isa 14:25; 28:3; Jer 23:29; 30:23; Ps 68:22 (MT 23); 110:1; Rom 16:20.

David proclaims that his enemies fell under his feet (2 Sam 22:39/Ps 18:38, MT 39), and the conquering warrior in Isa 63 boasts of the way that he has "trodden (דרך) the winepress alone" (63:3a). It is clarified that there were not grapes but rebellious people in the winepress: "I trod (דרך) them in my anger, and I trampled them down (רמס) in my fury; and their blood spattered on my garments" (63:3b–c).[76] This thought is reiterated in verse 6, "I trampled down (בוס) the peoples in my anger."[77]

In Mal 4 (MT 3), the seed of the woman crushing the head of the serpent takes the form of the ones who fear the name of Yahweh (4:2, MT 3:20) trampling down (עסס) the wicked, and the wicked being ashes under the soles of their feet (4:3, MT 3:21). This image is also employed in Ps 44:5, where the psalmist states, "In your name we trample down (impf. of בוס) those who rise up against us." The same verb appears in Zech 10:5, where the "cornerstone", the "tent peg," the "battle bow," "every ruler" comes from the house of Judah (10:3–4), trampling foes in the clay of the streets (בּוֹסִים בְּטִיט חוּצוֹת) (10:5).

In Ps 60:12 (MT 14) we read, "With God we shall do valiantly, and *he shall trample* (impf. of בוס) *our foes*" (emphasis added, same text as Ps 108:13, MT 14). And then among the blessings enumerated by the psalmist in Ps 91 we find a statement about protection for the foot of the one who trusts in Yahweh (91:2): "he will command his angels concerning you, to guard you in all your ways (דֶּרֶךְ). On their hands they will bear you lest you smite (נגף) your foot on the stone. Upon the lion and the venomous serpent you will tread (דרך); you will trample (רמס) the young lion and the dragon" (91:11–13). This text appears to interpret Gen 3:15 such that Yahweh will command his angels so that when the seed of the woman goes on its way (דֶּרֶךְ) to tread

---

[76] Cf. the words of the Targum of Pseudo-Jonathan on Gen 49:11, "the king, Messiah,... With his garments dipped in blood, he is like one who treads grapes in the press" (as cited in Charlesworth, "From Messianology to Christology," 15).

[77] Depending on how Isa 41:2 is translated, it too might fit with the motif being exposited here. The phrase in question reads, וּמְלָכִים יַרְךְ. If the form יַרְךְ derives from either רדד or רדה, it can mean something like "trample down" (see BDB, 921–22). This seems to be the way several translations take it: "he tramples kings underfoot" (ESV, NRSV, RSV). The reading יורד appears in 1QIsᵃ, which could derive from ירד (go down). Thus, other translations render the phrase, "he subdues kings" (KJV, NIV, NASU, NET).

(דרך) on the head of the serpent, though the foot of the seed of the woman is in danger and might suffer harm, the angels will bear it up so that it is not destroyed.[78]

9. Licking the Dust

As the restoration of Zion is proclaimed in Isa 49, Yahweh announces the return of the sons and daughters of Israel (49:22). The next statement articulates the subjugation of the enemies of the people of God: "Kings shall be your foster fathers, and their princesses shall be your nursemaids. Noses to the ground, they shall bow down to you, and the dust of your feet they shall lick (לחך). And you shall know that I am Yahweh; the ones who wait for me shall not be put to shame" (49:23). Here the triumph of Yahweh in restoring his people will result in the nobility of the seed of the serpent licking their father's food, dust. Incidentally, their heads are close to the feet of the righteous, as it is the dust of the feet of the righteous that they lick.[79]

Micah 7:1–7 details a woeful condition (cf. 7:1). But verse 7 transitions with an expression of trust, and beginning in verse 8 hope dawns through the rest of the chapter. In the midst of these statements describing the triumph of Yahweh in the salvation of Israel and the judgment of her enemies, as the subjugation of the seed of the serpent is described, we read, "And they shall lick the dust (לחך) like serpents, like the crawling things of the ground" (7:17). With Ps 72:9, which was noted above, these texts seem to draw on the imagery of Gen 3:14.[80] When the Bible describes the defeat

---

[78] See the discussion of Ps 58:10 (MT 11) below. Cf. also the imagery from Gen 3:15 in T. Sim. 6:6, "Then all the spirits of error shall be given over to being *trampled underfoot*;" T. Levi 18:12, "And Beliar shall be bound by him. And he shall grant to his children the authority *to trample on* wicked spirits" (cf. T. Dan 5:10); and Jub. 31:18, "And to Judah he said: 'May the LORD give you might and strength *to tread upon* all who hate you. Be a prince, you and one of your sons for the sons of Jacob; may your name and the name of your son be one which travels and goes about in all the lands and cities'" (emphasis added throughout).

[79] See too the allusion to Gen 3:14 in Isa 65:25, "And as for the serpent, dust is his food."

[80] Several of these images (enemies licking the dust, enemies underfoot, enemies crushed, and the righteous triumphantly reigning forever) appear in the Qumran War Scroll. The text is partially in brackets, but 1Q33 (1QM) 12:14–15 reads, "Open your gate[s] continuously so that the wealth of the nations can be brought to you! Their kings shall wait on you, all your oppressors lie prone before you, the dust [of your feet they shall lick (לחך)]." These lines are addressed to the "war hero" (גבור מלחמה), who is also called "Man of Glory" (איש כבוד) and "Performer of Valiance" (עושי חיל). This individual is

of enemy nations, it uses language reminiscent of the curse on the serpent.

10. Stricken Serpents

Along with the broken heads of broken enemies who are trodden underfoot and lick dust, there are several references in the OT to serpentine foes whom Yahweh has pierced, broken, crushed, or otherwise defeated. The image of the defeated worm seems to reflect the snake of Ge 3.

Isaiah 27:1 refers to "Leviathan" as both a "serpent" and a "dragon." The text reads, "In that day Yahweh will bring visitation—with his sharp, great, and strong sword—upon Leviathan, the fleeing serpent, even upon Leviathan, the crooked serpent, and he will slay the dragon in the sea." Here the eschatological victory of Yahweh amounts to killing the dragon, slaying the snake.

In Isa 51:9 "Rahab" and "the dragon" are set side by side, and Yahweh's victory at the exodus seems to be cast in terms of his victory over the dragon. We read,

> Arise, arise, clothe yourself with strength, O arm of Yahweh. Arise as in the days of old, generations of long ago. Are you not he, the one who cleaved Rahab, piercing the dragon? Are you not he, the one who dried up the sea, waters deep and wide, who made the depths of the sea a way for the redeemed to pass over?[81]

From this text and Isa 27:1, it seems that Isaiah can describe Yahweh's victories past and future as the killing of the great snake. Psalm 74:12–14 is very similar to Isa 51:9. The psalmist states, "God is my king from of old, working salvations in the midst of the land. You divided by your strength the sea, you shattered (שבר in the piel) the heads of the dragons (תַּנִּין) upon the waters. You crushed (רצץ) the heads of Leviathan" (Ps

---

urged to put his foot on the piles of the slain and to crush (מחץ) the peoples (12:9–11). The passage climaxes, after the statement about the enemies licking the dust, with the words, "Rule over the king[dom of …] [… and] Israel to reign forever" (12:15–16). This text is repeated in part in 19:1–8 and 4Q492, where the licking is corroborated.

[81] This text could be influencing T. Sol. 25:7, where the demon from the Red Sea, who claims to have hardened Pharaoh's heart and performed signs and wonders for Jannes and Jambres (25:3–4), explains that he was buried beneath the waters with the defeated Egyptians.

74:12–14a).[82] The same note is sounded in Ps 89:10 (MT 11): "You crushed (דכא) Rahab as one who is profaned."[83]

In Ps 44:19 the psalmist claims that instead of breaking the dragon, Yahweh broke his servants. The text reads, "For you have crushed (דכה) us in the place of dragons,[84] and you cover us with the shadow of death."[85] Psalm 58:4–6 (MT 5–7) describes the wicked as having venom like that of a serpent (58:4, MT 5) who cannot be charmed (58:5, MT 6), and then God is called upon to break (הרס) their teeth (58:6, MT 7).[86] Psalm 58 then concludes with the words: "The righteous (sg.) will rejoice (sg.) because he sees vengeance; he will bathe (sg.) his feet (sg.) in the blood of the wicked" (58:10, MT 11). Here those who are likened to a serpent in verse 4, whose

---

[82] Cf. T. Ash. 7:3, "Until such time as the Most High visits the earth. [He shall come as a man eating and drinking with human beings,] *crushing the dragon's head* in the water" (emphasis added, brackets indicate suspected Christian interpolation). Perhaps this imagery gives rise to the imprecation in Pss. Sol. 2:25, "Do not delay, O God, to repay to them on (their) *heads*; to declare dishonorable the arrogance of the *dragon*" (trans. R. B. Wright, *OTP*, 2:653, emphasis added). See also the reference to the subversive serpent in Pss. Sol. 4:9. In Pss. Sol. 17:4 we read, "Lord, you chose David to be king over Israel, and swore to him about his *seed* forever, that his kingdom should not fail before you." Verses 5–6 speak of a rival monarchy set up in place of the "throne of David," whose destruction is described by verse 7: "But you, O God, overthrew them, and uprooted their *seed* from the earth, for there rose up against them a man alien to our race" (I have altered Wright's translation emphasizing *seed* for σπέρματος in v. 4 and σπέρμα in v. 7—Wright renders both as "descendants"). The "man alien to our race" (Pompey?) is perhaps viewed as Yahweh's agent of judgment, and yet this judgment is both purging and defiling (17:11–20). In response to this, the psalmist calls on God to raise up the "son of David" (17:21) who will "smash the arrogance of sinners like a potter's jar" and "shatter" them "with an iron rod" (17:23–24; cf. Ps 2:9). With the reference in Pss. Sol. 17:32 to the Lord King Messiah, this seems to set up a picture of a Davidic King whose seed has been challenged by those who are likened to a "dragon," on whose head God is implored to visit judgment (2:25), and whose seed God is described as overthrowing (17:7). The author of the Psalms of Solomon seems to be reading reality through a lens colored by Gen 3:15.

[83] Wifall, "Gen 3:15—A Protevangelium?," 363.

[84] BDB suggests that this form, תַּנִּים, is erroneous for תַּנִּין, "serpent, dragon, sea-monster" (1072). But it could be the plural of תַּן, "jackal." Some manuscripts do read תַּנִּין.

[85] Cf. 2 Esdr (4 Ezra) 5:29, which voices a similar complaint regarding being trodden underfoot, "And those who opposed your promises have trodden down on those who believed your covenants" (*OTP* 1:533).

[86] Another text dealing with the defeat of the serpent is Ps 91:13, which has been noted above, where the serpent is trodden underfoot. See also 1 En. 46:4, "This Son of Man whom you have seen ... shall ... crush the teeth of the sinners."

teeth God is called upon to smash in verse 6, have apparently been trampled down under the feet of Israel's warrior king (cf. the superscription and the singulars), who bathes his feet in their blood in verse 10.

Twice in Job we read of God's power over the serpent. First, in Job 26:12 we find the verb "shatter" (מחץ), which we have seen at numerous points in this study. We read, "By his power he stilled the sea, and by his understanding he shattered Rahab. By his breath the heavens are fair, his hand pierced the fleeing serpent" (26:12–13; cf. Isa 27:1).[87] Again in Job 41:1–34 (MT 40:25–41:26) Yahweh's uniqueness is stressed by an elaborate description of the power of Leviathan (41:1, MT 40:25).[88] The text is forcing the realization that only Yahweh can triumph over this grand dragon.[89]

11. Saving Smashing

Thus far I have briefly commented on a number of texts that, it seems to me, reflect the imagery of Gen 3:14–15. We have seen skulls crushed, enemies broken, the rebellious trodden underfoot, the defeated seed of the serpent licking the dust, and we have seen serpents smashed. Before looking to the use of these motifs in the NT, we will briefly note an unexpected development in this idea of the crushing of the enemy of God.

Twice in Isa 53 we read that the servant was crushed: first in verse 5, "he was crushed (דכא in the pual) for our sins;" and then in verse 10, "Yahweh was pleased to crush (דכא in the piel) him." Here again the crushing judgment first announced in Gen 3:15 seems to be due to Israel because of its sin, but the servant takes their sin upon himself and is crushed for their iniquity, with the result that Yahweh is satisfied (cf.

---

[87] The descriptions of Yahweh as one who has power over storms in this context (see the statements on clouds in 26:8 and the thunder in 26:14) may be a polemic against the Hittite world-view reflected in "The Storm-God and the Serpent (Illuyanka)," trans. Gary Beckman *COS* 1:150–51. In Job Yahweh is the Storm God who triumphs over the serpent.

[88] Cf. Robert S. Fyall, *Now My Eyes Have Seen You*, NSBT 12 (Downers Grove, IL: InterVarsity, 2002), 157: "when Leviathan fills the picture he is no newcomer, nor is he simply an inflated picture of the crocodile. Rather,... he is the embodiment of cosmic evil itself."

[89] It might be significant for this discussion that we read in 2 Kgs 18:4, "And he beat to pieces (כתת) the bronze serpent that Moses made." See too the Targum on the Song of Songs at Song 8:2, where the King Messiah will be led into the temple and the righteous will feast on Leviathan, drinking wine from the day of creation and eating fruits prepared in the Garden of Eden.

53:4, 5, 6, 10, 11, 12).[90]

12. Genesis 3:15 in the New Testament

We can be confident of several allusions to Gen 3:15 in the NT. For instance, in Luke 10:18–19 we read, "[Jesus] said to them, "I was beholding Satan falling as lightning from heaven. Behold, I have given to you the authority to tread upon snakes and scorpions,[91] and upon all the power of the one who is at enmity.""[92] Luke 10 portrays Jesus telling his disciples that they will tread upon snakes and overcome the enemy, and in Rom 16:20, as noted above, Paul tells the Romans that God will soon crush Satan under their feet.[93] Earlier in Romans, Paul wrote that "the creation was subjected to futility ... in hope" (Rom 8:20). If, as most commentators think, the subjection to futility in view is the curse of Gen 3, the corresponding hope would

---

[90] For discussion of this text within its ancient Near Eastern context, see John H. Walton, "The Imagery of the Substitute King Ritual in Isaiah's Fourth Servant Song," *JBL* 122 (2003): 734–43. On another matter, it was noted above that the term גֻּלְגֹּלֶת (skull) is used to describe the crushing of Abimelech's head in Judg 9:53. This term appears to have been transliterated (perhaps via Aramaic) into Greek as γολγοθα (cf. BDAG, 204), which is transliterated into English as Golgotha, and the three Gospels that use the term observe that it means "the place of the skull" (Matt 27:33; Mark 15:22; John 19:27; cf. Luke 23:33). Davies and Allison acknowledge the possibility that the place could have in some way resembled a skull, but state that the reason the place "was named 'Golgotha' is unknown" (*Matthew*, 3:611). The Testament of Solomon depicts a "three-headed dragon" reporting to Solomon that he would be "thwarted" by a "Wonderful Counselor" who would "dwell publicly on the cross" at the "Place of the Skull" (12:1–3 [*OTP*, 1:973]). It is interesting that the one born of woman (i.e., her seed, Gal 4:4) who "nullified the one who has the power of death, that is, the devil" (Heb 2:14)—one might say he crushed the serpent's head—did so at "the place of the skull." Perhaps this gave rise to the name?

[91] Cf. the collocation of snakes and scorpions in Deut 8:15, as well as in "A Ugaritic Incantation against Serpents and Sorcerers," trans. Dennis Pardee, *COS* 1:327–28, lines 1–8 (interestingly, this text seems to link sorcerers with serpents), and in "The London Medical Papyrus," trans. Richard C. Steiner, *COS* 1:328–29, Numbers 30–31 (Number 33 makes reference to a "demon").

[92] I am taking ἐχθρός substantivally, but instead of translating this "the enemy" with other translations (ESV, NASU, NET, NIV, RSV), I am rendering it "the one who is at enmity" to bring out the connection to Gen 3:15. See too the subjugation of the "Prince of Demons" to the son of David, Solomon, in T. Sol. Greek title; 1:7; 3:1–6. See further D. C. Duling, "Solomon, Exorcism, and the Son of David," *HTR* 68 (1975): 235–52. This tradition of Solomon, son of David, triumphing over the demonic host could have been fostered through the kind of interpretation of Gen 3:15 being offered in this study. See too Solomon's authority over evil spirits in Josephus, *Ant.* 8.2.5 and in Targum Sheni to Esther (cited by Duling, *OTP* 1:947).

[93] See Thomas R. Schreiner, *Romans*, BECNT (Grand Rapids: Baker, 1998), 804–5.

appear to be the promise of one who would defeat the serpent in Gen 3:15.[94]

The scene in Rev 12 is also surely influenced by Gen 3:15.[95] As a woman is giving birth to her seed (12:1–2), a dragon appears hoping to devour the child (12:3–4). Clearly there is enmity between the seed of the woman and the snake. She gives birth to a male child, who is identified as a scion of David through an allusion to Ps 2, and child and mother are supernaturally protected from the dragon (12:5–6). The dragon is thrown down to earth after a battle in heaven (12:7–12), whereupon he again pursues the woman and her seed (12:13). They again benefit from divine protection (12:14–16), so the dragon leaves off pursuit of the singular seed that he might make war on the rest of the collective seed of the woman—those who obey God and hold to the testimony of Jesus (12:17).[96] In Rev 13:3 we read of a beast with a head that seems to have a mortal wound, and as Beale comments, "Such a wound on the head of the grand nemesis of God's people reflects Gen. 3:15, especially when seen together with Rev. 12:17."[97]

Alexander, Schreiner, and Wifall have rightly noted other passages in the NT that incorporate imagery from Gen 3:15. These texts mainly describe the enemies of the seed of the woman (or in some cases, "all things") being placed under his feet (Matt 22:44 and parallels; Acts 2:35; 1 Cor 15:25; Eph 1:20–22; Heb 2:5–9, 14–15; 10:13).[98] Wifall also notes the relevance of the fact that Jesus is named as being born

---

[94] So also C. E. B. Cranfield, *A Critical and Exegetical Commentary on the Epistle to the Romans*, ICC, vol. 1 (Edinburgh: T&T Clark, 1975), 414; and D. J. Moo, *The Epistle to the Romans*, NICNT (Grand Rapids: Eerdmans, 1996), 516.

[95] Cf. Beale, *Book of Revelation*, 679–80, who cites P. S. Minear, "Far as the Curse Is Found: The Point of Rev. 12:15–16," *NovT* 33 (1991): 71–77.

[96] Beale (*Book of Revelation*, 640) notes that "*Odes Sol.* 22 is one of the earliest interpretations of Revelation 12," and that this text (*Odes Sol.*) alludes to Gen 3:15 in 22:5, "He who overthrew by my hands the dragon with seven heads, and placed me at his roots that I might destroy his seed" (*OTP* 2:754).

[97] Beale, *Book of Revelation*, 688. So also Grant R. Osborne, *Revelation*, BECNT (Grand Rapids: Baker, 2002), 496. See too what appears to be an interpretation of Gen 3:15 in T. Sol. 15:10–12, where the stretching of the Son of God on a cross thwarts the whole demonic host. The text states that this man's mother will "not have sexual intercourse with a man" (15:10) and that he is the one "whom the first devil shall seek to tempt, but shall not be able to overcome … he is Immanuel" (15:11). Cf. also T. Sol. 22:20.

[98] Alexander, "Messianic Ideology," 27–28; Schreiner, "Foundations for Faith," 3; Wifall, "Gen 3:15—A Protevangelium?," 364–65.

of (i.e., the seed of) the woman (Gal 4:4) and the seed of David (Rom 1:3; 2 Tim 2:8).[99]

13. Conclusion

I began this study with the suggestion that if we adopt the hypothesis that the Old Testament is a messianic document, written from a messianic perspective, to sustain a messianic hope, we might find that the interpretive methods employed by the authors of the NT are legitimate hermeneutical moves that we can imitate today. This hypothesis would work under the assumption that in the Bible's metanarrative,[100] from the moment God uttered his judgment against the serpent, the seed of the woman (the collective of those who trust God) were hoping for *the* seed of the woman (the man who would achieve the ultimate victory over the serpent).[101] If the books of the Bible were written by and for a remnant of people hoping for the coming of this person, we would expect to find in these texts various resonations of this promise of God. I have argued that we do, in fact, find imagery from Gen 3:15 in many texts across both testaments. We have seen the seed of the woman crushing the head(s) of the seed of the serpent, we have seen shattered enemies, trampled enemies, dust eating defeated enemies, and smashed serpents. I find this evidence compelling. Hopefully others will as well, even if they do not entirely agree with the thesis that the OT is, through and through, a messianic document. There are, no doubt, those who will remain unpersuaded. We do not yet see all things under his feet. May that day come soon.[102]

---

[99] Wifall, "Gen 3:15—A Protevangelium?," 364.

[100] See Richard Bauckham's defense of the term "metanarrative" with reference to the Bible (he prefers to call it a "Nonmodern Metanarrative") in his essay "Reading Scripture as a Coherent Story," in *The Art of Reading Scripture*, ed. Ellen F. Davis and Richard B. Hays (Grand Rapids: Eerdmans, 2003), 47–53.

[101] A shadow of the biblical story of the one who vanquishes the serpent (Jesus) and wins for himself a bride (the church) may be reflected in the West Semitic "Ugaritic Liturgy against Venomous Reptiles," trans. Dennis Pardee, *COS* 1:295–98, where the god Horanu defeats the venomous serpents and gains for himself a bride (lines 61–76).

[102] I wish to express my gratitude to my research assistant, Travis B. Cardwell, for his help formatting this essay. I am also grateful for those who read this piece and offered helpful feedback, especially Profs. Thomas R. Schreiner and Scott R. Swain. Deficiencies or errors that remain are, of course, my responsibility.

WEAL AND WOE IN GENESIS

—David W. Baker

1. Introduction

As the first canonical biblical book, Genesis introduces the reader to people and themes, some of which will receive significant elaboration throughout the Bible, and some of which quickly fade into relative obscurity. "God" (אֱלֹהִים; Gen 1:1) is an example of the former, with that specific lemma occurring over 2,600 times in the Hebrew Bible, while the "tree of life" (עֵץ הַחַיִּים), though having considerable impact on humanity early in the Genesis narrative (2:9; 3:22, 24), is not referred to again until the intertestamental (2 Esdr 2:12; 8:52) and New Testament (Rev 2:7; 22:2, 14, 19) periods.[1]

An important concept, which is of particular interest for the honoree of this volume,[2] is that of the זֶרַע "seed/descendant(s)," which occurs in Genesis fifty-nine times in its nominal form as well as six times as a verb. In his discussions, Alexander points out the key initiating role that Gen 3:15 plays in understanding the term. As part

---

[1] The phrase is used four times in Proverbs (3:18; 11:30; 13:12; 15:4), where it metaphorically compares positive human attributes to a vivifying tree but with no specific allusion to that in Paradise.

[2] E.g., T. Desmond Alexander, "From Adam to Judah: The Significance of the Family Tree in Genesis," *EvQ* 61.1 (1989): 15–19; idem, "Genealogies, Seed and the Compositional Unity of Genesis," *TynBul* 44 (1993): 255–70; idem, "Further Observations on the Term "Seed" in Genesis," *TynBul* 48 (1997): 363–67; idem, "Royal Expectations in Genesis to Kings: Their Importance for Biblical Theology," *TynBul* 49 (1998): 198–212; idem, "Seed" in *New Dictionary of Biblical Theology: Exploring the Unity & Diversity of Scripture*, ed. T. Desmond Alexander, *et al.* (Downers Grove, IL: InterVarsity Press), 769–73; idem, "Messianic Ideology in the Book of Genesis", in *The Lord's Anointed: Interpretation of Old Testament Messianic Texts*, ed. P. E. Satterthwaite, R. S. Hess, and G. J. Wenham (Carlisle: Paternoster; Grand Rapids: Baker, 1995), 22–39; idem, *From Eden to the New Jerusalem: An Introduction to Biblical Theology* (Nottingham: Inter-Varsity Press; Grand Rapids: Kregel), 104–11; idem, *From Paradise to the Promised Land: An Introduction to the Pentateuch*, 3rd ed. (Grand Rapids: Baker Academic, 2012), 100–109 and *passim*.

of his curse spoken to the serpent, God stated: "And enmity I will put between you and the woman, and between your seed and her seed."[3] This programmatic text, or *protevangelium*,[4] contrasts two lines of descent "belonging either to the unrighteous 'offspring of the serpent' or to the righteous 'offspring of the woman'."[5] It "refers to a conflict between good and evil which will eventually result in victory for the righteous 'seed of the woman',"[6] from whose seed will come blessing (Gen 22:18; 26:4; 28:14).[7] While Alexander helpfully examines "seed" as it develops a royal application,[8] this study will take a different tack, looking at the spectrum of "good–evil" as well as "blessing" that is associated with Gen 3:15 and the understanding of "seed," and also trace the seed line, in light of these findings, to Judah, Abraham's fourth son.

We begin with trying to understand the polar terms "good" (טוֹב) and "bad/evil" (רַע), since the Genesis narrative lays a foundation for an understanding of what is beneficial for life and what is detrimental to it, what is weal and what is woe. The terms do not receive specific definition in the text but are part of the world view shared by author and audience, terms which Sailhamer describes as *thema*.[9] "Good" and "evil" are among a small number of "semantic primitives," terms which, while understandable, cannot be explained or reduced through simpler terms.[10] While clear

---

[3] Unless otherwise indicated, all translations are those of the author.

[4] Walter Wifall, "Gen. 3:15—a Protevangelium?," *CBQ* 36 (1974): 361–65.

[5] Alexander, *From Eden*, 107.

[6] Alexander, "Messianic Ideology," 31.

[7] Ibid., 26.

[8] E.g., "Royal Expectations"; *From Paradise*, 141–42; see also "The Regal Dimensions of the תולדות־יעקב: Recovering the Literary Context of Genesis 37–50," in *Reading the Law: Studies in Honour of Gordon J. Wenham*, ed. J. G. McConville and Karl Möller (New York: T&T Clark, 2007), 196–212.

[9] John H. Sailhamer, *The Pentateuch as Narrative: A Biblical-Theological Commentary* (Grand Rapids: Zondervan, 1992), 30; see Mignon R. Jacobs, "The Conceptual Dynamics of Good and Evil in the Joseph Story," *JSOT* 27 (2003): 311.

[10] Anna Wierzbicka, "Semantic Primitives," in *Frames, Fields, and Contrasts: New Essays in Semantic and Lexical Organization*, Adrienne Lehrer and Eva Feder Kittay, eds (Hillsdale: L. Erlbaum Associates, 1992), 209–28; Anna Wierzbicka, *Semantics: Primes and Universals* (Oxford: Oxford University Press, 1996), 51–54, 130–31.

to the original audience, they might not be clear for later readers since, according to Wierzbicka, "everywhere in the world, people may disagree whether something is 'good' or 'bad,' but in doing so, they rely on the concepts 'good' and 'bad' ... (experience can teach us to regard certain things as 'good' or 'bad,' but it cannot teach us the concepts of 'good' and 'bad')."[11] One therefore needs to investigate the terms' textual usage, observing what the terms describe and how they are seen to be "good" or "bad."

This study will start by exploring the semantic field of the "good-evil/weal-woe" polarity within the biblical book of Genesis.[12] This commences by not only including the two adjectives/substantives, but also other forms derived from the same roots (verbs יטב and רעע; nouns טוב, מֵיטָב, רָעָה and רֹעַ). It will note what is described as "good" or "bad" as well as the basis for that consideration, where discernible. After laying this foundation, it will move on to the analysis of the sometimes overlapping semantic field of "blessing" (ברך). Finally, the results of this research will be used to explore the path of "the seed of the woman" as it leads to Judah in Genesis.

2. Moral/ethical usage

In a religious text such as the Bible, one could expect terms from the religious, theological, or moral/ethical spheres to have prominence. This sphere is occupied by some occurrences of רָע in particular. Just prior to the flood, humanity is described in

---

[11] Wierzbicka, *Semantics*, 52.

[12] On semantic field analysis in general, see Adrienne Lehrer, *Semantic Fields and Lexical Structure*, North-Holland Linguistic Series 11 (Amsterdam: North-Holland, 1974); D. A. Cruse, *Lexical Semantics* (Cambridge: Cambridge University Press, 1986); Adrienne Lehrer and Eva Feder Kittay, eds., *Frames, Fields, and Contrasts: New Essays in Semantic and Lexical Organization* (Hillsdale, NJ: L. Erlbaum Associates, 1992). For Biblical Hebrew, see James Barr, "The Image of God in the Book of Genesis—A Study of Terminology," *BJRL* 51 (1968–1969): 11–26; idem, *Biblical Words for Time*, 2nd ed., SBT 1, 33 (London: SCM, 1969); J. F. A. Sawyer, *Semantics in Biblical Research: New Methods of Defining Hebrew Words for Salvation*, SBT 2, 24 (London: SCM, 1972); Moisés Silva, *Biblical Words and their Meanings: An Introduction to Lexical Semantics*, rev. ed. (Grand Rapids: Zondervan, 1995); Robert B. Chisholm, Jr., *From Exegesis to Exposition: A Practical Guide to Using Biblical Hebrew* (Grand Rapids: Baker, 1998), 41–44; Susan Anne Groom, *Linguistic Analysis of Biblical Hebrew* (Carlisle; Waynesboro: Paternoster, 2003), 103–30.

strongly negative moral terms, with God perceiving that "the evil of humanity (רָעַת
הָאָדָם) was great, and every inclination of his heart was only evil (רַע)" (6:5; see 8:21)
and that, in contrast to righteous Noah, the entire earth was corrupted and violent (vv.
11–12), truly depraved (Ps 14:1), and deserving of punishment to the extent of
eradication (Gen 6–8).

The immorality of the Sodomites was noted by the narrator, stating that they
were "evil (רָעִים) and very sinful against YHWH" (13:13), placing the two descriptors
within the same ethical semantic field. Lot also described the same men's intended
forcible rape of his two foreign visitors as "doing evil (תָּרֵעוּ)" (19:7), which they
themselves acknowledged when they said to Lot that, due to his meddling in their
affairs, they would treat him "more despicably (נָרַע) than them" (v. 9). While their
response was likely a sarcastic variation on the wording of Lot's statement in v. 7, it
indicates their awareness of the moral unacceptability of their actions. As he flees from
the condemned city, Lot himself is concerned that the catastrophic punishment (הָרָעָה)
consequential to their evil actions might lead to his own death as well (v. 19).

Judah's son Onan, by practicing *coitus interruptus* with Tamar, acted counter
to God's command to populate the earth (1:28; 9:1), while also thwarting his promise
to provide offspring (17:6, 20, etc.), an unethical action. The narrator noted that "what
he did was evil (וַיֵּרַע) in YHWH's eyes, so he killed him also" (38:10). His older
brother, Er (עֵר), was also "evil" (רַע; a wordplay on "Er" through consonantal
inversion) in God's estimation and suffered his brother's fate (v. 7). The nature of Er's
failing is unspecified, though it was likely similar in some way to that of Onan, since
Er also left no offspring through Tamar.[13]

Another sexual impropriety, adultery with Potiphar's wife, was deplored by
Joseph when he met her solicitation with the question "how shall I do this great evil
(רָעָה) and sin against God?" (39:9). Both parties recognized the immorality of the
suggested liaison, since she did not want it known, proposing it in secret (v. 11).

Joseph provided for his brother's needs when they came to Egypt for supplies

---

[13] Gordon J. Wenham, *Genesis 16–50*, WBC 2 (Dallas: Word, 1994), 366–67.

(Gen 43), but he did not trust their motives due to their earlier mistreatment of him (37:12–36). He tested them, concocting an apparent theft and accused them by asking, "Why have you paid back evil (רַע) for good?... You did evil (הֲרֵעֹתֶם) in what you did" (44:4–5). He was accusing them of an ethically inappropriate response to his beneficial treatment of them. When their despicable treatment of him earlier in their relationship is mentioned later, in addition to being called "evil" (רַע), it is also described as being a "crime" (פֶּשַׁע) and "sin" (חַטָּאת; 50:17; see vv. 15, 20). Their attempted fratricide and lying in order to cover it up were morally repugnant. This could shed light on "their evil report (דִּבָּתָם רָעָה)" which he delivered to his father early in the Joseph story (37:2). The narrator indicated that their unacceptable acts bracket the entire story.

In contrast to the רעע root, טוֹב and its cognates have few clear ethical/moral representatives in Genesis. One of the trees in God's garden is "the tree of the knowledge of good and evil" (2:9; see 3:22) which is forbidden for human consumption (2:17), though the serpent indicates that the knowledge thus gained from it is godlike (3:5). An ethical/moral interpretation regarding "right and wrong" has been proposed by some (e.g., CEV; see TLB, "the Tree of Conscience, giving knowledge of good and bad") and the combination has this connotation elsewhere (Deut 1:39; Isa 7:14–15). It is unlikely that God would desire for his creatures a state of perpetual moral ignorance and lack of ethical discernment, since an ability for such discernment seems presumed if a command is given. A better understanding here seems to be that, rather than following the parameters derived from God, humanity is precluded from self-determination or personal autonomy regarding morality.[14]

Cain seemed to be faced with a divinely offered moral choice when he was angry that his offering was refused by God (4:5). While the verse's translation is extremely problematic, he is offered two choices: acceptance "if you do good (תֵּיטִיב)," or sin, with its implied negative consequences, was lurking, if he made the wrong choice (v. 7). The context suggests that the desired response involved following implied ritual instructions concerning acceptable offerings to God, but instead he made

---

[14] Gordon J. Wenham, *Genesis 1–15*, WBC 1 (Dallas: Word, 1987), 64.

the wrong choice, fratricide leading to banishment (vv. 8–16).

3. Secular usage

Most occurrences of the two roots under discussion lie outside of the moral/ethical sphere. In several instances, the text explicitly states what something is "good for."[15] The first thing so described is each tree planted in Eden that is "pleasant (נֶחְמָד) looking and good for food" (2:9). The utilitarian evaluation[16] (provision of nourishment) is preceded by an aesthetic one. The same utilitarian description is given in 3:6 for "the tree which is in the middle of the garden" (3:3), with additional utilitarian ("desirable [נֶחְמָד] for bringing wisdom") and aesthetic evaluations ("delight [תַאֲוָה] for the eyes"). Other animal foodstuffs are similarly described: the calf, also described as "tender" (רַךְ, as yet untoughened by age, 33:13), which Abraham had prepared for his guests (18:7), and the two goat kids which Rebekah requested of Jacob as a means of misleading his father (27:9). In the first two instances, the evaluation is provided by the narrator, while in the latter two, it is given by actors within the story. The final utilitarian evaluation is provided by Joseph who considers God's choice to preserve him despite his brother's evil machinations was done "in order to … preserve many people alive" (50:20; see 45:7), including the preservation of those very brothers.[17]

While not explicitly stating the purpose of the "good" as in the examples noted, other uses of the term seem to share a similar utilitarian evaluation. Two additional comestible items appear as "good" in the dreams which Pharaoh shared with Joseph: cattle (41:35) and grain ears (41:5, 22, 24). The latter were also described as "fat" (בְּרִיאוֹת, v. 5, see v. 7) and "full" (מְלֵאֹת, v. 22, see v. 7). The former were also

---

[15] See R. P. Gordon, "טוב", *NIDOTTE* 2, 353 who indicates that the root means "a state or function appropriate to genre, purpose, or situation." Also, Claus Westermann, *Creation,* translated by John J. Scullion (Philadelphia: Fortress, 1974), 61, who writes, "good or suited for the purpose for which it is being prepared."

[16] I. Höver-Johag, "טוב *ṭôb*," *TDOT* 5, 304, a "utilitarian meaning in secular usage".

[17] The same preservative function (also using the *hiphil* stem of the verb חיה) is fulfilled by bringing animals and birds into the ark (6:19, 20; 7:3), directing Lot away from Sodom (19:19), and Joseph providing food to Egypt during famine (47:25).

"fat/healthy" (vv. 2, 4, 18, 20) as well as "fine looking" (יְפוֹת מַרְאֶה, vv. 2, 4; וִיפֹת תֹּאַר,
v. 18), combining aesthetic with utilitarian evaluations. Their utility appears also to
relate to the suitability for preserving life through their consumption. In contrast were
the "wild (רָעָה) animal" which Joseph's brothers claim devoured him (37:20, 33).
Unlike grain or cattle which provide for humanity, carnivores, through no moral failure
but by their very nature, put life in jeopardy.

God evaluated elements of his initial creation in the same utilitarian manner,
pronouncing them "good" since each fulfills his purpose in creating them: light (1:4),
dry land and sea (1:10), seed-bearing plants (1:12), the greater and lesser celestial
lights with their regulatory functions (1:18), creatures of sea, air (1:21), and land
(1:25). The totality of his creation, even the expanse (1:6–8) and humans (1:26–30)
which had previously received no independent evaluation, were evaluated even more
emphatically as "very good" (1:31). This latter designation does not, however, indicate
that all of creation is perfect or even complete, since Gen 2:18 indicates that the first
man's state of aloneness was "not good" (לֹא־טוֹב). This does not indicate something
that is the opposite of "good," "bad" or "evil," but indicates rather something yet
lacking, since it was to be rectified through providing "a helper as his counterpart" (v.
18). This lack is potentially met through the animals presented to the man (vv. 19–20),
but he quickly recognized that they did not fill this need, which would only be
addressed when an ontological equivalent, a "counterpart," was presented to him (v.
23). Only the woman was able to make "good" the lack of companionship, and
secondarily allow humanity to fulfill its original mandate, "to be fruitful, and multiply,
and fill the land, and subdue it" (1:28).

Humans receive the same aesthetic evaluation as did the cattle and grain of
Pharaoh's dreams, since "fine looking" described Sarai (יְפַת־מַרְאֶה, 12:11, see v. 14),
Rebekah (טֹבַת מַרְאֶה; 24:16; 26:7), Rachel (יְפַת־תֹּאַר וִיפַת מַרְאֶה, 29:17), and Joseph (יְפֵה־
תֹּאַר וִיפֵה מַרְאֶה, 39:6).[18] The "human daughters" were simply described as "good" (6:2),
apparently with this same nuance. This could be strictly an aesthetic judgment, but

---

[18] Höver-Johag, "טוֹב ṭôḇ," 306.

since each case also involved a sexual component, a utilitarian evaluation of mates with reproductive capabilities appears also to have been in play. Such fruitfulness seems to have been also in view when Issachar in his blessing from his father saw "a resting-place which is good" paralleling "the land which is pleasant" (49:15), combining utilitarian and aesthetic evaluations.

Leah considered her giving birth to a sixth son, Zebulun, to be a "good gift/dowry" (זֶבֶד טוֹב, 30:20) since it would serve to win from her husband Jacob the respect she so desired. Laban saw a relative advantage (טוֹב) of marrying off his daughter Rachel to Jacob rather than to another (29:19). The context of negotiating for laborer's wages (v. 15) shows that Laban's evaluation was based on economic self-interest. Relative value is likely also in mind when one of the natural resources found in the land of Havilah is designated as "good gold" (2:12), gold of a high quality. Value is also found in living long and well, to a "good old age" (שֵׂיבָה טוֹבָה, Gen 15:15; 25:8).

At times, "good," like beauty, is in the eye of the beholder, as when the phrase "the good in your eyes" (הַטּוֹב בְּעֵינַיִךְ) was used by Abraham regarding Sarah's treatment of Hagar (16:6), or similarly of Lot offering his virgin daughters to the Sodomites (19:8). In these cases, one could say that what is designated "good" was only so for one party of the transaction, with Hagar and Ishmael facing mistreatment and Lot's daughters' potential gang-rape. In another case, Abimelek offered Abraham land to live "wherever appears good to you (good in your eyes)" (20:15). These examples show that, as noted by Wierzbicka,[19] in at least in some cases, the meaning of "good" was relative to the perception of the evaluator.[20]

Using the *qal* verbal form of the root "to be good" (יטב), Joseph interpreted the cupbearer's dream as a time of restoration for him, asking that the cupbearer keep Joseph in mind when "it is well" with him (40:14).[21] Twice the verb anticipated matters being evaluated positively "in the eyes of" Pharaoh regarding Joseph's suggestion for Egypt to survive impending famine (41:37), as was the news of the safe arrival of

---

[19] See n.3.

[20] Höver-Johag, "טוֹב *ṭôb*," 308, "subjective estimate".

[21] The royal baker also saw that this dream interpretation was "good" (40:16).

Joseph's family to join him in Egypt (45:16). Hamor and Shechem made the same hopeful evaluation of the suggestion by Jacob's sons concerning how to win Dinah, but their perception proved wrong (34:18). With the causative *hiphil* form of the same stative verb, in several cases the verb's subject performed a beneficial action for another. Abraham used the subterfuge of having his wife pretend to be his sister so that Pharaoh might "treat him well" through sparing his life (12:13), which he did (v. 16), with Abraham also reaping considerable economic gain. Jacob also reminded God that he had promised to "do him good," blessing him with offspring (32:10, 13).

Economic advantage or gain describes several other uses of the טוב root. Joseph's beneficence to his undeserving brothers (44:4) has already been mentioned. When Abraham sent a servant to find a wife for Isaac, he took along with him "every good thing (טוב) of his master" (24:10), which included gold jewelry and other expensive gifts (v. 22, 53). The bountiful produce of the land of Egypt defined its "good years" (41:25), and Pharaoh promised the "good (טוב) of the land," including the "fat of the land," to Jacob and his sons (45:18, 20, 23). Even surpassing this, he also promised them "the best part (מֵיטָב) of the land" in Goshen (47:6) or Raamses (v. 11).

Not every occurrence of the רעע root constituents has ethical/moral connotations, as is clear from 31:7. There Laban's unethical treatment of Jacob (he "schemed against me, changing my wages on ten occasions") is placed in contrast to this root, since "God has not allowed him to deal harmfully (לְהָרַע) with me." Here deprivation of economic advantage was in mind. A רַע/טוב combination provides a merismic spectrum in describing speech (24:50; 31:24, 29), with this combination occurring in Genesis only in the Aramaean context of speech between Laban and Jacob. Actions were also described through both ends of this spectrum, as in Abimelek's suing for a treaty with Isaac based on beneficial rather than harmful action (רָעָה, טוב, 26:29). At times, however, only the negative, harmful side of the spectrum was noted (רַע, 31:29; 48:16; רָעָה, 31:52 x 2).

Economic disadvantage was also found in Pharaoh's dreams mentioned earlier. In contrast to the good cattle in Pharaoh's dream were another group designated as "bad/ugly looking" (רָעוֹת מַרְאֶה, 41:3, 4; רָעוֹת תֹּאַר, v. 19; see there also רֹעַ "ugliness") which were further described as "thin" (רַקּוֹת, vv. 19, 20, 27; דַּקּוֹת, vv. 3, 4) or "weak" (דַּלּוֹת, v. 19). Aesthetics played a role in their evaluation, but so too did economic value, since emaciated, low-quality cattle were of no use for meat or milk.

Mental "distress" was precipitated for Abraham by Sarah's mistreatment of Hagar and Ishmael (וַיֵּרַע, 21:11, 12), for Jacob by the possibility of Esau marrying "displeasing" (רָעוֹת) Canaanite women (28:8), Joseph's prison mates in the dejection of their imprisonment (40:7), and Joseph when his father seemed to wrongly bless two of his sons (48:17). Jacob was afflicted by "misery" when the existence of his remaining son, Benjamin, was revealed (הֲרֵעֹתֶם, 43:6; see 44:34), since his possible death would lead to Jacob's death "in misery" (בְּרָעָה, 44:29), and he finally evaluated the days of his own life as being "few and miserable" (רָעִים, 47:9).

4. Blessing

Related to the field of "good" and "evil" is that of "blessing," which is the bestowal or wish for favor or good upon someone. For example, Jacob called blessing upon his two grandsons, Ephraim and Manasseh, by saying "The angel who delivers me from all harm (רַע) may he bless (יְבָרֵךְ) the lads" (48:16, see vv. 9, 15). This adds the idea of blessing to the semantic field of "good" (that which is here desired) and "evil" (to which the blessing is in contrast). In this context, the blessing is a desire for numerical increase (רֹב) through offspring (v. 16) so that they might become a model of blessing (v. 20). Numerous other blessings include increase of various types, as indicated in the CHART OF "BLESSINGS" IN GENESIS on the following page.

In several instances, YHWH blessed economically, through increased crops and wealth for Isaac (26:12–13), land possession for Jacob (28:4), and Laban's increased flock yield through Jacob's innovative breeding practices (30:27–30). Esau was tricked out of his blessing, the central theme of Genesis 27, in which the verb "bless" occurs seventeen times[22] and the noun "blessing" six.[23] The context also contains economic elements ("heaven's dew," "earth's abundance," "plenitude (רֹב) of

---

[22] Gen 27: 4, 7, 10, 19, 23, 25, 27 (bis), 29 (bis), 30, 31, 33 (bis), 34, 38, 41.
[23] Gen 27:12, 35, 36 (bis), 38, 41.

CHART OF "BLESSINGS" IN GENESIS						
Ref.	Subject blessing	Object or Person being blessed	"Make fruitful" פרה	"Multiply" רבה	"Fill" מלא	Other Actions
1:22	God	Sea and water creatures[24]	X	X	X	
1:28	God	Humans[25]	X	X	X	Subdue כבש Rule רדה
9:1	God	Noah and sons	X	X	X	
9:7	God	Noah and sons	X	X	X	Abound שרץ
12:2	YHWH	Abram				Great nation, great name
17:16 x 2	God	Sarah				Give son, mother of nations and kings[26]
17:20	God	Ishmael	X	X		Princes, great nation
22:17	YHWH	Abraham		X		Offspring inherit enemy's gates
24:35–36	YHWH	Abraham				Wealth, possessions, son
24:60	Laban and his mother	Rebekah		[X][27]		Offspring inherit enemy's gates
26:3–4	YHWH	Isaac		X		Give lands
26:12	YHWH	Isaac				100–fold increase
26:24	YHWH	Isaac		X		
28:1, 3–4, [6]	God Almighty through Isaac	Jacob	X	X		Land[28]
35:9–12	God	Jacob	X	X		Become nations, kings, land
48:3–4	God Almighty	Jacob	X	X		Become nations, given land

grain and sweet-wine," v. 28, see vv. 37, 39) in addition to a position of authority over other nations as well as his own kin (v. 29, see vv. 37, 40). Humans also blessed in

---

[24] After the flood, Noah was commanded to bring out birds and terrestrial creatures from the ark so they could "abound (שרץ), be fruitful, and multiply" (8:17), though there is no explicit mention of blessing.

[25] God blessed humanity also in 5:2 at the beginning of a genealogy, demonstrating that fruitfulness and increase took place.

[26] Abraham, through a covenant with God, was promised increase (17:2), to be father of nations (vv. 4, 5, 6), fruitfulness (v. 6), and fathering nations and kings (v. 6), though these were not designated in the context as being a "blessing." Previously, Abraham's surrogate Hagar was promised increase (16:10), though this too was not identified as a "blessing."

[27] "May you have a thousand-fold increase (אַלְפֵי רְבָבָה)."

[28] Though not designated as a blessing, in 35:11–12 God Almighty commands fruitfulness and increase, promising nations, kings, and land.

this way, as with the blessing gifts which Jacob gave to Esau (33:10, 12–13), which consisted of considerable animal wealth (vv. 14–15), to some extent ameliorating the blessing which he had stolen.[29] Joseph's administrative skills brought blessing to Potiphar in both house and field (39:5). Jacob also wished blessing on his son Joseph, including "blessings of the breast and womb," fruitfulness and progeny (49:25).[30]

At times, blessings by God or by people do not specify of what they consisted.[31] Elsewhere, blessings appear to have been formal greetings or expressions of thanks, given by one of lower rank to a superior (Noah, 9:26, Melchizedek, 14:20, Abraham's servant blessing God, 24:27, 48, and Jacob blessing or greeting Pharaoh, 47:7, 10).

One other blessing is that of the seventh day by God: "And God blessed the seventh day and set it apart (וַיְקַדֵּשׁ) because in it he ceased from all of his work" (2:3). This blessing is unspecified as regards its nature if the blessing and sanctifying are in fact two separate acts conjoined by "and." The second verb might instead be explicative,[32] showing what this unique blessing of a period of time might entail, namely its designation as a ceasing from toil, in which its benefit would be indirect, for those workers who could cease on that day.

5. "Her Seed"

As noted earlier, Gen 3:15 initiates a trajectory in which two different "seeds," one (that of the woman) viewed positively and the other (that of the serpent) negatively, will be in conflict. The former is the focus here. According to the Genesis narrative, the first two offspring of the woman did not establish this trajectory, since

---

[29] Yair Zakovitch, "Inner Biblical Exegesis," in *Reading Genesis: Ten Methods*, ed. Ronald Hendel (New York: Cambridge University Press, 2010), 112.

[30] For a study of blessing in relation to economics or possessions, see Paul D. Vrolijk, *Jacob's Wealth: An Examination into the Nature and Role of Material Possessions in the Jacob-Cycle (Gen 25:19–35:29)*, VTSup 146 (Leiden: Brill, 2011), 310–23.

[31] God: 12:3 (all who bless Abram); 14:19 (Abram); 24:1 (Abraham "in every way"), 31 (Abraham's servant); 25:11; 26:29 (Isaac); humans: 12:3; 18:18; 22:18; 28:14 (nations of the earth through Abram and his descendants); 33:55 (Heb 32:1, Laban his daughters and grandchildren); 32:26, 29 (Heb 27, 30, wrestling foe blesses Jacob).

[32] For studies of the explicative function of other forms, see, e.g., David W. Baker, "Further Examples of the *Waw Explicativum*," *VT* 30 (1980): 129–36; idem, "Explicative *wāw*," *EHLL* I: 890–92.

the first, Cain, murdered his brother Abel and was consequently exiled (4:1–18), though his line is traced for a further six generations (vv. 17–22). Neither son is designated as "seed" in the text, but the third son, Seth, is given this designation by his mother (4:25) and it is he and his descendants whose line is traced through Noah (5:1–32). Noah's "seed," Shem, Ham, and Japheth, receive God's covenant (9:9), though the narrative narrows the focus as it moves on through Noah's son Shem to Abram (11:10–26; see 10:21–29).

Abram received special promises of blessing (e.g., 12; 15; 17) applicable also to his "seed" (e.g., 12:7; 13:15–16). Even in times when he practiced deceit, Abraham received good from those whom he harmed (12:16; 20:14–15). It is the second of Abraham's sons, Isaac, through whom the line is traced (17:19), even though his first son, Ishmael, the "seed" of an Egyptian handmaid, also receives blessing through his father (16:10; 17:20). Isaac showed the same deceitful tendencies as his father, with his victim repaying good for evil just as he had done with Abraham (26:29). The usurpation of the expected priority of the firstborn happens with the next generations as well. Isaac's firstborn, Esau is shown to willingly cede his firstborn birthright to his younger brother Jacob (25:29–34), who then also gains the firstborn blessing through trickery, aided by their mother Rebekah (27:1–41). This fulfilled YHWH's prognostication of the reversal at the babies' birth (25:23). Jacob himself received the promise of "seed" who would be blessed (26:24; 28:4, 13, 14), a promise fulfilled by his fathering thirteen children from four different mothers (29:31–30:24; 35:16–18).

Jacob's sons continued the trend of the loss of firstborn status. Reuben, the firstborn, lost the privileges of that position through incest with his father's concubine, Bilhah (35:22; 49:4; 1 Chr 5:1–2),[33] and the next two sons, Simeon and Levi, also usurped a father's responsibility, this time when they, rather than Jacob, avenged the rape of their sister Dinah (34:25–31; 49:5–7).[34] The "seed" line in the rest of Genesis is somewhat ambiguous. Jacob, laying his hands upon and blessing his grandsons

---

[33] Kenneth A. Mathews, *Genesis 11:27–50:26* (Nashville: Broadman & Holman, 2005), 626–27.

[34] Ibid., 609.

Ephraim and Manasseh, designated them as full sons ("seed") and heirs just like
Reuben and Simeon (48:5, 11, 19). According to the Chronicler, in an interpretation
which is unique in the Old Testament, they inherited the birthright privileges of
firstborn (1 Chr 5:1–2). Alexander has argued that their positioning, as well as the way
their father Joseph is treated in the narrative, in particular in the blessings of 49:22–
26, bestow upon him the status of firstborn.[35] Pride of place in these blessings,
however, seems to be given to Judah (vv. 8–12), who was given royal authority over
his brothers, who bow down to him like they would to Joseph in his earlier vision
(37:5–10). Alexander suggests that he also can be identified as "firstborn."[36] Judah's
descendants are given primary status later in the history of Israel, as when their banner
leads that of the other tribes, including Reuben, Ephraim, and Manasseh, when they
departed from Sinai (Num 10:14). His royal standing is illustrated by his descendants,
one of whom is Israel's great king, David (1 Chr 2:3–15; Matt 1:2–6; Luke 3:31–33),
and another is Jesus (Matt 1:2–16; Luke 3:23–33).

The importance of Judah in the line of the "seed of the woman" shows that
there is not a one-to-one correspondence between election and merit, between good
action and blessing. In the incident in which Judah impregnated his daughter-in-law
Tamar, he himself acknowledged that his action in withholding his youngest son from
bearing a child with her, and thus failing to perpetuate the family name, was less
righteous than hers, which, while deceitful, was done to protect and perpetuate that
line (38:26). It was this heroic act by Tamar which in fact led to the conception of
Perez, an ancestor of king David (38:29; Ruth 4:18–22). Judah is also not portrayed in
a positive light in his treatment of his brother Joseph. When his brothers determined
to kill Joseph, Reuben sought to save his life (37:21–22). Judah did as well, but for
less noble reasons, since he suggested that profit was better than fratricide (vv. 26–
27). Judah later proved himself more honorable than the previous two events might
indicate, offering himself as a replacement for his youngest brother Benjamin (44:33–
34). As Jacobs states regarding this incident, "according to the conceptuality of the

---

[35] Alexander, "Regal Dimension," 204–6.
[36] Ibid., 206–07 and references there.

story, the agents in the dynamics of good and evil are not limited to good or evil by virtue of their identity or quality of their previous actions. The capacity for good and evil may be a part of the same person."[37]

6. Conclusion

The semantic field of the "good–bad/evil" spectrum in Genesis can function in the moral/ethical as well as the secular spheres. At times the relegation of something to either pole of the spectrum is from the perspective of divine evaluation, but at other times it may be determined by a human evaluator, showing that the designations good/evil can be somewhat subjective. The field of "blessing" is associated positively with the "good" side of the spectrum, while "bad" can indicate its lack. Many examples of the two fields in Genesis of necessity relate to the "seed of the woman" (Gen 3:15) as it is traced through the promised line through Abraham and beyond, since this is the main focus of the narrative. The foundations of an understanding of good/evil and blessing were laid, however, prior to the establishment of this particular line. They have human, rather than simply Abrahamic, applicability, and in fact are more universal than creaturely, since they are applied to days, in particular the seventh day. There are within these fields links between the "sacred" and the "secular." Ethics is at times related to work, to economics. Blessing, or economic weal, the good, is derived from a proper relationship with the Creator, but that is not always exemplified by equating ethical action with blessing. At times, as in the case of Judah, his position as one of the promised "seed of the woman," and any blessing which he might receive, are not predicated on "good" acts, but rather center on the mysteries of divine election.

---

[37] Jacobs, "Conceptual Dynamics," 321.

Ephraim or Judah? Divine Sovereignty and the Potential for Kingship in Joshua–Judges[*]

—*Sarah Dalrymple*

1. Introduction

The programmatic statement of Gen 3:15 announces the defeat of the serpent by the seed of the woman. The promises to the patriarchs in turn highlight a distinctive family lineage, anticipating the establishment of a royal dynasty from that "seed" (Gen 17:6, 16; cf. 35:11). While Gen 25–36 is relatively silent on the subject of kingship,[1] the final section of the book (chs. 37–50) presupposes the royal concept and prepares for the future stages of its development.

In these chapters, the issue of the identity of the son who will succeed Jacob in the unique line of "seed" and the tribe that will produce the future royal line finds its focus in the person of Joseph. To some extent, Jacob's predilection for Joseph is understandable. Joseph is the son of his beloved wife Rachel, and his birth apparently marked the beginning of a new episode in Jacob's life (Gen 30:25). Chronologically, Joseph is Jacob's eleventh son, but Jacob treats him as his firstborn.[2] For Van Groningen, the royal concept is "a central and dominating factor in the Genesis account of Joseph."[3] The specific regal terminology of his dreams, together with the

---

[*] I respectfully dedicate this brief offering to T. Desmond Alexander: theologian, supervisor, and fellow heir according to promise.

[1] The most obvious exceptions are God's promise to Jacob in Gen 35:11 and the reference to Edomite kings in Gen 36 (see below). Isaac's blessing of Jacob (27:27–29), though lacking any explicit "royal" terminology, contains allusions to nationhood and sovereignty, and anticipates the experiences of Joseph (37:7, 9, 10; 42:6; 43:26, 28).

[2] Reuben, the firstborn, is thus displaced by a younger brother, reflecting a recurring pattern (cf. Seth/Cain; Isaac/Ishmael; Jacob/Esau; Ephraim/Manasseh; Perez/Zerah).

[3] W. Van Groningen, *Messianic Revelation in the Old Testament* (Grand Rapids: Baker, 1990), 150–53. Van Groningen's aim is to show how the text presents Joseph as a "messianic type."

reaction of his brothers and father to their obvious content, confirm their clear prediction of his future sovereignty. In Egypt Joseph's leadership qualities are recognized by Potiphar and in the royal prison. His divinely given ability to interpret Pharaoh's dreams results in his accession to royal status, where his rule is characterized by wisdom and the pastoral qualities of protection and provision.

Joseph's pre-eminence is not limited to his exile in Egypt or even to his own lifetime. Jacob's gift to Joseph of a portion of the land and his adoption of Joseph's sons Manasseh and Ephraim (48:1–20) indicate the patriarch's designation of Joseph and his descendants as those destined to take a leadership role in the fulfilment of the divine promises to Abraham. Jacob intentionally transmits the patriarchal blessing to Ephraim, Joseph's younger son. Once again, circumvention of the law of primogeniture highlights the distinction between alternative lines and the special line of seed. Ephraim's family line is destined for future ascendancy, and Jacob's blessing initiates the tradition that Ephraim would be the channel of a royal dynasty.

Joseph, however, is not the only protagonist whose leadership is articulated using royal terminology. Indeed, what is unarguably the clearest expression of royal status in this section of Genesis is ascribed to his brother Judah in 49:8–12. While Joseph continues to play a crucial leadership role that reflects kingly rule, the insertion of some surprising biographical material in Gen 38 registers the importance of the lineage associated with Judah. In a reversal that may well be symbolic of the larger story Perez, the fruit of Judah's unseemly union with Tamar, "breaks out" in front of the firstborn twin Zerah.[4] The Testament of Jacob in Gen 49 addresses all the sons of Jacob, but the blessings given to Joseph and Judah are distinctive by their content and extent. While Jacob's blessing declares the future royal status of Judah (49:8–12), the prolific nature of his blessing upon Joseph confirms his privileges as firstborn.[5] The focus on "blessing" in and through the life of Joseph, the one "who was set apart from his brothers," further supports the expectation at this stage in biblical history that royal

---

[4] T. Desmond Alexander, *From Paradise to the Promised Land: An Introduction to the Pentateuch*, 3rd ed. (Grand Rapids: Baker Academic), 106.

[5] Compare 1 Chr 5:1–2.

leadership will continue through his line.

The supremacy of Joseph is reiterated in the Blessing of Moses (Deut 33:13–17), where the tribes of Ephraim and Manasseh are personified in their eponymous ancestor. In anticipation of the conquest and settlement of the land, the blessings focus on the fertility of their territory and their military prowess. Joseph's strength is like that of "a firstborn bull,"[6] while the horns of the wild ox represent the troops of Ephraim and Manasseh, with Ephraim taking pre-eminence. As Israelite history begins to unfold, therefore, the center of gravity lies with Joseph, the "prince among his brothers."[7]

This brief contextual overview sets the stage for further exploration of the biblical-theological process linking the promises of "royal progeny" in Genesis with the coming of the messianic King. This essay will focus on two potential messianic trajectories as portrayed in Joshua–Judges, in anticipation of the divine rejection of one royal lineage (and its associated worship place) for the election of another (Ps 78:59–72). From this divinely elected royal lineage will emerge the Messiah who, through suffering, will climactically defeat the serpent (Gen 3:15).

2. The Potential for Kingship in the Book of Joshua

In the wake of the exodus and Sinai events, the prospect of a successor to Moses emanating from the tribe of Ephraim is far from improbable. It comes as no surprise, therefore, to discover that the figure most closely associated with Israel's conquest of the land of promise is that of the Ephraimite Joshua. Meanwhile, as Joseph's royal profile is maintained through his descendants, the status of the tribe of Judah continues to "shadow" it: Caleb, Joshua's Judahite counterpart, is present "in the wings." The profile of these two leaders in the book of Joshua epitomizes the prominence of the tribes they represent.

---

[6] Scripture references in this essay are mainly from the ESV, with some exceptions which are indicated as appropriate.

[7] The same epithet is used of Joseph in Gen 49:26.

2.1. Joshua as a Leader

Israel's first Ephraimite leader carries impressive credentials. His role as Moses' aide reflects a close association between the two men, anticipating his commissioning as Moses' legitimate successor and preparing for his leadership role "after the death of Moses" (Josh 1:1). Joshua's first appearance is as a warrior who leads the Israelites in their first military encounter after the exodus (Exod 17:8–13). His crucial role in the defeat of Amalek, the archetypal enemy of Israel, is encapsulated in his name יְהוֹשֻׁעַ ("Yahweh is salvation"), and anticipates future victories over Canaanite kings.[8]

The selection of Joshua as Ephraim's representative in the reconnaissance team dispatched by Moses suggests that he had a tribal leadership role separate from his special relationship with Moses. The twelve spies are described as "leading men" (Num 13:3 NRSV). Their designation by tribe, proper name and paternal association confirms the impression that Joshua, like the other spies, was an influential man whose report could sway the community. The focus on Hebron recalls God's command and promise to Abraham at that location (Gen 13:14–17). The patriarch's acquisition of a burial plot was an act of faith, anticipating the eventual fulfilment of the promise.[9] Similarly, the spies' expedition was to be a symbolic claim to possession.[10] Among the twelve "leading men," however, only Caleb and Joshua focus on the divine promises and "unreservedly" follow the LORD (Num 32:12 NRSV). The actions of the two faithful spies adumbrate their future leadership roles.

In Num 27, Moses' imminent death necessitates the commissioning of his legitimate successor. While Joshua's succession ensures continuity, his major task will be to lead Israel in conquest and to "go out before them and come in before them" (Num 27:17). This idiom, combined with the image of the leader as shepherd, connotes royal leadership.[11] The commissioning of Joshua initiates a focus on Israel's future

---

[8] L. D. Hawk, "Joshua" in *DOT:P*, 478.

[9] G. J. Wenham, *Numbers*, TOTC (Leicester: Inter-Varsity Press, 1981), 120.

[10] J. Milgrom, *Numbers* (Philadelphia: JPS, 1990), 100.

[11] The only other occurrence of this combination is applied to David (2 Sam 5:2). See also Isa 40:11; 44:28; Ezek 34; cf. Ps 78:71.

leadership, which carries on through the book of Deuteronomy and into Joshua and Judges. Joshua's commissioning, therefore, signals continuity with the past, but also marks the development of a paradigm for leadership for the covenant community and its life in the land.

2.2. *Joshua: A royal Leader?*

This vision for future leadership is reflected in the second account of Joshua's succession, related in Deut 31. For McConville, the account is "highly climactic in the flow of Deuteronomy" but also points forward to the continuing narrative in Josh 1:1–9.[12] A major element here is the completion of the Book of the Law (Deut 31:9–13 and 24–27), which provides the contextual framework for Joshua's appointment.

Unsurprisingly, the close association between Joshua's leadership and the Book of the Law resurfaces in Josh 1:1–9. The charge given to the new leader could be interpreted as a call to bravery in battle. However, verses 7–9 make clear that he will need to be "strong and very courageous" in obeying the precepts of the law. Not only is Joshua himself obedient to the commands of Moses, he also teaches "the book of the law" to the people and takes measures to ensure its transmission to future generations (4:1–9; 5:9; 7:24–26; 8:28–29; 8:30–35; 23:1–24:27).

The association between leadership and Torah is unambiguous—nowhere more so than in the law on the king in Deut 17:14–20 and in Yahweh's words to Joshua in Josh 1:2–9. This raises the question as to whether Joshua can be considered a "royal" figure without the political and social structures that go along with the office. For Butler, "Deuteronomy 17:14-20 gave a legal standard by which to measure Israel's leaders. Joshua 1:1-9 gives a corresponding paradigm. The remainder of the book then gives flesh and blood to that paradigm in the figure of Joshua."[13]

While the biblical picture of Joshua does not embody kingship in its fully developed form, some "royal" characteristics are not easily discounted. In the light of earlier canonical statements regarding the future status and pre-eminence of the Joseph

---

[12] J. G. McConville, *Deuteronomy*, ApOTC (Nottingham: Apollos, 2002), 440.
[13] T. Butler, *Joshua*, WBC 7 (Waco, TX: Word, 1983), 13.

tribes, Joshua's profile gives weight to the expectation of a royal lineage emanating from the tribe of Ephraim and may well provide a paradigm for the future institution of the monarchy.

2.3. Caleb: The Leader from Judah

At the same time, the potential of a royal dynasty from the tribe of Ephraim is not portrayed without acknowledgement of the tribe of Judah and its future rise to pre-eminence. The account of Joshua's leadership also subtly registers the profile of the Judahite leader Caleb. Joshua and Caleb are frequently mentioned together by the biblical author as the sole survivors of the exodus generation (Num 14:30, 38; 26:65; 32:12). As such, they embody a faithful remnant within Israel; their unreserved faithfulness to Yahweh guarantees their entry into Canaan and sets them apart from the rest of their generation.

The profile of these two leaders in turn reflects the prominence of their respective tribes. To some extent, their interaction is symbolic of the relationship between their precursors Joseph and Judah, where the former takes the leadership role while the latter stands somewhat "in the shadows." Thus, while Joshua's leadership is undisputed, the insertion of material highlighting the profile and leadership qualities of Caleb indicates that he too, with the tribe he represents, is a key player in the unfolding drama of the fulfilment of God's promises to the patriarchs.

The references to Caleb's extra-Israelite paternity (Josh 14:6, 14) in no way diminish Caleb's role as a Judahite leader. Indeed, the uncertainty about his ancestry reflects the social and ethnic "discontinuity" that is by no means foreign to the tribe of Judah. The tribe's eponymous ancestor had a Canaanite wife, and his sexual union with his daughter-in-law Tamar resulted in the continuation of the family line through the most unlikely channel (Gen 38).

As a Judahite leader with a non-Israelite ancestry, Caleb seems an unlikely candidate for leadership. Yet his courage and initiative lead him to play a key role in the conquest of the land. Moreover, Caleb himself is the beneficiary of a divine promise (Num 14:24), the terminology of which clearly echoes God's promises to

Abraham (Gen 15:18 and 17:8). His loyalty is rewarded with a special inheritance in Canaan, which "his descendants" will "possess."[14] It is of no little significance that "Caleb son of Jephunneh the Kenizzite," a proselyte, is the first to receive an inheritance in Canaan "because he wholeheartedly followed the LORD, the God of Israel."

The divine promise begins to be fulfilled in the account of the allotment of Judah's inheritance (Josh 14:6–15:63). Caleb's special interest in the strategic city of Hebron dates back to the reconnaissance mission to that region (Num 13–14). This city, with its strong associations with Abraham, became the first inheritance given to the Israelites west of the Jordan, and the initiative of Caleb secured it. Joshua reaffirms the gift of Hebron to Caleb and pronounces a blessing on the Judahite leader (Josh 14:13).

In the book of Joshua, therefore, the leadership and authority of Joshua are portrayed alongside the energy and initiative of Caleb. The focus falls once more on the two Israelite leaders, from the two leading tribes, who play parallel leadership roles in the process of the emerging identity of the nation.

2.4. The Parallel Roles of Judah and the House of Joseph in Joshua 13–19

The narratives of land distribution in Josh 13–19, similarly, draw parallels between both tribes, and in turn contrast their profiles with those of the remaining tribes. The first distinctive in relation to Judah and the Josephites is reflected in the fact that the biblical writer has integrated narratives into the descriptions of their allotments. The descriptions of the allotments for the other tribes contain no such narratives. These narratives recount the requests made by various individuals/groups for the allotment of territory: Caleb to Joshua (Josh 14:6–13); Achsah to Caleb (Josh 15:18–19); the daughters of Zelophehad to Eleazar, Joshua and the leaders (Josh 17:3–6); and the Josephites to Joshua (Josh 17:14–18).

As Hess rightly points out, Caleb's acquisition of Hebron (Josh 14:6–15), together with Othniel's conquest of Debir (Josh 15:13–19) are the only narratives of

---

[14] Note particularly the use of the Leitwort יָרַשׁ. Cf. also Deut 1:36.

individual conquests among the allotments of Josh 13–19.[15] By focusing on the success of the Judahite leader (and that of his close relative), the narrative focuses on the success of the tribe (Josh 14:6): Caleb's story is the first instalment in the larger Judah allotment. The depiction of Judahite territory—by far the most detailed and complete—is bracketed by the first "Caleb story" (Josh 14:6–14) and the second (15:6–15), which in turn precedes an extensive list of Judahite towns. The summary in 15:20 indicates that the territory occupied by Caleb, Othniel and Achsah forms part of the inheritance of "the tribe of the people of Judah according to their clans."

The Achsah vignette might seem somewhat inapropos in the context of military conquest, but this concise father-daughter anecdote highlights the determination of a resourceful woman. Achsah's request—"Give me a blessing"—echoes her father's in Josh 14:12 and holds the key to her (and Othniel's) future: full rights to the water supply. Clearly, she shares her father's commitment to the ongoing agenda of taking and possessing "the inheritance of the tribe of the people of Judah" (Josh 15:20). Her commitment fully integrates the story into the surrounding context.

This story is in turn embedded within a larger unit that broadens the perspective to include the Joseph tribes. The Caleb and Othniel/Achsah narratives in the description of Judah's territory are mirrored by the inclusion of two narratives in the description of the Josephite allotments, both of which deal with requests for territory. The four individual narratives yield a symmetrical arrangement:

> A the Caleb narrative
>> B the Othniel/Achsah narrative
>> B´ the Zelophehad narrative
> A´ the Josephite narrative

The literary structure of this section highlights once more the parallel roles of Judah and the house of Joseph. However, Joshua's encounter with the Josephites leads to a very different outcome from his encounter with Caleb. First, the Josephites complain

---

[15] R. S. Hess, *Joshua*, TOTC (Leicester: Inter-Varsity Press, 1996), 218.

about the inadequacy of their portion, since they are unable to conquer the Canaanites in the lowlands (Josh 17:16, 18), and unwilling to clear the forested hill country. However, as Joshua points out, their numerical superiority ought to enable them not only to clear more land for settlement, but to drive out the Canaanites. Joshua's concluding statement to his fellow tribesmen reiterates the crucial task: "possessing" their inheritance "to its farthest borders" (17:18). Earlier, Caleb had stated his intentions in similar terms (Josh 14:12).

The second distinctive is the keyword חָזָק, which features in both the Caleb and the Josephite (Josh 14:11; 17:17–18) narratives. Once more, however, there is a marked contrast between the attitude of Caleb and that of the Josephites who, with their numerical "strength," had the potential to deal definitively with the "strong" Canaanite challenge (17:12–13, 18). Third, as noted above, the Caleb narrative prompts an elaborate and detailed description of Judah's territory. The Josephite narrative, on the other hand, concludes the descriptions of their inheritance with the difficulties they encounter. Joshua's exhortation to his fellow tribesmen echoes that of his Judahite counterpart, Caleb, whose initiative inspired the comprehensive occupation of that tribe's territory.

The other two elements in this structure (the Achsah vignette and the Zelophehad narrative) are also interrelated. In both, women take the initiative to request a portion of land, but in each case the rationale is different. Whereas the daughters of Zelophehad make their request on the basis of prior entitlement, Caleb's daughter requests a "blessing" in addition to what she has already been allocated.[16] Like Caleb's, the Achsah narrative is linked to conquest and the request for land in return. Like the Josephites, the daughters of Zelophehad request a portion without reference to a conquest.

Given the structural arrangement and the interplay of these short narratives, their literary and theological impact is clear. In general terms, they highlight the initiative and profile of Judah and the house of Joseph, and demonstrate how Judah,

---

[16] The background to this story is found in Num 27:1–7.

and to a lesser extent Manasseh and Ephraim, fulfilled the task of settlement and conquest. There are no such narratives in the allocations for the remaining seven tribes. The account of the second division of the land at Shiloh (18:2) begins in a negative vein: it seems that Joshua himself must organize and motivate them to claim their allotted portions.

This dichotomy between the "big three" and the seven landless tribes is also reflected in the sequence of allotments in Joshua; the Judges account reflects a similar order. The textual space assigned to the Judah and the Joseph tribes far exceeds that of the other seven, and significantly refers to promises or decisions given by Moses regarding their allocation (Josh 14:9, 17:4; cf. Judg 1:20). There are no comparable references regarding the allotments for the seven remaining tribes. Judah and the Josephites actively set about procuring their inheritance (Josh 15–17). The other seven tribes do not, which accounts for Joshua's reprimand (Josh 18:3). Though "the land lay subdued before them," they had not even begun "taking possession" of it.

Joshua's survey commission (Josh 18:4) is reminiscent of the episode of the spies in Num 13, and it is difficult not to draw the analogy between the ten spies and the seven landless tribes. The "slackness" with which Joshua reproaches them (18:3) calls to mind the failure of the remaining spies to believe the divine promises.[17] Joshua solemnly reminds them that "the LORD, the God of your ancestors" had "given" the land to them as an "inheritance" (Josh 18:2). Their lack of enterprise and the need for a detailed, systematic intervention by Joshua stands in stark contrast to the initiative of the three primary tribes.

This brief examination points up the prominence of the tribes of Judah and the house of Joseph in the mind of the biblical writer.[18] This is epitomized in the portrayal of Joshua and Caleb. It is fitting, therefore, that the two leading characters have the first and final word in this section of Joshua. Caleb, the Judahite, receives Hebron (Josh 14:6–15), and Joshua, the Ephraimite, receives Timnath Serah (19:49–50).

---

[17] Cf. Num 13:30; 14:8.

[18] Joshua's installation of the ark of the covenant at Shiloh in the territory of Ephraim may further contribute to the picture of Ephraimite pre-eminence at this time.

The portrayal of the two men and the tribes they represent points once more to the existence of two potential royal lines in the Israelite consciousness. At the same time, the more positive portrayal of Judah (in the person of Caleb) and the negative remarks about Ephraim anticipate later developments.

2.5. Judah: First among Equals?

It is clear from both Joshua and Judg 1 that Judah is viewed in a more positive light than any other tribe, including the Joseph tribes. Whereas the portrait of Judah's inheritance was detailed and coherent, the account of the Josephite allotment is surprisingly brief and incomplete. Joseph's border descriptions are abbreviated, and only the overall outlines are intelligible. This territorial imprecision manifests itself in "urban islands"[19]—cities or towns belonging to one tribe but located within the general territory of another. Ephraim thus possesses towns within Manasseh's territory (Josh 16:9), while Manasseh possesses a string of Canaanite strongholds located within the territory of Issachar and Asher yet fails to dislodge their Canaanite population (Josh 17:11–12). The picture of Josephite occupation is far from perfect.

The status of the descendants of Joseph in Josh 16–17 reflects the situation prevailing since Jacob's adoption and blessing of Joseph's sons, when Joseph as "firstborn" received a double portion of the patrimony (Gen 48). Following the pattern established in Gen 48, Manasseh, the biological firstborn, receives his allotment after his younger brother Ephraim, prefiguring the eventual precedence of Ephraim over Manasseh. The references to Joseph as a unit at this crucial stage may well function as a "flashback," alluding to Joseph's royal status and continuing prominence as a leading tribe. Nevertheless, the issues of ethnic and territorial confusion appear to signal the onset of a decline in the fortunes of the Josephites.

2.6. Judah and the House of Joseph in Judges

Analysis of the narrative in Judg 1 yields a similar conclusion, but by different means. The writer's particular interest in the tribe of Judah is obvious: in terms of

---

[19] R. D. Nelson, *Joshua* (Louisville, KY: Westminster John Knox, 1997), 197.

textual space, half the chapter is devoted to this tribe.[20] Two of the three anecdotes are associated with the Judahite conquest of two significant cities (Jerusalem and Hebron). Once more, Caleb and his family are singled out for special attention: Caleb will appear as a representative of "the elders who outlived Joshua" and in whose days Israel still served Yahweh (Judg 2:7); Othniel will reappear as the first judge (Judg 3:7–11), and his marriage to Achsah will assume greater significance in the light of ensuing events.

The positive emphasis on Judah's achievements is often interpreted as a tendentious glorification of the tribe at the expense of its northern counterparts. However, this reading fails to take account of the implicit criticism of Judah in the chapter, and of the significant profile of the house of Joseph in comparison to the other tribes. The parallel focus on Judah and the house of Joseph in Judg 1 echoes that of Josh 13–19, and is reflected in the text's structure and content.

As Webb has observed, the key word עָלָה frames the section and opens each of the major divisions (Judg 1:4, 22; 2:1).[21] When Israel asks, "Who shall go up first for us against the Canaanites, to fight against them?" (Judg 1:1), only Judah and the house of Joseph are said to "go up" (Judg 1:2, 22). In both cases, the initial picture is one of success. Detailed descriptions of the exploits of Judah and Joseph set the accounts of the occupation of their allotted territory apart from those of the other tribes. At the same time, consolidation of victories through full occupation of the territories is not complete. In Judah's case, there is a passing reference to their failure to drive out the inhabitants of the plain, which is attributed to superior Canaanite armaments (Judg 1:19). The summary of Judah's exploits in vv. 18–19 is the first indication that Judahite success is not as decisive as it could have been.

The record of the house of Joseph's failure, however, seems more intentional. Like Judah, the Josephites enjoy divine accompaniment (Judg 1:22b, cf. 1:19), but their strategy is seriously flawed. The conquest of Bethel entails making a deal with

---

[20] See K. L. Younger Jnr., "The Configuring of Judicial Preliminaries: Judges 1:1–2:5 and its Dependence on the Book of Joshua," *JSOT* 68 (1995): 92, Figs. 5 & 6.

[21] B. G. *Webb, The Book of Judges: An Integrated Reading* (Sheffield: JSOT Press, 1987), 103.

the inhabitants of the land, an action expressly forbidden in Judg 2:2. This compromise results in the establishment of another Canaanite city (albeit at a distance). The contrast with the Judahite Caleb's capture of Hebron is at the least implicit.

Significantly, this compromise marks the beginning of a general decline in Josephite tribal success, signaled by the recurring formula "did not drive out."[22] The writer's tone becomes increasingly negative as the campaign is beleaguered by complacency, compromise and co-residency with the Canaanites.[23] This progressive failure on Israel's part culminates in Judg 2:1–5, when the angel of the LORD "went up" (עָלָה) from Gilgal, where Judah and the house of Joseph had received their inheritance, to Bochim, where the people weep on hearing of Yahweh's displeasure.

This situation recalls the account of the second land distribution in Josh 18:1–19:51. However, the Judges account is markedly less subtle: there is no longer any differentiation between Manasseh-Ephraim and the remaining tribes, and none of the tribes (including Judah) attracts unqualified commendation from the biblical writer. While the structure of Judg 1 once more throws into relief the prominence of Judah and the house of Joseph, the demarcation between these tribes and the remaining seven is no longer as clearly drawn as it was in Josh 13–19.[24] As the leadership problem intensifies throughout the book of Judges, the profile of the Joseph tribes, in particular, becomes increasingly vulnerable.

3. Judges: The Need for Leadership

The biblical writer's portrayal of the "royal" leadership characteristics of Joshua and the exemplary qualities of Caleb constitutes a key stage in the emerging picture of two potential royal lines associated with the tribes of Joseph and Judah. The double statement of Joshua's death (Judg 1:1; 2:8–10), however, signals a new phase in the story of leadership in Israel. It may also provide a subtle indication that the dynamics of Ephraimite pre-eminence are about to be overturned.

---

[22] See Judg 1:27, 28, 29, 30, 31, 32, 33.

[23] Note [וּ]בקרב (in [their] midst) in Judg 1:29b, 30b, 32a and 33b.

[24] Webb, *Judges*, 101.

It would be difficult to overstate the centrality of the theme of leadership in the book of Judges. As was the case in Joshua, the issue is addressed in the first sentence. The notice of the death of Joshua (Judg 1:1) evokes memories of the leader *par excellence*. In Judges, however, there is no direct transition of leadership, since Joshua has appointed no successor. This absence of human leadership is reflected in the book's opening question: "Who shall go up first for us?" (Judg 1:1). In the final story the same formula of oracular inquiry is employed (Judg 20:18), recalling the opening question and clearly expressing the book's programmatic concern for leadership. The intervening narratives catalogue the failure of tribal leadership, where Ephraim's claim to pre-eminence is increasingly undermined. Failure to perpetuate the covenant fidelity characteristic of Joshua's leadership calls for an alternative solution.

3.1. Leadership in Judges

In this post-Joshua era, the leadership issue does not initially concentrate on a specific office to be filled but rather on a task to be implemented: the occupation of tribal allotments. The programmatic question in Judg 1:1, therefore, does not necessarily raise the issue of a possible dynastic line or a monarchy at this stage, but simply which tribe will take the lead in initiating the process of settlement.

The question presupposes a united effort ("for us"), as an ethnic and religious unity in the initial stages. In the course of time, however, this sense of unity and collaboration is gradually replaced by intertribal rivalry and self-interest. This disturbing development reaches its nadir in the book's epilogue, where internecine war leads to the near eradication of a tribe.

The issue of who should lead Israel—and how—quickly emerges as a central theme. There are, periodically, some indications of a movement towards centralized leadership—most notably under Gideon (Judg 8:22–28). Meanwhile, Ephraim's leadership status is increasingly undermined. God addresses the leadership vacuum by "raising up" judges, who function as *ad hoc* rulers in a climate of political, religious and cultural decentralization. The increasing fragmentation and corruption of the nation is starkly illustrated in the potential conflict between Gideon and the envious

Ephraimites (Judg 7:24–8:3), the fratricide of Abimelech (Judg 9:1–6), the intertribal feud and ensuing slaughter of forty-two thousand Ephraimites by Jephthah (Judg 12:1–6), and the full scale internecine civil war resulting in the near-extinction of the tribe of Benjamin (Judg 20). Clearly, the tribal coalition is in danger of dissolution.

3.2. What Kind of Leadership?

The core of the book of Judges (3:7–16:31) focuses on how a leader is identified, the qualities required, and the problems associated with flawed leadership. The judges were "charismatic" leaders "raised up"[25] by Yahweh, endued with power by God's spirit,[26] who were able to rally the people against foreign oppression and achieve striking short-term successes against incredible odds. However, as each successive cycle shows, they were powerless to rescue the people from their apparent predisposition to apostatize. The paradigm established in Judg 2:16–18 and most closely followed in the account of Othniel's judgeship becomes progressively more unstable.[27]

Thus, the gradual religious and moral decline of Israel is reflected in the progressive degeneration of the judges.[28] The leadership problem in Israel becomes critical in the closing chapters: there is no longer any cry for deliverance, and no judge is raised up to "deliver" Israel. At the same time, however, the deficiencies of charismatic leadership as portrayed in the narratives should not detract from the divinely appointed office of "judge-deliverer" (Judg 2:16–19). Clearly, it was not the creation of a new institution (i.e., kingship) that would secure Israel's future. Rather, the nation needed leadership that would demonstrate fidelity to the covenant. Joshua provides a model for the type of leadership that kings were to exercise, based on the Mosaic paradigm of Deut 17:14–20. The question then arises: to what extent, if at all,

---

[25] See 2:16, 18; 3:9, 15.

[26] Later this same "gift" would empower kings (1 Sam 10:10; 11:6; 16:13–14).

[27] J. C. Exum, "The Centre Cannot Hold: Thematic and Textual Instabilities in Judges," *CBQ* 52 (1990): 412.

[28] See, for example, Webb, *Judges*, 175–76; G. J. Wenham, *Story as Torah: Reading the Old Testament Ethically* (Edinburgh: T&T Clark, 2003), 48; D. I. Block, *Judges, Ruth*, NAC (Nashville: Broadman & Holman, 1999), 37.

was that model implemented in the post-Joshua era?

The deployment of "kingship" vocabulary in Judges is economical but also strategic. The first explicit and extensive references are found in the Gideon cycle and its sequel, which describe Israel's first experiment with the institution and its disastrous consequences. Following his successful resolution of the Midianite crisis, the Israelites offer Gideon dynastic rule over the nation (8:22–27). The offer (clearly that of kingship), is wrongly motivated in several respects. The Israelites attribute their deliverance directly to Gideon, as the final clause of Judg 8:22 shows.[29] The offer also flouts the Mosaic legislation for kingship, which decreed that kings were to be divinely chosen (Deut 17:14). The Israelites clearly intend a hereditary regime, which may well confirm that they had in fact adopted their kingship model from surrounding nations (cf. 1 Sam 8:5, 19–20). While many read Gideon's refusal in Judg 8:22–23 as one of the clearest statements in the OT against kingship, others interpret his rejoinder as less than sincere.[30] Despite his theologically correct statement, the portrayal of Gideon's "royal" lifestyle, together with the obvious shift towards political and religious centralization under his leadership, confirms that he acts like a king over the nation in all but name.

The story of Abimelech is a necessary sequel to that of Gideon, and a climax to both stories. Abimelech's reign reflects all the worst aspects of kingship: conspiracy, family intrigue, the purge of political opponents, and the violent abuse of power (Judg 9:5, 34–52). For Block, Jotham and his parable (Judg 9:7–21) function as the alter ego of the narrator, representing the latter's view of Israelite kingship as he knows it.[31] While Jotham clearly perceives Abimelech's reign as negative, the parable's main focus is not a general critique of kingship as such. Rather, it highlights the absence of integrity in Shechem's leaders, the inadequacy of leadership that is not divinely appointed, and the wrong motivations of those who desire it.

---

[29] Note particularly Judg 7:2 in this regard, and compare 6:14, 15, 36, 37; 7:2, 7.

[30] See further D. I. Block, "Will the Real Gideon Please Stand Up?," *JETS* 40 (1997): 353–66.

[31] Block (*Judges*, 315 n.772) points out the assonantal links between Jotham's name and תמם, the *Leitmotif* of Jotham's interpretation of his fable (vv. 16, 19).

The third set of references to kingship in Judges occur in the book's epilogue: "In those days there was no king in Israel" (17:6; 18:1; 19:1; 21:25). Scholarship almost unanimously interprets this editorial refrain as "an apology for the monarchy," written from a Judahite perspective.[32] On the other hand, some have argued for an anti-monarchic polemic by an exilic writer who saw the key to Israel's survival as a return to direct divine intervention and theocratic leadership.[33] This discussion demonstrates scholarship's propensity to reduce the book's programmatic purpose to the advocacy of one form of leadership or another. It seems preferable to see its portrayal of a variety of leaders as an invitation by the writer to reflect on what the best form of leadership might be. In particular, the authorial/editorial intent of the refrain in the epilogue to Judges acquires its significance in its specific context (Judg 17–21). The book of Judges represents another stage in the ongoing quest for a leader who will keep Israel faithful to the LORD and give her victory over her enemies. By the end of the book, Israel is a step closer to the historical fulfilment of Yahweh's rejection of Ephraim's leadership and his choice of Judah (Ps 78:67–72).

3.3. The Contenders for Leadership

As noted above, the Judges 1 narrative of Israel's possession of their allotted inheritance traces a progressive decline in tribal success. While the campaign of occupation begins positively with Judah (1:3–20), it then moves to the failure of Benjamin (Judg 1:21) and that of the northern tribes, ending negatively with the displacement of Dan by the Amorites (Judg 1:34). The Book of Deliverers follows a similar scheme, beginning in the south with Othniel (Judah) and Ehud (Benjamin), and culminating with Samson, the Danite whose tribe eventually settled in the north. Similarly, the epilogue also reflects this south-to-north schematization, showing particular interest in Judah with references to Jerusalem and Bethlehem (Judg 19:10–11; 19:1, 2, 18), the Joseph tribes (Judg 17:1, 8; 18:2, 13; 19:1, 16, 18), and, in reverse

---

[32] See, for example, M. A. Sweeney, "Davidic Polemics in the Book of Judges," *VT* 47 (1997): 517–29.

[33] W. J. Dumbrell, "In those days there was no king in Israel; every man did what was right in his own eyes. The Purpose of the Book of Judges Reconsidered," *JSOT* 25 (1983): 23–33.

order, Dan (Judg 17–18) and Benjamin (Judg 19–21). For many, tribal-political pre-eminence controls the arrangement of the accounts.

In view of the positive performance of Judah in chapter 1, it is not without significance that the first judge should be one whose Judahite connections and credentials are already well-known. In many ways the reader has been well prepared for the reappearance of this Judahite hero-figure by the vignette of Judg 1:11–15. The reader is left in no doubt that the Othniel of Judg 3:9 is the same Othniel who captured Debir and won Caleb's daughter Achsah as his prize in Judg 1:12–15.[34] Othniel's story is pivotal in that he represents the lasting impact of the Joshua/Caleb leadership and serves as a final link between the exodus generation and the one to follow. As Webb rightly points out, the Judahite judge is "the embodiment of an institution; all the key words applied to judgeship in chapter 2 are applied to Othniel here, and his career conforms to the paradigm given there."[35]

The designation of Othniel as first judge follows the shocking reference to one inevitable outcome of co-existence with the Canaanites—that of intermarriage (3:5–6).[36] The tragedy of Israel's downfall through cohabitation and intermarriage with Canaanites stands in sharp contrast with Othniel's marriage which, like his judgeship, is exemplary. As Block remarks, the Achsah vignette portrays "positive social relationships" between father and daughter, husband and wife that function with boldness, creativity and respect. It is worth noting at this stage also that these relationships stand in stark contrast to the abusive and violent treatment perpetrated against the Levite's concubine in Judg 19 and the daughters of Shiloh in Judg 21.[37] Moreover, the first judge Othniel's marital status stands in bold relief with that of Samson, the last judge.

Othniel's encounter with Israel's first oppressor, King Cushan-rishathaim of Aram-naharaim, also sets him up as model. The identity and origin of this tyrant has

---

[34] Webb, *Judges*, 127.
[35] Webb, *Judges*, 127.
[36] See Webb, *Judges*, 128.
[37] Block, *Judges*, 96–97.

engendered much discussion: it is impossible to link him with any known historical figure. However, the same may be said for virtually every other oppressor named in Judges.[38] Many commentators construe the tyrant's name as a mocking and pejorative pseudonym—"Cushan of Double Wickedness," so that, "The clash between Othniel and Cushan-rishathaim is a clash between two institutions, but both alike are seen as expressions of Yahweh's rule over Israel; kingship in punishment, and judgeship in deliverance."[39]

The significance of the Othniel cycle cannot be reduced to some kind of allegorical "scorecard" for assessing the rest of the narratives.[40] On the contrary, the positive portrayal of Othniel as the first judge seems entirely appropriate in its context. No other tribe produces a comparable judgeship. Inevitably, this becomes the paradigm for his successors: "As in [Judg] 1:1–3:6, where Judah is the model tribe, so in 3:7–16:31 the Judean judge is the model. Both one tribe and that tribe's judge become the standard against which to measure all the other tribes and all the other judges."[41]

3.4. Model Leader, Model Tribe?

The paradigmatic portrayal of Othniel and his tribe leads to the conclusion that, if one tribe in Israel is preeminently qualified to produce a royal leader for Israel, then that tribe would be Judah. However, while the prologue and epilogue recognize Judah's divinely sanctioned leadership in the holy war, this tribe is by no means idealized in the book. Judah is noticeably missing in the roll call of tribes in the Song of Deborah (5:14–23) and does not appear to respond to any deliverer's call to arms (cf. 3:27; 4:10; 6:35; 7:23; 11:29). In the days of Samson, the men of Judah were prepared to turn over their own countryman to protect themselves (Judg 15:9–13). Indeed, Judah does not enjoy leadership profile again until the final story (Judg 20:18).

---

[38] K. A. Kitchen, *On the Reliability of the Old Testament* (Grand Rapids: Eerdmans, 2006), 212; cf. Block, *Judges*, 152.

[39] Webb, *Judges*, 128.

[40] L. G. Stone, "Judges, Book of," *DOT:HB*, 600.

[41] Victor P. Hamilton, *Handbook on the Historical Books* (Grand Rapids: Baker, 2001), 112.

At the same time, while Judah's profile is not entirely pristine, the impression left with the reader is that of a force to be reckoned with. It is surely significant that Judah's emergent leadership role is corroborated in the book's frame and as such confirms the divine appointment of this tribe to provide future royal leadership in Israel (cf. Gen 49:8–12; Ps 78:68).

Clearly, the Joseph tribes also play a prominent role in the nation of Israel. It has already been noted that, whereas in the book of Joshua Judah and the house of Joseph were portrayed in parallel roles, in Judges chapter 1 Manasseh and Ephraim become more closely identified with the failures of the remaining tribes than with the successes of Judah. The tribe of Ephraim, together with the territory it occupies, continues to have a *Leitmotif* function throughout the book, not least in the epilogue.[42]

In the first half of the book of Judges, Ephraim's profile is relatively positive, particularly in terms of its military contribution (see, for example, Judg 3:26–29; 7:24). However, despite their military prowess, the men of Ephraim prove to be a source of tension and conflict among the tribes. Gideon barely avoids violent confrontation with them as they accuse him of overlooking them at the outset of his campaign against the Midianites (Judg 6:35; 7:24; 8:1). Under Jephthah's judgeship, the attitude of the Ephraimites again precipitates a crisis, this time with dire consequences. Once more, the tribe is involved in challenging a judge's leadership, and the feud escalates into a full-scale intertribal war, resulting in the slaughter of forty-two thousand Ephraimites.

In the narrative of these two incidents alone, the status of Ephraim as the tribe of leadership is seriously challenged. Other negative portrayals of Ephraim are perhaps less obvious but no less instructive. Judges 9 relates what one commentator refers to as "The Canaanite Kingship of Gideon's Son Abimelech."[43] The setting is Shechem, the principal center in the hill country of Ephraim (Josh 20:7). Shechem was still a center of Canaanite worship, with a motley population that was partly Israelite, partly Canaanite. The civil war that erupts under Abimelech is a harbinger of things to come (Judg 12:1–6; 20:1–48). All this takes place in the heartland of Ephraimite hill country

---

[42] Cf. Judg 3:27; 5:14; 7:24–8:3; 10:1; 12:1–6, 15; 18:22–26.

[43] Block, *Judges*, 308.

and reflects Ephraim's failure to expel the Canaanites and its acceptance of intermarriage and idolatry. Shechem is not the only Ephraimite city where Canaanite influence is prevalent; Bethel is also portrayed as being in the grip of Canaanite idolatry and immorality, as is Benjaminite Gibeah.

3.5. 'No king in Israel'

It is in the book's epilogue, however, that the tribe of Ephraim, through events unfolding in its territory, is painted in the darkest of colors. These extended narratives disclose further shocking evidence of the cultic and moral chaos that reigned in Israel. They are distinguished from Judg 3:7–16:31 by their content in that no judges feature. They are also distinctive by their structure, which seems to indicate a different preoccupation on the part of the writer/editor:

A	(17:6)	In those days there was no king…
		every man did what was right in his own eyes
B	(18:1)	In those days there was no king…
B´	(19:1)	In those days there was no king…
A´	(21:25)	In those days there was no king…
		every man did what was right in his own eyes[44]

In the first narrative, the editorial comment is inserted at critical junctures in the narrative; in the second, the formula frames the entire narrative. The formula, however, serves as much more than a literary marker, for by its strategic use the writer clearly states his negative assessment of both episodes. The expanded form—"All the people did what was right in their own eyes" (Judg 17:6, cf. 18:1)—is a clear echo of the Mosaic expression "to do what is right in the eyes of the LORD," and reflects the general lack of covenant commitment among the Israelites.

The symmetry of the two stories is marked by several common features. In both cases a nameless, wandering Levite sets in motion a series of catastrophic events. In both, the Levite has connections with Bethlehem-Judah and with "the hill country

---

[44] Webb, *Judges*, 182.

of Ephraim" (Judg 17:1, 7–8; 19:1–2). In the first episode, the presence of the Levite in Micah's house attracts the attention of the Danites and leads to further cultic aberration; in the second, the presence of the Levite and his concubine in Gibeah triggers the horrific crime committed there and the civil war that results.

This final, dark section ominously begins with its geographical setting: the "hill country of Ephraim" (17:1). The phrase is deployed four times in all (17:1, 8b; 18:2b, 13), as if to evoke the previous negative portrayal of the tribe. The story of Micah's idolatry will now expose the cultic crisis unfolding in Ephraim's territory. The hill country of Ephraim, and Bethel in particular, continue to provide geographical references for the increasingly grim narrative in Judges 19–21.[45] It is noteworthy that, following huge losses in battle against Benjamin (Judg 20:26; 21:2) the Israelites weep at Bethel, the place where co-existence and compromise with the Canaanites first began (Judg 1:22–26). This manifestation of grief recalls a similar event at Bochim[46] (Judg 2:1–5). Thus, in the book's prologue as well as its epilogue, Bethel is associated with misfortune for Israel, the source of idolatry and the near destruction of an Israelite tribe.

The marital and social relationships portrayed here also function as a foil to their positive counterpart in the prologue. The story of Caleb, Othniel and Achsah portrays how family relationships function with creativity and initiative, but also with dignity and propriety. The contrast between Achsah and the nameless, voiceless concubine of Judg 19 could scarcely be more striking.

Following the summons issued by the Levite (Judg 20:1), the Israelites rise up "as one man"—a response that far exceeds anything achieved previously in Israel's wars against the Canaanites. Having already established their strategy they proceed to inquire of God at Bethel (Judg 20:18). The contrast between the question in 20:18 and the corresponding question in the book's prologue (Judg 1:1) is marked; the same may be said of Yahweh's response. Most notable, however, is the absence of a

---

[45] See Judg 20:18, 26, 31; 21:2 and 19 (2x).

[46] Bochim is probably a pseudonym for Bethel, as both recensions of the LXX seem to confirm (see Webb, *Judges*, 105 and 241 n.94).

corresponding divine promise of success, as in Judg 1:2. The contrast with the successful campaigns in the opening verses of the book is maintained as the narrator recounts three engagements between Israelites, each resulting in defeat and loss.

The bleak picture of moral corruption continues as the Israelites desperately seek a solution to the problem they have created. This further back-reference to the book's prologue is strikingly unambiguous. The manner in which Othniel "won" his wife as a promised reward in the context of a divinely sanctioned holy war stands in stark contrast to the manner in which the Israelites now procure wives for the Benjaminites.

The contrasts between the story of Othniel and Achsah and events in Judg 19–21 create a strong affinity between the opening and closing sections of the book. Othniel's leadership is the antithesis of the status quo in the epilogue, where there was "no king in Israel," and anarchy reigned. It seems reasonable to conclude, therefore, that the book is framed by two scenarios focusing on the theme of leadership. The first scenario, as we have seen, describes successful leadership raised up and empowered by Yahweh. The second scenario describes the disastrous consequences of the absence of such leadership.

The above analysis of the book of Judges reveals the book's programmatic concern for leadership through successive cycles of crisis at both the tribal and national levels. At the tribal level, Ephraim is the natural successor to Joshua. While the Ephraimites lay claim to pre-eminence, however, they fail to implement the leadership qualities of their illustrious tribal chief. Instead, Ephraim's profile becomes increasingly vulnerable as the tribe and its territory become identified with intertribal rivalry, civil strife, and covenant infidelity. Judah fares better, with the book's prologue and epilogue acknowledging this tribe's divinely sanctioned leadership role in the holy war.

4. Conclusion

The rise of kingship in Israel follows a complex path.[47] The portrayal of two potential messianic trajectories in Joshua–Judges culminates in 1 Sam 4, when the definitive blow to Ephraimite pre-eminence is realized in the divine rejection of the tribe's associated worship place—the pre-Davidic sanctuary at Shiloh. Perhaps the most succinct theological commentary on this climactic event is furnished by one of ancient Israel's songwriters:

> He rejected the tent of Joseph;
>> He did not choose the tribe of Ephraim,
> But he chose the tribe of Judah,
>> Mount Zion, which he loves.
> (Ps 78:67–68)

Asaph's statement encapsulates "the story so far": Judah's is the divinely elected royal lineage from which the messianic king will one day emerge. In fulfilment of the divine promise in Gen 3:15 the "seed of the woman" will, through suffering, climactically defeat the serpent. In so doing, he will redeem people from every nation who will reign with him on "Mount Zion," his royal abode.

---

[47] Space does not permit a substantial discussion of the function of Saul's kingship. For the purposes of this study, it will suffice to note that his kingship bridged the gap between Ephraim and Judah.

MESSIANIC TRAJECTORIES IN RUTH—A REDEEMER AND GREAT NAME

—James McKeown

1. Introduction

The relevance of the book of Ruth to the main themes of this volume may not be immediately obvious. Apart from the reference to King David and his genealogy, the little book of Ruth does not at first glance make a significant contribution to the themes that develop the programmatic statement in Gen 3:15. In studies of the overarching message of Genesis to Kings, it would be easy to neglect this small book which is not technically part of the Deuteronomistic History. However, Desmond Alexander has not neglected Ruth and he has described it as a bridge between Judges and Samuel.[1] This chapter in the book dedicated to him, seeks to confirm and highlight his findings that Ruth provides a useful sequel to the books that precede it and a significant introduction to those that follow. As Alexander has shown, the links between Ruth and Genesis are unmistakable. The people, themes and traditions mentioned in Genesis are not only known but are regarded as central to the story.

A good starting point is to note that well-known names in the Genesis narratives are also known to the author of Ruth: Rachel, Leah (Gen 29–35; Ruth 4:11), Perez, Hezron (Gen 46:12; Ruth 4:18), and Tamar (Gen 38:6–30). Tamar is especially significant since, like Ruth, she is not an Israelite and if Ruth's method of obtaining a husband, as directed by Naomi, was risky and unorthodox, this fades into insignificance when compared with Tamar's desperate and dangerous strategy. Furthermore, Genesis mentions the beginnings of the Moabite people and does so in sordid terms showing that the nation's beginnings were the result of incest (Gen 19:30–38). Ruth was a Moabite and her behavior must be under scrutiny in the light

---

[1] T. Desmond Alexander, *The Servant King* (Leicester: Inter-Varsity Press, 1998), 49–54.

of this tradition. On the other hand, the man she married could trace his ancestry back to the illicit relationship between Judah and Tamar (Gen 38).

Many scholars have drawn attention to the unmistakable thematic continuity between Genesis and Ruth. While the Moabite background, and the link with Judah, together with the other names mentioned, provide an explicit connection with the Genesis traditions, an implicit connection is provided through thematic concurrence. In particular, this chapter will discuss the themes of blessing, offspring (seed), and land. It will be argued that the book of Ruth develops these themes beyond Genesis and brings us one stage closer to their denouement in King David and ultimately, the Messiah. These themes may also be identified throughout Genesis to Kings but within the limited scope of this chapter, the main focus will be the interrelationship between Genesis and Ruth.

2. The Theme of Blessing in Genesis and Ruth

The book of Genesis exhibits a sense of movement. Many of the main characters are involved in travelling but the plot of the book is also moving from alienation from God towards harmony and blessing. This alienation led to the expulsion of the first human couple from the Garden of Eden. Outside Eden the unrelenting descent of humankind into violence and rebellion led to alienation from God and the pronouncement of divine curses (Gen 1–11). From Gen 3 onwards, the long shadow of sin and its consequences pervades the history of humanity. The turning point came in chapter 12 with the call of Abraham and the unmistakable pronouncement of blessing on Abraham and his offspring.[2] Thus, the book of Genesis witnesses a move from alienation to blessing.

This trajectory from alienation to blessing is also evident in the book of Ruth which is set in the period when the judges ruled. This was a time when Israel's unfaithfulness to YHWH was very evident and women were the focus of much of the abhorrent violence that was endemic in that period.

---

[2] For convenience the patriarch's later name "Abraham" is used throughout this chapter. Also, his wife will be referred to as "Sarah."

Against this violent backdrop, the book of Ruth tells a story about women who showed resilience and initiative in the most difficult circumstances.[3] The heroine of the book of Ruth came from a nation that was at enmity with Israel, but she was treated with respect and integrated into Israelite society. The final chapters of the book of Judges emphasize the message that in those days there was no king and everyone did what was right in his own eyes (Judg 17:6; 21:25). Although the book of Ruth has the same pre-monarchic setting as the book of Judges, Ruth's story points forward to King David who will bring law and order to the country and victory over their enemies. Remarkably Ruth the Moabite was his ancestress.

The book of Ruth begins with a litany of tragic events that leave Naomi bereft of her husband and her two sons. During her darkest hour news reached her in Moab that YHWH had "visited his people and given them food" (Ruth 1:6).[4] Naomi was not comforted by this news, since she was not in Israel where the provision had been made, but in the foreign territory of Moab. The text emphasizes this by repeating "land of Moab" in verse 6. Naomi's decision to return to Bethlehem presented her daughters-in-law with a dilemma, whether to accompany her or to stay in Moab. Orpah decided to follow Naomi's advice and stayed in Moab. She did what Naomi requested, and she is not criticized for making this decision. Ruth, on the other hand, refused to leave Naomi and expressed her commitment to remain with her until death would separate them (Ruth 1:16–18). Together they made the journey to Bethlehem, uncertain about what would happen there.

Whereas Abraham approached the land of Canaan with the promise of blessing to support him, Naomi had no such reassurance as she returned to Bethlehem and she even complained that the "hand of YHWH" was against her (Ruth 1:13). Although her arrival in Bethlehem coincided with the barley harvest, the atmosphere of blessing evoked by fruitful fields did nothing to assuage her sense of alienation and bitterness.

---

[3] As Katharine Doob Sakenfeld argues, "The entire story in the book of Ruth serves as counterpoint to this picture of the era of the judges" (*Ruth*, IBC [Louisville: Westminster John Knox, 1999], 18).

[4] Unless otherwise stated biblical citations are from the ESV.

Unlike Abraham she had not been promised a great name and she even protested that her present name with its connotation of pleasantness was inappropriate (Ruth 1:21).

Having presented this bleak scene of unhappiness for Naomi, the narrative of Ruth begins the journey towards blessing. Abraham's blessing was bestowed against the dark backcloth of the downward spiral into sin and rebellion (Gen 1–11). Ruth received blessing after a very dark period in her life with the loss of her husband and the difficulty of being accepted as a stranger in Bethlehem.

The main difference between how the theme of blessing is developed in the book of Ruth in comparison to Genesis, is that blessing is promised to Abraham, introducing an important stage in the fulfilment of Gen 3:15, whereas for the main part of the story, Ruth is not even aware that she is being blessed. Her entrance into the field of Boaz was by chance: "she happened to come to the part of the field belonging to Boaz, who was of the clan of Elimelech" (Ruth 2:3).[5] From his first appearance in the narrative, Boaz is presented as the source of blessing. The vocabulary of blessing resounds even in his daily conversation. Thus, he announced his arrival in the harvest field with the warm greeting "the LORD be with you!" to which his harvesters reply, "The LORD bless you" (Ruth 2:4).

His reference to the presence of YHWH is the prerequisite for the blessing that the workers invoke in response. It is possible to dispute the claim that Boaz's greeting to the workers and their reply highlight the theme of blessing. It can be argued that words used in greetings are usually bereft of any meaning. For example, when people say "goodbye" they are probably not aware that this is a contraction of "God be with you." My counter argument is that if Boaz was simply saying "Hello" this would not have been recorded and I concur with Sakenfeld that, "Boaz's blessing should be read with its full theological meaning."[6] This view is supported by Hubbard who argues that the objective of the greeting "was to encourage the workers that Yahweh was

---

[5] However, as Sakenfeld observes, "what appears as chance is better to be understood as divine providence" (*Ruth*, 40). Block argues that "in reality the text screams, 'See the hand of God at work here!'" (*Ruth: The King is Coming*, ZECOT [Grand Rapids: Zondervan, 2015], 151–52).

[6] Sakenfeld, *Ruth*, 41.

present 'with them,' blessing their work."[7] The narrator is portraying Bethlehem as a place of refuge and blessing, since not only are the greetings articulated in blessing vocabulary but the whole atmosphere in the harvest field of ripe grain is evocative of blessing, peace, and harmony.

Ruth entered this scene of blessing from a standpoint of one who was an outsider. She had experienced barrenness and death in Moab and was in desperate need of blessing. After the initial attempts of Naomi to deter her and the lack of a warm reception from the townsfolk, Ruth received such a warm welcome from Boaz that she reacted with surprise and exclaimed, "Why have I found favor in your eyes … since I am a foreigner" (2:10). While he was aware of her foreign identity, Boaz also recognized her as a pilgrim seeking security under the "wing" of Israel's deity. The language he used is reminiscent of the call of Abraham. Like the renowned patriarch, Ruth had left her homeland and her family to go to the land that YHWH had blessed.

> All that you have done for your mother-in-law since the death of your husband has been fully told to me, and how you left your father and mother and your native land and came to a people that you did not know before. The LORD repay you for what you have done, and a full reward be given you by the LORD, the God of Israel, under whose wings you have come to take refuge! (2:11–12).

Boaz was aware that Israel's story began when Abraham left Babylon in obedience to God's call and became a stranger in Canaan where he experienced YHWH's presence and blessing. He accepted Ruth into his harvest field and shared its blessing with her because he believed that she had not only shown commitment and loyalty to Naomi but she had also shown faith in Israel's God.[8] The mention of the wings of God is reminiscent of the exodus story when God is portrayed as carrying his

---

[7] Robert L. Hubbard, *The Book of Ruth*, NICOT (Grand Rapids: Eerdmans, 1988), 144.

[8] L. Daniel Hawk makes a similar point, "Boaz, who has been the recipient of Yahweh's blessing (v. 4), now signals Yahweh's acceptance of Ruth into the covenant community by conferring a blessing through 'Yahweh, the God of Israel' (v. 12)" (*Ruth*, ApOTC 7B [Nottingham: Inter-Varsity Press, 2015], 81).

people out of Egypt on eagles' wings (Exod 19:4). Wings signified blessing in terms of protection and the same word is used later in the book of Ruth when she asked Boaz to spread the corner (wing) of his garment over her (Ruth 3:9). However, in spite of the warm welcome that Ruth received from Boaz, she was still not a full member of the community. This is accentuated by the repeated description of her as "Ruth the Moabite" throughout the account (1:22; 2:2, 6, 21; 4:5, 10).

The next mention of blessing in the Ruth narrative occurs when Ruth returned to Naomi. Boaz had generously provided about an ephah of barley. Daniel Hawk comments that an ephah "is well beyond what anyone could expect to glean in a day" and he suggests, following Sakenfeld, that this was sufficient "to feed two individuals for five to seven days."[9] Ruth also had retained some of the cooked food that she had received at mealtime to share with Naomi (2:14, 18).

Naomi had initially not shown any enthusiasm for Ruth's initiative (cf. 2:2). When she saw the large quantity of food that Ruth had acquired, she was obviously surprised and blessed the person who had been so generous (2:19). Upon hearing that this person was her late husband's relative, Naomi, who had previously felt bitter, made a statement that may be regarded as a turning point in this story:[10] "And Naomi said to her daughter-in-law, 'May he be blessed by the LORD, whose kindness has not forsaken the living or the dead!'" (2:20).

This statement is ambiguous because she does not clarify whether the one "whose kindness has not forsaken the living or the dead" refers to Boaz or to YHWH. Block argues that Boaz is the subject.[11] Schipper, on the other hand, argues that "although not conclusive, the syntax favors interpreting YHWH as the implied subject of the clause."[12] Hawk, makes the interesting suggestion that this ambiguity is "probably intentional, suggesting that Naomi sees Boaz and Yahweh acting in concert

---

[9] Hawk, *Ruth*, 84. Cf. Sakenfeld, *Ruth*, 46.

[10] Sakenfeld, comments that we are at "the turning point of the story both theologically and rhetorically" as Naomi began to move from despair to hope and from bitterness to gratitude (*Ruth*, 47).

[11] Block, *Ruth*, 145.

[12] Jeremy Schipper, *Ruth, A New Translation with Introduction, Notes and Commentary*, AB 7D (New Haven: Yale University Press, 2016), 134.

as agents of blessing."[13] Either way, Naomi who had accused YHWH of afflicting her, had at last seen a glimmer of hope in this meeting with Boaz.

A similar statement is found in Genesis when Abraham sent his servant to find a wife for Isaac. The servant, because of his relationship with Abraham, was very conscious that YHWH was with him and was guiding him. The story reaches its climax when he exclaimed: "Blessed be the LORD, the God of my master Abraham, who has not forsaken his steadfast love and his faithfulness toward my master. As for me, the LORD has led me in the way to the house of my master's kinsmen" (Gen 24:27).

His exclamation expressed his relief that YHWH had made his mission possible through his presence and guidance. Both statements in Genesis and in Ruth are found in the context of blessing, showing that guidance and protection were afforded to those living in harmony with YHWH. Naomi, who had not previously revealed to Ruth the identity of Boaz, now explained to her daughter-in-law that this man whom she had met was one of their next of kin (literally, one of our redeemers).

In chapter 3, Naomi takes the initiative to find "rest" for her daughter-in-law. This concept of "rest" is closely linked to the theme of blessing in Genesis. "Rest" is epitomized by the seventh day (the day of rest) which is the only day that is explicitly the recipient of blessing (Gen 2:3). Outside Eden, the first humans are refugees who need a resting place. This theme is developed negatively in the story of Cain who is a restless wanderer (Gen 4:10–16).

This link between the themes of blessing and rest that is prominent in the creation narratives appears again in the book of Ruth. According to Block, the concept of rest "speaks of the tranquility, peace, satisfaction, and security that a woman in Israel longed for and expected to find in the home of a loving husband."[14]

Naomi had envisaged that only in Moab could Ruth find rest (Ruth 1:9) and this is probably one of the reasons why she was so reluctant to take Ruth and Orpah back with her to Bethlehem. Naomi did not believe that Bethlehem could be a place of rest for two Moabite widows. However, in chapter 3 she realized that Ruth will never

---

[13] Hawk, *Ruth*, 86.
[14] Block, *Ruth*, 167.

return to Moab and that she must find rest in Israel. Naomi recognized her own responsibility to facilitate her daughter-in-law in finding this elusive rest.

Naomi apparently knew what Boaz would be doing in considerable detail, and she knew that he would be sleeping at the threshing floor. She instructed Ruth to approach him after he had gone to sleep. Ruth was to prepare for the encounter by washing and dressing in her cloak. Bush suggests that Ruth had been wearing the garments of a widow in mourning and that she was to lay these aside and wear garments that showed that she was available for marriage.[15] Naomi's initiative was full of risk. Prostitutes might be expected to ply their wares in the darkness, but not a respectful widow. This is even more poignant since Moabite women had a reputation for seduction and as Schipper observes, "Ruth's encounter with Boaz on the threshing floor has striking similarities in context and vocabulary with the story of Moab's birth in Gen 19:30-38."[16]

Ruth must have known that this strategy involved risk, but she also knew that doing nothing was also fraught with danger since she needed the security and blessing that Naomi had envisaged for her. She carried out Naomi's instruction and approached the sleeping Boaz at midnight. Startled and alarmed to find someone close to him in the darkness, Boaz asked, "Who are you?" Ruth requested that he spread the corner (wing) of his garment over her. She used the same word that Boaz had used earlier in relation to Ruth seeking refuge under YHWH's wing (Ruth 2:12). According to Block, this was a request for marriage and Ruth was asking Boaz "to be the answer to his own invocation of blessing upon her in 2:12."[17] Boaz's reaction was entirely positive, and his response was to invoke a further blessing, "May you be blessed by the LORD, my daughter."

Early in the morning, Ruth returned to Naomi with six measures of grain of indeterminate weight. She explained to Naomi that Boaz had given her the grain so that she would not "go back empty-handed" to her mother-in-law (Ruth 3:17). Naomi, who had previously complained that YHWH had brought her back to Bethlehem

---

[15] Frederic W. Bush, *Ruth, Esther*, WBC 9 (Dallas: Word, 1996) 150–52.

[16] Schipper, *Ruth*, 41.

[17] Block, *Ruth*, 180.

"empty," was now enjoying blessing that she had not anticipated. The next mention of blessing relates to the birth of Obed and that will be dealt with in the section below on the theme of "offspring" since these two themes are inextricably linked.

3. The Theme of Offspring (Seed) in Genesis and Ruth

A close correlation between Ruth and Genesis is also found in relation to the theme of "seed." The prominence and significance of the theme of seed has been highlighted and explained by Alexander.[18] Following the expulsion of humankind from the Garden of Eden, the storyline of Genesis becomes an annotated family tree following the ups and downs of the line of the promised seed who will break down the barrier—erected by sinful disobedience—between God and his created order.

It can be argued that it this is not only one of the main unifying themes of Genesis but also the most significant, since the other themes—such as blessing and land—are meaningless without a line of offspring through which they can be realized. We first encounter the concept of "seed" in the creation narratives which highlight the fact that, even among plants, the concept of seed ensures the continuation of the species (Gen 1:11–12). The programmatic statement in 3:15 develops this theme since two lines of seed are introduced as protagonists (the seed of the woman and the seed of the serpent). Although it is not easy to pinpoint to whom the seed of the serpent refers, it is undoubtedly the seed of the woman that is highlighted in the main genealogies that are followed and delineated in Genesis. This theme is continued throughout the patriarchal narratives beginning with the story of Abraham. As Alexander observes, the "Abraham narrative builds on the divine promise given in Genesis 3:15 regarding the 'seed of the woman' overcoming the 'seed of the serpent.'"[19] Thus, an important aspect of Genesis is that it functions as a family tree pointing forward to the promised seed.

This line of promised seed is carefully traced throughout Genesis by a contrast

---

[18] T. Desmond Alexander, "Genealogies, Seed and the Compositional Unity of Genesis," *TynBul* 44 (1993): 225–70.

[19] Alexander, "Royal Expectations in Genesis to Kings: their Importance for Biblical Theology," *TynBul* 49 (1998): 205.

between those who are chosen and those who are not. Foils are provided for the main characters in the chosen line of seed. For example, the beneficent deed of Shem and Japheth is made possible by the misdeed of Ham. Abraham's faithfulness to his calling and to the land that YHWH has shown him is highlighted by the failure of Lot. A contrast is also apparent between the way that Isaac is born following divine promises and the way that Lot's children are born, resulting from incest. Similar comparisons and contrasts characterize both the Jacob and Joseph narratives. The goal of this genealogical thread is the tribe of Judah, which points forward to the royal line with the programmatic prophecy given by Jacob: "The scepter shall not depart from Judah, nor the ruler's staff from between his feet, until tribute comes to him; and to him shall be the obedience of the peoples" (Gen 49:10).

In the book of Ruth similar comparisons add tension and interest to the story line. Ruth is compared to Orpah. Orpah's return to Moab is not criticized in the text and, indeed, it is what Naomi requested. However, her decision helps to highlight the commitment of her sister-in-law and as Block observes, "Orpah represented an effective foil for Ruth."[20] Furthermore, Boaz's selflessness is highlighted by the understandable desire of the unknown redeemer to protect his own inheritance, whereas Boaz acts selflessly for the benefit of others.

The theme of "offspring" in Genesis involves many setbacks and the special genealogical line that began in Gen 3:15 is frequently under threat. Examples of this include the action of Pharaoh in taking Sarah into his harem (Gen 12:15) and the barrenness of Sarah (Gen 15:2). The book of Ruth also highlights threats to this line of seed. When Elimelech died, those who would have been expected to continue this line were Mahlon and Chilion. The meanings of these names are uncertain, but Hawk suggests that, "Mahlon and Chilion sound to the ear like derivatives of the Hebr. root *ḥlh*, which means to be 'weak', 'sickly' or 'finished.'" He concludes that we "might call them 'Wasted' and 'Weakling.'"[21] This does not augur well for the promised royal line of Judah. The situation is exacerbated when both men die leaving their widows

---

[20] Block, *Ruth*, 109.

[21] Hawk, *Ruth*, 56 cf. Schipper, *Ruth*, 82.

childless. Block emphasizes the seriousness of this situation:

The hope that Moab represented for Elimelech and his family was dashed, and ultimately the hope for Israel's royal line was jeopardized, when first the head of this household and then Naomi's two sons died leaving only three surviving widows.[22] Naomi's despair as she expressed regret that she was bereft of her husband and sons, not only presents us with a family tragedy but also suggests a threat to the line of Judah.

A clear connection between Genesis and Ruth exists through the story of Judah. The similarities between the two stories are unmistakable. Judah was living away from his family and his daughter-in-law, Tamar, was bound by the rules of levirate marriage. When two sons died, Judah treated her badly and kept her waiting for a levirate marriage that he was determined would never happen. When the levirate marriage failed to materialize, Tamar was forced to take drastic action to ensure the continuation of the family line.[23] Pretending to be a prostitute, she became pregnant with twins through her father-in-law, Judah. As a result, Perez and his brother were born outside marriage and the levirate system that should have protected Tamar was inadequate (Gen 38:1–30).[24]

This raises a question that has been the most debated issue in the book of Ruth. Was the levirate system more successful in Ruth's situation? Was Ruth's marriage a levirate marriage or did that system fail her as it had failed Tamar?

When Boaz began negotiations at the city gate, the second redeemer was willing to purchase the property that had belonged to Elimelech. However, when Ruth was mentioned, he changed his mind since he was worried that her involvement would endanger his inheritance. Two main explanations have been given to explain what changed his mind. The first approach follows the recommended masoretic reading (*qere*) in the margin of the Hebrew Bible. This approach assumes that the rules of levirate marriage applied to Ruth and that the purchase of the land involved a legally-

---

[22] Block, *Ruth*, 69.

[23] The failure of the levirate system was not the result of a defect in the system itself but was the consequence of Judah's refusal to fulfil his obligation.

[24] Judah's encounter with Tamar was not marriage and he never intended to marry her. Her deception of her father-in-law is reminiscent of the deception of Lot by his own daughters.

binding obligation to marry her. The Masoretes did not invent this interpretation and we know that it goes back at least as far as Josephus.[25] However, serious problems are raised when we understand Ruth's marriage in this way. Levirate rules applied when blood brothers were involved (Deut 25:5 cf. Matt 22:23–28). Although the redeemer was a relative of Elimelech, he was not a blood brother. Furthermore, as Eskenazi and Frymer-Kensky demonstrate, "Biblical laws about redemption of land or slaves say nothing about marrying the widow. And levirate marriage does not apply here."[26] If this man wanted to buy the land without marrying Ruth, there was nothing to stop him from doing so.

This conundrum has given rise to a second approach that follows the Hebrew text before the Masoretes inserted the vowels (*ketiv*) and presents Boaz as declaring that he had decided to marry Ruth.[27] Thus Sasson offers the following translation of Ruth 4:5: "Boaz declared further: 'know that on that very day you are purchasing the field from Naomi, I am acquiring Ruth of Moab, wife of the deceased.'"[28] Boaz explained that the purpose of this marriage was in order "to perpetuate the name of the dead in his inheritance" (4:5, 10). This declaration complicated matters for the second redeemer as he faced the possibility of the children of Ruth and Boaz having a legal claim on his land. This would clearly endanger his inheritance and was a risk that he was not prepared to take. Despite Boaz's intention to "perpetuate the name of the dead," it was not a levirate marriage since the genealogy is traced through Boaz. If levirate rules had applied the genealogy would have been through Mahlon.

We now have a clear comparison between the situation of Tamar and that of Ruth. Both faced the extinction of their family lines. As Ellen van Wolde explains, "they share the same purpose: to give birth to a male heir in order to make the names

---

[25] Paul L Maier, *Josephus: The Essential Writing. A New Translation* (Grand Rapids: Kregel Publications, 1988), 98.

[26] Tamara Eskenazi and Tikva Frymer-Kensky, *Ruth*, JPS Bible Commentary (Philadelphia: Jewish Publication Society, 2011), 76.

[27] Block accepts this approach and argues that "Boaz offered to go beyond legal duty and fulfil the moral obligation to which he had committed himself on the threshing floor" (*Ruth*, 214).

[28] Jack M. Sasson, *Ruth, A New Translation with a Philological Commentary and a Formalist-Folklorist Interpretation* (Baltimore and London: John Hopkins University Press, 1979), 6.

of the dead husbands survive."[29] The legally-binding system of levirate marriage failed Tamar and did not apply to Ruth. Tamar was forced to trick her father-in-law in order to resolve the situation. Ruth found herself in a similar predicament and her visit to the threshing floor was an act of immense risk in order to convince Boaz to act.

Finally, the book of Ruth concludes with a genealogy that follows the line of Judah's son Perez for ten generations. This provides a close link with Genesis and the same term תּוֹלְדוֹת (toledot) is used. Alexander points out that in Genesis the toledot formulae "in part, function like the lens on a zoom-camera by focusing attention on a single individual and his immediate descendants."[30] Zvi Ron explains that the use of the term toledot in Ruth "hints that the list should be viewed as part of the Genesis family of genealogical lists."[31] As Irmtraud Fischer comments, this list of names in Ruth is particularly significant because it picks up the genealogical information from Genesis in order to "declare the line of Judah the main line after Jacob-Israel, a line directly leading to the House of David."[32]

The similarity between the structure of this genealogy and those in Genesis has been recognized by several scholars. The genealogy in Ruth covers ten generations and there are two genealogies in Genesis that, likewise, cover ten generations (Gen 5:1–32; 11:10–26). It has been noted that the tenth position in these genealogies is particularly significant. In tenth place in the Gen 5 genealogy we find Noah and in Gen 11 it is Abraham, while in Ruth the tenth place belongs to David. If we take the three genealogies together, Noah is tenth in line, Abraham is twentieth and David is thirtieth. Zvi Ron argues that the emphasis on these three characters is significant because each began a new epoch. Noah represented the beginning of the post-flood world. Abraham as the father of many nations, especially Israel, also signified a

---

[29] Ellen van Wolde, "Texts in Dialogue with Texts: Intertextuality in the Ruth and Tamar Narratives," *BibInt* 5.1 (1997): 12.

[30] Alexander, "Royal Expectations," 203.

[31] Zvi Ron, "The Genealogical List in Ruth," *JBQ* 38 (2010): 86. Block makes the same point (*Ruth*, 253).

[32] Irmtraud Fischer, "The Book of Ruth: A 'Feminist' Commentary to the Torah?," in *Ruth and Esther: A Feminist Companion to the Bible,* Second Series, ed. Athalya Brenner (Sheffield: Sheffield Academic Press, 1999), 48.

turning point in history. Furthermore, as Ron points out, "David began the dynasty that will ultimately lead to messianic times under the Messiah son of David."[33] Thus, the family tree that is traced from Seth to Perez in Genesis, is continued in the book of Ruth from Perez to David. Ruth is not an isolated story but part of the program of redemption that began in Gen 3:15.

4. The Theme of Land

When Ruth was sent to the threshing floor by Naomi, the instructions did not include any reference to the land, but Ruth went beyond these instructions and raised the subject from her own initiative by reminding Boaz that he was a kinsman redeemer (Ruth 3:9). Until this point the reader is not aware that Naomi had land to sell but apparently the family had not sold their land before going to Moab. During the harvest there would have been no market for land that had been left fallow but after harvest there was an opportunity to realize its value and gain resources to provide for herself and Ruth. The land could not be put on the open market but had to be sold within the family. For ten years the land may have been barren—just like the family itself—but now the conditions are right for a new start and Naomi connected the two enterprises: getting benefit from the land by selling it and finding rest for Ruth through marriage.[34]

This emphasizes the close relationship between the theme of seed and that of land, since the land belongs to a particular family group and can only be bought by that line of descendants (seed). This is where the idea of redemption was important. In Israel, provision was made for those who encountered difficult times and needed someone to buy their land and keep it within the family group (Lev 25:23–28). The person who did this was the kinsman-redeemer. In the story of Ruth there was more than one possible redeemer. At the threshing floor Boaz revealed that someone has a closer relationship to the deceased than he, so this person must be given the first opportunity to redeem the land (Ruth 3:12–13).

---

[33] "Genealogical List," 86.

[34] Some scholars argue that the land was not left fallow but was farmed by others during the absence of Elimelech and his family.

This other redeemer seemed interested in adding to his own territory but had no interest in getting involved for the sake of Naomi and Ruth. This is reflected in the rich symbolism evoked by the motif of names. The second redeemer is known as Peloni Almoni (so and so) but Boaz is described as one who will "call a name in Israel" and his son is accorded similar acclaim (Ruth 4:11). The term Peloni Almoni simply indicates that his name is missing or has been forgotten.[35] This is not to be understood as pejorative. This unknown person does not do anything amiss and his forgotten name is not judgment. Like Orpah, the second redeemer is behaving normally, protecting his own interests. However, the missing name does facilitate the elevation of the name of Boaz whose generosity provided a haven for Ruth and essential resources for Naomi.

The concept of a great name is prominent in Genesis. In the enigmatic story of Gen 6 we are introduced to the "men of renown" (literally men of a name), and in Gen 11 the builders of the Tower of Babel are motivated by the desire to make a name for themselves. In both cases divine restrictions are imposed to limit the achievements of those attempting to promote their own names. On the other hand, YHWH promised to make Abraham's name great and it is his great name that is associated with the line of chosen seed (Gen 12:2). This title (great name) is also ascribed to King David (2 Sam 7:9). The book of Ruth is, therefore, taking us on the journey from Abraham to David and one of the trajectories in the story is the theme of the great name through the line of offspring (seed) who are heirs to God's blessing.

5. Were Boaz and Obed Messianic figures?

Both Boaz and Obed are described as redeemers and this concept of redemption is, of course, an important theme for biblical theology since it is found in both testaments. In particular, Boaz is an important link in the rhetorical arc that begins in Gen 3:15 and ends with Jesus the Messiah. Although he is not mentioned again after the story in Ruth, apart from the appearance of his name in genealogies, Boaz is recognized as a significant figure by Alexander who comments, "Although the concept of kinsman-redeemer is not associated with the Israelite King elsewhere in the Old

---

[35] Hawk translates the term as "Nobody Special." *Ruth,* 127.

Testament, it is highlighted as an aspect of God's activity on behalf of Israel.... Since this is how the divine king rescues his people, it might be expected that his royal servant would fulfil a similar role."[36]

Block observes that Boaz is portrayed "as a model of personal righteousness" but points out that he is not understood as a messianic figure since he is never mentioned as such in either the Old or New Testaments. Block concludes that it is really Obed rather than Boaz who "functions typologically" as the Messiah in the book of Ruth.[37] Obed's credentials that qualify him as a messianic figure include his birth through a woman who was previously barren until God opened her womb (Ruth 4:13). Block also draws attention to the significance of the name Obed which means servant and he points out that this name "anticipates David the anointed servant of YHWH (2 Sam 7) and ultimately the Isaianic servant.[38]

6. Conclusion

While closely linked with the covenantal relationship between YHWH and Israel, the line of seed promised in Genesis was not primarily about ethnicity. It included people like Tamar and Ruth who displayed faithfulness in adverse circumstances. It was more about commitment rather than birth-right. At the beginning of the story, the lives of Ruth and Naomi reflected the ongoing effects of the rebellion of humankind related in Gen 3 and exemplified in the judges period. These consequences of sin included famine, barrenness and death. Through the generosity and faithfulness of Boaz, the kinsman-redeemer, the situation was changed to abundant blessing manifest in redemption, fruitfulness and a continuation of the line of promise that began in Gen 3:15 and passed through David to Jesus Christ—who is introduced in Matthew in a genealogy that not surprisingly includes the names we have encountered in the book of Ruth.

---

[36] Alexander, *Servant King*, 53.

[37] Block, *Ruth*, 55.

[38] Block, *Ruth*, 55.

"WE THREE KINGS …"—AN EXAMINATION OF THE MESSIANIC TRAJECTORY OF THE BOOKS OF KINGS WITH SPECIAL REFERENCE TO SOLOMON, HEZEKIAH, AND JOSIAH

—J. Gary Millar

1. Introduction

For many years, studies of the books of Kings have been dominated by issues surrounding the history of composition of the work, and the (often competing) ideologies which have contributed to its formation.[1] This has meant that literary and biblical-theological connections and trajectories within the final form of the book have often been neglected. One such trajectory is that of God's ideal King, the messiah, particularly as reflected in the narratives dealing with the three "best" kings of God's people, Solomon, Hezekiah and Josiah.

The significance of the Solomon narratives in 1 Kgs 1–11 for the overall message of the books of Kings has often been overlooked.[2] There have been many studies of the structure of this part of the text, and many attempts to locate the apparently competing perspectives and ideologies of contrasting statements about Solomon.[3] Often, dealing with the thorny issues concerning the putative origins and concerns of the Deuteronomistic Historians have filled the frame to the detriment of

---

[1] See the comprehensive collection of essays dealing with the "state of play" on this issue: André Lemaire, Baruch Halpern, and Matthew J. Adams. *The Books of Kings: Sources, Composition, Historiography and Reception*, VTSup 129 (Leiden: Brill, 2010).

[2] See, e.g., Lowell K. Handy, *The Age of Solomon: Scholarship at the Turn of the Millennium*, Studies in the History and Culture of the Ancient Near East 11 (Leiden: Brill, 1997). Despite the vast number of articles, very little attention is paid to the theological significance of Solomon.

[3] See, e.g., Marc Brettler, "The Structure of 1 Kings 1–11," *JSOT* 49 (1991): 87–97, who sees a negative frame around positive material; also, see Kim I. Parker, "Solomon as Philosopher King? The Nexus of Law and Wisdom in 1 Kings 1–11," *JSOT* 53 (1992): 75–91, who argues for a positive portrayal followed by a negative one.

some even more fundamental issues, including why so much space is devoted to the highly nuanced and ambiguous account of the reign of the first (and only) "son of David" to sit on the throne of the united kingdom for his entire reign.

Given the fact that the books of Kings routinely view those ruling in both Judah and Israel through the lenses of 2 Sam 7 (particularly in the case of the kings of Judah) and Deut 17, evaluating each reign against a fused Mosaic/Davidic ideal, the extended treatment of Solomon (occupying almost a quarter of the text of Kings) might reasonably be expected to take on a certain paradigmatic significance. Hermeneutically, one would expect such a major discussion of one king to provide an extended worked example of how God views those who ascend to thrones, and in particular, how these kings contribute to or detract from the evolving/diminishing messianic hope in these narratives. At a *prima facie* level then, a re-examination of the Solomon narratives is warranted, particularly given the puzzling (and intriguing) ambiguities which emerge on any careful reading of the text. But Solomon is not alone, either in being neglected or in receiving a highly nuanced treatment from the writer(s) of Kings.

On working through the books of Kings, it rapidly becomes apparent that most of the procession of monarchs who are presented in the narrative are straightforwardly abject failures, at least in terms of Yahweh's expectation of the kings of his people.[4] However, two kings stand out as those who are faithful to the vision and legacy of their forefather David.

In 2 Kgs 18:3, Hezekiah is commended because "he did what was right in the eyes of the LORD, according to all that David his father had done."[5] He is exemplary in that, according to verse 5, "he trusted in the LORD, the God of Israel, so that there was none like him among all the kings of Judah after him, nor among those who were before him." This true Davidide (who even takes on and overcomes Philistines; cf. 18:8) also, according to verse 6, appears to live up to the Mosaic ideal: "For he held fast to the LORD. He did not depart from following him, but kept the commandments

---

[4] Of course, in some cases, the gap between their political impact as judged by other ancient Near Eastern material, and the divine verdict on their reign may be substantial (e.g., Omri).

[5] All biblical quotations are from the ESV.

that the LORD commanded Moses." For the first time since Solomon, it appears that Judah has a king who has the potential to be the kind of Davidic Messiah anticipated in 2 Sam 7. However, in a way which is strongly reminiscent of the extended Solomon narratives, the ensuing events described in the rest of chapters 18–20 present Hezekiah in a highly ambiguous way.

Similarly, the discussion of the reign of the godly Josiah in 2 Kgs 22–23 hits significant high points. In 2 Kgs 23:24, the writer of Kings identifies Josiah's distinctive commitment to the word of Yahweh in terms of purging idols from the nation "that he might establish the words of the law (הקים את־דברי התורה) that were written in the book that Hilkiah the priest found in the house of the LORD." He goes even further, however, in verse 25, to describe him in similarly exalted terms to Hezekiah, as a king without peer who manages to conform to both Davidic and Mosaic ideals: "Before him there was no king like him, who turned to the LORD with all his heart and with all his soul and with all his might, according to all the Law of Moses." In this case, the text goes a step further by adding "nor did any like him arise after him."[6] This note has the effect of "closing the loop" with regard to godly Davidic Kings, and establishing the triumvirate of Solomon, Hezekiah and Josiah as central to the messianic concerns of the books of Kings, and therefore to the entire flow of biblical theology.[7] It would not be unreasonable, given their theological significance and literary prominence, to assume that these three kings taken together make an important contribution to the overall shape and message of kings.[8]

---

[6] Sweeney provides a helpful comparison of the discussion of Solomon and that of Josiah, but makes no mention of Hezekiah; see Marvin A. Sweeney, "The Critique of Solomon in the Josianic Edition of the Deuteronomistic History," *JBL* 114 (1995): 607–22. However, see also the criticisms of Sweeney in David A. Glatt-Gilead, "The Deuteronomistic Critique of Solomon: A Response to Marvin A. Sweeney," *JBL* 116 (1997): 700–703.

[7] Studies of Hezekiah and Josiah tend to focus on the apparent political agendas behind the text—for one short study that typifies the dominant approach, see, e.g., E. W. Todd, "The Reforms of Hezekiah and Josiah," *SJT* 9 (1956): 288–93.

[8] Over 100 years ago, Edward Day gave an account of how the Deuteronomistic History assesses the kings of Judah, although not considering how the Solomon narratives related to this ("The Deuteronomic Judgements of the Kings of Judah," *JTS* 11 [1909]: 74–83). Presumably, such a fragmentary approach precluded drawing any literary or theological conclusions across the work as a whole.

In a 1992 article entitled, "'There Was None Like Him': Incomparability in the Books of Kings," Gary Knoppers helpfully highlights the connections between these three kings in particular. In 1 Kgs 3:12, incomparable wealth and wisdom is attributed to Solomon; in 2 Kgs 18:5–6, incomparable trust is attributed to Hezekiah and in 2 Kgs 23:25, incomparable reforms are attributed to Josiah.[9] Knoppers is convinced that "the incompatibility formulae do not conflict with one another and indicate unity rather than disunity within the Deuteronomistic history. The incomparability formulae are one means by which an exilic Deuteronomist highlights the exceptional accomplishments of major figures within his history."[10] Knoppers' basic contention that these three figures tie the whole presentation of Kings is an important one. However, we can go further. The delicate nuance and ambiguity with which each of these "peerless" kings is depicted takes us right to the heart of the overall message of the books of Kings.[11] The presentation of these three kings not only adds further depth to the emerging picture of the suffering and glory of the messiah, but clarifies precisely how the promise of a rescuer in Gen 3:15 is to be fulfilled.

The rest of this chapter then, will be devoted to examining how the presentation of these three kings, both individually and together, establishes and sets out a vision for a Davidic Messiah which will prove foundational both for the rest of the Old Testament, and for understanding Jesus Christ, the one "greater than Solomon" himself.

2. King Solomon: The hermeneutical Key to the Books of Kings

2.1. A Tension Introduced

Any discussion of the reign and significance of Solomon has to come to terms with the tension between the stunning interaction between Yahweh and his king in 1

---

[9] Gary N. Knoppers, "'There Was None Like Him': Incomparability in the Books of Kings," *CBQ* 54 (1992): 411–31.

[10] Knoppers, "Incomparability," 413–14.

[11] Alison L. Joseph provides a stimulating discussion of Solomon and Josiah in particular (*Portrait of the Kings: The Davidic Prototype in Deuteronomistic Poetics* [Minneapolis: Augsburg Fortress: 2015]). However, her focus is also on tracing the evolving concerns of various redactional stages, rather than investigating the deliberate tensions present within the final form of the text. She also says little about Hezekiah in his own right.

Kgs 3:3–15, where Solomon asks for and receives "wisdom" in the form of an understanding and discerning mind, and the gradual declension of his devotion to God throughout the narrative, culminating in the damning summary of 1 Kgs 11:1–8. The admission in 11:1 that "King Solomon loved many foreign women, along with the daughter of Pharaoh: Moabite, Ammonite, Edomite, Sidonian, and Hittite women" leads to the assertion in verses 3–4 that "his wives turned away his heart … after other gods, and his heart was not wholly true to the LORD his God, as was the heart of David his father."

It is often noted that this downward slide was foreshadowed as early as 1 Kgs 3:1, where the narrative of Solomon's request for wisdom is preceded by the announcement in 1 Kgs 3:1 that "Solomon made a marriage alliance with Pharaoh king of Egypt. He took Pharaoh's daughter and brought her into the city of David until he had finished building his own house and the house of the LORD and the wall around Jerusalem." Clearly, political expediency is at least part of his motivation, but the fact that his reign starts and ends with references to his marriages to foreign women suggests that there are deeper issues in the mind and heart of this wisest of kings. What is less often discussed, however, are the dark events of 1 Kgs 2, which introduce the idea of royal wisdom, and cast the events which follow in an ambiguous light.

In 1 Kgs 2:1–4, David, after the sad inactivity with which the book opens (1 Kgs 1:1–4), finally springs into action. As he galvanizes his son in the wake of Adonijah's rebellion and before his own passing, he first draws on both 2 Sam 7 and Deut 17 in a way which sets a precedent for the evaluation of all the kings to follow: "Be strong, and show yourself a man, and keep the charge of the LORD your God, walking in his ways and keeping his statutes, his commandments, his rules, and his testimonies, as it is written in the Law of Moses, that you may prosper in all that you do and wherever you turn, that the LORD may establish his word that he spoke concerning me, saying, 'If your sons pay close attention to their way, to walk before me in faithfulness with all their heart and with all their soul, you shall not lack a man on the throne of Israel'" (2 Kgs 2–4). At this point, however, David's words take on a very different tone.

David reminds Solomon of two incidents narrated in the books of Samuel: Joab's execution of Abner and Amasa (2 Sam 3:26–30; 20:1–13) and Shimei's cursing of David (2 Sam 16:5–14; 19:16–23). In both of the earlier narratives, David highlights the wickedness of Joab and Shimei, but does nothing to bring them to account for their actions. In fact, he insists that Shimei be treated with mercy, despite cursing David to his face, and simply gives Joab his old job back (2 Sam 20:23). It now appears that these (presumably politically expedient) actions masked a strong desire for vengeance.

David's long-harbored desire for justice (if not revenge) comes to the surface in the rest of his speech to his son, as he calls Solomon to "act therefore according to your wisdom" (1 Kgs 2:6). Lest there be any confusion over what David is asking his son to do, he qualifies his instructions by urging Solomon not to "let his grey head go down to Sheol in peace." Joab is clearly to be given a taste of his own brutal medicine. Similarly, after parading his own integrity, displayed by keeping his vow, Shimei is to receive similar treatment, which is again directly linked to Solomon's wisdom (1 Kgs 2:9). [12]

It is not accidental that the first mention of wisdom in connection with Solomon is not a positive one. This wisdom is decidedly worldly, and the narrative of 1 Kgs 2 reflects badly on both David and Solomon. In particular, this casts a shadow over the descriptions of Solomon's wisdom to follow. It is not simply that Solomon starts well and loses the plot at the end. There are significant question marks over the nature of his wisdom from the very beginning.[13]

It is not, of course, that "wisdom" becomes a negative category in the books of Kings. In the narrative which follows, Solomon is highly commended for seeking a discerning mind (3:9–10). However, this striking introduction is determinative for the narrative which follows. It introduces a darker note of tension which then plays out

---

[12] This is noted, for example, by Jerome T. Walsh in "The Characterization of Solomon in 1 Kings 1–5," *CBQ* 57 (1995): 475, but he simply comments: "His repeated references to Solomon's wisdom (vv. 6, 9) warn his son to read between the lines."

[13] It is also worth noting that Solomon is the one also called Jedidiah, "loved of the LORD," whom God has established as king ahead of his older sibling (see 1 Kgs 2:15, 24). See the helpful discussion in Isaac Kalimi, "Love of God and Apologia for a King: Solomon as the Lord's Beloved King in Biblical and Ancient Near Eastern Contexts," *JANER* 17 (2017): 28–63.

through the rest of the Solomon narrative. Neither this dark note, nor the paradigmatic role played by the Solomon narratives in 1 Kgs 1–11 for the books of Kings as a whole, has been given sufficient attention.

2.2. A Tension Lived out—Wisdom in a World of Power, Money, and Sex

2.2.1. Power

If one needed confirmation that the presentation of Solomon is not a straightforward or hagiographic presentation of Israel's greatest king, it comes in the understated note of 1 Kgs 3: that Solomon married Pharaoh's daughter. The *hitpael* of the verb "to marry" carries with it the implication of forming an alliance or making common cause (see, e.g., Deut 7:3, where the Canaanites are in view).[14] It seems that the first act of Solomon on securing power and neutralizing potential internal enemies, is to make a prohibited alliance with an international ally. These events, like much of the rest of Kings, played out against the background of Deut 17:14–20, especially verse 16. In marrying Pharaoh's daughter, Solomon not only takes God's people "back to Egypt," but introduces Egypt to the very heart of Israel.

This is then confirmed by the author's highlighting the fact that Solomon the "Wise" installs Pharaoh's daughter in the city of David, the citadel at the South-eastern corner of Jerusalem (also 1 Kgs 3:1), at least until her palace was finished (1 Kgs 7:8). However, even the fact that his Egyptian Queen has such national prominence (and apparently pre-eminence) contributes to the growing sense of uncertainty in the text. Add to this the fact that according to 1 Kgs 3:2, "the people were sacrificing at the high places," and we have a growing picture of a reality of life in Israel which is a long way from a depiction of some messianic ideal. Whilst the context suggests that Solomon, at least, went there to worship Yahweh (see on 3:3–4 below). Nonetheless, the fact that failure to remove the high places is the standard by which many later Kings are judged (see, e.g., 2 Kgs 14:4; 15:35; 18:4, 22; 23:19) suggests that even in this context, the existence of the high place is a further reflection on the ambiguities

---

[14] On the historicity of this alliance, see K. A. Kitchen, *On the Reliability of the Old Testament* (Grand Rapids: Eerdmans, 2003), 1.

of Solomon's kingship.

These observations then go some way to temper the soaring accolades. Uniquely in the Old Testament, "Solomon loved the LORD" (1 Kgs 3:3). There are several OT figures who receive striking commendations (e.g., Caleb, who followed the LORD wholeheartedly; Deut 1:36) but there are none who are praised quite like this. Solomon alone is commended for his love of God, which reveals itself by his "walking in the statutes of David his father." This covenantal love is both affective and practical. Along with Asa, Hezekiah and Josiah (1 Kgs 15:11; 2 Kgs 18:3; 22:2; see also, e.g., 2 Kgs 14:3), Solomon follows in the footsteps of David, which, in the eyes of our writer, is the definitive mark of a godly king.[15] However, our writer has already made clear, that even this wisest of kings will come up short when it comes to exercising power in a godly way.

2.2.2. Money

The second member of the deadly triumvirate of money, sex and power to be highlighted in the Solomon narrative is money. In two key passages, his exorbitant wealth is discussed in a way which makes clear that for the writer at least, the way in which he handles prosperity is lacking in godly wisdom.

As we have already seen, the writer's preferred pattern seems to be to preface a glowing report of Solomon's attributes with a more worrying analysis of his flawed behavior. This has the effect of creating doubt and ambiguity, rather than simply damning his behavior.

First Kings 4:7 introduces the elaborate system that Solomon had created to ensure that his household were well provided for. The fact that the names of those officials responsible for each month, and their jurisdictions, are included in full, suggests that the writer of Kings is highlighting just how carefully Solomon organized things to ensure his own comfort. The fact that according to 4:19, a governor was required to take overall responsibility for delivering these provisions, underlines what

---

[15] Despite this commendation, and the fact that "he was wholly true to the LORD all his days," Asa does not make it into this chapter, because he did not remove the high places (1 Kgs 15:14), nor was he praised as "uniquely" godly.

a major operation this was. However, the details supplied in verse 22 go some way to explaining why this was necessary.

The grocery order for the royal court is very impressive (4:22–23). A cor of flour was roughly equivalent to 125 kg. This emphasizes both the size and opulence of Solomon's court. Whilst this was not atypical of ancient kings, it does not sit well with Deut 17. The seven kinds of meat consumed are striking both for their luxury and quantity. This is a far cry from the diet of the general population, and even through some of this at least comes from other nations as tribute, this cannot and does not eradicate the aroma of exploitation from the atmosphere.

First Kings 4: 26–27 notes that Solomon also had 40,000 stalls of horses for his chariots, and 12,000 horsemen. Had there been any doubt, this clarifies the unfavorable comparison to the model king of Deut 17. The officials charged with ensuring that Solomon and his court are well-supplied, also get the task of ensuring that this vast quantity of animals are well-looked after.

It is in this context that Solomon is lauded as an outstanding example of the ancient wise man, and his wisdom attributed to God himself (4:29–31). However, as we have already seen, this wisdom is tinged with ambiguity by the preceding narrative.

Solomon's compromised attitude to wealth (especially when measured against the proscription of amassing gold in Deut 17:17) comes to the fore when his income and interior decorating practices are discussed in 1 Kgs 10. Earlier in the piece (in 1 Kgs 7:45–50), the Temple furnishings are described in lavish detail. Hiram seems to have donated a large number of bronze vessels and implements. Solomon himself augmented this with gold, both to line the Holy of Holies, and to make more ancillary items. However, when we come to chapter 10, it seems that this would not have made a significant dent in Solomon's personal wealth.

Every year, Solomon could count on an income of 666 talents of gold (well over 20 metric tons) presumably from his own mining/prospecting activities, an amount which is fairly typical of significant empires in the ancient world. Add to that the gold which he gathered through taxation and tribute (including duty paid for access to trade routes through Israelite territory by foreign kings and territories), and he was an extremely wealthy man. Some of this gold was used to create 500 ceremonial shields (300 of these were full length, with 5–10 kg of gold hammered onto base metal, and 200 were smaller and lighter, using 1.5–3 kg of gold), which provided a stunning backdrop for the daily life of Solomon's court in the Hall of the Forest of Lebanon.

The vaguely troubling description of Solomon's wealth then gives way to a description of his throne. The fact that the throne had six steps may be an allusion to the Babylonian idea that the king ruled the cosmos from "level 7" of creation.[16] In any case, the lion carvings (two lions standing beside the armrests, while twelve lions stood there, one on each end of a step on the six steps) bring together both the symbol for the House of Judah and make a grand statement about Solomon's power and significance. The details of the throne are typical of the period, but the fact that the like of it was never made in any kingdom makes it clear that not only was Solomon a king like the kings of the other nations, but in many ways surpassed them. The cumulative weight of these opulent details does create the impression that Solomon's decadence outstripped even his wisdom.

It is hard to avoid the conclusion that the writer is pushing us to this conclusion, when he reports on Solomon's dishware in 10:21–22. In both Solomon's own quarters, and the "State Hall" of the House of the Forest of Lebanon, only gold utensils were used. The difference between gold and pure gold is not clear, but the fact that silver was not considered as anything in the days of Solomon is confirmation that the royal court of Israel was truly "world class," with the quality of its kitchenware matched by regular, exotic deliveries from the ends of the earth of gold, silver, ivory, apes, and peacocks. Yes, Solomon has been granted spectacular wisdom and material blessing by God, but the shameless array of wealth is surely included to produce a growing disquiet in the reader. Yes, Solomon has been richly blessed by God (1 Kgs 3:3), but the way in which Solomon has used it appears foolish.

The final piece in this worrying puzzle comes in a reiteration that Solomon not only flouted the Deuteronomic prohibition of chariots, but actively sourced them (and

---

[16] Lissa M. Wray Beal, *1 & 2 Kings*, ApOTC 9 (Nottingham: Apollos, 2014).

the horses to pull them) from Egypt, as well as exporting them to former enemies including the Hittites and Arameans (10:28–29). Prosperity under Solomon came at a price. Trading in chariots and horses was a tell-tale sign that the king had abandoned the ways of Yahweh. In addition, Solomon the Wise is arming his neighbors in a way which amounts to recklessness. At every level, this narrative closes on a note of alarm.

2.2.3. Sex

The other major issue which casts a long shadow over Solomon's world, and the presentation of his wisdom is his attitude to sex. The summary of his reign in 1 Kgs 11 exposes a fissure in his character and reign which, it turns out, throws the whole question of his wisdom into sharper relief than ever before, effectively bracketing the account of his rule between two negative assessments of his choices (see the comments on 1 Kgs 2 above).

The fact that "King Solomon, however, loved many foreign women besides Pharaoh's daughter—Moabites, Ammonites, Edomites, Sidonians and Hittites" (1 Kgs 11:1) makes explicit what was hinted at in chapter 3. The alliance with the daughter of Pharaoh was, it turns out, much more than an astute political move (or even an unfortunate affair of the heart). It was indicative of a deep-seated flaw in his moral make-up. The motivation for these marriages is not the political standing of the nation but Solomon's own desires. The phrase "Solomon loved many foreign women" (שלמה אהב נשים נכריות רבות) makes that very clear. The writer is also not subtle in highlighting the heart issues that are operative here: behind the divine prohibition stood the fear that "'they will surely turn your hearts after their gods.' Nevertheless, Solomon clung to [or, with the NIV, held fast] to them in love" (11:2 NIV). Solomon's "wisdom" does not stretch to submitting to the prescriptions of Deuteronomy.[17]

In a way which is quite unlike the normal *modus operandi* of the writer of Kings (who generally prefers subtlety and nuance to bald editorial comment, particularly in the "body" of the discussion of particular kings), Solomon's excesses are spelled out in

---

[17] See the discussion of the negative aspects of 1 Kgs 3–11 in Sweeney, "Critique of Solomon," 613–618.

painful detail—so verse 3: "He had seven hundred wives of royal birth and three hundred concubines, and his wives turned away his heart." In particular, their influence in effectively wooing him away from the Davidic ideal is underlined. This is one of the most important motifs in the entire books of Kings.[18] The great hope for Solomon was that he would be his father's true heir. However, chapter 2 had hinted at the fact that he may be a "chip off the old block" in ways that are not entirely helpful. The ensuing narrative holds out hope in key ways—not least that he is the temple builder in chapter 7, but reveals himself in chapter 8 to be an insightful and godly "Davidic Theologian." Now, however, on closer examination, his life is revealed as a significant declension from the Davidic ideal (11:4). His love for his wives appears to have triumphed over his heralded love for Yahweh (see 1 Kgs 3:3).

As is often the case in the Old Testament (and the books of Kings in particular), infidelity in marriage (whether adultery or marrying outside the limits defined by God for his people) slides inexorably into idolatry, which for Solomon, is made explicit in 11:5. Solomon's failure is spectacular and specific. Often, the condemnation of kings of both Israel and Judah to follow is generic, and largely based on their failure to take sufficient action against existing practices.[19] Startlingly, with Israel's "wisest" king, his sin is clearly and worryingly detailed (also 11:7–8) Given all this, the verdict on the great hope of God's people—the original descendant of David—is deeply depressing, if not surprising in verse 6: "So Solomon did what was evil in the sight of the LORD and did not wholly follow the LORD, as David his father had done."

2.3. Interim Conclusion: Reading Kings in the Light of Solomon

Solomon's accession and reign dominates the opening of the books of Kings. The simple fact that eleven chapters are devoted entirely to the account of his rule should surely point us to the paradigmatic significance of this king. However, we can go much further. This wisest of kings is both introduced and held up throughout as a highly ambiguous figure, who is capable of moments of profound insight and

---

[18] This is reflected, for example, in the way in which Josiah reverses the corruptions of worship which arose under Solomon in 2 Kgs 23:13–14.

[19] E.g., 2 Kgs 13:11 (Jehoash of Israel), 2 Kgs 14:4 (Amaziah of Judah).

godliness, yet the trajectory of whose life is steadily downhill, from Davidic wholeheartedness to consistent idolatry.

How then should this affect how we read the books of Kings? Reading the Solomon narratives in the light of the ambiguities concerning his wisdom on the one hand sets us up to read the ensuing accounts of the kings of Judah and Israel *pessimistically* and on the other to read them *messianically*.

The innate pessimism of these books has often been realized and given their denouement (and probable genesis) in the Babylonian exile, is hardly the most startling exegetical or theological insight! However, this negative vision is not often rooted in the extended and careful exposure of Solomon as an anti-David in the first eleven chapters. Similarly, the natural extension of this assessment of Solomon to a search for a "better king than the son of David" has not been recognized as the controlling theological concern of Kings, despite the fact that it is borne out by the accounts of virtually every king, both north and south of the border which follows.

To trace these themes for every king is beyond the remit of this essay; however, the mirroring of this basic perspective in the assessment of the two other "best" kings of Judah, Hezekiah and Josiah, who dominate the closing section of the books of Kings, should confirm the importance and validity of reading these books in this light.[20] These narratives take their place in the unfolding picture of the promised one who would undo the curse of sin.

3. King Hezekiah: The Inevitability of Disappointment in the Davidic King

After narrating the tragic demise of the northern kingdom of Israel in 2 Kgs 17, attention turns to the question of "Is there any hope for Judah?" and the reign of one of two nominees for the "most godly king Judah ever had" award, Hezekiah. Not since the reign of Solomon has a Davidic king been given this much airplay. The long section of text that occupies chapters 18, 19 and 20 then offers a glimmer of hope that

---

[20] For more detail see J. Gary Millar, "1 & 2 Kings," in *ESV Expository Commentary*. Volume 3. *1 Samuel–2 Chronicles*, ed. I. M. Duguid, J. M. Hamilton Jr. and J. Sklar (Wheaton, IL: Crossway, 2019).

at last, the right kind of king might reign in Jerusalem, who fulfils the promise of 2 Sam 7, and lives up to the ideals of Deut 17.[21]

Right at the beginning of the Hezekiah narratives, the writer goes to great lengths to ensure that the reader picks up on the fact that at last, we have a king like David, who did "what was right in the eyes of the LORD, according to all that David his father had done" (2 Kgs 18:3). Unlike Solomon, Hezekiah had a flawless record of dealing with idolatry, succeeding where almost every king of Judah failed.[22] The verdict on Hezekiah's reign in 2 Kgs 18:4 is more positive than any other Judean king: "He trusted in the LORD, the God of Israel, so that there was none like him among all the kings of Judah after him, nor among those who were before him." He also "held fast to the LORD" in faithfulness to the Torah of Moses.[23] The word is "cleaved," as used in Gen 2:24 and elsewhere of an intimate relationship. So, Solomon "cleaved" to his foreign wives (1 Kgs 11:2). However, Hezekiah follows the injunction of Deuteronomy to cleave to the LORD (see Deut 4:4; 10:20; 11:22; 13:4 etc.). In 2 Kgs 18:7, it is stated that "the LORD was with him," and as a result, he was successful in all he did. David is the only other king spoken of in these terms (1 Sam 16:18; 18:12, 14; 2 Sam 5:10).

The connection with David is enhanced by the note that Hezekiah "struck down the Philistines as far as Gaza and its territory, from watchtower to fortified city" (2 Kgs 18:8; see 1 Sam 18:27; 19:8). From the outset then, Hezekiah is presented as one of Judah's truly great kings. In the wake of the Assyrian destruction of Israel, there is a glimmer of hope that things might turn out differently in Judah.

---

[21] Mordechai Cogan has provided a concise and beautifully presented overview of the details we know of Hezekiah from the biblical text and other ancient Near Eastern material in *Understanding Hezekiah King of Judah: Rebel King and Reformer* (Jerusalem: Carta, 2017).

[22] See 1 Kgs 8:1–9 for other items associated *with* Moses which were kept at the Temple.

[23] Many earlier commentators simply deleted this phrase as, for example, "an exaggeration that is unsatisfactory in content and syntax," Gwilym H. Jones, *1 and 2 Kings,* NCB, 2 vols. (Grand Rapids: Eerdmans, 1984), 2:562. This may explain the relative neglect of Hezekiah in discussions concerning the ideal king/messiah.

3.1. Wisdom or Weakness?

It must be said that Hezekiah lived in the most demanding of times. The Assyrian threat is real and looming large, which is noted as soon as the summary of his reign is concluded (2 Kgs 18:9–12). However, Hezekiah's response to the Assyrian threat aligns him not with David, but with the procession of faithless kings who have tried to buy off foreign oppressors rather than trusting Yahweh.

His message to the King of Assyria in 2 Kgs 18:14 seems like an unwarranted capitulation. The king then proceeds to use temple silver and gold to buy vassal status, which he can purchase for three hundred talents of silver (approximately 12000 kg) and thirty talents (1050 kg) of gold. Hezekiah only manages to scrape together this enormous sum by giving him "all the silver that was found in the house of the LORD and in the treasuries of the king's house. Additionally, he stripped the gold from the doors of the temple of the LORD and from the doorposts that Hezekiah king of Judah had overlaid and gave it to the king of Assyria" (2 Kgs 18:15–16). In other words, Hezekiah has to take back his own donations to the Temple in order to pay off this pagan king. He now joins the rather depressing list of those kings who paid off foreign powers with the riches of the temple: Rehoboam (1 Kgs 14:25–28); Asa (1 Kgs 15:17–19); Jehoash (2 Kgs 12:18–19); Amaziah (2 Kgs 14:11–14) and Ahaz (2 Kgs 16:7–9).

In Hezekiah's defense, this situation and the ensuing humiliating negotiations detailed in the rest of chapter 18, cause him substantial distress, which he expresses in a godly way (2 Kgs 19:1), as well as seeking a word from the LORD through the prophet Isaiah. After Yahweh speaks through his prophet (19:5–7), there is word both of the Assyrians' temporary withdrawal to deal with a threat from Cush, and of the Assyrian King's determination to march on Jerusalem (2 Kgs 19:11–13). The challenge and affront to God himself is very clear. So what is Hezekiah to do?

For the first time since Solomon in 1 Kgs 8, a king of Judah is recorded as praying a rich and substantial prayer to Yahweh (2 Kgs 19:14–19). And this is a rich prayer. The prayer begins in verse 15 by asserting the sovereignty of Yahweh in the face of the Assyrian (and every other) threat: "O LORD, the God of Israel, enthroned above the cherubim, you are the God, you alone, of all the kingdoms of the earth; you have made heaven and earth." He then moves to ask God to recognize the mockery of the Assyrian by placing before him the boasts of the Rabshakeh and the king himself; namely, that the Assyrians have overcome the gods of every nation that ever stood in their way by exposing it as an empty claim because the defeated "gods" were only idols, the work of human hands (vv. 16–19). This time, they are in a different kind of fight! This basic conviction allows Hezekiah to bring the request of 19:19 to God with confidence: "So now, O LORD our God, save us, please, from his hand, that all the kingdoms of the earth may know that you, O LORD, are God alone." His prayer is not ultimately for himself, or for his nation, but for the honor of God. In that, it aligns perfectly with the prayer of Solomon in 1 Kgs 8:23, 53–54.

God's dramatic response to this prayer, and the ensuing decimation of the Assyrians narrated in the following verses is one of the most striking triumphs in the Old Testament, and might even hold out the prospect of a new golden age under the reforming (and godly) king Hezekiah. However, in 2 Kgs 20, events take a rapid and disappointing downturn.[24]

The fact that the events of chapter 20 occur *after* those of chapters 18 and 19 (see 2 Kgs 20:6) makes sense if, as I am arguing, Hezekiah, like Solomon, is being held up as a godly king who nonetheless falls short of what is required. This same point has been made convincingly by Sehoon Jang concerning the virtually identical material in Isa 36–39.[25] Whilst other factors may also be at play in Isaiah, it is clear that in Kings, the primary concern is to highlight the shortcomings of Hezekiah. [26]

In marked contrast to the prayer of 2 Kgs 19, Hezekiah's interchange with Yahweh in chapter 20 is myopic and self-concerned. God's announcement to him on

---

[24] Song-Mi Suzie Park has helpfully shown that there is a significant interplay between positive and negative portrayals of Hezekiah embedded in the biblical text (*Hezekiah and the Dialogue of Memory* [Minneapolis: Augsburg Fortress, 2015], 256–58). Her conclusion that this arises in large part from a rivalry between Hezekiah and Josiah "parties" is less convincing.

[25] Sehoon Jang, "Is Hezekiah a Success or Failure? The Literary Function of Isaiah's Prediction at the End of the Royal Narratives in the Book of Isaiah," *JSOT* 42 (2017): 117–35.

[26] Motyer argues that in Isaiah, the reversing of the order of events serves the transition from the Assyrian crisis to the looming threat of Babylon, which dominates Isa 40–66 (*The Prophecy of Isaiah* [Leicester: Inter-Varsity, 1999], 276–97).

his death bed that he would not recover from the unspecified illness is both confronting and shocking, given the hopes raised by the earlier narrative for the kingdom. But the focus falls not on the fate of Judah, but on Hezekiah's own state of mind. In a way reminiscent of Ahab in 1 Kgs 21:4, "Hezekiah turned his face to the wall," presumably in despair. However, to his credit, he does the right thing and prays (2 Kgs 20:3). The language and claims here are reminiscent of some of David's Psalms.[27] However, a significant question remains over whether or not Hezekiah is justified in making such exalted claims about himself.

This uncertainty is confirmed by two things—the weeping in verse 3, and request for a miracle which follows in verses 9–11. When Hezekiah breaks down in the face of his own mortality, *weeping bitterly*, whilst understandable, does raise a question about his ability to prioritize the wellbeing of his people over his own personal future. This preoccupation is borne out in the exchange in the wake of God's promise to heal him, given through Isaiah in 20:7.

In keeping with the suggestion above that Hezekiah was acting more out of panic than faith, in 20:8 he asks for a sign. Uniquely the prophet offers Hezekiah a choice of signs. In a way which is reminiscent of Gideon's faithlessness in Judg 6:33–40, Hezekiah asks that the shadows move in the opposite direction to that normally produced by the setting sun. As with Gideon, God responds to this dubious request—but for the sensitive reader, there is a growing sense of disquiet, which is only intensified by what happens next.

3.2. Humility or Hubris?

Shortly after gaining relief from the Assyrian threat, Hezekiah received an approach from Merodach-baladan the son of Baladan, king of Babylon (2 Kgs 20:12). This seems like an inspired moment of opportunism, which is aided and abetted by Hezekiah's lack of discernment, for he falls for the Babylonian subterfuge, and welcomes them wholeheartedly. More than that, the naïve, and presumably boastful king decides to show the visiting Babylonians his treasury (20:13). The narrator makes

---

[27] See, e.g., Ps 18:20–24.

sure we don't miss the significance of this foolishness at the end of verse 13—"There was nothing in his house or in all his realm that Hezekiah did not show them." Hezekiah even boasts to Isaiah about his boasting to the Babylonians (20:14–15).

The word that the prophet brings in verses 16–19, and the king's response, confirm the fact that we are right to see Hezekiah as a new Solomon who likewise shares some tragic—and devastating faults. In 2 Kgs 20:17, Isaiah announces bluntly that the exile is coming. It is a hammer-blow to God's people. Isaiah is quick to point out that this won't simply be a matter of property being taken, but the very people of God will be taken and forced to serve as eunuchs in Babylon. The response to this tragically sad word from God is as shocking as it is unexpected: "The word of the LORD that you have spoken is good." (20:19). How can this word from God possibly be construed as good news? The second half of verse 19 makes it explicit: "For he thought, 'Why not, if there will be peace and security in my days?'"

This is hard to fathom. Solomon's greatest descendant (so far) has just been told that not only will the glories of Solomon's day not be recovered, but the very kingdom itself will be lost. And his response? "It's OK – I'll survive!" It seems that this assessment of himself (2 Kgs 20:3) revealed more than he may have intended. Even the most godly king of Judah proves to be both foolish and utterly selfish. The reigns of Solomon and Hezekiah bracket the books of Kings with two "golden ages"— and yet it is very apparent that both of these kings, Israel's best, were dogged by key flaws that not only affected the future of their empires, but beyond that, highlighted the need for a better anointed king even than these.

4. King Josiah: The Confirmation of the Inadequacy of the Davidic King

During the dark interlude provided by the reigns of Manasseh and Amon, God confirms the word spoken to Isaiah that Judah's fate is sealed (see 2 Kgs 21:10–15). This bleak picture is then relieved by the accession of King Josiah as an eight-year-old at the beginning of 2 Kgs 22.

Josiah is introduced in glowing terms, reminiscent of his great-grandfather Hezekiah, and before that, King David himself: "he did what was right in the eyes of the LORD and walked in all the way of David his father, and he did not turn aside to the right or to the left" (2 Kgs 22:2). This final accolade is typical of Deuteronomy, and in particular, the ideal king described there (see Deut 5:32; 17:11, 20; 28:14 etc.). The portrayal of Josiah is so positive that one could be forgiven for thinking that there *might just* be some hope for Judah yet.

4.1. Too little, too late?

This burgeoning optimism is backed up by the account of what seems to be the most thoroughgoing reform ever carried out in Judah. It begins with a review of the affairs of the temple (see also Jehoash's initiative in 2 Kgs 12:9–16). This in itself was a positive development, but the most significant moment arose serendipitously, when Hilkiah the high priest stumbles on what he calls "the Book of the Law." (2 Kgs 22:8–10).[28]

Eventually, the book is read to Josiah, who shreds his clothes as an expression of grief, and then seeks help in understanding this book (2 Kgs 22:12–13). Josiah seems clear that the words of this book are an indictment of the long-term behavior patterns of Judah. Josiah is presented as a model of piety—albeit a model which comes too late to influence the course of events in Judah.[29]

In 2 Kgs 22:14–20, the otherwise unknown prophetess Huldah confirms that there is no way back for the people; namely, the same judgment that befell Ahab (1 Kgs 21:21) and Jeroboam (1 Kgs 14:10) will now be visited on Judah. However, Huldah adds another message for Josiah himself: because he repented—even in the face of judgment—God's mercy is extended to Josiah in the form of an early death (2 Kgs 22:19–20).[30]

---

[28] For the term "the Book of the Law" see Deut 28:61; 29:21; 30:10; 31:26; Josh 1:8; 8:30, 35; 23:6; 24:6.

[29] David Janzen makes the intriguing suggestion that both Josiah and Hezekiah fail initially (in Josiah's case simply by continuing on a Manasseh-like trajectory), but recover, to hold out hope to the exiles if the Davidide will only follow in the steps of Hezekiah and Josiah ("The Sins of Josiah and Hezekiah: A Synchronic Reading of the Final Chapters of Kings," *JSOT* 37 [2013]: 349–70). Ultimately, however, he fails to give an adequate account for the reversal of events in Hezekiah's life, and the early death of Josiah.

[30] In the light of the events which follow, it seems that Huldah predicts both Josiah's death (in battle) and his peaceful burial.

It is worth pausing to reflect on the implications of this for a moment. Judah (finally) has a godly king who appears to be a model of hearing and obeying God's word. But unfortunately, it is a case of "too little, too late." Nothing can be done at this stage to avert the coming wrath. Even the best of kings is apparently impotent in the face of the wrath to come.

This, of course, does not stop Josiah continuing to model what it means to respond wholeheartedly to the word of Yahweh. Like a new Moses (see 31:9–13), he gathers the nation in Jerusalem and "read in their hearing all the words of the Book of the Covenant that had been found in the house of the LORD" (2 Kgs 23:1–2). Standing as Jehoash had done in earlier reforming times (2 Kgs 11:12–14), Josiah uniquely made a covenant before the LORD. This is the closest thing we have seen to a "Deut 17" type of a king in the entire history of the people of God.[31] The fact that "all the people joined in the covenant" sets this moment apart in the history of Judah and Israel. This is national repentance of a kind that we have not seen up to this point. Nor have we seen anything like the reform which he then embarks on.

Now Josiah finally purges Judah from the influence of the gods introduced by Solomon in 1 Kgs 11 (see 2 Kgs 23:13–14; also detailed in verses 4–12 is the idolatrous legacy of Jeroboam, Ahaz and Manasseh). Such was the king's reforming zeal that he extended his campaign even to Samaria. No king (or prophet or priest) had ever mounted such a sustained and thoroughgoing campaign to bring the worship of God's people into line with his word, nor had any king since Solomon claimed authority over the whole of the land. Perhaps, after all this time, a king worthy of the name has come—and yet we already know that this king's life will be cut short!

Second Kings 23:21–23 records the pinnacle of Josiah's achievements as the Passover is re-established at the heart of the nation. Having read of it in "the Book of the Covenant" (see Deut 16:1–8), Josiah commands that it be celebrated. This really is a high point in the life of God's people. The last recorded national Passover is mentioned in Josh 5:10–12. But given what the reader already knows (that the die of

---

[31] Joseph points out that Josiah is the first king to read the Torah at all, let alone read it every day as prescribed in Deut 17 (*Portraits*, 156).

divine judgment has already been cast), this is a bitter-sweet moment. An ideal king has arrived, but it is too late for God's people!

Solomon's reign was marked by ambiguity because of the gap between his wisdom and his behavior. Hezekiah managed to institute reform and hold the Assyrians off, but then, he sowed the seeds for national destruction, being more concerned about his own longevity than anything else. The ambivalence around Josiah is simply that his rule cannot change anything. Despite his thoroughgoing reforms, which were admirably motivated—he did it all that "he might establish the words of the law that were written in the book that Hilkiah the priest found in the house of the LORD" (2 Kgs 23:24)—nothing actually changed for the better.

The tragedy is that the affirmation he receives outstrips even that of Hezekiah: "Before him there was no king like him, who turned to the LORD with all his heart and with all his soul and with all his might, according to all the Law of Moses, nor did any like him arise after him" (23:25). Josiah is the only king who manages to live out Deut 6:4–5, or to embody the qualities of Deut 17:14–20 consistently throughout his reign, but as 2 Kgs 23:26–27 makes clear, God has spoken and will not change his mind. Even Josiah cannot alter the fate of Judah.

4.2. The Triumph of Foolishness

The conclusion of the account of Judah adds weight to the contention that in the overall flow of Kings, the reign of this king is more than a short relief before the tragedy of the exile. Having held Josiah up as a paragon of virtue, the abrupt account of his tragic death has the effect of affirming that even the best, most godly king, cannot deliver the kind of kingdom which God has promised.

In 2 Kgs 23:28–30, Josiah is summarily dispatched by Pharaoh Neco, who was on his way to a climactic showdown with the Assyrians. Second Chronicles confirms that this really wasn't Josiah's fight (see 2 Chr 35:20–23). Kings and Chronicles speak with one voice—Josiah makes an inexplicably foolish choice, which costs him his life.[32]

---

[32] See the detailed discussion of how Josiah's death is handled in biblical and extrabiblical

In the kindness of God, Josiah's violent death and peaceful funeral (reflected in the quiet dignity of 2 Kgs 23:30), means he does not have to witness the awful scenes which would ensue as the Babylonians march on Jerusalem. But that is not the only concern of the text. It makes painfully clear that even this most godly king cannot rule forever. Like Solomon and Hezekiah before him, his wisdom is flawed. We need a better king than this.

5. Conclusion

At a macro level, the text of Kings is bookended by the extended discussion of the rule of Solomon the Wise in 1 Kgs 1–11 at the beginning, and the rule of Hezekiah and his great grandson Josiah in 2 Kgs 18–23 at the end. There are significant similarities between these great kings. On the positive side, each of them is described in ways which set them apart as uniquely godly. Solomon *loved* Yahweh like none before or since. Hezekiah *trusted* Yahweh like no other, and Josiah *turned* to Yahweh as the embodiment of Deuteronomic piety. And yet each of these three great kings ultimately failed. Solomon's wisdom did not save him from decadence. Hezekiah's faith did not protect him from self-pity and self-preoccupation. Josiah's piety did not prevent him from getting involved in a conflict he could not possibly win.

The significance of these three kings for reading the books as a whole has often been overlooked, as the focus tends to have fallen on redactional and historical-critical issues that seek underlying political or propaganda explanations for the tone of the narrative with a focus on the latter reforming kings in particular. Such studies are, of course, not without value. However, it is important to realize that the primary function of these narratives seems to lie elsewhere.

By framing the history of Israel and Judah with these towering figures who all ultimately fall short of fulfilling their potential, and more importantly, seeing the fulfilment of the kingdom promises of God, the focus of the reader is inexorably thrown forward to look for a king who does display Solomon's wisdom, Hezekiah's

---

texts: Steve Delamarter, "The Death of Josiah in Scripture and Tradition: Wrestling with the Problem of Evil?," *VT* 54 (2004): 29–60.

faith and Josiah's relentless, word-driven piety, to the extent that when Jesus Christ announces that "one greater than Solomon is here" (Matt 12:42), it comes as no surprise. The quest for the one who will crush the serpent's head, which begins in Gen 3:15, is significantly advanced by the extended treatment of the best of Israel and Judah's rulers.

Jesus Christ, the King, steps into the biblical narrative as one who does not succumb to the pressures or temptations of money, sex or power. When under pressure, his focus does not shift inward, but to those whom the Father has given him (see, e.g., John 17). And despite appearances to the contrary, his death is not a tragic accident, nor the result of a headstrong dash into an unwinnable fight—rather, he voluntary lays down his life for his friends, in order that we might have life.

On reading of Solomon, Hezekiah and Josiah, the three best kings God's people ever had, and seeing their flaws so clearly exposed, the messianic fabric of the books of Kings becomes plain. The mysterious figure introduced in the Protoevangelium is starting to emerge from the shadows, and it becomes clear that he comes wearing a crown. These kings ensure that the sensitive reader of these books is already searching for, longing for, the one in whom every promise of God is yes and Amen.

THE END OF HISTORY AND THE LAST MAN

—Stephen G. Dempster

1. Introduction

The title of this essay in honor of the scholarship of Desmond Alexander is also the title of an influential and highly controversial book published in 1992 by the political theorist Francis Fukuyama.[1] He argued that with the end of the cold war and the ostensible triumph of capitalism and liberal democracy, world history had reached its final political goal. There were not to be many surprises about the ideal form of government for the world. The last man of liberal democratic capitalism had arrived and history had nothing more to offer.[2] There have been many critics, of course, of Fukuyama's thesis, and after 9-11 and the rise of Islamic fundamentalism, the intransigence of Chinese authoritarian capitalism, and other ideologies centered around identity politics and nationalist/ethnic tribalism, all bets are off regarding the end of history and its last man, as even the author now admits.[3]

I use this example from the world of twentieth century politics and history as a means of providing insight into the structure of the Hebrew Bible, while trying to shed light on what has been a hermeneutical crux, the last four verses of Kings (2 Kgs 25:27–30), regarding the release of the exiled king Jehoiachin from prison in Babylon. I would also like to honor Desmond Alexander's groundbreaking work in the area of hermeneutical thinking about the Old Testament messianic promise and contribute this study as both a complement and a compliment to his essay on a major theme in the

---

[1] Francis Fukuyama, *The End of History and the Last Man* (New York: Penguin, 1992).

[2] As Fukuyama wrote in his initial presentation of his ideas, the end of history was "the end point of mankind's ideological evolution and the universalization of western liberal democracy as the final form of human government." *The National Interest* 16 (1989):1.

[3] Stephen Holmes, "The Identity Illusion," *New York Review of Books*, 2019.

narrative from Genesis to Kings. Alexander remarks in that study that Jehoiachin's release "possibly anticipates better times to come."[4]

2. A Hermeneutical Crux

It is not often understood that this crux occurs at the virtual middle of the Hebrew Bible, at the end of what has been termed the Primary History.[5] Thus at the end of this first history of Israel,[6] spanning Genesis to Kings, there is also a last man standing—Jehoiachin, a descendant of David. Like Fukuyama's man standing at the end of history, he does not represent himself but a form of government, the Davidic monarchy, which had been eternally guaranteed by divine covenant (2 Sam 7:12–16; Pss 89:2–4; 132:11–13, 17–18). But unlike Fukuyama's last man, this one does not represent the triumphalist winner in a political competition who has defeated all of his opponents, but rather a loser—a virtual dead man but one who has been raised from the graveyard of exile:

> In the thirty-seventh year of the exile of Jehoiachin king of Judah, in the year Awel-Marduk became king of Babylon, he released Jehoiachin king of Judah from prison. He did this on the twenty-seventh day of the twelfth month. He spoke kindly to him and gave him a seat of honor higher than those of the other kings who were with him in Babylon. So Jehoiachin put aside his prison clothes and for the rest of his life ate regularly at the king's table. Day by day the king gave Jehoiachin a regular allowance as long as he lived.[7]

In a very real sense 2 Kgs 25:27–30 presents the end of the Primary History and the last man standing from the nation of Judah, a king in exile, one who has been as good as dead, but who has now been released from prison.

---

[4] Desmond Alexander, "Royal Expectations in Genesis to Kings: Their Importance for Biblical Theology," *TynBul* 49 (1998): 208.

[5] David N. Freedman, "The Law and the Prophets," in *Congress Volume: Bonn*, 1962, VTSup 9 (Leiden: Brill, 1963), 251–59.

[6] The second history covers the same ground but is more extensive, going beyond the exile. This history is the book of Chronicles.

[7] 2 Kgs 25:27–30 (NIV).

3. Hermeneutical Solutions

3.1. Martin Noth—Pessimism

As mentioned above, it is well known that these last four verses of the History are a real exegetical and hermeneutical crux in modern scholarship, ever since Martin Noth's groundbreaking work on the Deuteronomistic History. Noth viewed these verses as nothing more than the last historical note that the Deuteronomist had available to him for his Deuteronomistic History, a work spanning the books of the so-called Latter Prophets: Joshua, Judges, Samuel and Kings. Thus, the author of this history was able to edit older sources and punctuate them with transitional speeches, as well as provide a frame for the work of Deuteronomy which functioned to introduce the history. [8] Noth concluded that his Deuteronomistic History was largely a pessimistic work whose main note was that of judgment. The last chapter of the destruction of Judah and the exile of its population in Babylon ended "the hopes and fears of all the years"[9] and the *coup de grace* was the historical source provided in the last four verses of Kings. There is no hope for the future—only fear—even if the exiled king has been released from prison. To imagine anything more significant is but wishful thinking:

> [T]here is no thought of a new dawn of a new future with the release of Jehoiachin in 2 Kings 25:27–30. For irrespective of the fact that the reported occurrence was suited in no way to serve the advancement of one such far reaching meaning, according to the sources DTR had no conception of this view. On the contrary he has with all due conscientiousness and respect simply communicated the actual happening of this last fact known to him of the Judean history of the kings.[10]

---

[8] Martin Noth, *Überlieferung-Geschichtliche Studien: Die Sammelnden und Bearbeitenden Geschichtswerke im Alten Testament*, 2nd ed. (Tübingen: Max Niemeyer, 1957).

[9] This allusion to a possible messianic motif found in the Christmas carol, "O Little Town of Bethlehem," is used by Donald Murray in his paper arguing for a non-messianic interpretation of these last four verses of Kings. See Donald F. Murray, "Of All the Years the Hopes—or Fears? Jehoiachin in Babylon (2 Kings 25:27–30)," *JBL* 120 (2001): 245–65.

[10] Martin Noth, *Überlieferunggeschichtliche Studien*, 108 (my translation).

This suits Noth's view that the history of Israel is a history of judgment and fear because of the nation's disobedience to the law of Moses.[11]

3.2. Gerhard von Rad—Optimism

While there have been many who have agreed with Noth over the years since his proposal,[12] Gerhard von Rad stated his disagreement sharply, arguing that the covenant with David in 2 Sam 7 and the constant reference to the preservation of a Davidic descendant on the throne—the "lamp of David" in Kings provided a strong constraint for reading the ending of Kings differently (1 Kgs 11:36, 15:4, 2 Kgs 8:19). Like Noth, von Rad saw the ominous motif of judgment running through the historical work as he wrote about the historian, "none was less in a position than he to minimize the terrible severity of the judgment"[13] caused by the violation of the laws of Deuteronomy. But unlike Noth, von Rad argued that the historian

> could not, indeed must not, believe that the promise of Yahweh might fail, and that the lamp of David would finally be extinguished, for no word of Yahweh pronounced over history could ever fall to the ground. For this reason there can be no doubt to our mind that the mention of Jehoiachin's release from prison at the very end of the Deuteronomist's work (II Kings 25:27-30) must be of particular theological significance.... Obviously nothing is said here in strictly theological terms, but a carefully measured indication is given: an occurrence is given which has an immense significance for the Deuteronomist, since it provides a basis upon which Yahweh can build further if he so willed. At all events the reader must understand this passage to be an indication of the fact that the line of David has not come to an irrevocable end.[14]

---

[11] Noth, *Überlieferunggeschichtliche Studien*, 108–9.

[12] For many examples see Murray, "Of All the Years the Hopes—or Fears?," 246–47 n.6.

[13] Gerhard von Rad, "The Deuteronomic Theology of History in 1 and 2 Kings," in *The Problem of the Hexateuch and Other Essays* (Edinburgh; London: Oliver and Boyd, 1966), 219.

[14] Von Rad, "Deuteronomic Theology of History," 220, cited in Murray, "Of all the Years the Hopes—or Fears?," 245 n.3.

3.3. Frank Cross—Redactional History

Since these interpretive lines have been drawn, interpreters have lined up on both sides of this debate.[15] Frank Cross, with his double redaction theory, posited a redactional history which sought to have it both ways.[16] Cross essentially agreed with both Noth and von Rad by arguing that the redactional history explains both the negative and the positive strains in the Deuteronomistic History: the Deuteronomic code with its stress on curse for disobedience as well as the irrevocable covenant with David. By positing a double edition of the history, Cross could argue that there was an optimistic first edition caused by the Davidic covenant which culminated in the arrival of King Josiah, whose coming had been prophesied 300 years in advance. But his unexpected death and the ensuing exile necessitated a second pessimistic edition which had to deal with the bad news. Consequently, Cross states about the last verses of Kings:

> We must admit that Noth has the better of the argument when it comes to the interpretation of 2 Kings 25:27-30. That Jehoiachin was released from prison and lived off the bounty of the Babylonian crown—still in exile for the remainder of his days—is a thin thread upon which to hand the expectation of the fulfillment of the promises to David.[17]

Thus, the redactional history of the text is used to explain the optimism and pessimism but pessimism ultimately triumphs as the last few verses would be a very thin thread indeed on which to hang any future hope.

3.4. Hans Walter Wolff—Moderate Hope

Many have taken a fourth position, a more mediating position, such as Hans Walter Wolff, who claimed that repentance was a key motif throughout the history

---

[15] For those following von Rad, see Murray, "Of all the Years the Hopes—or Fears?," 246 n.5.

[16] Frank Moore Cross, "The Themes of the Book of Kings and the Structure of the Deuteronomistic History," in *Canaanite Myth and Hebrew Epic: Essays in the History of the Religion of Israel* (Cambridge, MA: Harvard University Press, 1997), 274–90.

[17] Cross, "Themes of the Book of Kings," 277.

which would offer hope for exiles, particularly since it was mentioned as the basis for hope for exiles in Solomon's prayer at the dedication of the temple (1 Kgs 8:46–51). The idea that the historian would go to great trouble to produce a history without any hope would be unthinkable: "one can only ask why an Israelite of the sixth century B.C. would even reach for his pen if he only wanted to explain the final end of Israel's history as the righteous judgment of God."[18] But for Wolff it was clear that that hope would be found in repentance not "in the lone brittle piece about Jehoiachin's elevation."[19] In fact "when Jehoiachin is allowed to take off his prison garments, this means little more than that God is still acting for his people."[20] The final verses do not hold out hope for a Davidic descendant. John Gray similarly argues for a hopeful conclusion but again a modest one with absolutely no messianic overtones:

> We cannot agree with von Rad that the mention of this incident is an indication of a modified Messianic hope, an idea of royalty which was expressed in the liturgy, e.g. Psalms, Isa 9:2-7, 11:1-9…. Significant as the survival and release of Jehoiachin was in the prospects of Israel, the specific mention of it may have been motivated by the primitive superstition that to close the book on a despondent note was to bring the future under the same evil influence, whereas to close it on an auspicious note was to open up a brighter prospect…. The note on the relief of Jehoiachin implies rather the prospect of grace for Israel after her delinquency and punishment in accordance with the general pattern of the Deuteronomic History, most clearly apparent in the Book of Judges.[21]

Thus this "may encourage readers to see exile as a state of unexpected opportunities."[22]

---

[18] H. W. Wolff, "The Kerygma of the Deuteronomic Historical Work," in *The Vitality of Old Testament Traditions*, ed. W. Brueggemann and H. W. Wolff (Atlanta: John Knox, 1982), 85.

[19] Wolff, "Kerygma of the Deuteronomic Historical Work," 86.

[20] Wolff, "Kerygma of the Deuteronomic Historical Work," 99.

[21] John Gray, *I & II Kings*, OTL (Philadelphia: Westminster Press, 1976), 773.

[22] Dominik Markl, "No Future without Moses: The Disastrous End of 2 Kings 22–25 and the Chance of the Moab Covenant (Deuteronomy 29–30)," *JBL* 133 (2014): 712.

This mediating position has become the dominant one in recent scholarship. Donald Murray is one of the leading exponents for this interpretation of the final four verses of Kings, which tempers both Noth's pessimism and von Rad's optimism, theological minimalism versus maximalism.[23] In an exhaustive study of the various views with a detailed exegesis of the passage he concludes:

> Latent within the dispirited limitation of events of this final episode is some positive movement that is incompatible with a totally pessimistic reading of the text. If there is as an attenuated conclusion to 1 Kings 8:50b, it serves as a token presaging not a hopeful future for an heir to the Davidic promise, but a more tolerable future for all vanquished Judeans. In contrast to the relentless devastation depicted in the preceding episodes of 2 Kings 25, that is a hope not to be despised. But, since at the end of 2 Kings 25:27–30, all power continues in the hands of their conqueror, and any promise latent in the amelioration of Jehoiachin's release is not attributed to the agency of Yahweh, it is also a hope that is not to be exaggerated.[24]

In support of such a modest hope—not to be despised but neither to be exaggerated, Christopher Begg in an earlier work, provides the most cogent arguments. He argues that one has to be careful not to be guilty of eisegesis by reading into the text more than is actually there.[25] Since Jehoiachin was released by a pagan king and not by Yahweh, there cannot be any *heilsgeschictliche* significance. Secondly, there is no explicit fulfillment formula attached to this note about the release of the king, suggesting it lacked any prime theological importance for the Deuteronomist. For example, there is no mention of what is a leitmotif in the book of Kings that the line of David provides Yahweh's lamp for the dark times in Judah, that on account of

---

[23] For the language of minimalism and maximalism see Christopher T. Begg, "The Significance of Jehoiachin's Release: A New Proposal," *JSOT* 36 (1986): 49.

[24] Murray, "Of All the Years the Hopes—or Fears?," 265.

[25] Begg, "Significance of Jehoiachin's Release."

Yahweh's covenant with David, both temple and monarchy are preserved. Thirdly, there is no mention of any repentance or contrition of Jehoiachin, which would lead to divine mercy—a key theological motif of the Deuteronomistic History. Fourthly, there is no commensurate mercy shown to Jehoiachin's descendants nor release for the exiles of Judah. Finally, a supposed covenantal formula by the Deuteronomist, i.e., "he spoke kindly to him" (2 Kgs 25:28), used to describe Jehoiachin's new status may mean nothing more than good will be shown by the Babylonian monarch. Begg further argues that a close study of the immediate narrative context, which is ignored by both von Rad and Noth, shows a pro-Babylonian stance, with an emphasis on serving Babylon. "There are no other options since Babylon is unassailable."[26] This points to a modest hope for the exiles if they keep submitting to Babylon.

Of course, none of these objections are insurmountable even within the context of the Deuteronomistic History. It is clear for the narrator that pagan kings as well as Israelite kings are under the sway of the God of Israel. After all, the Aramean, Hazael, is anointed by an Israelite prophet (2 Kgs 8:7–13), and the twin judgments of the Assyrians and Babylonians of Israel and Judah respectively show that their kings serve the judgmental purposes of Yahweh (2 Kgs 17, 24–25). Yahweh is not just a god of the mountains or the plains but all nations, as stories about battles (1 Kgs 20), lepers (2 Kgs 5), and prophets of Baal attest (1 Kgs 18). Why could not a Babylonian king like Amel-Marduk serve the saving purposes of Yahweh? The fact that there is no explicit fulfillment formula recorded regarding Jehoiachin's release is not difficult to understand since there are other examples of fulfilled prophecy in the absence of a formula. For example, the historian does not explicitly mention that Joash's rescue from Athaliah's massacre of the royal house keeps the Davidic promise intact, but who could argue that such an explicit theological conclusion was necessary? (2 Kgs 11:13). One just simply has to connect the historical dots.[27] Moreover, the lack of mention of

---

[26] Begg, "Significance of Jehoiachin's Release," 56.

[27] See, e.g., von Rad on this very point: "Actually in this particular respect, the Deuteronomist demands the close attention of his readers and considerable vigilance on their part, if they are to realize that everywhere there is a self-fulfilling relationship between the divinely inspired prophecy and the historical occurrence, even at those points where it is not expressly mentioned.... By and large one can

repentance on Jehoiachin's part may simply be an argument from silence. While repentance and return from exile is an important theme in the Deuteronomistic History (Deut 4:25–38, 30:1–10; 1 Kgs 8:43–51), there is no mention of the end of exile here, because it simply has not happened yet.[28] Similarly the lack of mention of Jehoiachin's descendants is also a tenuous argument from silence. It is known from other texts both biblical (1 Chr 3:17–20) and extrabiblical,[29] that such existed, and it can be implied by the evidence in Kings.[30] Also, the fact that a covenantal formula can be interpreted as an expression of good will is true, but this language specifically contrasts Jehoiachin's fate with that of his uncle Zedekiah (2 Kgs 25:6; cf. 2 Sam 7:28). Moreover, the language echoes David's prayer of response to the Davidic covenant which praises God's faithfulness to his divine promise (2 Sam 7:28–29). Finally, while the immediate context suggests the importance of serving Babylon, the idea that Babylon is "unassailable" is clearly at variance with the theological message of the book of Kings.

By widening the horizon of the text to include other texts in the history from Genesis–Kings, some recent studies have strengthened the moderating position. Although they do not argue on the basis of the Davidic covenant, that there is hope, they suggest that previous texts foreshadow a good future for the exiles if not for Jehoiachin himself. Thus when similar language of Jehoiachin's release is used for the exaltation of Joseph in Egypt from prison to the throne (Gen 41), and the ensuing exodus from Egypt, it is difficult not to see these themes as portending a future for Jehoiachin and his people in Babylon.[31] Similarly, David's elevation of Mephibosheth

---

work on the assumption that the Deuteronomist makes explicit mention of the fulfillment of a prophecy more particularly in those cases where the fact is not so immediately perceptible to the reader, whilst in those instances where the events speak for themselves he was able to dispense with this." Von Rad, "The Deuteronomic Theology of History in 1 and 2 Kings," 211–12.

[28] David N. Freedman, "The Earliest Bible," in *Backgrounds for the Bible*, ed. Michael Patrick O'Connor and David N. Freedman (Winona Lake, IN: Eisenbrauns, 1987), 29–37.

[29] Weidner Chronicles. See David Winton Thomas, ed., *Documents from Old Testament Times* (New York: Harper & Row, 1961), 84.

[30] E.g., 2 Kgs 24:14 mentions Jehoiachin's wives. While he is only 18 years old, the importance of heirs would be doubly important for any member of the royal family.

[31] Paul S. Evans, "The End of Kings as Presaging an Exodus: The Function of the Jehoiachin

to eat at the king's table is a striking reversal of status and a striking resemblance to Jehoiachin's new status (2 Sam 9). As the sole remaining heir of the now defunct Saulide dynasty, Mephibosheth would have viewed himself under the new Davidic regime as a *persona non grata* (2 Sam 9:8). But because of David's חֶסֶד, he has been rehabilitated. However, such a rehabilitation of Saul's descendant should in no way imply hope for the Davidic line since it did not imply such for Saul.[32] All it offers is hope for a modest life in exile. Such texts are regarded as providing a more hopeful future for the exiles and not for the messianic status of a Davidic descendant.

3.5. David Janzen—Maddening Ambiguity

Finally, to bring this discussion of interpretation regarding the end of the Primary History to a conclusion, there is a fifth view, one which assumes the unity of the text but argues that the last few verses are intentionally ambiguous, even "maddeningly" so. David Janzen's study ends up claiming that the historian's conclusion was a case of simply hedging his bets.[33] Within the history, there is the pervasive evidence of northern dynasties perishing because of sin, and even an eternal covenant being broken. Yet at the same time there was the promise to David of an everlasting covenant. Was it possible that such an inviolable covenant could even be annulled because of sin? Maybe. Maybe not. In favor of the former possibility was the story of Mephibosheth's rehabilitation, when David brought him to his table and gave him a high status in his kingdom. But this in in no way meant a rehabilitation of the Saulide dynasty. In favor of the latter possibility was the example of the preservation of the royal seed of Joash during Athaliah's bloody purge of his male siblings. According to Janzen, the last four verses of Kings represent an historian's best guess

---

Epilogue (2 Kgs 25:27–30) in Light of Parallels with the Joseph Story in Genesis," *McMaster Journal of Theology and Mission* 16 (2014): 65–100. For similar points, cf. Michael J. Chan, "Joseph and Jehoiachin; On the Edge of the Exodus," *ZAW* 125 (2013): 566–67; Ian Douglas Wilson, "Joseph, Jehoiachin and Cyrus: On Book Endings, Exoduses and Exiles, and Yehudite/Judean Social Remembering," *ZAW* 146 (2014): 521–34.

[32] Jeremy Schipper, "'Significant Resonances' with Mephibosheth in 2 Kings 25:27–30: A Response to Donald F. Murray," *JBL* 124 (2005): 521–29; David Janzen, "An Ambiguous Ending: Dynastic Punishment in Kings and the Fate of the Davidides in 2 Kings 25.27–30," *JSOT* 33 (2008): 55.

[33] David Janzen, "Ambiguous Ending," 58.

about the future: there is no certainty, only ambiguity.[34]

Thus, to summarize, the interpretive options for the last man appearing at the end of Israel's history are as follows: 1) downright pessimism as the verses are the final nail in the coffin of a history of judgment; 2) optimism as the verses echo God's irrevocable covenant with David; 3) a redactional pessimism after initial optimism; 4) a modest optimism, not to be despised but neither to be exaggerated; 5) an intentionally ambiguous ending, which leaves the outcome to history.

What is significant about virtually all of these interpretations is that they very rarely look beyond the Deuteronomistic History—the Former Prophets—for elucidation of these verses. In other words, they are in some sense noncanonical readings. Noth admits as much when he sees his reading of Dtr as at variance with the messages of the Latter Prophets, who predicted the catastrophe of the exile but looked beyond it to a new future of hope. Similarly, John Gray in the quotation cited above specifically contrasts the message of Dtr with the passages about an eschatological David in Isaiah and the Psalms. This is precisely the point that Iain Provan makes in a perceptive article in which he argues that not only does the ending of Kings "hang on tenaciously in difficult circumstances to the words of 2 Sam 7:15-16" emphasizing the irrevocable nature of the Davidic covenant, but that read in concert with the Latter Prophets, the Davidic king becomes almost "Messianic."[35] Recently Konrad Schmid argues that a fuller canonical understanding changes everything when he observes that "Genesis to Kings in the arrangement of MT segues into the account of the *corpus propheticum* where we encounter decisive statements about Israel's future."[36] In fact

---

[34] Richard Nelson is more optimistic than Janzen but writes that although the immediate context of Kings is pessimistic, within the entire context of the book of Kings Jehoiachin's release is "richly ambiguous." Although the covenant is broken God is always a "wild card" whose grace may bestow hope: *First and Second Kings* (Louisville: Westminster John Knox, 2012), 267–68.

[35] Iain W. Provan, "The Messiah in the Book of Kings," in *The Lord's Anointed: Interpretation of Old Testament Messianic Texts*, eds. P. E. Satterthwaite, Richard Hess and Gordon J. Wenham (Carlisle: Paternoster, 1995), 76 (and see esp. 80–83).

[36] Konrad Schmid, *Genesis and the Moses Story: Israel's Dual Origins in the Hebrew Bible*, Siphrut: Literature and Theology of the Hebrew Scriptures 3 (Winona Lake, IN: Eisenbrauns, 2010), 44, cited in Markl, "No Future without Moses," 727.

this is one of the points that I have made in a recent study on the Former and Latter Prophets in the Tanak.[37] The pairing of the two in MT resolves any ambiguity in the Former Prophets for the future of Israel. For example, at the beginning of the Former Prophets all the promises to the patriarchs are not in doubt but by the end of Kings, they have all been called radically into question. But the subsequent Latter Prophets confirms that these promises are still in effect, and shows that beyond the judgment is God's salvation. Thus, Jeremiah announces a new covenant, Ezekiel a new temple, Isaiah a new heavens and earth, and the Twelve a new David. Thus, Jehoiachin's release is indeed seen as radically good news when viewed through the lens of the Latter Prophets.

4. Two Recent Canonical Studies on the Last Man

Two monographs on Jehoiachin have recently made a similar point and have therefore firmly planted themselves on the side of von Rad. James Critchlow examines all the evidence surrounding Jehoiachin in the biblical canon, as well as in the intertestamental literature and argues that when viewed in this expanded context, the last four verses of Kings give reasons for hope in a coming Messiah. If "The exile of king, queen mother, wives, children and officials looked like the dead end of the Davidic kingdom,"[38] and the "death of the remaining Davidide [Jehoiachin] should have stamped closed on the line of kings, the optimistic account [Jer 52:31-34=2 Kgs 25:27-30] portends that Yahweh was indeed doing something different."[39] Thus, examined within its immediate and local context, the last four verses of Kings suggest a radical departure from the calamity of exile and thus an offer of hope. But any latent ambiguity is resolved once the broader scope of the canon is shown: e.g., when Jeremiah's curse on Jehoiachin is reversed not only by Jeremiah himself but later by

---

[37] Stephen G. Dempster, "The Tripartite Canon and the Theology of the Prophetic Word," in *Interpreting the Old Testament Theologically: Essays in Honor of Willem A. VanGemeren*, ed. Andrew T. Abernethy (Grand Rapids: Zondervan, 2018), 74–94.

[38] James R. Critchlow, *Looking Back for Jehoiachin: Yahweh's Cast-Out Signet*, Africanus Monographs (Eugene: Wipf & Stock, 2013), 52.

[39] Critchlow, *Looking Back for Jehoiachin*, 25.

Haggai (Jer 22:14–20; Hag 2:22–23).

Secondly, a more expansive work by Matthew Patton considers Jehoiachin explicitly within the framework of a biblical theology. Thus, there is much more theological reflection in this monograph. Patton particularly argues that it is only when the global canonical view is taken into consideration that it can be understood why a person who reigned a mere three months became the subject of so much prophetic discussion. Accordingly, Patton begins his study,

> Jehoiachin reigned a mere three months before Nebuchadnezzar took him into exile. He was one more Judean king who did evil in the eyes of Yahweh and his one recorded action as king was to surrender to the Babylonians. How significant can a king be whose reign ended when it had scarcely begun?[40]

However, by looking at Jehoiachin from the perspective of the grand narrative of Scripture, he comes to a similar view as Critchlow but one more grounded in biblical theology. He thus asks: "If the various books of the Bible bear witness to one grand storyline, what is the significance of Jehoiachin within that story?"[41] Patton concludes that when this story is viewed in terms of its global context and the prophecies of restoration in Deuteronomy one can only reach the conclusion:

> Reading 2 Kings 25:27-30 in light of the prophecies of restoration provokes the unsettling feeling that the book is ending when the story is not yet over: the PH [Primary History] itself is not self-contained. In lieu of a satisfying ending Jehoiachin's emergence from prison functions syndochically for the ending that is not (yet) there. Rather than decisively concluding the story, the emergence of this key figure from prison is a muted but insistent reminder that the story that began long ago in Genesis

---

[40] Matthew H. Patton, *Hope for a Tender Sprig: Jehoiachin in Biblical Theology* (Winona Lake: Eisenbrauns, 2017), 1.

[41] Patton, *Hope for a Tender Sprig*, 2.

is not yet over. It opens a fresh chapter, inviting the reader to read the rest of the canon to see how this story will end.[42]

In my own work I have noted along with other scholars the importance of the Primary History, but also the structure of the Tanak for understanding the Old Testament/Hebrew Bible. In my judgment it is when the total canonical scope is taken into view, that von Rad's keen theological judgment about the Deuteronomistic History is validated.[43] Yes, there is judgment and curse to be sure, but the fact that the last man standing at the end is a Davidide surely has ramifications for the exiles. This is not a pathetic pessimism, nor a slim but cautious optimism, nor a hedging of future bets, but rather a lightning rod of hope.

I would like to consider this within the MT structure to show its cogency, looking at the macro-structure from one of the oldest orders in the Tanak to see its importance.[44] In this order the first half of the Hebrew Bible consists of the Torah plus the Former Prophets. This constitutes virtually one-half of the Hebrew Bible. The second half consists of the Latter Prophets and the Writings.[45] In virtually all orders of the Tanak the first half exhibits little variety, the Latter Prophets some diversity, and the Writings much more variation.[46] The main point of this essay does not depend on a particular sequence of the Writings, but one of the earliest sequences nonetheless reinforces it.

5. Torah

Kingship is important from the very beginning of Genesis which clearly uses royal imagery to describe what it means to be human in the creation of humanity.

---

[42] Patton, *Hope for a Tender Sprig*, 74.

[43] Stephen G. Dempster, *Dominion and Dynasty: A Biblical Theology of the Hebrew Bible* (Downers Grove, IL: InterVarsity Press, 2003), 155–56.

[44] Dempster, *Dominion and Dynasty*, 33–35. See in particular *Baba Bathra* 14b.

[45] For further elaboration on the two halves of the Hebrew Bible see David Noel Freedman, *The Unity of the Hebrew Bible* (Ann Arbor: University of Michigan Press, 1993).

[46] For orders for the Prophets and the Writings see Roger T. Beckwith, *The Old Testament Canon of the New Testament Church: And Its Background in Early Judaism* (Grand Rapids: Eerdmans, 1984), 449–67.

Terms which were used in ancient Near Eastern cultures for a special class of human beings are here used for all human beings. Thus "when kingship descends from heaven,"[47] all humans are invested with it. The terms "image" and "likeness" used to describe human beings are not uniquely biblical terms as the Tell Fakireyeh inscription clearly shows (Gen 1:26–28). The "synonymous" terms have different pragmatic purposes, functioning to identify a statue of a ruler in a province in Northern Syria in the ninth century BC, Hadad-Yithi.[48] The word "likeness" emphasizes a private connection to the deity, and has a votive function. The word "image" shifts the focus to a more public dimension with humanity's presentation to the world as God's image with a ruling role. Human beings consequently have a unique relation to God (likeness) and a unique relation to the rest of creation (image).[49] Both of these royal aspects are also present in Gen 2 which uses different terminology to express the image and likeness. Clearly in the creation of humanity likeness to the creator is stressed, as God fashions first the male and breathes into him his divine breath (Gen 2:7). The fact that the female is made from the same substance as the male and is crafted by the creator exemplifies the same important relation (Gen 2:21–22). Secondly, the pair have a task to face outward toward the creation, i.e. to keep and serve it, and to face inward toward each other (Gen 2:15, 23–25).

Of course, the ensuing history shows their fall from this position. Not satisfied with their divine image, they try to become like God in a new way, by disobeying his word, and trusting in the word of a serpent (Gen 3:1–7). They do become like God, to be sure, but this is a recipe for disaster as their moral autonomy must be curtailed with

---

[47] *Sumerian King List* line 1. See *The Electronic Corpus of Sumerian Literature*, http://etcsl.orinst.ox.ac.uk/ section2/tr211.htm.

[48] Randall E. Garr, "Image and Likeness in the Tell Fakhariyeh Inscription," *IEJ* 50 (2000): 227–34. See also the recent essay by Peter Gentry who further develops the work of Garr: "The Imago Dei and its Relation to Humanity as God's Vice-Regents on Earth," Unpublished Paper: Evangelical Theological Society, Denver: November, 2018. Gentry's influence has been formative for my understanding of the image. See also J. Richard Middleton, *The Liberating Image: The Imago Dei in Genesis 1* (Grand Rapids: Brazos Press, 2005).

[49] For more on the royal imagery of these twin features and the idea of the image of God, see John Van Seters, "The Creation of Man and the Creation of the King," *ZAW* 101 (1989): 341.

death as not only a judgment but also a form of grace (Gen 3:22). Rather than as loving servant kings who have been given as their stewardship the creation, humanity tyrannizes the earth and it becomes filled with violence. This is the serpent's way and not God's (Gen 4:17–24; 6:1–7, 11–13).[50] Everyone is living as if there is no divine king, and everyone is doing what is right in their own eyes.[51] Consequently instead of a world filled with goodness, it is a world filled with violence. The biblical genealogy of Cain accentuates this. Cain is a killer and his distant descendant, Lamech, is a child-killer whose titanic vengeance knows no human bounds (Gen 4:23–24). It may be his ilk who view themselves as divine beings who takes wives to themselves and populate the word with tyrants like their ancestor,[52] some of whom lead to Nimrod (Gen 10:8–9), and his plan to build a huge tower to assault heaven itself (Gen 11:1–9).

But if this distorted kingship is the problem, there is a solution and it is found in a new ruler, one who will defeat the serpent. Found in the curse on the serpent, Gen 3:15, the so-called *Protoevangelium*, charts out a future which leads to the expectation of a human descendant who will restore human beings to their glorious position.[53] Consequently this explains why there are numerous genealogies to follow in the book of Genesis—not just ones which accentuate the growth of evil, but ones which trace a line of descendants, which will not only bless the world, but which culminate in a

---

[50] Cf. Gen 18:19 for Yahweh's way.

[51] Cf. the moral chaos at the end of the book of Judges in 17:6 and 21:25.

[52] There is much debate over the "erratic boulder" in the literary landscape of Gen 5–6 (6:1–4). Without going into the debate, a dominant early interpretation was the fact that the Nephilim were the product of angelic beings (sons of God) uniting with human beings (daughters of men). This has been modified by some scholars recently who argue that ancient Near Eastern evidence which presents kings arrogating to themselves divinity (e.g., Gilgamesh, Naram-Sin), and therefore exploiting women, produced people who lived in this same manner of exploitation and oppression, thus contributing to a horrific pre-flood situation. See Meredith Kline, "Divine Kingship and Genesis 6:1-4," *WTJ* 24 (1962): 187–204. Waltke modifies this understanding by seeing these individuals as demon-possessed kings: Bruce K. Waltke, *Genesis: A Commentary* (Grand Rapids: Zondervan, 2016), 117–18. For a different and comprehensive recent perspective see Rita F. Cefalu, "Royal Priestly Heirs to the Restoration Promise of Genesis 3:15: A Biblical Theological Perspective on the Sons of God in Genesis 6," *WTJ* 76 (2014): 351–70.

[53] The royalty of this conqueror is assumed since humanity is made in God's image and likeness.

coming king who will someday rule the world.[54] Thus while Lamech in Cain's genealogy boasts about killing a child for wounding him, Lamech in Seth's genealogy begets a child, and sees in his birth a hopeful sign for relief from the earth's curse (Gen 5:28–29). Here we see hope for world redemption through a descendant, whose name aptly recalls God's grace (Gen 6:8).[55] It is no accident that it this new Adam named Noah who builds an ark that provides a future for the world.

There is another new Adam and Eve in Abram and Sarai. Called out to establish a great nation, they are promised a great name—clearly royal terminology, which echoes the ancient heroes or men of renown in the primal history (Gen 12:1–2).[56] It is in their descendants that all families of the earth will be blessed. It is in their progeny that the conditions of paradise will be restored.

The first time the word "king" explicitly occurs in the Bible is in Gen 14 where it occurs 27 times and in the context of war. But it is Abram with his 318 men who surpasses all of them, as he is able to defeat four kings from Mesopotamia, save his nephew Lot, and he is honored and blessed by the holy figure of King Melchizedek, who bestows upon him the blessing of the most high God, creator of heaven and earth (Gen 14).

Later the changing of Abram's and Sarai's names indicates their roles to become father and mother of a new humanity (Gen 17:5–6, 15–16). The lengthening of Abram's name to Abraham means that he will be father of many nations, not just one, and the change from Sarai to Sarah reaffirms her royal stature as the mother of a new humanity.[57] Significantly they will give birth to a line of kings! Thus, by the end of Genesis it is clear that one of these kings will be from the tribe of Judah, and it will be he to whom the nations will someday give homage. He will be a like an unstoppable

---

[54] See, e.g., Desmond Alexander, "Royal Expectations in Genesis to Kings: Their Importance for Biblical Theology," *TynBul* 49 (1998): 204–5.

[55] There is wordplay here in Hebrew as the word "grace" reverses the consonants of the name "Noah" (וְנֹחַ מָצָא חֵן בְּעֵינֵי יהוה).

[56] Note Yahweh's desire to make David's name as great as the great ones of the earth (2 Sam 7:9) a clear echo of Gen 12:2. Note also Gen 6:4, 10:8–9, and the desires of the builders in 11:1–9.

[57] The names Sarah and Sarai probably both mean "princess" but Sarah means more generally princess as opposed to "my princess," or Sarai is a more archaic form.

conquering lion (Gen 49:8–12).

The theme of kingship continues in Exodus where despotic rulers seek to tyrannize God's people by attacking their future through destroying their descendants. But another ark is fashioned for a new Noah to save the world (Exod 2:1–10).[58] This time the survivor emerges from the flood as a baby and it is in this baby's cry that the entire edifice of a despotic Egyptian empire will come tumbling down.

When this prince of Egypt grows up, he rejects Egyptian royalty to be a leader for a motley group of oppressed slaves. He leads his people out of bondage and they go through hell and high water before their divine king triumphs over the forces of chaos at the Red Sea and they sing a song of victory whose climax is God's rule once again on the earth: May Yahweh rule forever and ever! (Exod 15:18).

But how will this rule take place? It not only will defeat chaos in Egypt but also in Israel. Israel at Sinai is called to be a different type of kingdom, a kingdom that does not enslave but liberates. It is to be a holy nation and a *royal* priesthood (Exod 19:5–6). As priesthood defines a role to God and for God, and royalty stresses a ruling and leadership dimension, Israel as God's people has a calling to the nations. The backstory to this new calling is Abraham's election to bless the world through his descendants (Gen 12:3).[59] But no sooner does Israel accept its calling than it miserably fails in keeping the stipulations of God's Sinai covenant. Only an intercession by Moses and a new Levitical cult of sacrifices will keep them in the divine presence (Exod 32–34; Lev 1–16).

Meanwhile on the way to their new land where the divine rule will be established through them, the plan is jeopardized not only by Israel itself (Num 14), but by a formidable enemy, whose curses could threaten even the greatest power (Num 22–24). The assumption behind the hiring of Balaam by king Balak of Moab was to defeat Israel the nation, but the backstory presents this as an attempt to thwart the divine plan

---

[58] Cf. Keith Bodner, *An Ark on the Nile: Beginning of the Book of Exodus* (Oxford: Oxford University Press, 2016).

[59] See John A. Davies, *A Royal Priesthood: Literary and Intertextual Perspectives on an Image of Israel in Exodus 19.6*, JSOTSup 395 (London: Continuum International, 2004).

for universal blessing. In case the reader misses this, the narrator specifies why Balaam is hired: his word really works—the one whom he blesses is blessed and the one whom he curses is cursed (Num 22:6). This resoundingly echoes God's election of Abraham and determination to bless him in spite of all opposition to the contrary (Gen 12:3). But Balaam himself soon learns the lesson that Israel cannot be cursed, "because he is blessed!" (כי ברוך הוא).[60] Thus every time that Balaam is to curse Israel, he in fact blesses them! These blessings, situated as they are at the end of Israel's march to the promised land, reaffirm God's commitment to bless his people. They also announce the coming of a leader over the nations who will defeat an archenemy, an anti-God figure named Gog,[61] and this conqueror will be like a lion (Num 24:9), who will crush his enemies "at the end of the days" (Num 24:14–22, esp. v. 17).

In the next book, Deuteronomy, provision is made for a king in Israel as the nation is about to enter the promised land (Deut 17:14–20). There are other models of kingship available, as is clear from Israel's anticipated desire to have a king like the other nations. But this text makes the point that Israel must have a different model of kingship: "Not so shall it be among you" (Mark 10:.43). Israel's king must be one who leads by trusting in God (likeness) and serving his people (image). Negatively, he must not multiply his army, his wives, and his wealth. In particular he must not lead his people back to Egypt, which implies slavery! Positively he must write out a copy of the Torah and meditate on it day and night so that he might have a Torah mind. This will enable him to see himself properly and be humble, and therefore serve his God and his people by following the divine will.

At the beginning and end of Deuteronomy, Moses predicts that the people will eventually end up in exile as a result of covenant violation (Deut 4:25–28; 30:1a; 31:16–21, 29). Indeed, some of them will experience the worst form of curse by being

---

[60] Num 12:6.

[61] Reading "Gog" in Num 24:7 in agreement with the LXX. The question here is whether the MT is de-eschatologizing the text with the reading "Agag" or whether the LXX has preserved the original, eschatological meaning. In favor of "Gog" as the original reading, it is worth noting that Gog's identity is known in an early tradition in Ezekiel (cf. 38:17). In my judgment, this can best be explained as originating with the Balaam oracle in Num 24.

led back into Egypt (Deut 28:68),[62] which assumes that not only will the people fail to observe the Torah, but so will their king. The good news is that if repentance takes place in exile, God will have compassion on his people in accordance with the Abrahamic covenant, and they can take up their role again to bless the world.

6. Former Prophets (Joshua–Kings)

The transference of leadership from Moses to Joshua does not explicitly mention kingship, but it does stress the importance of the new Israelite leader meditating on the book of the Torah day and night to ensure success and victory (Josh 1:8–9). The success of the Israelites in the conquest assumes that good leadership based on the Torah has taken place. The subsequent book of Judges at its beginning shows a dichotomy between divine and human kingship when Gideon emphatically rejects being made a king. For him a human king and a divine king are incompatible (Judg 8:22–23). But this is probably because Gideon's view of kingship is based on the surrounding culture and not on the Torah. Indeed when his son Abimelech seizes kingship all of these fears come to fruition as his brutal quest for power eliminates all the competition but one, Jotham (Judg 9:1–5), whose famous parable of the bramble bush shows how kings were often viewed (Judg 9:7–20). Yet at the same time, by the end of the book of Judges, moral anarchy rules Israel so much so that the narrator virtually laments the fact that there is no king in Israel (Judg 17:1, 6; 21:25). His refrain assumes that the presence of a human king would not be incompatible with divine rule, but would ensure the elimination of moral disorder.

The book of Samuel is framed by such a concern as the days of the Judges— thankfully—end . Hannah sees in the birth of a child Yahweh's new world order (1 Sam 2:1–10). She has been delivered from her own personal oppression by the birth of a future kingmaker, Samuel, and she sees in his birth the fact that the real "movers and shakers" of history are not the mighty, the well-fed wealthy, and the mother of seven children (i.e., the social "somebodies"), but the weak, the hungry poor and the barren woman (i.e., the social "nobodies"). Why? Because the real mover and shaker

---

[62] Indeed, this is the last, most ignominious curse!

of history is Yahweh:

> The LORD deals death and gives life,
>
> Casts down into Sheol and raises up.
>
> The LORD makes poor and makes rich;
>
> He casts down, He also lifts high.
>
> He raises the poor from the dust,
>
> Lifts up the needy from the dunghill,
>
> Setting them with nobles,
>
> Granting them seats of honor.[63]

But what goal does Yahweh have in mind? Nothing less than a world in which his rule extends to the ends of the earth: "The LORD will judge the ends of the earth" (1 Sam 2:10). But how? "He will give his king strength and raise the horn of his anointed" (1 Sam 2:10). The last image, that of a raised horn is clearly an ancient image of victory reminiscent of Hannah's victory over her own personal oppression (1 Sam 2:10; cf. 2:1). Thus, Hannah's personal victory anticipates an eventual universal triumph.[64]

It is not long before the "mighty" begin to fall in the book of Samuel. The exploitative and lustful house of Eli comes falling down like kingpins as first Hophni and Phinehas are killed in battle, and then their doting father, old Eli, falls from his throne and breaks his neck (1 Sam 4:11–18). Then the Philistine statue of Dagon falls in worship before the captured ark of the covenant, and when raised the next day to take its seat of supremacy in the Philistine pantheon, it falls again, this time decapitated and "disarmed" before the holy ark (1 Sam 5:1–4). When Israel wants a king like the other nations, such a king is seen for who he is in the narrative—a king who will lead

---

[63] 1 Sam 2:6–8 (JPS).

[64] For a study of this important theme see my study "Hannah's Song, A New World Order and the Right Side of History," in *Ecclesia Semper Reformanda Est: A Festschrift on Ecclesiology in Honour of Stanley K. Fowler*, ed. Michael A. G. Haykin, David G. Barker, and Barry H. Howson (Dundas: Joshua Press, 2016), 3–32.

them back to "Egypt," enslaving the people once again (1 Sam 8).[65] When Israel's first king is noted for his height (1 Sam 10:23), this is a bad omen and it is not long before he begins to be abased and someone insignificant—a shepherd boy, the son of Jesse, becomes elevated.[66] It is the small boy who decapitates and disarms the tall Goliath, and he is able to become the king *de facto* if not *de jure* despite living in exile which is the result of being persecuted by Saul. The night before the tall Saul meets his demise, Yahweh brings up the dead prophet, Samuel, from the grave to pronounce the *coup de grace* (1 Sam 28:16–19; cf. v. 20). Soon after David becomes king in Israel *de jure*.

The crowning moment in David's kingship is his desire to build a house for Yahweh—a temple—for he sees the incongruity between his palace—the human symbol of reign—and the humble accommodation for the ark of the covenant, in the tent of meeting—the divine symbol of rule (2 Sam 7). It is at this point that Yahweh raises up David to heights unknown as David himself recognizes. Yahweh decides that the king will not build him a house—a temple—but rather that he will build David a house—a dynasty—forever! This becomes the Davidic covenant, and thus David's line is marked for rulership in accordance with ancient prophecies in Genesis and Numbers. Torah obedience is necessary but even if his descendants fail to keep the Torah and evoke God's punishment, Yahweh will still never take away his חֶסֶד from David's house. Clearly this covenant is intended to develop the Abrahamic covenant with its focus on a great name and God's choice of Israel to be his people. David is overwhelmed and he concludes by asking God to ensure the good word of his promise:

> And now, O Lord GOD, you are God, and your words are true, and you
> have promised this good thing to your servant; now therefore may it
> please you to bless the house of your servant, so that it may continue
> forever before you; for you, O Lord GOD, have spoken, and with your
> blessing shall the house of your servant be blessed forever.[67]

---

[65] I am using the term Egypt metaphorically here.

[66] Note that when Samuel is selecting David from Jesse's sons God tells him explicitly not to pay attention to height! 1 Sam 16:7.

[67] 2 Sam 7:28–29 (ESV).

David emphasizes here the divine guarantee of the good thing—the promise—of the eternal covenant, and then finally he reaffirms that this means an everlasting blessing on his house.

This clearly clarifies a number of points. David's kingship will not be like Saul's. God will never take his חֶסֶד from David's house. This is an eternal dynasty and it is difficult not to see this house as the eventual answer to Hannah's thanksgiving song that God will reign unto the ends of the earth, by giving a king his power and raising the horn of his anointed.

But if this is true, it is clear from the subsequent narrative that this king will not be David nor many of his sons. The checkered history of this line is continued through David's sin with Bathsheba and murder of Uriah (2 Sam 11), and with the rape of Tamar by Amnon (2 Sam 13:1–19), Absalom's murder of Amnon (2 Sam 13:20–36), the treason of Absalom and his death (2 Sam 15–19), and the uprising of Adonijah (1 Kgs 1–2). Who, reading this narrative for the first time, would have ever expected the next king to be the result of a union between David and his former paramour, Bathsheba? But it is in fact Solomon who is the next king, and he soon proves not to be a Messiah, with his clear violation of the Deuteronomic laws of kingship, with royal ambitions of power, an extraordinarily large harem, and wealth often acquired at the expense of others. Ahijah presides over the disintegration of his kingdom, but explicitly preserves Judah because of the Davidic covenant (1 Kgs 11:29–36). Kings come and go in the south but there always remains a king on the throne except for a period of seven years during the reign of Athaliah. Here the Davidic house is all but at an end because of the brutality of a feminine Pharaoh, Athaliah, as the infant Joash represents the last Davidic descendant alive, the last man from the Davidic history (2 Kgs 11:1–3). But a royal sister, like Miriam before her, saves her brother from the royal genocide. After a seven year hiatus, the vacant throne of David is filled again with Joash raised up as it were from the grave (2 Kgs 11:4–20).

The checkered history of the Davidic line of descendants continues until the exile of Judah and the complete destruction of the Jewish nation (2 Kgs 25). Zedekiah, the presiding puppet monarch of Babylon, who rebels against his masters, is captured, sentence is pronounced, and his sons destroyed before his eyes, after which these same eyes are gouged out (2 Kgs 25:4–7). Nebuchadnezzar, the king of Babylon, leads him away to exile, to join his nephew, Jehoiachin, the last legitimate king of Judah, who had been exiled to Babylon ten years before. The final mention of the nation before the last four verses of Kings, the closing verses of this history which began at creation in Genesis 1, relate that the remnant population in Judah returns to Egypt with their leader, in a stark realization of the culmination of the curses in Deuteronomy for the violation of the Torah (2 Kgs 25:26; cf. Deut 28:68).

7. The End of History and the Last Man

So as the history draws to a conclusion, a history that started at creation, a history of human beings fashioned as royalty, descended from heaven, but a history of disobedience and fallen and distorted kingship, there seems to be no one left. Where is the promise of a descendant from this royalty that would restore humanity to its former glory? (Gen 3:15). Where is the promise of a descendant who would provide relief from the curse? (Gen 5:28–29). Where is the promise of a line of descendants who would someday bless the world? (Gen 12:3). Where is the promise of a lion-like king from the line of Judah, who would put the world to rights? (Gen 49:8–12; Num 24:9). Where is the king and anointed one who would rule to the ends of the earth? (1 Sam 2:10). Where is the God who would abase the proud and elevate the humble, who would kill and make alive again, who would bring down to the grave and bring up from that place of death? (1 Sam 2:6–8). What has become of the Davidic covenant and God's promise never to remove his חֶסֶד from his descendants? (2 Sam 7:12–16).

This is the context for the last four verses of Kings. As the problematic history of Israel and now that of Judah draws to a close, the last descendant of David emerges from the graveyard of an exilic prison, suited with new clothes, a seat at the king's table, a "throne" and "a good thing" spoken to him ("he spoke kindly to him"). What do such words echo in the readers' ears? The most salient at a time like this is certainly David's words about God guaranteeing the Davidic covenant and about blessing his house forever because of the promise (2 Sam 7:28–29).

Thus, the history from Genesis to Kings is at an end but there is a last man standing, and he is a Davidide! The house of David is still alive. Perhaps this is akin to resurrection. Resonances in the early history of such resurrections show the truth of Hannah's song of killing and resurrecting, of abasing and elevating. If one were to use boxing terminology to describe these last four verses and the ancient promises of God, one might use the terms, "down but not out." This may be "a thin thread," but sometimes a thin thread is all that is needed.

8. The Latter Prophets: Jeremiah–The Twelve

Thus, at the halfway point in the Hebrew Bible, the end of history and the last man points to hope and a new history. And this is exactly what the rest of the Hebrew Bible demonstrates. Whereas Jeremiah addresses the nation with words of judgment and even pronounces a curse on Jehoiachin (Jer 22:24–30), declaring that Yahweh has ripped his signet ring off his hand, his symbol of rulership, the prophet does not give up on the Davidic promise, pronouncing that someday a righteous branch will grow from the tree of David and in his days Judah and Israel will be saved (Jer 23:5–6, 33:14–16). Even the curse on Jehoiachin will be reversed, since God will bless him and his exilic family.[68] In fact only if God could break his covenant with the day and night, would he break his covenant with the house of David! (Jer 33:20–21).

Ezekiel promises that Jehoiachin will be like a new sprig taken from the cedar tree in exile and raised to become a great tree under which all the birds of the forest will take shade and shelter. This is because Yahweh elevates and humbles, he nourishes and dries up (Ezek 17:22–24).[69] A new David, a true shepherd, will become king after the exile (Ezek 34:23–31).

Isaiah promises that a shoot will rise up from the stump of Jesse and bring justice and healing to the nations. There will be a new world order in which the lion will lie down with the lamb. Dangerous serpents will be obsolete, and death and

---

[68] "Surprisingly, the humiliation of exile is the source of hope concerning Jehoiachin's future. Indeed, Jehoiachin was no sooner exiled than Jeremiah began to speak of him as a "good fig" and as an heir to restoration promises with the rest of the gôlâ" (Jer 24:4–7) [Patton, *Hope for a Tender Sprig*, 292].

[69] For detailed exegesis see the excellent study by Patton, *Hope for a Tender Sprig*, 173–97.

destruction will vanish as the earth will be covered with the knowledge of God as the waters cover the sea (Isa 11:1–9).

The Twelve sing a song in harmony with this as no one less than a new David will appear after the exile (Hos 3:5). The fallen house of David will be restored (Amos 9:11–13). God even restores Jehoiachin by investing his grandson Zerubbabel with his signet ring so that he can continue the Davidic house (Hag 2:22–23).[70] The Latter Prophets make it clear that a new chapter of the history has to be written, one in which the last man standing at the end of the first history becomes the channel by which a new history can begin.

9. The Writings

In the Writings, it is no accident that David becomes thematized. Whether it is in the startling ending of the book of Ruth, the constant drumbeat of David's name in the titles of the psalms in the final form of the Psalter, the dominant imprint of his house in some of the wisdom literature, or in the last historical narrative of the Tanak focusing on the Davidic house—Chronicles—David seems virtually omnipresent. Why, for example, is there such a hope in a Davidic descendant for the postexilic community in the final form of the Psalter? (Pss 2; 72; 89, 110; 132).[71] There is no Davidic ruler on the throne, and yet all the kings of the earth are required to bow before him. Is this not the eschatological David? (Ps 2).

Though there are a variety of orders for the Writings, there is a second history, comparable to the Primary History, extending from creation to the exile and even beyond. Like Genesis, the first book in the Primary History, Chronicles has many genealogies, but these genealogies essentially conclude with the arrival of David on the historical scene (1 Chr 1–9). But this history, while produced after the exile, and covering the tragic events which led to exile, including the history of Israel's

---

[70] For further detailed exegesis and theological reflection see the studies by Critchlow (Critchlow, *Looking Back for Jehoiachin*) and Patton (*Hope for a Tender Sprig*).

[71] Note also the ubiquitous presence of Psalm titles and David the choir conductor (145) for the last great flurry of praise psalms (146–50).

intransigence and violation of the Sinaitic covenant, does not end with the dynasty's revival—the house of David understood genealogically. It ends with the temple's revival. The last word is not Amel-Marduk proclaiming the release of Jehoiachin, and thus the revival of the house of David—the Davidic dynasty, but the word of Cyrus a generation later proclaiming release to the exiles and charging them to return and build the house of David—the temple (2 Chr 36:22–23). This indicates that repentance has taken place and the command ends with a plea to "the one whose God is with him" to go up! This last word "go up" is the same word that Hannah proclaimed when she praised God's power which could bring down to the grave and raise up. Perhaps there is even here an anticipation of someone from the Davidic house going up to build the temple—the one whose God is truly with him! And who could that be in Chronicles but David?[72]

This focus on the Davidic House at the end of the two histories of Israel becomes even sharper if Chronicles closes the canon, which it did in an early arrangement which is preserved as a *baraita* in the Talmud, which may date back to at least the first century AD or before.[73] Thus in the middle of the Hebrew canon is the word about the revival of the Davidic house understood genealogically—the dynasty, and at the end of the Hebrew canon is the word about the revival of the house understood architecturally—the temple. Thus, the last words of the history are words of hope in which to build a new future—a house which God builds! And it is presented as if Israel is still in exile.

---

[72] John H. Sailhamer, "Biblical Theology and the Composition of the Hebrew Bible," in *Biblical Theology: Retrospect and Prospect*, ed. Scott J. Hafemann (Downers Grove, IL: InterVarsity Press, 2002), 137.

[73] Baba Bathra 14b. See Roger T. Beckwith, *The Old Testament Canon of the New Testament Church and Its Background in Early Judaism* (Grand Rapids, Eerdmans, 1984). See also Hendrik J. Koorevaar, "Die Chronik als intendierter Abschluss des alttestamentlichen Kanons," *JET* 11 (1997): 42–76; Stephen G. Dempster, "Canons on the Left and Canons on the Right: Finding a Resolution in the Canon Debate," *JETS* 52:1 (2009): 47–77.

10. Conclusion

As the New Testament begins with the book of Matthew, it begins with a new Genesis, in which the old history is sketched leading to a new man, who will build a new temple (Matt 1:1).[74] The genealogy of Matthew moves from Abraham in whose seed the entire earth would be blessed to David, to Jesus (Matt 1:1–17). Jesus is thus the *telos* of Israel's history, the last man, the new David. Since the genealogy is structured in a triad of 14 generations, and the numerical value of the name David is 14, it is clear that when Jesus arrives he is history's last man, the goal of Israel's history. Significantly Jehoiachin is featured twice in the genealogy: he is clearly no longer the last man but someone who straddles the beginning of the exile to its end, a history of judgment to its beginning of promise:

> Jeconiah is a complex figure, for in straddling the deportation he marks both the lowest point of Israel's history and also a new beginning.... Jeconiah also functions positively in the third part of the genealogy, for his continuance shows that there is a future beyond deportation, nebulous though it may be. The Davidic line is exiled, but it nevertheless continues...[75]

Thus, Jehoiachin as the Primary History's last man continues to the goal of the Old Testament history. When Jesus arrives, he is the true son of David, the end of the line, and he is the one who by going into exile, leads Israel out of exile. He dies as a result of all the violations of the covenant but that is not the end. By virtue of his resurrection he is able to be a blessing to the entire world by reigning from the exalted throne of David (Acts 2:30–35). Then, the great news at the end of Matthew is that this last man—the goal of the Davidic house—gives instructions to go out to the entire world and preach good news to everyone so that they can become part of a house of David—the temple—which is so expansive it includes the entire world (Matt 28:18–

---

[74] As noted by many scholars, there is a definite reference to Gen 5:1 if not the entire book of Genesis: "A book of the genesis of Jesus Christ..."

[75] Patton, *Hope for a Tender Sprig*, 270.

20). Thus, the last man is the first man of a new humanity, a countless number who will rule as kings and queens of a new creation, thus fulfilling their magnificent destinies. In this new world, they will fully face God (likeness) and the world (image). This is very different from the last man of a liberal capitalism, where economic oppression and human selfishness and greed remain unchecked.[76] This biblical end of history and this last man give way to a new history of restored queens and kings of creation who will reign forever, in love with their exalted Lord. (Rev 22:1–5, esp. v. 5).

---

[76] Cf. Fukuyama, *End of History*.

SUFFERING SAINTS, GLORIOUS KINGS, AND DIVINE DELIVERANCE: CONTEXT AND *RELECTURE* IN THE PSALMS

—Philip S. Johnston

1. Psalms and the Christian

The Psalms are undoubtedly the best loved part of the Old Testament for the vast majority of Christians, and have been throughout the centuries.[1] Recited or chanted, the psalms have formed part of the daily and weekly liturgy of churches and religious houses from earliest records. Psalm 23 still remains the best-known passage of Scripture after the Lord's Prayer, even in an era of minimal memorisation. The Psalms are included in many pocket editions of the New Testament, and are frequently cited in guides of what to read in various circumstances. No other part of ancient Israelite Scripture is as read, sung or enjoyed as the Psalms.

There are several reasons why the Psalms appeal to Christians. Different readers weigh these differently, but all contribute to their popularity. One is their form. Psalms are poetry, appealing to our imagination as much as our reason. In contrast to the more prosaic nature of historical, legal and prophetic material, here are texts which resonate with a side of human nature often overlooked in doctrinally-centred Protestantism. The poetic form is straightforward, with short lines and simple vocabulary. The language is ordinary, down-to-earth and direct. The topics covered are relevant to all: the wonders and horrors of the world, the joys and sorrows of life, the hopes and fears of faith. Further, this poetry is easily understood since its key feature is that of matching ideas, the typical couplet having lines which support each other in a wonderful variety of repetition. As often noted, this form of poetry translates

---

[1] I am delighted to contribute to this volume honoring Desi Alexander, one-time supervisor, occasional collaborator and long-time friend. Unless otherwise indicated, all references cited are from NIV 2011, with English versification even when referring to the Hebrew text.

into any language and culture, unlike poetry based on rhythm or rhyme. The psalms are imaginative, direct, and resonant.

A second, equally important reason is that the psalms are the response of faith, and of faith "from bottom up." In the rest of the Hebrew Bible, God addresses Israel "top down" through his agents: laws for life and worship, accounts of obedience or disobedience, and proclamations of God's response to this. By contrast, in the Psalms, the direction is the opposite: it is Israelites who address God, occasionally as a community but more often as individuals. Hence communities and individuals today feel they can identify with and appropriate their prayers. These prayers do not seem to come from expert specialists like leaders, law-givers, priests, scribes, historians and prophets.[2] Instead they seem to come from the ordinary believer, expressing the whole gamut of personal experience: hardship, persecution, barrenness, resolution, praise, joy, hope, and everything in between. Even many of the psalms ascribed to David portray the struggles and setbacks of an ordinary Israelite rather than a king.[3] Ordinary Christians of all cultures and eras have therefore identified closely with the psalms, and found in them scriptural expression for their own experience.

An important factor in this appropriation is the non-specificity of most psalms. There are numerous references to plots, snares, enemies and battles, as well as to rescue, victory and celebration. But rarely are any protagonists named or historical references included. The specifics have been removed, whether in original transcription or later transmission, enabling the text to be repeatedly reused in multiple similar contexts from then on.[4]

---

[2] Scholars have long debated the extent of professional composition of psalms, whether specifically for the cult (so S. Mowinckel, *The Psalms in Israel's Worship*, trans. D. R. Ap-Thomas. 2 vols. [Oxford: Basil Blackwell, 1962]) or for private use within a temple setting (so others), or otherwise.

[3] Regardless of the issue of authorship. Many are anonymous, some attributed to groups, about half to David (see further below).

[4] The same phenomenon is observable in Christian hymnody, with original compositions shorn of excessive length or inappropriate material, e.g., "All things bright and beautiful" no longer includes the original verse "The rich man in his castle, the poor man at his gate; God made them high and lowly, and ordered their estate." Similarly, the hymn-like British national anthem no longer has added verses entreating English victory against the Scots and the French!

Within the wide range of human responses, two stand out: lament and praise. Hermann Gunkel rightly described lament as the backbone of the Psalter, comprising a good third of its contents.[5] What this founder of form-criticism observed has long been noted by those who work systematically through the Psalter in liturgy or private devotion: the first lament-dominated half is hard work, personally when all seems well, and communally when worship services focus on praise. And yet many other Christians especially appreciate these psalms, written by suffering saints who vividly portray similar struggles to their own. Such modern believers find particularly pertinent the hope in divine deliverance which glints through in nearly all these lament psalms.[6]

The third main reason for Christian affection for the psalms is that evangelists, apostolic preachers and writers from the early church onwards interpret them as "messianic," seeing predictive portrayals of Jesus which affirm him to be the awaited messiah.[7] The Hebrew term מָשִׁיחַ (origin of the English term "messiah," which sounds very similar) simply meant *anointed*: anointing with oil was applied to prophet, priest and king in Israel, and to similar appointments throughout the ancient Near East. So each king of Israel was successively "the anointed one" on taking office. However, as each king successively failed to live up to the high ideals, and especially as the kingship was not re-established on return from exile, the Jews (as they came to be called) increasingly looked for an idealised future anointed one. Jesus was of course this *messiah*, but in such a different way to the common expectation that he was misunderstood by his contemporaries, followers as much as opponents. Only after

---

[5] H. Gunkel, *Introduction to Psalms: The Genres of the Religious Lyric of Israel*, comp. by J. Begrich, trans. J. D. Nogalski (Macon, GA: Mercer University Press, 1998; German orig., 1933).

[6] Claus Westermann astutely simplified categorization to praise and lament, and also showed how most laments move at least partly towards praise. However, he was unwise to absolutize this, since Ps 88 at least does not. C. Westermann, *Praise and Lament in the Psalms* (Edinburgh: T&T Clark, 1981), 74, 266; and for critique: P. S. Johnston, "Distress in the Psalms," in *Interpreting the Psalms: Issues and Approaches*, ed. P. S. Johnston and D. G. Firth (Leicester: Apollos, 2005), 63–84 (esp. 79–80).

[7] By citation or allusion, the NT references at least Pss 2, 8, 16, 18, 22, 34, 35, 40, 41, 45, 68, 69, 97, 102, 110, 118.

Pentecost did the apostles finally piece all the evidence together. Alongside direct prophecies elsewhere, they noticed how descriptions of the psalmists' various misfortunes and hopes bore an uncanny resemblance to the experience of Jesus, or how their descriptions of royalty surpassed any ancient king but were gloriously accomplished in the person and mission of Jesus. In this perspective the psalms were re-applied to a new situation, a process already evident within some psalms.[8] Both the general trend and a few key psalms will be explored further below.

The early church took this approach much further, often in defence against Jewish critique of this Jesus-focussed interpretation of their Scriptures. Two broad Christian approaches developed, the Antiochene, which kept more to the original sense of the ancient texts, and the Alexandrian, which veered more towards allegory. Sadly the latter eventually dominated, leading to all manner of fanciful interpretations and a tendency to ignore the original context and find instead some application to Jesus, however tenuous. Not every mention of wood implies the cross, nor every mention of standing/rising indicates the resurrection. Nevertheless, we must take seriously the apostolic interpretation of the Old Testament, including its very occasional use of allegory.[9]

2. From Psalms to Psalter

Lay Christians are usually content to take the psalms simply as sacred texts, and not worry about how they came to be preserved, transmitted and recognised as authoritative. Yet this is highly relevant to the issue of their messianic perspective.

By contrast, scholars discuss at great length the issues of authorship, compilation and transmission of biblical books. While their arguments for other books are often based on inference, with the psalms we have some of the clearest evidence,

---

[8] This interpretation via "re-application" or *relecture* differs from the traditional view that the psalms included messianic prediction from the outset. It flows both from viewing the psalms as responses to immediate situations, and from noting their re-application to new situations within the Old Testament itself, as discussed further below.

[9] For fuller discussion of this approach, see P. S. Johnston: "Old Testament and Christ," in *New Dictionary of Christian Apologetics*, ed. C. Campbell-Jack and G. J. McGrath (Leicester: IVP, 2006), 506–10.

both internal and external to the text.

First, there is clear evidence in the text itself of a long and complex process of collation of the psalms. The most obvious include:

- Division into five books by doxologies placed at the end of each book but not integrated into their final psalms (except for Ps 150, which is completely doxology).[10]

- Various collections grouped (with an occasional exception) by a key term of their headings: David (Pss 3–41; 51–70; 138–145);[11] Asaph (Pss 73–83); Sons of Korah (Pss 42–49; 84–88); Songs of Ascent (Pss 120–134).[12]

- Psalm 72 adds after its doxology: "This concludes the prayers of David son of Jesse." This postscript (a) shows an early collection, since there are Davidic psalms later in the Psalter; and (b) implies a meaning of "prayers of David" wide enough to include a psalm described at its start as "Solomonic."[13]

- Editorial preference for divine names, with 'YHWH' (LORD) dominating in Bks I, IIIb, IV and V, and 'Elohim' (God) in Bks II and IIIa.[14]

- Duplication, with Pss 14 and 40B repeated almost verbatim in Pss 53 and

---

[10] The five books are: Pss 1–41, 42–72, 73–89, 90–106, 107–150. Ps 150 closes the whole Psalter and is a complete doxology in itself. The books are not indicated as such in the Hebrew text, but are discerned by these doxologies and other features. The division is usually thought to reflect the five 'books of Moses', as noted in the 10th century AD Jewish midrash on Ps 1:2.

[11] The preposition ל before David and other names in the Hebrew psalm titles has traditionally been taken to indicate authorship (cf. Hab 3:1). However, prepositions in all languages are complex, and there are other plausible interpretations. For present purposes, it is sufficient to refer to such psalms simply as "Davidic," etc.

[12] Some exceptions also suggest editorial activity, e.g., the anonymous 10 and 43 may originally have been part of 9 (same original acrostic) and 42 (same refrain) respectively.

[13] Ps 72 may have been read later as a prayer *by* David *for* Solomon, so e.g., M. E. Tate, *Psalms 51–100*, WBC 20 (Dallas: Word, 1990), 222. If the postscript referred initially to Pss 51–72, this collection also included the anonymous Pss 66, 67, 71 (unless these were inserted later). If it referred to Bk II (or even Bks I–II), then the collection also included Korahite and other non-Davidic psalms.

[14] The disparity is strong. In Bks I, II, IV and V, the dominant name is used in at least 85% of all occurrences. In Bk III it is slightly less: IIIa (Pss 73–83), 69%; IIIb (Pss 84–89), 78%.

70 respectively.[15]

Secondly, there is evidence for change of text, notably in the adaptation of individual psalms to the community. For example:

- Psalm 25 is individual (I/me/my) in its alphabetic acrostic, yet ends with a communal coda ("Deliver Israel") appended to the acrostic.
- Psalm 129 begins similarly as an individual prayer, but is collectivized by v. 1b ("let Israel now say") and by vv. 5–8.
- Psalm 51 is a well-known confession of guilt.[16] The body of the psalm (vv. 1–17) is deeply personal, and concludes that God prefers a contrite heart to sacrifice. Yet the closing two verses then pray for the rebuilding of Jerusalem's walls (previously irrelevant) and restoration of its sacrifices (previously spurned)! It looks like this individual psalm was reoriented during the exile as a communal confession of sin and prayer for restoration.

This application of older material to a new context, whether it involves change to the text itself or not, is called *relecture* (i.e., "re-reading"). It shows that the Israelites and later the Jews already recontextualized revered texts in a way not dissimilar to that of the NT writers concerning Jesus, or of Christian believers regarding themselves. There are obvious differences in these three types of re-reading, but the impulse is similar. What is important at this point is that this *relecture* can sometimes be seen within the biblical text itself.

Thirdly, though less well known, there is some evidence that the Psalter was still a work in progress at Qumran, about a century before the turn of the eras. The psalms were obviously popular, and the Dead Sea scrolls include some 20 different fragments which contain two or more psalms, thus indicating their respective ordering.[17] This evidence shows that the first half (Books I to III) was pretty well

---

[15] Also, Pss 14 and 40B (Book I) use "YHWH" more, while Pss 53 and 70 (Book II) use 'Elohim' more.

[16] The heading specifies David's confession after adultery, though the psalm itself gives no such indication.

[17] There are many other psalms fragments which are too short to be helpful in this respect. See

finalised, with the same psalms that became canonical and in the same order. But this is less clear for the second half (Books IV and V). One scroll (11QPs[a]), which only contains the second half, has several interesting peculiarities: it has a different ordering of these psalms; it omits some psalms which became canonical; and it includes other passages which did not.[18] The Psalms Septuagint, translated in roughly the same period,[19] follows what later became the canonical order, but with slightly different numeration and an additional Psalm 151. Some scholars have concluded that there were actually two versions of the psalter in circulation in the late Second Temple period, one with what became the canonical order (represented by most of the scrolls and the LXX), the other with a different second half (represented by 11QPs[a]).[20]

After publication of 11QPs[a] in 1965, many scholars initially suggested that it reflected a liturgical collection rather than a different version of the psalter, and this view still finds support.[21] However, most scholars now think that it reflects a slightly different collection of psalms, and that the completion of the psalter as a canonical book occurred later than conservative scholars previously thought.[22]

This is more relevant to the interpretation of the Psalms than often realised. If

---

particularly P. W. Flint, "Unrolling the Dead Sea Psalms Scrolls," in *The Oxford Handbook of the Psalms*, ed. W. P. Brown (Oxford: Oxford University Press, 2014), 229–50 (one of the last of his numerous publications); also D. Swanson, "Qumran and the Psalms," in *Interpreting the Psalms: Issues and Approaches*, ed. P. S. Johnston and D. G. Firth (Leicester: Apollos, 2005), 247–61.

[18] 11QPs[a], also called the Great Psalms Scroll, contains: 101–103, 109, 118, 104, 147, 105, 146, 148, 121–32, 119, 135–36, *Catena*, 145 (with postscript), *154*, *Plea for Deliverance*, 139, 137, 138, Sirach 51, *Apostrophe to Zion*, 93, 141, 133, 144, *155*, 142–143, 149–150, *Hymn to the Creator*, David's Last Words [2 Sam 23:7], *David's Compositions*, 140, 134, *151*. (List from Flint, "Unrolling the Scrolls," 232, with italics indicating noncanonical inclusion. *Pss 154 & 155* are also found in the Syriac Bible.) This different collection and order are partly supported by the much shorter 11QPs[b], and possibly by 4QPs[e].

[19] The Pentateuch was translated into Greek first, probably in the mid-third century BC, the other books later, though probably by the mid-first century BC.

[20] E.g., Flint, "Unrolling the Scrolls," 240.

[21] Recently by A. D. Hensley, *Covenant Relationships and the Editing of the Hebrew Psalter*, LHBOTS 666 (London: T&T Clark, 2018), 33–41.

[22] E.g., N. deClaissé-Walford: "The book of Psalms appears to be one of the latest books of the Old Testament to achieve … final form." N. deClaissé-Walford *et al.*, *The Book of Psalms*, NICOT (Grand Rapids: Eerdmans, 2014), 24.

the inclusion or exclusion of specific psalms and the ordering of the Psalter was open to adjustment down to the century before Jesus, the same could be true of the text itself. We know from other sources that the Maccabean revolt (167–164 BC) and subsequent Hasmonean dynasty engendered a gradual but steady development of messianic expectation towards the form witnessed in the New Testament. In particular, this growing messianism may have influenced the Hebrew text and early translation of the royal psalms, with original references to ancient Israelite kings now being recast in expectation of a future ideal king. Indeed, recent decades have seen various proposals of theological editing of the psalter. The first half ends with Ps 89 and the dramatic collapse of the Davidic monarchy; so the second half may well have been edited in response to this. One proposal is that Book IV (Pss 90–107) strongly proclaims divine kingship in order to fill the human vacuum, at least in part.[23] Another is that there is an increased portrayal of the Davidic king as an ideal, future figure.[24] In any case, despite disagreements between their proponents, these perspectives could well be complementary. So rather than being problematic, these insights may actually help us interpret the grandiose and seemingly exaggerated language of these psalms.

3. Interpreting Royal Psalms

Hermann Gunkel based his form-critical study on the similarities of form or structure (*Gattung*) and the regular contexts of use (*Sitz im Leben*) which fostered this similarity.[25] However, as he recognised himself, the royal psalms do not fit this analysis, since their occasions of use are so rare and distinctive that there is no typical pattern. Nonetheless, his wider approach emphasised the possible reuse of such psalms at coronations, royal weddings and battle victories, and their focus on the immediate king rather than a future deliverer.[26]

---

[23] So G. H. Wilson, *The Editing of the Hebrew Psalter*, SPLDS 76 (Chico, CA: Scholars Press, 1985). Wilson was the pioneer of such study, and his work opened up a whole need area of research.

[24] So D. C. Mitchell, *The Message of the Psalter: An Eschatological Programme in the Book of Psalms*, JSOTSup 252 (Sheffield: Sheffield Academic Press, 2007); Hensley, *Covenant Relationships*, 33–41.

[25] See his *Introduction to Psalms*.

[26] G. H. Wilson, "The Use of Royal Psalms at the 'Seams' of the Hebrew Psalter," *JSOT* 35

In one of his earliest articles, David Clines helpfully notes and critiques the different ways the ideology of Israel's kingship has been understood in scholarship, starting with the most elevated.[27]

a) *Divine kingship*, i.e., the king was an incarnation of the deity, and played the part of a dying and rising god annually in the New Year festival, as in other ancient Near East cultures. However, such a festival is unattested in the OT and the concept clearly goes against the biblical histories, e.g., the way prophets address kings (1 Sam 15:22–23; 2 Sam 12:1–14; 1 Kgs 18:18) and the way kings react (also 2 Kgs 5:7, 6:27).

b) *Sacral kingship*, i.e., while not actually a god, the king mediated divine blessing to the people, and represented their humiliation and restoration in the New Year festival. However, as noted above, this festival and the concept behind it are unattested in the Old Testament, as is any reference to the king as holy or sacral.

c) *Charismatic kingship*, i.e., the king ruled not by dynastic succession but by virtue of a divine gift (charisma) usually conveyed through a prophet, a tradition practised in Israel more than Judah. However, kings throughout the ancient Near East claimed divine appointment, as also in Israel and Judah (Pss 2, 110; see below). Further, for the biblical historian, even in turbulent northern Israel the monarchy was a succession of dynasties, however short-lived, rather than one in which each king required charismatic anointing.

(1986): 85–94, discusses their distinctive placing, e.g., Ps 2 as a second introduction, Pss 72 and 89 at the close of Bks II and III.

[27] D. J. A. Clines, "The Psalms and the King," *TSF Bulletin* 71 (1975): 1–6; reprinted in his *On the Way to the Postmodern*, vol 2 (Sheffield: SAP, 1998), 687–700. The article contains a wealth of detail and argument beyond this brief summary. Clines cites as proponents of the five approaches outlined: a) the "Myth and Ritual" school of I. Engnell, G. Widengren, S. H. Hooke; b) S. Mowinckel, A. R. Johnson; c) A. Alt, M. Noth, J. Bright; d) Widengren again (many others think the king performed priestly functions); e) Clines himself.

    d) *Sacerdotal kingship*, i.e., the king not only performed priestly functions but was himself the high priest. David inherited the functions of Jerusalem's Jebusite priest-kings (Ps 110:4; cf. 2 Sam 6:12–18; 24:25), and various successors were involved in priestly activities: Solomon, Ahaz, Hezekiah, Manasseh and Josiah (1 Kgs 8; 9:25; 2 Kgs 16:10–11; 16:12–13; 18:4; 21:3–6; 22:3–23:3). However, Ps 110:4 (if indeed a reference to the king) is unique in describing him as priest. Other references could imply a supervisory role for the king, as also exercised by patriarchs and Nehemiah, and the latter at least was clearly not a priest.[28]

    e) *Divinely appointed kingship*, i.e., the king was appointed by Yahweh, enjoyed his blessing and protection, and was described and praised in extreme terms (see further below). Nevertheless, Clines argues that, once appointed, the king was mainly responsible for military, diplomatic and judicial spheres rather than religion, as the historical books indicate. So in sum, while the psalms give a religious understanding of kingship, they do not portray it as essentially a religious institution.

This certainly accords with the wider Old Testament perspective. But this argument needs to be supported by close attention to the relevant key psalms.

4. Psalms and the King

Psalm 2 grandly and forcefully affirms YHWH's choice of his king on his holy hill Zion, with worldwide dominion despite the rebellion of subservient kings. In contrast to later psalms where the king is God's agent for global peace and plenty, here there is a strong sense of military might and suppression of revolt, which should lead to due reverence of both Zion's king and YHWH himself.

Four expressions invite further comment. First, the king was "anointed" (v. 2):

---

[28] Also, though unmentioned by Clines, King Uzziah was punished with leprosy for burning incense and usurping the role of the Aaronic priests (2 Chr 26:16–21).

this was normal for Israelite and Judean kings on appointment to office, so the obvious original application is to an immediate Israelite context rather than a future one.[29] Then YHWH declares: "You are my son; today I have become your father" (v. 7). Again this reflects a common perception, widespread in the ancient Near East though seldom attested in Israel, of the king in some way adopted by the supreme deity. Some Egyptian and Mesopotamian records refer to the pharaoh or the king as actually divine—Israel never took that step (see above, and below on Ps 45). But the Israelite king was God's primary agent to bring justice, harmony and prosperity to humanity, and thus had a unique relationship with him which this proclamation captures. Thirdly, the king would shatter his enemies (v. 9). This also is a common ancient motif,[30] repeated in the royal psalms,[31] and probably the closest echo of Gen 3:15 in the psalter. Finally, the fractious kings are told to "Kiss the son" (v. 12), in an age-old sign of a subject's loyalty to their monarch.[32] This again has immediate reference, and fits within the cultural expectations of human kingship.

Psalm 2 may well have been written or adopted as a coronation psalm, as most scholars argue. If so, its repeated use at coronations of kings who serially disappointed the psalm's proclamation may well have led to its gradual projection onto a future ideal king, chiming with prophetic oracles of such a figure. Any such preexilic dynamic would have gained considerable momentum when the absence of a postexilic monarchy became the norm. Further, many scholars interpret the placement of Ps 2 as part of an edited double introduction to the psalter, where Ps 1 presents Israel's torah-

---

[29] Earlier editions of the NIV had "Anointed One," implying a specific and possibly messianic reference (with "anointed one" as a footnoted alternative). However, NIV 2011 has simply "anointed," implying the common practice of royal anointing noted above. For Son/son and Father/father in vv. 7 and 12, there is a similar pattern of upper case in earlier NIV editions and lower case in NIV 2011.

[30] See e.g., S. Parpola, *Assyrian Prophecies*, SAA 9 (Helsinki: Helsinki University Press, 1997), 17–18, no. 2.5 lines 21–23 and 31.

[31] See also Ps 72: 8–9; 89:23.

[32] The term "son" here is in Aramaic, and most scholars find the whole phrase problematic, whether they retain the traditional translation (as P. C. Craigie, *Psalms 1–50*, WBC 19 [Waco, TX: Word, 1983], 63–64), or emend to "Serve the Lord in fear; in trembling kiss his feet" (as reluctantly R. A. Jacobson, in N. deClaissé-Walford et al., *The Book of Psalms*, 67–70). In the latter case, the kiss would express fealty loyalty to God himself.

centered piety and Ps 2 gives God's messiah-centered rulership. This also suggests later re-reading of Ps 2 as eschatological.

Psalm 45 has perhaps the most obvious primary context of all the psalms, explicitly stated in the heading as a royal wedding. The king sits enthroned, resplendent in full regalia, surrounded by royal guests and lauded to the skies for his great virtues (vv. 2–9); the princess bride, arrayed in golden gown, enters the king's palace with her bridesmaids (vv. 10–15); and their future sons will perpetuate the dynasty (vv. 16–17). Rhetorically, it addresses in turn the reader (v. 1), the groom (vv. 2–9), the bride (vv. 10–15), and finally the happy couple (vv. 16–17).

However, within all this pomp and pageantry, v. 6a is problematic. The Hebrew is succinct, in typical poetic style, with four common Hebrew words and no significant textual variation. These words taken separately would normally mean "your-throne, God, always, and-ever," and their straightforward reading is therefore "Your throne, O God, will last forever and ever." There are four main interpretations of this phrase:

a) This refers to the king whom Israel considered divine, as in many surrounding nations. However, nowhere else in the Old Testament is this concept evident, as noted by Clines (above).

b) This refers to God, whom the poet turns to address directly. However, there is no indication of a change of addressee for this phrase from king to God,[33] or back again to the king afterwards. The whole section reads as an encomium to the king.

c) The term אֱלֹהִים is not the noun "God" but an adjective "godly," giving "Your godly throne..." in words addressed to the king.[34] However, אֱלֹהִים is an extremely common Hebrew term which always elsewhere is a noun meaning "God" (or occasionally "the gods"), not an adjective, and there are other grammatical ways (like the construct) to use a noun adjectivally.

---

[33] Possibly for the whole verse, since the "scepter of justice" (v. 6b) could be divine rather than human.

[34] So RSV (but not NRSV), NEB, JPS 1999 (also called NJPS).

Nevertheless, this could still be a unique form, and poetry often throws up unusual expressions.

d) The first Hebrew term is not the noun "throne" but a verb meaning "enthrone," giving "God has enthroned you."[35] In Hebrew, as in most languages, the same stem can be used for noun and verb. This neatly resolves the theological or rhetorical dilemma of other translations. It also gives the phrase the same grammatical structure as declarations earlier and later in the same psalm: "God has blessed you" (v. 2); "God has set you" (v. 7). It is true that there is no evidence elsewhere of this Hebrew stem used as verb, and that none of the ancient versions understood the term in this way. But the Old Testament has a significant number of unique words or grammatical forms, so this does not invalidate the interpretation. On the contrary, the distinctiveness may explain why later translators into Greek and other versions misunderstood this term, and aligned it with the stem's common meaning.[36]

In sum, unless we posit a unique reference to the king as divine, or an unscripted change of addressee, this phrase fits the rest of this hymn of praise to a king whose throne or enthronement is divinely blessed.

Psalm 110 has a military flavour, reminiscent of Ps 2. YHWH will extend the king's rule, his troops are poised, he will crush other kings and judge their nations, and be sustained in the task (vv. 2–3, 5–7). Alongside this are two significant proclamations. The first confers favoured status: "Sit at my right hand" (v. 1). The right hand was a common ancient metaphor for privileged relationship, even legal heir.[37] Here Ps 110 aligns with Pss 2 and 45 in conferring exceptional status on Israel's

---

[35] Its suffix is then the object of the verb (enthroned *you*), not the possessor of the noun (*your* throne). So REB, following M. Dahood, *Psalms 1–50*, AB 16 (New York: Doubleday, 1966), 273, and P. C. Craigie, *Psalms 1–50*, 366–67. For the second radical of a Piel form (כִּסַּאֲךָ, as denominative verb) with *shewa* and without *dagesh forte*, see GKC §52.d.

[36] They may also have interpreted the phrase in line with growing messianic expectation.

[37] See Pss 45:9; 80:17; 1 Kgs 2:19 (also Gen 48:14–20). In 7th century Assyria, the elderly Esarhaddon placed his younger son Ashurbanipal on his right hand as nominated successor, with the older, less favored son on his left.

king as God's key agent on earth.

The second proclamation is very different, and unique in the Old Testament: "You are a priest forever, in the order of Melchizedek" (v. 4). Melchizedek was the king of ancient Salem (the likely precursor of Jerusalem), about whom we have only one brief paragraph (Gen 14:18–20): after Abram defeated an invading coalition and rescued Lot, this "priest of God Most High" (אֵל עֶלְיוֹן) blessed Abram, who then presented him a tenth of the booty. The ancient world often attributed priestly status to kings, whose role included supporting numerous temples. Here Melchizedek simply pronounces a blessing, and offers food and drink.[38] Later, David himself is reported twice as performing sacrifice: after bringing the ark to Jerusalem, and after God stopped a plague (2 Sam 6:18–19; 24:25). These texts imply close personal involvement, though he could simply have overseen the ceremonies. The latter interpretation was obviously the case for Solomon after dedicating the temple, since "the king and all Israel with him offered sacrifices," and the enormous number of animals surely necessitated a professional priesthood (1 Kgs 8:62–63). So the king's function as priest could be largely titular and need not usurp the Levitical priesthood. In any case, the only recorded aspect of Melchizedek's priesthood was prayer and blessing.

Psalms 2, 45 and 110 are all quoted in the New Testament and their texts applied to Jesus. From Ps 2, the anointed one against whom the nations conspire is cited by Peter and John on release from detention (v. 1; Acts 4:25–26), the son-father decree by Paul preaching in Pisidian Antioch (v. 7; Acts 13:33; similarly Heb 1:5; 5:5), and the king's iron rule in the apocalypse (v. 9; Rev 2:27). From Ps 45, the everlasting throne and following lines are referenced in Hebrews (vv. 6–7; Heb 1:8–9). And from Ps 110, the most extensively quoted psalm, the opening royal elevation is applied by Jesus himself and then by Paul at Pentecost (v. 1; Matt 22:44; Mark 12:36; Luke 20:42; Acts 2:34); and both this and the Melchizedek oracle feature similarly in Hebrews (vv. 1, 4; Heb 1:13; 5:6; 7:17, 21; implicitly 12:2). Clearly Jesus,

---

[38] The text leaves unspecified whether the bread and wine are ritually significant or simply sustenance, and whether only intended for Abram or also for his men.

his apostles and the inspired writers read these psalms taking their grandiose language to its full extent, and thus seeing the only possible fulfilment in a messiah who surpassed human limits and expectations. This prophetic application does not negate an original contextual one, even if the earlier application is superseded by the later. It is a good example of *relecture* in light of wonderful new divine intervention.

5. Psalms and Endless Dominion

Psalm 72 begins with a prayer to God to "endow the king with justice," then continues as a statement of the many glorious benefits which a righteous king brings to his own people and indeed throughout the world. For Israel there will be prosperity for all and protection for the poor (vv. 2–4); the nations will bring tribute and offer service (vv. 5–11);[39] all peoples will prosper, and all the needy will be protected (vv. 12–17). Interspersed in this paean of praise are several grandiose claims that the king's rule will be flawless (vv. 2, 6, 17), limitless (vv. 8, 11, 17) and endless (as long as sun and moon, vv. 5–7, 17).

Such accolades easily outstripped David and Solomon, however godly the former and however large their joint empire, still more so their many successors. It clearly could not be realised by any human king, and would only be fulfilled to the letter by God incarnate in Jesus. Nevertheless, grandiose language was the vernacular of ancient royal courts and has remained so throughout the ages. Indeed, it continues to this day in the British national anthem, with "Long to reign over us" sung without embarrassment or irony to a nonagenarian monarch. It is difficult to deny the same use of hyperbole to ancient Israelites and Judeans affirming the divine promise to endow their king and his maximal role in the nation and the world—however much each successive holder of office failed to exemplify it.

Psalm 89 powerfully juxtaposes contradictory themes in the immediate aftermath of Jerusalem's catastrophic destruction. It opens with another glorious hymn of praise to YHWH (vv. 1–18), noting his unrivalled supremacy in the heavens (vv.

---

[39] The catena of accolades includes v. 9b, "may ... his enemies lick the dust," which echoes Gen 3:14; though here it is enemies who lick the dust, not a serpent who eats it.

5–8), his mighty creative power (vv. 9–13), his love, faithfulness and righteousness vis-à-vis his people (vv. 1–2, 14–18), and most notably his unending covenant with David (vv. 3–4). The next section (vv. 19–37)[40] elaborates this at length in terms similar to Ps 72, and even surpasses it in the specifics of longevity: he will be faithful to YHWH; his rule will be irresistible and extensive; and his line will be endless despite the many failings of his offspring. But the third section (vv. 38–45) apparently contradicts this: God has rejected the Davidic king and renounced the covenant, while city and palace now lie ruined. The psalm closes (vv. 46–51) with a prayer for restoration: "where is your former great love, which in your faithfulness you swore to David?" (v. 49).

Psalms 72 and 89 use similar hyperbolically grandiose language of the king, with the subtle differences that in the former a psalmist provides the royal depiction, attributed generally to "the king," whereas in the latter YHWH himself has given the description, attributed specifically to David. Again though, this could only be truly fulfilled in "great David's greater son." However, Ps 89 differs substantially from Ps 72 in that it acknowledges the rupture of covenant and its promise, and then longs for its renewal. Implicitly it pleads for restoration of the Davidic monarchy, and the psalmist's horizon remains national and immediate, not international and atemporal.

Neither of these psalms is directly quoted in the New Testament, though some of their prominent themes are clearly echoed there: universal blessing through an individual (Ps 72:17; Luke 1:48 of Mary); unending reign (Ps 89:4; Luke 1:33 of Jesus); and status as God's firstborn (Ps 89:27; Col 1:15). This illustrates the way the New Testament writers mine the language and theology of their ancient Scriptures, instinctively as well as explicitly, to describe Jesus the Messiah.

---

[40] The catalogue of accomplishments includes v. 23a, "I will crush his foes...," which echoes Gen 3:15; though here it is YHWH striking the foes, not the woman's seed crushing the serpent, and the verb is כתת (Piel), not שׁוּף. Nevertheless, Tate, *Psalms 51–100*, 423, notes the cosmic language of the section and warns against interpreting it in purely sociogeographic terms.

6. Psalms, Death and New Life

Psalm 22, titled "Davidic," for its first two-thirds is the intensely graphic prayer of a person feeling abandoned by the God he trusted, and instead surrounded by savage enemies who taunt him verbally and threatened him physically (vv. 1–21). But its final third changes: first it expects divine deliverance (as do many laments) and promises praise and vow-fulfilment in the great assembly (vv. 22–26); then it widens the horizons of praise in space and time, to all nations and unborn generations (vv. 27–31). The main part relates an experience of extreme anguish. If written by David himself, it could express his pre-royal experience as an outlaw hunted by Saul, or his later royal humiliation when on the run from his usurper son Absalom. The concluding third would then present a royal perspective of leading worship and of limitless praise. If written by an unknown psalmist (and later included in a Davidic collection) it reflects an equally harrowing experience and an equally strong faith—indeed, all the more so for a psalmist lacking the benefit of royal perspective.

For Jesus and the New Testament writers, Ps 22 was more than an Israelite evocation of extreme suffering and unquenchable faith. It was a prefiguring of the unique suffering and status of Jesus himself. Jesus quotes its opening words in that moment of indescribable isolation from God the Father, and various other verses are used by the evangelists to depict his anguish on the cross.[41] For the author of Hebrews, the psalmist's praise amongst his people betokens Jesus' identification with (and sanctification of) the Christian family.[42] The traumatic experience of the abandoned, taunted and death-bound psalmist becomes an uncanny portrayal of the unimaginable suffering and death of Jesus.

Psalm 16, also titled "Davidic," is a prayer of a troubled individual who sides with "holy people" rather than idolaters (vv. 2–4),[43] but primarily expresses faith in

---

[41] Cf. Matt 27:34–35, 43, 46; Mark 15:24, 29, 34; Luke 23:34; John 19:24. These cite variously Ps 22:1, 7, 8, 18.

[42] Heb 2:11–12, citing Ps 22:22.

[43] There is uncertainty over the identity of "holy people" (קְדוֹשִׁים), as noted widely by commentators and in NIV 1984 footnote. However, this does not affect the interpretation of the final verses.

God as his refuge, counsellor and security (vv. 1, 5–8). This faith leads him to the startling affirmation that God will not abandon "me / your faithful one" to Sheol or to decay in a grave, but instead will furnish unending joy "in your presence" (vv. 10–11).

This is startling in its ancient context, since there was no developed sense of the afterlife in Israel: death was the end of meaningful existence; there was a shadowy ill-described underworld called Sheol; its denizens somehow persisted in somnolent inactivity; there was no further communion with God, who should therefore be worshipped during this life on earth; Sheol is seen as a fitting fate for the wicked, but rarely for the godly; but there is no alternative for the godly, apart from a few rare glimpses.[44]

Given this backdrop, many scholars interpret the rare glimpses of continued communion with God as the psalmists' fear of an early death (as often desired for their enemies), and their desire instead to prolong their experience of God in this life. However, while the number of dissenting texts is small, they are sufficient in number and content to argue that within Israel there was a strand of faith which looked to an alternative outcome.[45] As I have summarised elsewhere: "The form of this continued communion with God remains tantalizingly vague: no spatial location is indicated, no name (contrasting with the name Sheol) is mentioned, no fellow beneficiaries are acknowledged – in fact no details are given at all."[46] Nonetheless, this psalmist and a few other Israelites hoped for some form of God-centred future for themselves.

For Christians, there is the further interpretation in the New Testament. At Pentecost Peter quoted this passage as David predicting Jesus' resurrection, since

---

[44] For detailed argument and full references, see P. S. Johnston, *Shades of Sheol: Death and Afterlife in the Old Testament* (Leicester: Apollos, 2002). This research is summarised in various dictionary articles, notably: *NDBT*, 443–47; *DOT:P*, 532–36; *DOT:HB*, 215–19; *DOT:WPW*, 5–8; *DOT:Pr*, 1–5; *NIDB* 5, 277; *OEBT* 2, 399–402.

[45] These glimpses occur particularly in Pss 16, 49 and 73 (possibly also 17), and in the resurrection verses of Isa 26:19 and Dan 12:2.

[46] *Shades of Sheol*, 201–202. This section summarizes an earlier article: P. S. Johnston, "'Left in Hell'? Psalm 16, Sheol and the Holy One," in *The Lord's Anointed*, ed. P. E. Satterthwaite *et al.* (Carlisle: Paternoster, 1995), 213–22.

David "died and was buried" (Acts 2:29).[47] Peter takes the reference to Sheol and decay literally, and gives a *relecture* of the Psalms as predictive proof of Jesus' resurrection. The new reading, however glorious for the first believers and all since, does not negate the original Davidic hope; it simply bursts its bounds in a previously unimaginable way in applying it to the one who fulfilled all Israel's hopes and dreams.

7. Conclusion

As noted at the start, many Christians use the psalms regularly and profitably, and have already developed good reading strategies. These are often instinctive rather than articulated, often moulded over the years by godly instruction in home or church. Nevertheless, it is valuable to try to summarise these, noting good practice to emulate and difficulties to avoid.

First, much of the contents of the psalms can be appropriated directly to the Christian today. These ancient prayers of ordinary believers in a different dispensation speak from the human heart to God above. Even after the coming of the Messiah and the gift of the Spirit, they can still wonderfully encapsulate our prayers. Their directness and vividness in praise and distress cuts through our often cerebral approach to express our deepest emotions, and teaches us how to be fully ourselves before God. These prayers were adapted, generalised, sometimes anonymised, reapplied to new circumstances, then collected and edited over the millennium before Christ. Christians today can join this long tradition of fruitful reapplication, and make the psalms their own.

At the same time, the psalms remain part of a different dispensation. They reflect a very different spiritual era with aspects which do not apply to Christians: ethnic nation, geographical territory, chosen capital, king and dynasty. Their religious practice and outlook are often foreign to us: sacrifice and temple, vows and oaths, divinely revealed civil law, communal culpability, capital punishment, human vengeance, and perspectives on death. Christian readers often instinctively overlook these elements, but spelling them out reminds us that we cannot and must not assume

---

[47] Ps 16:8–11; Acts 2:25–28. This interpretation is repeated by Paul in Pisidian Antioch (Acts 13:35–37).

the psalms are necessarily Christian prayers. The addition of a doxology like "Glory be to the Father" does not baptise a psalm, *pace* many liturgies. Nor does the judicious use of square brackets around problematic verses such as the vengeful elements of Ps 137 (vv. 7–9) or Ps 139 (vv. 19–22), or the non-penitential coda of Ps 51 (vv. 18–19), *pace* some lectionaries. In reading the psalms, we are reminded that we read Israelite Scripture, all of which is pre-Christian, and some of which is non-Christian in that it has been surpassed by a new revelation. We must read and appropriate this ancient prayer through a Christian lens. Thankfully, many a traditional hymn gives us a good model for this, e.g., "Saviour, if, of Zion's city, I, *through grace*, a member am…"

Finally, Christians will read the psalms through the messiah of the New Testament. They rejoice that many of the impossibly grandiose royal descriptions were gloriously fulfilled in Jesus. He confounded all messianic expectations, especially at the extremes of human experience: in his humility in life, humiliation in death and triumph in resurrection. But beyond the use of a few psalms in doctrine and apologetics, Christians follow Jesus as the model reader of the psalms: he inhabited them throughout his life, expressed their joy and praise in his own prayers, experienced their difficulties and anguish, was surrounded by enemies without taking vengeance, plumbed the depth of separation, and by rising from death showed what truly lies beyond it. We do not need to look for a Christology for every psalm, let alone every verse. But we can and must reread all the psalms in the light of Jesus, and recontextualize them in the light of the whole New Testament.

WISDOM'S TESTIMONY TO MESSIAH'S SUFFERINGS AND GLORY

—*Graeme Goldsworthy*

1. Introduction

There is a logic to Biblical Theology that suggests that the study of any theme should begin at the beginning, that is, with the earliest expressions of the theme in the Old Testament's narrative framework. I personally favor starting with our own situation as Christians by looking at how the developed theme is dealt with in the New Testament, and especially at how it effects the presentation of Jesus as the Christ. Constant references or allusions in the Gospels to Old Testament antecedents mean that we will need then to go back to look at those antecedents, all the time engaging in the hermeneutic spiral by adjusting our understanding of the Old by the New and *vice versa*.

2. Jesus as Israel's true Wise Man

The Gospels depict Jesus as the Wise Man of Israel *par excellence*. In his account of the postresurrection appearances of Jesus, Luke gives a comprehensive view on the relationship of Jesus to the Old Testament Scriptures (Luke 24:25–27, 44–49). It is reasonable to conclude from this pericope that Jesus claims that the whole of the Old Testament, including the wisdom books, testify to him.[1] Furthermore, there is a continuity between the Old Testament wisdom distinctives and wisdom in the New Testament. Collectively, the Gospels portray Jesus as the ultimate Wise Man in what he taught, and how he did so, including his use of the well-worn idioms of the wisdom literature. But, the very process whereby Jesus showed himself to be the wise man of Israel inevitably aroused tensions between his definitive wisdom and the wisdom of

---

[1] Luke 24:44 indicates that all three parts of the תנך testify to Jesus. This includes the כתובים, which contains the wisdom literature, and almost certainly is referred to under Jesus' heading of "Psalms."

162

those who opposed him. Similar tensions existed within Old Testament wisdom, particularly in Job and Ecclesiastes. Hans Heinrich Schmid referred to that situation as "the crisis of wisdom."[2] In Job, the crisis is seen in the clash of ideas between Job and his companions. These *friends* try to apply a rigid view of natural retribution to Job's situation.[3] They are not totally in error, but they cannot see that the retributive perspective of empirical and proverbial wisdom does not apply here, for Job is indeed a righteous man. In the Gospels, there is a similar clash between the wisdom of Jesus and the distorted wisdom of the contemporary Jewish teachers. This crisis highlights the way in which the Gospels show Jesus to be the source of wisdom, thus being greater than the sages of Israel (Matt 7:28–29). This is one aspect of the widening hermeneutical divide between Jesus and the Jewish teachers who fail to acknowledge him as Messiah.

The only Gospel record of Jesus as a growing child is in the account of the twelve-year-old boy among the wise men at the temple: "And the child grew and became strong, filled with wisdom. And the favor of God was upon him" (Luke 2:40).[4] It concludes with: "And Jesus increased in wisdom and in stature and in favor with God and man" (Luke 2:52). We note, then, that on the one hand, Jesus taught using the rhetoric of wisdom, and on the other hand, while his wisdom amazed some, it was so completely unacceptable to the commonly held wisdom of his Jewish contemporaries that he was rejected by them and even hated. As to his rhetoric, Jesus uses lists, a characteristic of wisdom (Matt 5:1–11); he was a master of metaphor and the parable (Matt 5:13–16; 7:12–20). He concluded his Sermon on the Mount with a classic contrast of the wise man and the fool that is a feature of the Book of Proverbs.[5] Matthew's comment on this is that Jesus spoke unlike the scribes, the successors to the sages, in that he not only possessed wisdom, but was the source of it and thus had unique authority (Matt 7:24–29). The growing conflict between Jesus and the scribes and Pharisees marks

---

[2] Hans Heinrich Schmid, *Wesen und Geschichte der Weisheit* (Berlin: Alfred Töpelmann, 1966), 173–95.

[3] That is, wise actions lead to good outcomes, and foolish actions lead to bad outcomes.

[4] Unless otherwise indicated, biblical citations are from the ESV.

[5] Especially in Prov 10–15.

a new crisis in Israel's wisdom that would lead eventually to the cross.

One key passage in this regard is Luke 11:29–54 dealing with the conflict between Jesus and the Jewish teachers. The queen of the south, a Gentile who was versed in the wisdom of the ancient Near East (1 Kgs 10:1–9), came to hear the wisdom of Solomon but, says Jesus, "something greater than Solomon is here" (Luke 11:31). Solomon's wisdom included the glories of his kingdom (1 Kgs 3–4 along with 1 Kgs 10 form a wisdom *inclusio* around chapters 5 to 9); a messianic glory that is now outshone by Jesus the Messiah, the true fount of wisdom. Luke's account follows with woes against Israel's teachers for their blindness and hypocrisy (Luke 11:37–54). Jesus accuses them of having taken away the key of knowledge, that is, of wisdom (Luke 11:52).

Matthew gathers many of the parables of Jesus together in a way that indicates how they functioned. They are the משלים of Jesus, and through the explanations that he gives to his bemused disciples he emphasizes the wisdom dimension. He explains the Parable of the Sower as belonging to those who not only hear, but who are attuned to God's wisdom. The quoted words of Isa 6:9–10 expand the implication of the "fear of Yahweh" as the key to wisdom and truth (Matt 13:10–17). That Jesus spoke to the crowds in parables is explained by the wisdom introduction to Ps 78.[6]

> All these things Jesus said to the crowds in parables; indeed, he said nothing
> to them without a parable. This was to fulfil what was spoken by the prophet:
> "I will open my mouth in parables [אפתחה במשל פי in Ps 78:2 MT];[7]
> I will utter what has been hidden since the foundation of world" (Matt
> 13:34–35).

As with the explanation of the Sower, Jesus here increases the sense that the wisdom of the parables is imparted to those who are already on the inside; they are the ones "who have" and to whom more will be given (Matt 13:10–13). This

---

[6] See below, section *3.5. Wisdom in the Psalms.*

[7] Literally, "I will open my mouth in a מָשָׁל." The translation of מָשָׁל as "parable" agrees with the LXX's: ἀνοίξω ἐν παραβολαῖς τὸ στόμα μου except that the latter uses the plural and is a possible source of Matthew's quotation. The LXX translates מָשָׁל as παραβολή in a number of places, including Deut 28:37; 1 Sam 10:12; 24:14; 2 Chr 7:20; Prov 1:6; Jer 24:9; and Ezek 12:22, 23; 18:2, 3.

reinforces the rubric to Proverbs that the fear of the LORD is the beginning of wisdom and knowledge. This rubric, in turn, constitutes the ancient Hebrew equivalent of the presuppositional perspective on the understanding of reality.[8]

3. Wisdom, Creation and World Order in the Old Testament

The New Testament testimony to Christ as Wisdom, provides a vital link between the person of Messiah and wisdom. The dramas of the four Gospels portray a wisdom in Christ that arouses opposition from the false wisdom of the scribes and Pharisees, and that is theologized by the Epistles as they show the salvific function of God's true wisdom in Christ. In doing so they embrace the moral dimension of righteousness as a matter of disorder being remedied, and of sin-warped order being redeemed through the perfect order of the incarnate God. The moral revolt of humanity in Gen 3, and of subsequent human history, is dealt with by the righteousness of God through the suffering, death and resurrection of Messiah.

Where did the Christology of wisdom spring from; what are its Old Testament antecedents? In dealing with the overall picture, let us take the matter of creation first. According to Prov 8:22–31 creation is the expression of God's wisdom. The personification of wisdom in this passage is, of course, a metaphor describing the creation as the original expression in time and space of the wisdom of God. Personified Wisdom speaks thus in Prov 8:22–31:

> [22] The LORD possessed me at the beginning of his work,
>
> the first of his acts of old.
>
> [23] Ages ago I was set up,
>
> at the first, before the beginning of the earth.

---

[8] The modern version of such presuppositionalism has been expounded and defended by Cornelius Van Til, e.g., in his "My Credo," in *Jerusalem and Athens: Critical Discussions on the Philosophy and Apologetics of Cornelius Van Til*, ed. E. R. Geehan, (Phillipsburg: Presbyterian and Reformed, 1971), 1–21; Cornelius Van Til, *The Defense of the Faith* (Philadelphia: Presbyterian and Reformed, 1975). See also Greg L. Bahnsen, *Van Til's Apologetic: Readings and Analysis* (Phillipsburg: P & R Publishing, 1998). This approach echoes Anselm's *"Credo ut intelligam,"* (I believe in order to understand), which harkens back to a similar statement by Augustine.

[24] When there were no depths I was brought forth,

   when there were no springs abounding with water.

[25] Before the mountains had been shaped,

   before the hills, I was brought forth,

[26] before he had made the earth with its fields,

   or the first of the dust of the world.

[27] When he established the heavens, I was there;

   when he drew a circle on the face of the deep,

[28] when he made firm the skies above,

   when he established the fountains of the deep,

[29] when he assigned to the sea its limit,

   so that the waters might not transgress his command,

   when he marked out the foundations of the earth,

[30] then I was beside him, like a master workman,

   and I was daily his delight,

   rejoicing before him always,

[31] rejoicing in his inhabited world

   and delighting in the children of man.

In verses 22–26 wisdom appears as having pre-existed while there was no ordered universe. In the beginning, wisdom was "possessed," "set up," "brought forth," "there," and "with him." Then, in verses 27–31, God creates, and establishes order and bounds for the various aspects of creation. So, it is said that God "established," "drew a circle," "made firm," "assigned a limit," and "marked out." The result is that God rejoices in wisdom and in its result: the world and the human race.

In the opening verses of the creation narrative chaos is overcome by God's creation of order. First there is תהו ובהו (Gen 1:2, "a formless void" NRSV), after which God establishes order by the creation of the various parts of the whole on separate days which are ordered by evening and morning. Light is separated from darkness; day from night; the waters above from the waters below; the sea from the dry land; the sun from the moon; the fish from the birds; each species of animal from the others. And man, male and female, alone is created in the image and likeness of God. The overarching order is settled by authority: God has spoken as supreme Lord over all his creation; he dictates to mankind its delegated sovereignty over the rest of creation; thus, the ordered hierarchy is established: God, man, world.

The second creation narrative (Gen 2:4–25) looks more closely at the ordering of human existence in terms of woman created out of man. Adam's naming of the animals establishes the distinction between the fitting female human helper for the male and all other living things. In naming the animals Adam exercises his God-given dominion, and also engages in the wisdom activity of making lists for classification. Then there is the order of marriage, which includes maintaining the distinction between the man and the woman while asserting their unity as "one flesh." This unity-distinction is part of being in the image of God, in whom such unity-distinction is a trinitarian property.

In God's judgment on Man's sin, an act of "un-creation" confuses the original order of creation (Gen 3:14–19). The human pair have repudiated the authority of God in favor of autonomous self-authentication. God's role as the creator who establishes order and relationships is rejected. This revolt against the person of the Creator and against the order that reflects his character, is a radical moral revolt that cannot be separated from the epistemological re-alignment. Because it is a moral revolt against the personal relationship between God and humans, any restoration of order must deal with the moral problem of lost righteousness. Furthermore, this righteousness in mankind reflects the righteousness of God which wisdom tells us has to do with order.[9]

In their rebellion, the humans have adopted a totally different presuppositional starting point for understanding reality. The most surprising element in the whole episode is that God did not end it there with the destruction of the entire creation. We subsequently learn that God had planned from all eternity that his response to human rebellion would be an expression of his mercy and grace. Such mercy and grace will

---

[9] The defining of righteousness in God and man as self-consistent orderliness was proposed by Hans Heinrich Schmid, *Gerechtigkeit als Weltordnung*, BHT 40 (Tübingen: Mohr Siebeck), 1968.

need to deal with the moral issue involved in the breakdown of personal relationships. We thus also learn that it is the prime expression of the wisdom of God, not only to create all things, but also to redeem his creation and to bring in a new creation. Human descent into disorder and unrighteousness will be redressed. The promised redress begins with Gen 3:15 and is expounded from then on in the covenant of grace.

4. Order and Creation: The Limits of Wisdom in the Wisdom Books of the Old Testament

The Christology of wisdom raises serious questions about the fragmentation of the biblical witness by those who assess Israel's wisdom as being out of touch with covenant theology. Nevertheless, we need to try to understand to what extent the Wisdom literature of the Old Testament provides sustainable antecedents for the wisdom Christology of the New Testament.[10]

4.1. Proverbs and the Perception of Order and Righteousness

The Book of Proverbs contains literary types, or idioms, that characterize empirical Wisdom as it focuses on the learning of wisdom from life's concrete experiences. The literary types in Proverbs include the short sentence aphorisms, the longer instructions, and the numerical sayings. Proverbial wisdom is always qualified by the rubric of the fear of Yahweh (Prov 1:7; 9:10).[11] As we observe the operation of retribution in Proverbs, we cannot escape the moral implications. Thus, the binary opposites of the wise and the foolish are constantly matched by the opposition of the righteous and the wicked (e.g., Prov 10–15). I suggest this device establishes the moral nature of wisdom and folly: righteousness is to wisdom as wickedness is to folly. Thus, while it is easy to regard retribution in Proverbs as purely natural, it is clear that such

---

[10] I have discussed this at greater length in my book, *Gospel and Wisdom: Israel's Wisdom Literature in the Christian Life* (Exeter: Paternoster, 1987), now included in *The Goldsworthy Trilogy* (Milton Keynes: Paternoster, 2000).

[11] One of the most substantial studies of "the fear of Yahweh" was done by Joachim Becker, *Gottesfurcht im Alten Testament,* AnBib 25 (Rome: Papal Biblical Institute, 1965). See also Roland E. Murphy, *The Tree of Life: An Exploration of Biblical Wisdom Literature* (Grand Rapids: Eerdmans, 1990), 16, 126 and Leo G. Perdue, *Wisdom and Creation: The Theology of Wisdom Literature* (Nashville: Abingdon, 1994), 79.

retribution belongs to the judgment of God who is righteous.

It has been rightly pointed out that the sentence literature of Proverbs arises from concrete events in human existence.[12] When, over time, one person's notable experience is shared by others, concrete events can be generalized but the original context is never eliminated completely. Thus, an aspect of empirical wisdom is learning when it is appropriate to apply an aphorism or proverb. For example, Prov 26:4–5 juxtaposes seemingly incompatible sayings that demand consideration of the circumstances to which each may apply. Failure to learn this lesson leads to the crisis of wisdom exhibited by Job's companions. One of the characteristics of the empirical wisdom of Proverbs is the constant activity of abstraction in order to show how different things belong together. Order is the presupposition, but often difficult to discern. We see this in the numerical sayings, for example:

> There are six things that the LORD hates,
>
> Seven that are an abomination to him (Prov 6:16).

Or:

> The leech has two daughters;
>
> "Give" and "Give" they cry.
>
> Three things are never satisfied;
>
> Four never say, "Enough" (Prov 30:15).[13]

But, through all this, Proverbs maintains the limits of human wisdom so that it is always subject to the sovereign will of God: "Many are the plans in the mind of a man, but it is the purpose of the LORD that will stand" (Prov 19:21).[14]

---

[12] Harmut Gese, *Lehre und Wirklichkeit in der alten Weisheit: Studien zu den Sprüchen Salomos und zu dem Buche Hiob* (Tübingen: Mohr Siebeck, 1958), 33–35; William McKane, *Proverbs: A New Approach*, OTL (Philadelphia: Westminster, 1970), 413–15; James G. Williams, *Those Who Ponder Proverbs: Aphoristic Thinking and Biblical Literature* (Sheffield: The Almond Press, 1981), 35–39.

[13] The formula n, n+1 is employed in a way that invites the reader to supply n+2, n+3 and n+x; that is, to include other things that can be classified with this group (Prov 6:16–19; 30:15–31). R. N. Whybray, *Proverbs*, NCBC (Grand Rapids: Eerdmans, 1994), 99–100; Raymond C. Ortlund, *Proverbs: Wisdom that Works* (Wheaton, IL: Crossway, 2012), 103.

[14] So also Prov 16:33.

4.2. Job and the Mystery of Hidden Order

While the main purpose of Job may appear, at first glance, to be a reflection on the problem of suffering, there are other matters that concern us here even if they are dealt with in the context of a righteous man who suffers. Three aspects of this book should be considered. First, there is the lengthy center section given over to the arguments with Job made by his four companions. These men illustrate the crisis of wisdom in that, for them, the paradigm of natural retribution becomes set in concrete and leads them to the wrong conclusion that Job's suffering is divine retribution for sin. The empirical connection between deed and outcome tends to indicate that bad deeds beget evil, good deeds beget good; Job experiences evil and thus must have sinned grievously. Yet, on the contrary, we know Job is righteous (Job 1:1, 8; 2:9–10). Second, the heart of the book is arguably articulated in Job's reflections in chapter 28. Here he deals with the mystery, the hiddenness, and surpassing value of wisdom which is ultimately known only to God. The theme of this soliloquy, that follows on from the previous chapter, is "where shall wisdom be found?" (Job 28:12) God alone truly understands wisdom, as shown by the way he ordered his creation (Job 28:20–27). Third, the solution to Job's desire to understand his suffering is that he is rebuked by God for his trying to plumb the depths of God's mind and wisdom. Job's "words without knowledge" (Job 38:2) lead to the series of blistering rhetorical questions beginning with, "Where were you when I laid the foundation of the earth?" (Job 38:4 ESV).

4.3. Ecclesiastes and the Corrupt Misuse of Wisdom

Of the biblical Wisdom books, Ecclesiastes is in many ways the most difficult to assess and has arguably aroused the greatest variety of interpretations. I have suggested elsewhere that it can be said to deal with the confusion of order.[15] Whatever the order expressed in the wisdom of Proverbs, and the protest in Job against the absolutizing of proverbial wisdom, Ecclesiastes expresses the reality of the pervading sickness of human wisdom. Commentators who see Ecclesiastes as dealing with a variety of human world-views, rejecting them as vanity, may be right.

---

[15] Goldsworthy, *Gospel and Wisdom*, ch. 8.

But, another dimension is the confusion within Israel's wisdom; the crisis of wisdom to end all crises! Qoheleth cries out for the redemption of human wisdom, even of the gifted wisdom of God's own people who struggle to be responsible in the world confused by sin. More than Proverbs or Job, Ecclesiastes illustrates and warns against the dangers of wisdom that has been detached from the salvation history of Israel. When a comprehensive world view, the goal of all philosophies, is attempted without the world view that is given by revelation of creation and redemption, it will evaporate and be as breath (Qoheleth's "vanity").

4.4. Wisdom in the Psalms

Scholars have long proposed that some Psalms are wisdom compositions. There has been some agreement over a few individual Psalms but, as with the identification of wisdom in other places, there has been little consensus. Elsewhere I have examined the relationship of empirical wisdom and salvation history in certain Psalms including Pss 25, 78, 111, 128 and 133.[16] Regarding wisdom in Psalms, Donn Morgan comments:

> Therefore, regardless of whether or not these psalms with wisdom characteristics testify to an active part by the wise in psalmody, it is clear that the Psalter witnesses to an interrelationship between the wisdom tradition and the cult, an interrelationship which must be taken seriously.... The virtual universal agreement that Ps 1 is a wisdom psalm is quite significant, for it provides an important framework for understanding the Psalter as a whole.[17]

Psalm 78 is relevant to our enquiry because it treats a crucial part of salvation history, the exodus from Egypt and the process of getting into the promised land, as a wisdom lesson. The related events are portrayed as a parable, or a wisdom instruction, that leads from the chaos of rebellious Israel to the establishment of order by David.

---

[16] G. Goldsworthy, "Empirical Wisdom in Relation to Salvation-History in the Psalms," Unpublished Ph. D. thesis, Union Theological Seminary in Virginia, 1973.

[17] Donn F. Morgan, *Wisdom in the Old Testament Traditions* (Atlanta: John Knox, 1981), 125, 128.

The psalmist begins as a wisdom teacher:

> Give ear, O my people, to my teaching;
>
> incline your ears to the words of my mouth!
>
> I will open my mouth in a parable;
>
> I will utter dark sayings from of old,
>
> things that we have heard and known,
>
> that our fathers have told us (Ps 78:1–3).

But he quickly moves on deal with a significant part of salvation history; the glorious deeds of the LORD (Ps 78:4–5). This involves the giving of the covenant law which they were to teach to their children (Ps 78:5–8). Their consequent disobedience showed that they had forgotten the miracles of the exodus from Egypt (Ps 78:9–16, 32–37, 42–55). Despite this, God is compassionate (Ps 78:23–29, 38–39), yet they remain stubborn. The solution to this is the election of Judah and David. Here then is the good shepherd of God's people: וירעם כתם לבבו ובתבונות כפיו ינחם (Ps 78:72). Translations of this final line vary, but we should note the use of the wisdom word תבונה. The ESV has: "and guided them with his skillful hand," which is a rather vague metaphor. I propose that the wisdom nature of this psalm would allow the translation: "and he guided them in the wisdom of his rule."

5. Wisdom, Covenant, and Redemptive History

5.1. Wisdom before Solomon

Scripture is interested in wisdom as a human trait that reflects the wisdom of God; the intelligence of animals is not the issue.[18] Basic to this concern is the creation of man in the image of God and the manifestation of this relationship in the way God speaks to his image. Humankind is thus defined first and foremost, not in physiological, evolutionary, psychological, or sociological terms, but in terms of relationships: first to God, then to other humans, and to the world. The earliest

---

[18] Although Proverbs sometimes uses animal or insect behavior as object lessons from which we can gain wisdom: Prov 6:6–9; 26:2–3, 11; 30:18–19, 24–31.

references to wisdom (חכמה) have to do with the skill of craftsmanship of those charged with the construction of the tabernacle (Exod 28:3, 31:3, 6; 35:26, 31, 35; 36:1–2). This skill is seen as an endowment of the Spirit of God. Next, Israel's obedience to God's Law will be its wisdom (Deut 4:6). Joshua is anointed with wisdom in order to assume Moses' role as leader (Deut 34:9). Wisdom is thus connected with the foretaste of the sanctuary that will become the glory of Solomon's wisdom, and with the leadership that foreshadows David's messianic role in history and prophecy. Wisdom is to a degree institutionalized with David's recourse to counsellors. With the monarchy, intelligent and godly human consideration appears to be replacing more direct prophetic revelation from God.[19]

5.2. The Wisdom of Solomon

It is surely not fortuitous that Israel's wisdom flourishes and reaches its height at the same time as, and within the ambit of, the zenith of covenant redemptive history in the reign of Solomon. In other words, the foreshadowing of the gospel reaches its fulness with David and Solomon and provides the framework for decision-making. Solomon has been declared to be the son of God in the covenant with David (2 Sam 7:12–14). But the manner of his covenant status is shown in 1 Kgs 3–10 to be the glories of Israel's power in the promised land with the temple as God's dwelling. Around the description of the temple being built and dedicated, along with the glories and riches of Solomon's kingdom, there is the *inclusio* of Solomon's wisdom and its function as a light to the Gentiles in 1 Kgs 3–4 and 10. That Proverbs is attributed to Solomon is surely significant. I believe that if those biblical theologians that worry about the lack of covenant and redemptive history in the Wisdom books had started with the history of wisdom in Israel, rather than with the Wisdom literature, they would have found that wisdom and covenant theologies are not only friends but have a symbiotic relationship.

---

[19] Goldsworthy, *Gospel and Wisdom*, 53–59.

5.3. Wisdom and Prophetic Eschatology

First, we note the prevalence of the crisis of wisdom in that a false wisdom needs be identified and renounced by the prophets. Such spurious wisdom will perish and with it the so-called wise men who have rejected the word of the LORD. Their treachery is against the covenant of salvation which stems from the wisdom of God (Isa 5:21; 29:14; 31:1–2; 44:24–25; Jer 4:22; 8:8–9). The wisdom of the world is condemned in the behavior of some of the nations that impinged upon Israel's history and cause her suffering (Isa 19:11–12; Jer 49:7; 51:57; Ezek 28:11–12, 17).

The positive side of wisdom within redemptive history is found in the way it is said to characterize the messianic kings and the promise of renewal of God's people. In Isa 9:6 (MT 5) the messianic child born to God's people is described as פלא יועץ ("a wonder of a counsellor"). He is the counsellor *par excellence* given to rule from the throne of David. Likewise, Isa 11:2–3 describes the messianic shoot from Jesse's root in terms that, in the use of distinctively wisdom words, match the description of personified wisdom in Prov 8:12–15:[20]

Isaiah 11:2–3	Proverbs 8:12–15
And the Spirit of the LORD shall rest upon him, the Spirit of wisdom [חכמה] and understanding [בינה], the Spirit of counsel [עצה] and might [גבורה], the Spirit of knowledge [דעת] and the fear of the LORD [יראת יהוה]. And his delight shall be in the fear of the LORD.	I, wisdom [חכמה], dwell with prudence, and I find knowledge [דעת] and discretion [מזמות]. The fear of the LORD [יראת יהוה] is hatred of evil. Pride and arrogance and the way of evil and perverted speech I hate. I have counsel [עצה] and sound wisdom; I have insight [בינה]; I have strength [גבורה]. By me kings reign, and rulers decree what is just.

Once again, we find wisdom as a key characteristic of the Davidic messiah.[21] Isaiah's

---

[20] Goldsworthy, *Gospel and Wisdom*, 122.

[21] The wisdom words and phrases common to both passages are: חכמה, דעת, יראת יהוה, עצה, and בינה. Although גבורה appears in both texts as an attribute of wisdom, it is not a distinctively wisdom idiom.

perspective is eschatological and foreshadows the Christ who is to come. But, the sage writing Prov 8 also spoke about more than he realized as he foreshadowed the Christ who was the Word of creation, and who became flesh for us (John 1:1–4, 14).

6. Paul's Wisdom Christology

6.1. 1 Corinthians 1–2; 2 Cor 1:12

While it is appealing to simply identify Paul's wisdom Christology (1 Cor 1:18–2:16) with the ethos of wisdom in the Old Testament Wisdom literature, we need to be clear that this connection exists theologically. Paul links wisdom with the suffering of Christ and our salvation. In 1 Corinthians, Paul's wisdom Christology grows out of his pastoral concern for a church that lacks unity (1 Cor 1:10–17). Disputes over baptism, spiritual gifts, and misuse of the Lord's Supper, all need to be dealt with in this "carnal" Corinthian church (1 Cor 3:1–3). Paul was sent to preach the gospel, and that not with words of eloquent wisdom—that is, the wisdom of the world. To the perishing, the cross is foolishness; to those being saved, it is the power of God (1 Cor 1:17–18). Here the crisis of wisdom is at its high-point as God's wisdom clashes with the wisdom of the world that Christians were all too prone to adopt. The wisdom of God in the gospel is folly to the world (1 Cor 1:18). Worldly wisdom is destroyed by the cross (1 Cor 1:18–19). Christ is both the power and wisdom of God (1 Cor 1:24). God's "foolishness" is wiser than men (1 Cor 1:25). What the world considers to be God's foolishness will shame the wise of the world (1 Cor 1:27). God has made Christ to be our wisdom, righteous, sanctification and redemption (1 Cor 1:30).

There is a certain ambiguity in the syntax of 1 Cor 1:30: ἐξ αὐτοῦ δὲ ὑμεῖς ἐστε ἐν Χριστῷ Ἰησοῦ, ὃς ἐγενήθη σοφία ἡμῖν ἀπὸ θεοῦ, δικαιοσύνη τε καὶ ἁγιασμὸς καὶ ἀπολύτρωσις. A literal translation is: "But from him you are in Christ Jesus, who has become wisdom to us from God: righteousness and sanctification and redemption." The KJV, NRSV (1989), and ESV all imply that wisdom is the first in a list of attributes. But the NIV takes a different approach: "It is because of him that you are in Christ Jesus, who has become for us wisdom from God — that is, our righteousness, holiness, and redemption."

The exegetical question is whether Paul makes "wisdom" the first of a series of attributes, or whether he defines "wisdom" epexegetically by "righteousness and sanctification and redemption." I believe it is reasonable to propose the latter: God has made Christ to be our wisdom, which includes all the rest. Because the Greek places ἀπὸ θεοῦ, after ὃς ἐγενήθη σοφία ἡμῖν the NIV treats δικαιοσύνη τε καὶ ἁγιασμὸς καὶ ἀπολύτρωσις as epexegetical and inserts the clarifying "that is" before this list. On this view Christ, as our wisdom, means that the fulness of our redemption is our wisdom in Christ. This certainly accords with the various statements about the wisdom of God in 1 Cor 1 and 2 where wisdom refers to the saving work of God in Christ. Nevertheless, the use of τε after δικαιοσύνη may allow the reading as a series.

6.2. Ephesians 1:7–10, 17; 3:10

Wisdom also figures in Paul's hymn of praise in Eph 1:7–10. This passage is important for our consideration of the link between wisdom and redemption:

> In him we have redemption through his blood, the forgiveness of our
> trespasses, according to the riches of his grace, which he lavished upon us,
> in all wisdom and insight [ἐν πάσῃ σοφίᾳ καὶ φρονήσει] making known
> to us the mystery of his will, according to his purpose, which he set forth
> in Christ as a plan for the fullness of time, to unite all things in him, things
> in heaven and things on earth.

Verse 10 in the Greek is εἰς οἰκονομίαν τοῦ πληρώματος τῶν καιρῶν, ἀνακεφαλαιώσασθαι τὰ πάντα ἐν τῷ Χριστῷ, τὰ ἐπὶ τοῖς οὐρανοῖς καὶ τὰ ἐπὶ τῆς γῆς ἐν αὐτῷ. Here Paul says that it is God's wisdom and insight by which he has revealed his will, in the fulness of time, to sum up all things in Christ. I take ἀνακεφαλαιώσασθαι to mean more than making Christ head *over* all things as ruler. Thus, I cannot agree with those commentators that confine this "summing up" or "uniting" to the eschatological process leading to the consummation at the return of Christ in glory.[22] The eschatological fulfilment of all God's promises was *within* the

---

[22] E.g., Francis Foulkes, *Ephesians,* TNTC (London: Tyndale Press, 1963); Peter T. O'Brien,

God-Man of the incarnation (2 Cor 1:20). God's wisdom is shown in that he first restores the order of the universe (things in heaven and things on earth) in the incarnate Christ. This is both the basis for, and the foretaste of, the eschaton which is now working within us and the creation, and of the consummation to come. But it is the redemption through his blood and by his grace (Eph 1:7) that is made known to us in all wisdom. The goal is ἀνακεφαλαιώσασθαι τὰ πάντα ἐν τῷ Χριστῷ. The restoration of creation's order comes only through his blood.

In the God-Man, God and created reality exist in perfect relationship. This agrees with the "new creation" passage in 2 Cor 5:17: ὥστε εἴ τις ἐν Χριστῷ, καινὴ κτίσις· τὰ ἀρχαῖα παρῆλθεν, ἰδοὺ γέγονεν καινά. Before καινὴ κτίσις, most English versions insert "he is," which the Greek lacks. But the antecedent to this implied "he" is ambiguous in that "he" could refer to either τις or Χριστῷ, or both. The insertion could just as easily be "who is" thus making the following clause a dependent adjectival clause qualifying "Christ." It would then read: "If anyone is in Christ, who is a new creation." The main clause then follows: "the old has passed away; behold, the new has come." I suggest that the new creation does refer to both τις and Χριστῷ, and more importantly to Χριστῷ. If Christ is not "new creation," then those who are ἐν Χριστῷ certainly are not.

Thus, all reality is *representatively* renewed in the incarnation of Christ. Paul may use different terminology, but he clearly regards the outcome of the person and work of Christ to be the re-ordering of the entire creation. That Jesus is the God-Man means that God and the created order are in perfect relationship in him. If this summing up does ultimately refer to the consummation at Christ's return, we must ask about the relationship of the incarnation to the consummation.

Paul refers twice to the fullness of time in his writings. In Gal 4:4, he uses almost the exact same phrase (τὸ πλήρωμα τοῦ χρόνου) as Eph 1:10 (εἰς οἰκονομίαν τοῦ πληρώματος τῶν καιρῶν). Various proposals have been made to distinguish between χρόνος and καιρός, but both contexts here indicate particularly significant

---

The Letter to the Ephesians, PilNTC (Grand Rapids: Eerdmans, 1999); Lynn H. Cohick, *Ephesians: A New Covenant Commentary* (Cambridge: Lutterworth, 2013).

moments in God's redemptive history. James Barr has shown that the common distinction between quantitative (χρόνος) and qualitative (καιρός) time cannot be sustained.[23] While Gal 4:4 clearly refers to the incarnation, I suggest Eph 1:10 refers to all stages of redemption in Christ. It is no novelty to propose that the τέλος of Scripture, the goal of God's work, is reached in three ways: FOR us, IN us, and WITH us.[24] The "end" (all of it!), the restoration of the kingdom of God, is reached *for* us representatively in the incarnation, and made redemptive in the life, death, and glorification of Jesus. It is in the process of being reached *in* us experientially through the preaching of the gospel and the ministry of the Holy Spirit, and it will be consummated *with* us, when Jesus returns in glory to judge the living and the dead. These vital distinctions simply reflect those between our *justification*, *sanctification*, and *glorification*.[25] It is important to note that the New Testament perspective is not that a part of the eschaton is reached in the incarnation, a further part at Pentecost, and the final part at the return of Christ. That position I judge to be the error of premillennialism, and especially dispensationalism. The whole of the end is involved in each stage, but in different ways. For the IN us work of God to occur, and finally the WITH us work to occur in the consummation, there must be the FOR us work of God in Christ, including the restoration of the moral dimension through the shedding of Messiah's blood. Paul typically deals with Christian living and the existence of the church, the "in us" work of God, as flowing from the justifying "for us" work of Christ (e.g., Eph 2:5–10; 3:8–10; Gal 2:19–20).

6.3. Colossians 2:1–3

Again, in Col 2:3 we have a reference to Christ as the repository of all wisdom and knowledge: ἐν ᾧ εἰσιν πάντες οἱ θησαυροὶ τῆς σοφίας καὶ γνώσεως

---

[23] James Barr, *The Semantics of Biblical Language* (London: Oxford University Press, 1961), 225–26; idem, *Biblical Words for Time* (London: SCM, 1962).

[24] This view is clearly set out in detail by Adrio König, *The Eclipse of Christ in Eschatology: Toward a Christ-Centered Approach* (Grand Rapids: Eerdmans; /London: Marshall Morgan and Scott, 1989).

[25] They also reflect the popular response to "Are you saved?" as "I have been saved; I am being saved; I will be saved."

ἀπόκρυφοι. It is clear from this context that "hidden" (ἀπόκρυφοι) does not mean that these treasures are unattainable. Rather, as Peter O'Brien translates, they have been stored up.[26] After all, Paul wants his readers to have the knowledge of God's mystery, that is, Christ himself (Col 2:2). It would be easy to dismiss this text as saying merely that Christ is the all-wise One who also knows everything. Surely, Paul means much more. All his wisdom-Christology passages support the view that God's Christ is the hermeneutical norm or touchstone for every fact in the universe. The ultimate meaning of anything is found in Christ. In him is the restoration of the order lost at the fall. The order was lost and confused, and its shadow ever since has been graciously preserved in the world according to the wisdom of God until the solid substance is fully restored in Christ.

Other New Testament passages refer to the wisdom of God, or to the wisdom that is imparted to Christians. But enough has been said for us to reach the conclusion that the New Testament's wisdom Christology has its antecedents in the wisdom ideals and the Wisdom literature of the Old Testament. It is a wisdom that is first manifested in the creation and which reflects the redemptive purposes of the God of the covenants and of prophetic eschatology.

7. Conclusion

The foregoing considerations of the links between wisdom and the redemptive plan of God that centers on the Davidic Messiah, the temple in Jerusalem, and the promised land, enable us to construct a sequence of Wisdom from creation to new creation with the redemptive means in the suffering and exaltation of Messiah.

That God's creation is "very good" (Gen 1:31), and that its pinnacle is the creation of the human pair in the image and likeness of God, indicates the personal relationships that establish the moral perfection that could not exist in a mechanistic universe. The rebellion of humanity (Gen 3) is thus a radical moral revolt against the person of God and the order he has established in the creation. Thus, what might appear to be "natural" retribution in the empirical wisdom of Israel shares the divine nature

---

[26] Peter T. O'Brien, *Colossians, Philemon,* WBC 44 (Milton Keynes: Word [UK], 1987), 95.

of God's righteous retribution on sin. If wisdom is about order, its confusion, and its ultimate restoration, then it shares the moral dimension that can only be dealt with through judgment and ultimate glorification.

The gracious promise of Gen 3:15 is the light of God's wisdom in suffering and redemption. The judgments of Gen 3 project all subsequent history into the fallen universe in which the wisdom literature of Israel struggles to understand the righteousness of God that sovereignly preserves life and order within the "un-creation" of a world in exile from Eden and which is dependent on the grace and mercy of God for restoration. The story of wisdom subsequent to this is messianic. It comes to its heyday with Solomon, notwithstanding his later betrayal of it. Wisdom appears to wither on the vine in Israel's history, but the prophets will not let it rest there. The wisdom of God will appear in Messiah and he will renew all things—the very universe itself—in the new creation. And so the Wisdom of God comes into Galilee preaching the gospel of God. In him, the God-Man, God has assembled the new creation. He has restored the righteous order of God and creation in the babe of Bethlehem and dealt with the moral problem of mankind's folly at the cross.

> "Worthy is the Lamb who was slain, to receive power and wealth and wisdom and might and honor and glory and blessing!" (Rev 5:12)

RHETORIC AND TRUTH IN ISAIAH: AN APPROACH TO MESSIANIC INTERPRETATION IN THE OLD TESTAMENT*

—J. Gordon McConville

1. Introduction

Walter Brueggemann notes about the capacity of prophetic speech and writing:
"a focus on rhetoric as generative imagination has permitted prophetic texts to be heard and reuttered as offers of reality counter to dominant reality."[1] In what follows, I want to consider what this might mean for reading Isaiah, with reflections on how the "Immanuel" sign might be taken as "messianic." The essay seeks to address what might be entailed in a messianic interpretation of Isaiah. In doing so, it does not confine itself to recognizably messianic texts, such as those that embody promises of a future royal figure, but considers underlying issues concerning the rule of God in history, in which messianic expectation is rooted. This is a necessary prelude to understanding what might be meant by messianic hope in Isaiah. The book itself gives a prompt to such an enquiry, in applying the term מָשִׁיחַ uniquely to the Persian king Cyrus (45:1), commissioned by Yahweh to set in motion the salvation of his people by delivering them from their captivity in Babylon.

The essay has a further premise, namely that the rule of God in history, that gives rise to messianic hope, is not merely declared, but offered to the discernment of faith. This offer takes form within prophetic discourse which seeks to persuade and convict. It also encounters contrary speech, aiming equally to persuade and convict. This contention over what is really true corresponds to a prophetic conception of the

---

* I am delighted to dedicate this essay to my old friend Desmond Alexander, in recognition of his enormous contribution to research and pedagogy in Old Testament study, not least on the topic of "messiah," to which Desmond has devoted so much of his insightful scholarship.

[1] Walter Brueggemann, *The Prophetic Imagination* 2nd ed. (Minneapolis: Fortress, 2001), xi.

moral issues that confront the hearers of Isaiah, and the readers of the book. The essay therefore examines ways in which the language of Isaiah seeks to expose those issues. It culminates in a consideration of the familiarly "messianic" topic of the sign of Immanuel (7:14). But this is inseparable from the argument as a whole.

2. Isaiah and Alternative Truth

It is in Isaiah's conception of "reality counter to dominant reality," together with the imaginative power of his/its rhetoric, that the book's extraordinary vision lies. We might add to Brueggemann's statement that, in Isaiah's perception, what seems to be "dominant reality" is often a delusion. And this is why it can be seen as an ironic vision, the irony lying both in the false perceptions by which the world is construed, and in the prophet's exposure of them through language.

Broadly, "dominant realities" take the form of the exercise of power by kings and empires, while the counter-reality, as claimed by the prophet, is the rule of Yahweh over history and nature. These "realities" are given shape in mind and word. Their claims are voiced, indeed made effective, by speech. The powerful have always known the power of the word. This is dramatized in Isaiah especially by the portrayal of Assyrian speech, operating as a vital tool of conquest and subjugation.[2] We see it in the siege of Jerusalem under Sennacherib (Isa 36–37), in which the words of his commander the Rabshakeh play a crucial part. And we hear in the background the accounts of Assyrian (and other ancient Near Eastern) triumphs, which form the choral accompaniment to the history of the first millennium.

By way of example, in his own report of his siege of Jerusalem in 701 BC, King Sennacherib of Assyria famously boasts that he has "shut Hezekiah up like a bird in a cage." It is a well-known case, giving credence by what it does not say to the main claim of the biblical account, namely that he failed to take Jerusalem (though he had ravaged the rest of Judah), because of the miraculous intervention of Judah's God (Isa

---

[2] See Danna Nolan Fewell, "Sennacherib's Defeat: Words at War in 2 Kings 18:13–19:37," *JSOT* 34 (1986): 79–90. I am reading the confrontation between the Assyrian forces and the Jerusalem garrison primarily through the account in Isa 36–37, but will have occasion to refer to the parallel account in 2 Kgs 18:13–19:37 in places.

37:36). Sennacherib makes much of his successes in Judah, and his glorying in victory is of a piece with his annals in general, and indeed with the typical self-congratulation of ancient Near Eastern despots. Not only horses and chariots are powerful; so too are words. The contention between Sennacherib and the God of Judah is an issue not only of power, but of truth.

The rival claims of these counter-realities are at the heart of the book of Isaiah, whose underlying goal may be said to expose delusion and establish true perception of reality. In furtherance of this goal, an ironic strain pervades Isaiah, and works in a number of ways, both in the structure of the book, and in its poetics. I will consider examples of both.

3. Isaiah and Assyria

In approaching the topic of speech and reality in Isaiah, I mean the book of Isaiah in its entirety.[3] The central theme of the book is difficult to state, because it is so large and varied.[4] There are, however, topics that run through it, such as justice and righteousness as both divine standard and obligation upon the people of Israel and Judah, the anticipation of an exalted Zion, vision and blindness, the kingship of Yahweh and the nature of human authority. There are also signs of careful structuring, as in the organization of Isa 2–12 so as to reflect theologically on the relation between judgment and salvation, the comparison and contrast between the responses of Kings Ahaz and Hezekiah to the prophetic word (Isa 7–8, 36–38), the persistence of the topics mentioned above, and intertextual allusions to parts of Isa 1–39 in chs. 40–66.[5]

---

[3] I take this to be a unified composition, not in the sense of having originated from a single author, but as the product of a long period of growth and reinterpretation. Its message and outlook, therefore, are worked out in relation to a long span of history, stretching from Isaiah's own time, during the increasing ascendancy of the neo-Assyrian Empire, through the time of Babylonian domination, and into the Persian, or Second Temple, period.

[4] Some question whether the book has a thematic unity at all, or is rather more like an anthology. For a discussion of this and the possibilities for holistic reading, see Jacob Stromberg, *An Introduction to the Study of Isaiah* (London: T&T Clark International, 2011), 77–93. See also H. G. M. Williamson, "Recent Issues in the Study of Isaiah," in *Interpreting Isaiah*, ed. David G. Firth and H. G. M. Williamson (Downers Grove, IL: IVP Academic; Nottingham: Apollos, 2009), 21–39.

[5] See Stromberg, *Introduction*, 64–72; Benjamin Sommer, *A Prophet Reads Scripture:*

One leading candidate to be the uniting theme, as argued by R. W. L. Moberly,[6] is that of exaltation. Its importance is established at the beginning of Isa 2, with an image of the elevation of the "mountain of the house of Yahweh," and developed throughout the chapter with an elaborate contrast between the true exaltation of Yahweh alone (2:11, 17) and the haughtiness, or false self-exaltation, of human beings. The topic is taken up again in 5:15–16, and in Isaiah's vision of Yahweh enthroned in 6:1. It is woven into the fabric of the book in relation to the exaltation of the Davidic king (9:2–7, MT 1–6), in contrast, for example, to the forcible humbling of the proud king of Babylon (14:12–15).

Isaiah's (and Yahweh's) controversy with Assyria may be regarded as the primary example of this theme in the book. The self-glorying of Assyria is depicted, notably, in Isa 10:5–14 and Isa 36–37. In the former, Assyria (or better the king of Assyria) is heralded as the instrument of Yahweh for Israel's punishment, yet misreading his own place in the divine purpose, and facing punishment in turn for his arrogance. The latter is the account of the siege of Jerusalem under Sennacherib. In both these cases, Isaiah shows acute insight into the Assyrian mentality and language. The catalogue of conquered cities in Syria (Isa 10:9–10; 36:19) finds an echo (for example) in the Aššur Charter, Sargon II, 720 BC, recording Assyrian victories over Hamath, Arpad and "Samerina," *inter alia.*[7] The description of the siege of Jerusalem in 2 Kgs 18–19 and Isa 36–37 has affinities with Assyrian records such as the account of Sennacherib's first campaign against Babylon (ca. 704–702 BC),[8] an event close in time to the siege of Jerusalem, and featuring none other than the Rabshakeh. Even the language of Assyria is borrowed and adapted at times, as shown classically by Peter

---

Allusion in Isaiah 40–66 (Stanford, CA: Stanford University Press, 1998); Richard L. Schultz, *The Search for Quotation: Verbal Parallels in the Prophets*, JSOTSup 180 (Sheffield: Sheffield Academic Press, 1999).

[6] R. W. L. Moberly, *Old Testament Theology: Reading the Hebrew Bible as Christian Scripture* (Grand Rapids: Baker, 2013), 162–75.

[7] See *The Context of Scripture. Volume 2. Monumental Inscriptions from the Biblical World*, ed. W. W. Hallo and K. Lawson Younger (Leiden: Brill, 2000), 295.

[8] Hallo and Younger, *Context of Scripture* 2:300–02.

Machinist.[9] In 10:5–14, Isaiah uses the vaunting words of the Assyrian to set him up for a fall. His boast in 10:9–11 is the stuff of his military propaganda. Isaiah allows him to ventilate his pride, and in vv. 13–14 the bragging becomes extravagant: he has achieved his splendid victories because of his wisdom and understanding; he has "gathered all the earth," as one gathers eggs (where אסף, "gather" also means "destroy"). The force of the boast is felt in the words: כל האָרץ אני אספתי—with the heavy emphasis effected by אני, "I". In the final line (of v. 14), Isaiah even lends him the benefit of his own poetic creativity: ולא היה נדד כנף ופצה פה ומצפצף, displaying alliteration, onomatopoeia, and a tailing off into stillness—"no wing fluttered, no mouth opened, or chirped." The impression of calm equilibrium thus created by the self-glorying king prepares only for the retort: "Shall the axe vaunt itself against the one who wields it?"— a scathing picture, leading into a taunt that carries irony close to sarcasm (in v. 18): "the *glory* (כבוד , cf. v. 16[10]) of his fruitful land Yahweh will destroy, as when an ailing man wastes away": והיה כמסס נסס (hear the fading away to nothing—perhaps echoing the ומצפצף of v. 14). The motif of the forest and fertile land—signs of wealth and source of pride—runs through the poem too, ending with the devastating "the remnant of the trees of his forest will be so few that a child can write them down" (cf. vv. 33–34). The fall, predicted here, comes about later in the book, when the king's rhetorical question: "shall I not do to Jerusalem and her idols as I have done to Samaria and her images?" is met with a resounding "no," when the siege of Jerusalem dramatically fails (note 10:16, "I will send wasting sickness among his stout warriors"; cf. vv. 24–27).

---

[9] Peter Machinist, "Assyria and its Image in First Isaiah," in *JAOS* 103 (1983): 719–37. Machinist argues that Isaiah evidently knew and adapted phraseology from the Neo-Assyrian royal inscriptions, as part of his wider argument that the Hebrew Bible's (Isaiah's) view of the Neo-Assyrian Empire largely confirmed that empire's own view of itself as an overwhelming and terrifying military power. Peter Dubovsky puts a slightly different slant on it, suggesting that in the HB texts (he deals with the siege in 2 Kgs 18) is a "historiography of representation," in effect a Judahite point of view; the accounts use "optics" and "focalization" to telescope events and sources in order to bring out things that are essentially true in that perspective ("The Assyrian Downfall through Isaiah's Eyes [2 Kings 15–23]: The Historiography of Representation," *Bib* 89 [2008]: 1–16, esp. 14–15).

[10] And the alliteration there: ותחת כבדו יקד יקד כיקוד אש.

The prophetic dispute with Assyria is built into the structure of the book, which as we have noted, covers a long span of time, and is the context of the portrayals of the kings of Judah. Thus, Ahaz (who did not "believe") is deliberately contrasted with Hezekiah, who did (ch. 7 compared with chs. 36–37). Chapter 39 closes off the Assyrian phase, with Hezekiah's dubious "at least there will be peace in my time," pointing forward to the Babylonian phase that will occupy chs. 40–55. In fact, while ch. 39 is the conventional boundary of "First Isaiah," there are reasons to see chs. 36–39 as prelude to chs. 40–55. In that case, the boasting of the Assyrian commander in chs. 36–37 becomes an occasion for the long sequence of passages in 40–48, in which it is matched by the "boasting" of Yahweh, as in 40:25: "To whom then will you compare me that I should be like him?"

One thread that winds through this careful composition is that of Yahweh's counsel, or plan, primarily carried by means of the noun עצה and related verb יעץ, but not confined to these.[11] In an oracle against Assyria, he declares his plan to destroy it in his (Yahweh's) land, and further that this is a plan that extends ultimately to the whole earth (Isa 14:24–27). Forms of עצה and יעץ occur four times in these verses, in addition to דמיתי in v. 24. His purpose can be traced then through the events in the reign of Ahaz to those in the time of Hezekiah. Thus, in Isaiah's oracle concerning Assyria at the time of Sennacherib's siege of Jerusalem, Yahweh says: "Have you not heard how, long ago, I undertook this (עשׂיתי), from days long gone I shaped it (ויצרתיה); now I am bringing it to fruition, that you should turn fortified cities into ruined heaps?" (Isa 37:26, my translation). The vocabulary is different, but the thought is clear, and probably refers back to the sayings in 10:16, 24–27; 14:24–27).[12]

This "planning" discourse too has an ironic dimension because the plan of Yahweh is counterposed to the "plans" of the nations. Ahaz is terrified because "Syria,

---

[11] For the range of vocabulary employed, see Edgar W. Conrad, *Reading Isaiah,* OBT (Minneapolis: Fortress, 1991), 53. Conrad identified "The LORD's Military Strategy" as an important motif in the book (52–82). See also Joseph Blenkinsopp, *Isaiah 1–39,* AB (New York: Doubleday, 2000), 363.

[12] Conrad, *Reading Isaiah,* 55–57. And note the alliteration on עשׂיתי (from עשׂה, "do, make"), and ויצרתיה, a form of יצר, "form."

together with Ephraim and the son of Remaliah, has plotted (יעץ) to harm you" (7:5, my trans.). This plan we know from the outset to be futile, because the outcome is declared beforehand in 7:1 (= 2 Kgs 16:5). So throughout the narrative of Ahaz, in which he refuses a sign from Yahweh (foreclosing any insight into Yahweh's "plans"), makes his own plans in the light of his fear of the wrong party, and throws in his lot with the party that is destined to destroy his kingdom, we know everything crucial that he does not know. The ironic tension in the narrative depends on this.

The "plan" motif reaches a new level in the Hezekiah narrative. The dramatic force of the Hezekiah story derives from the vivid account of Sennacherib's siege of Jerusalem, conducted by his commander, the Rabshakeh. The account of the siege in Isa 36–37 largely follows the (presumably original) parallel in 2 Kgs 18–19,[13] but here it is built into the thematic structure of Isaiah, notably in the critical contrast that it makes between Ahaz and Hezekiah.[14] It is less an account of the siege than of the war of words between the Rabshakeh (for the king of Assyria) and Isaiah (for Yahweh), followed by the pious prayer of the king and the miraculous deliverance of the city. The tone is set straight away when the Rabshakeh picks up the motif of the "plan": "Do you think that mere words add up to sound strategy (עצה) and military strength?" (36:5) The garrison in Jerusalem may try to resort to diplomatic speech-convention in an attempt to protect the city, but the "plan" and strength of Assyria are bound to prevail. As readers, we know what he (and the garrison) do not, that the "plan" that will determine the outcome of the encounter is Yahweh's. The Rabshakeh's project, in the discourse of Isaiah, is doomed from the start, just like that of Syria and Ephraim in the time of Ahaz (Isa 7:1). The whole story is one of ironic reversal, in which the apparently powerful party is shown to be weak, or in Isaiah's terms, claims to be

---

[13] As we have noted, it omits 2 Kgs 18:14–16, which reports a first encounter between Hezekiah and Sennacherib, in which Hezekiah agrees to pay tribute. It also reduces the Assyrian delegation at Jerusalem from three officials to one, the Rabshakeh.

[14] Notice, for example, the Rabshakeh's chosen location for the confrontation, namely "the conduit of the upper pool on the highway to the Fuller's Field" (36:2), echoing the meeting between Ahaz and Isaiah in 7:3.

"high," and is brought "low."[15]

We have noticed above how the book of Isaiah deliberately poses an opposition between the claims of Assyria and those of Yahweh. Here, these rival claims, and the Assyrian delusion, are subjected to the closest scrutiny. The Rabshakeh is fully aware of the power of words to create a perception of truth. He opens the dialogue by focusing precisely on words (2 Kgs 18:20 = Isa 36:5), apparently disparaging their power, yet in reality preparing to deploy them for his assault. He proceeds to speak in the vernacular of Judah, adopting a stance of thorough knowledge of the issues in the conflict. Like a skilled negotiator, he has done his homework ("fact-checking"), and he knows a lot about Judah. He knows about Hezekiah's religious reform, with its centralizing policy and closure of sanctuaries (2 Kgs 18:4–6, 22; Isa 36:7[16]), and he reckons that a certain conservative sentiment in Judah may regard this as dangerous, and their current predicament as a consequence of it. He acutely plays on the notion that he has been brought against Judah by none other than Yahweh (Isa 36:7)— precisely the view expressed by Yahweh through Isaiah (Isa 10:5–6). He knows of the Isaianic prophecies that Yahweh will defend Jerusalem against enemies (Isa 36:15; 37:10, cf. 29:5–8; 31:4–5). All of this he uses to weaken the resolve of king and people in the city, who are facing the overwhelming probability that the city is about to be destroyed. He even enters into the place of Yahweh, when he locates the future hope of Jerusalem, not in Yahweh, but in the king of Assyria, who claims to be able to give them precisely those things that their traditions attributed to Yahweh, namely fruitful land and prosperity (Isa 36:16–17; cf. Deut 7:13; cf. Exod 13:5).

The bravado of the Rabshakeh is accompanied by signals that the Assyrian

---

[15] The point is well made by Fewell: "The drama of the story is expressed through ironic reversal. The strong one fails while the weak one survives. The taunter comes to be taunted with his own words. The destroyer comes to be destroyed. The one who has defeated all the gods of all the lands is murdered in the presence of his own god, who is unable to deliver him," "Sennacherib's Defeat," 83. Mary Hom writes similarly of "the double irony that Sennacherib, who had declared that YHWH would be unable to protect his people, ultimately proves to be unprotected from his own god as well from his own flesh and blood"; Mary Katherine Hom, *The Characterization of the Assyrians in Isaiah: Synchronic and Diachronic Perspectives*, LHBOTS 559 (London; New York: T&T Clark, 2012), 178.

[16] The Isaiah version omits the content of 2 Kgs 18:1–16.

project is faltering. The king himself sends a parting shot across Jerusalem's bows (Isa 37:10–13), but, in reality, he is on his way home to deal with a crisis there, and we know this because of another prophetic word (Isa 37:6–7). The irony of the drama lies not only in the fact that the Assyrian has got it wrong, but in the fact that his own words expose the fundamental falsehood of his position. Whereas he thinks he has entered the religious and epistemological space occupied by Judah, our implied author and his (implied) audience—and we ourselves—have in fact entered his. The tables are turned, not only in the miraculous events that demonstrate the truth of Yahweh's purpose, but in the fabric of the discourse itself. The Assyrian lives in a false reality, and he is allowed to disclose this to us by means of his own arrogant speech.

Fewell, focusing on the account in 2 Kgs 18:13–19:37, brings out forcefully how the discourse in the siege is carefully constructed to lay heavy emphasis on both speech and hearing. [17] She describes a network of language around this topic, with an overwhelming emphasis on speech, and thirteen speech-formulas. Each speaker focuses on accusations of untruthfulness on the part of the other, in which Yahweh "mimics the tone, employs the same rhetorical devices, and rebukes the content of the earlier Assyrian speech."[18] This is integral to the rhetorical purpose, because Yahweh's judgment on the Assyrian is due to what he has *said*. In Yahweh's emphasis on the other's *deception*, he is echoing the Assyrian's accusation that Hezekiah has deceived the people (Isa 36:18; 2 Kgs 18:30–31). In Isa 37:26–29 (= 2 Kgs 19:25–28) he "ironically affirms one of the Rabshakeh's more powerful rhetorical ploys...," where he claims that it was Yahweh who brought him against Judah.[19] Running through this rhetorical strategy is a fundamental issue of "trust," as well as the implication of blasphemy in the Assyrian's false claims, conveyed by the three verbs גדף, חרף, (Isa 37:23) and רגז (37:28–29; 2 Kgs 19:22, 27–28). Finally, there is "ironic contrast" in Yahweh's promise of bounty, after the Rabshakeh had promised it on Assyria's account, together with famine in the case of resistance. Fewell concludes: "The story

---

[17] The following is an account of Fewell's argument in "Sennacherib's Defeat," 83–87.
[18] Fewell, "Sennacherib's Defeat," 84.
[19] Fewell, "Sennacherib's Defeat," 85.

as it now stands is an ironic story about words.... [It] depicts the deliverance of Jerusalem to be Yahweh's assertion of autonomy over life and death in the face of the Assyrian counter-claim."[20]

The point is supported by Mary Hom's observation: "What the Assyrian material in Isaiah offered in contradistinction to Assyria's ideology was, simply and powerfully, alternative understandings—alternative understandings of god, the cosmos, the empire..."[21] For Dubovsky, more strongly: "Only Isaiah understands the true problem of Assyria, namely putting itself in the place of Yahweh, and thus its 'blasphemy'."[22]

The authors of Isaiah and Kings have not concocted this scenario out of nothing. The Rabshakeh's words (like passages we have already noted) bear comparison with language and ideas known from Assyrian records. How far the narrative in Isa 36–37 is based either on historical actuality or documentary source is impossible to determine. For some it is a Deuteronomic composition. Benjamin Thomas, in an important recent work, finds differently. For him, the language of the Rabshakeh is not entirely congruent with Dtr, and he thinks that "the overlapping material in the Isaianic texts and in the Rabshakeh's speeches may derive from the larger context of Neo-Assyrian propaganda."[23] For our present purposes it is sufficient to observe a degree of familiarity with Assyrian military propaganda, which is here subtly, and triumphantly, subverted.

The controversy with Assyria relates to two important features of the book of Isaiah. First, it is connected with the motif of vision and blindness. This motif, set up in Isaiah's commission following his temple-vision of Yahweh (Isa 6:9–10), is an inability to perceive the truth that is declared by the word of Yahweh (note an echo of

---

[20] Fewell, "Sennacherib's Defeat," 87.

[21] Hom, *Characterization*, 206–07.

[22] Dubovsky, "The Assyrian Downfall," 11.

[23] Benjamin D. Thomas, *Hezekiah and the Compositional History of the Book of Kings*, FAT/2 63 (Tübingen: Mohr Siebeck, 2014), 364. He notes, for example, the occurrence of the expression "broken reed" in Assyrian propaganda; 364 n.70, citing C. Cohen, "The Neo-Assyrian Elements in the First Speech of the Biblical Rab-Šaqe," *IOS* 9 (1979): 32–48.

the "hearing" motif in 37:7, ושמע שמועה). It is pursued through the unfolding story of Judah itself in the book (e.g., 42:18–25). But it belongs essentially to the portrayal of Assyria, because it is profoundly unable to grasp its own role and significance in the way things really are, a failure of understanding that underlies its ruthless belligerence (10:7).

The second feature is that of language itself. The rhetorical style of the book of Isaiah, with its heavy ironies, is not accidental, but is a function of its theology of the human "heart," with its proneness to moral blindness, or self-deception. The point can be illustrated by observing a certain affinity between the Rabshakeh's speech and terms in Gen 6. In Isa 10:7 we read that while Assyria is the instrument of God's judgment, "his heart does not think so" (ולבבו לא כן יחשב). The combination of לבב and חשב recalls Gen 6:5, which characterizes the thoroughgoing sinfulness of the human heart in the days before the great flood. There may be a further echo of the flood-narrative (Gen 6:7) in "for he says," in Isa 10:8b, in a parody of the speech of Yahweh.[24] In this way, the speech of Assyria is characterized as rooted in, and perpetuating, the deepest kind of human delusion.

The analysis of the Rabshakeh's raises a question about the book's audience or audiences. To whom is its rhetoric directed? The question may be pursued by considering further examples of its rhetorical character.

4. Language and Imagery

The capacity of Isaiah's language to address the book's fundamental concerns is one of its outstanding features. As Peter Miscall puts it: "Isaiah places form, how it is said, on an equal footing with content, what is said. The encyclopedic style, the diversity amidst unity, manifests itself in terminology, phraseology, imagery,

---

[24] I have made some of these observations in "Human 'Dominion' and Being 'Like God': An Exploration of Peace, Violence and Truth in the Old Testament," in *Encountering Violence in the Bible*, ed. Markus Zehnder and Hallvard Hagelia, Bible in the Modern World 55 (Sheffield: Sheffield Phoenix, 2013), 194–206 at 199–200. I also suggested that the possible echo of Yahweh's speech in that of Assyria lies between the upbeat to Yahweh's judgment speech in Gen 6:7, ויאמר יהוה, and the prelude to Assyria's boasted conquests in Isa 10:8, כי יאמר. The issue addressed in that essay was whether human violence might ever be compatible with divine justice and truth.

wordplay, punning, etc." [25] This too has a rhetorical aim, to undermine false perceptions of reality. But whose false perceptions?

A clue to this is found in the book's opening chapter, where it is evident that the language works on more than one level. The first memorable image in the book is that of the battered human body representing Israel suffering at the hands of violent enemies (1:5–6). It is conveyed in the form of a rhetorical appeal: "Why would you (pl.) continue to be beaten?" The thought is connected with the preceding portrayals of Israel as historically unfaithful, rebellious children (vv. 2–4). The appeal is apparently leveled at the people of Judah who were actually suffering at the hands of the Assyrian invader under Sennacherib in 701 BC, as suggested by the isolation of Zion in a devastated land (vv. 7–8). It is implied that, if only they would turn and rely on the LORD, there might yet be relief from their suffering. The intertextual relationship with Isa 36–37 is evident.

In this case, the prophet employs enormous verbal dexterity to convey the message. The image is linked in language and thought to the preceding verses (vv. 2–4): Israel has "rebelled," they are children who, unnaturally, rebel against their "father," who have "acted corruptly" (בנים משחיתים), and are "utterly estranged." This has consequences: the broken body is a fruit of "corruption," and itself a kind of corruption; the "utter estrangement" expressed in the unusual phrase נזרו אחור (v. 4d), finds an echo in the wounds that are "not pressed out" (לא זרו, v. 6c). The deployment of sound is pursued hard, not least with variations on sibilants (ז, שׂ, צ, שׁ) together with ר (already met in נזרו, זרו). It begins with זרע מרעים (v. 4b), with its impossible possibility of a "[holy] seed" that is rooted in evil (here in parallel to בנים משחיתים). It continues: זרים אכלים אתה ("aliens devour it" [the land], v. 7b), a point that is tweaked further in כמהפכת זרים, "as in the overthrow of/by enemies" (v. 7c). The tweak lies in the evocation of Sodom in the term הפך/מהפכת, characteristic of the Sodom narrative in Gen 19–20 (19:21, 25, 29 [2x]), and also in the turnabout implied in the syntactical game whereby Israel may be the victim of an "overthrow" by foreigners (Sodom), rather than Sodom

---

[25] Peter D. Miscall, *Isaiah* (Sheffield: Sheffield Academic Press, 1993), 95.

being overthrown (by God)—itself a kind of conceptual "overthrow."

This rhetorical performance is presented as if operating right in the situation portrayed. To this the "heavens and earth" are called as witnesses (v. 2). Yet already by virtue of that call the rhetorical act is displaced to another setting, one in which it can be viewed from outside, as an accomplished thing. And this perspective is brought forcefully home by the unexpected shift in v. 9, in which suddenly a first-person plural voice intrudes: "If the LORD had not left us a few survivors…".[26] The effect of the oracles in vv. 4–8, therefore, is not confined to the impact they might have had when first uttered (though such an impact is part of the meaning of the text), but operates also in the world of those identified as "we." These may be, as Conrad has it, a "community of survivors," who are experiencing Yahweh's work of judgment and salvation in a situation later than the events of 701 BC, and whom he equates with the "implied audience" of the book.[27] Beyond that, however, it is also a voice that draws the reader in and invites their acquiescence in the judgments that are offered. But the relationship between this voice and the oracles is complex, for it is integrated with the rhetorical dexterity of the discourse.[28] The hints of Sodom and Gomorrah in v. 7 dovetail with the chastened reflection of v. 9b, in which the cities, paradigms of evil and due punishment, are named. And the shock effect continues into v. 10a, in which Sodom and Gomorrah become, not merely a reference-point in the past, but characterizations of the hearers themselves! The implied setting of v. 10 is back in a time which, from the perspective of the "we" voice is in the past. Yet the force of the rhetoric, in the wake of the logic of v. 9, still addresses the listening audience directly.

The composition, therefore, is designed to enable a prophetic word, presumably once spoken into the situation portrayed, to be heard with new force by a new audience. The running theme is that of false perception of reality. Those who persisted in their false trust in the face of dire threat (typified in the book by King Ahaz

---

[26] For the "we" voice in Isaiah, see Conrad, *Reading Isaiah*, 83–116.

[27] Conrad, *Reading Isaiah*, 116.

[28] The sibilant/ר sound-play continues here in כעיר נצורה ("like a besieged city," v. 8b), and הותיר לנו שריד ("left us a remnant," v. 9).

in ch. 7, the antitype to Hezekiah) were living in a delusion. But the prophetic argument has no intention of merely depicting past failures. The impact of the prophet's rhetorical genius is meant to be felt by new and contemporary hearers. What delusion might they, or better "we," be living in?

5. The Case of Immanuel

This tension between the prophetic word recalled and present reality underlies the force of much of the discourse in the book. A consequence is that many sayings have double or hidden meanings. The case of Immanuel (7:14–16, and throughout chs. 7–8) is an obvious example. The child who would be born to the unnamed young woman (7:14) is a sign given originally to King Ahaz. It comes with the explanation that the alliance of Syria and the kingdom of Israel, of which he was terrified, would come to ruin within a short space of time, that is, before the child was very old (7:16). He should therefore put his trust, not in military defenses or dubious alliances, but in the LORD (7:9). Put differently, he should turn from his false reality to embrace the true reality, namely that the LORD alone disposed over events.

Here too, however, a rhetorical situation is conveyed from a vantage point outside it. The composition has a retrospective dimension. Ahaz is portrayed as having refused the sign even before it was given (v. 12). In the composition, therefore, the sign takes on an ambiguous character. Does "God (is) with us" mean that God is "with us" for good or for ill? The enigmatic saying in 7:15, interposed between the sign in v. 14 and its plain-sense interpretation in v. 16, already hints at a longer perspective and a shift in meaning.[29] The point hits home in v. 17, in which "God with us" has an outcome in the invasion of Judah by Assyria. The multiple possibilities of "God with us" are carried forward in 8:8, 10. The logic of 8:1–8 is remarkably similar to 7:14–17. That is, first, a child is to be born signifying the imminent demise of the threatening alliance, and consequent relief for Judah (8:1–4), but then abruptly the specter of

---

[29] The echo of "curds and honey" in vv. 21–22 invites a reading of v. 15 in terms of the impoverished situation pictured there; so Stromberg, *Introduction*, 118–19, and more fully, idem, *Isaiah After Exile: the Author of Third Isaiah as Reader and Redactor of the Book*, Oxford Theological Monographs (Oxford: Oxford University Press, 2011), 222–28.

Assyrian invasion arises, Judah is overwhelmed, and the sign of Immanuel is invoked (8:8). In a further switch, an oracle of salvation in the context of aggression from many nations culminates in the assertion "God is with us" (Immanuel) (vv. 9–10).

In this sequence, Immanuel becomes the parade example of dual possibility in Isaiah's language. In 8:8 it comes as an arresting conclusion to an image of the Assyrian invasion as an overwhelming river, an evocation of the mighty Euphrates, contrasted with the gently flowing "waters of Shiloah," a modest stream irrigating Jerusalem. The vivid picture is inseparable from the message. The gently flowing waters of Shiloah suggest a peaceful Jerusalem, a possibility, however, that "this people" (Judah) has "refused." The reader will recall how King Ahaz was met by Isaiah at a place where water was conveyed into the city (7:14),[30] and how he refused the way of quiet trust. In consequence, instead of the rapid withdrawal of a minor enemy, there would come the unimaginably greater deluge of the superpower of the day.

The picture language, while powerful, is also questioning. What is the effect of the switch of metaphor from river to wings (vv. 7–8)? The former connotes clearly enough the terrifying splendor of the Assyrian army, the river image augmented by that of "glory" (v. 7), a key concept in Isaiah, for "glory" belongs truly only to Yahweh (5:16). Here it conveys the gleaming splendor of an army, the *melammu* of the king of Assyria. It is an image of invincibility that provides an intertextual comment on the fear of the city's garrison in Isa 36–37. But as the river flows on "even to the neck" of Judah (that is, overwhelming all but Jerusalem), the image is disturbed by the sudden change to one of a bird's wings.[31] Are these wings threatening, thus in keeping with the images of river and glory? Or could they be protective, overspreading and bearing up, as in texts where they bespeak God's care for Israel (Exod 19:4; Deut 32:11)? Opinions divide on the point. For Oswalt, among others, the image remains

---

[30] This was probably not the same stream as "the waters of Shiloah." Even so, there is a certain echo between them.

[31] It has been thought that the "wings" might be in keeping with the military metaphor, the "wings" signifying the diverging streams of the river, or perhaps the flanks of the army. H. G. M. Williamson notes, however: "Nearly all commentators … nowadays recognize that there is a change of image here to that of a bird," *Isaiah 6–12*, ICC (London; New York: T&T Clark, 2018), 255.

threatening; the bird hovers as if to attack, and will only be prevented from doing so, because the LORD will protect Immanuel.[32] On the other hand, the idea of the wings as protective has a long pedigree in the scholarly literature. For G. B. Gray, on the basis of Old Testament parallels, the outstretched wings "far more naturally imply protection," a view now also taken by Williamson.[33] For him, this entails taking the initial phrase in v. 8b as "*his* wings," that is, the LORD's, and he concludes that, in this case, the sign of Immanuel is unequivocally promise-bearing.[34]

However, it seems to me that, from the point of view of rhetorical effect, this is not readily resolvable. It is no accident that Isaiah couches his message here in metaphorical language, with its capacity for suggesting different meanings. In Isa 8:1–8, the movement from the relative clarity of Maher-Shalal-Hash-Baz to the ambiguity of Immanuel is essential to the discourse. As Maher-Shalal-Hash-Baz is overlaid by Immanuel, the initial sign of swift deliverance is artfully tweaked. The name Immanuel carries with it in this context the opening into uncertainty, the deferral of relief, that was created by 7:15. The rhetorical effect is to interrogate false appraisals of reality, the false trust of the sort exemplified by King Ahaz. Yet almost immediately the name of Immanuel is invoked again, now in an unequivocally positive oracle of salvation (vv. 9–10), in language that recalls the LORD's powerful victory over defiant warring nations in Psalm 2, with its theme of his protection of David and Zion.

The theological and compositional development of the Immanuel sign in chs. 7–8, therefore, defines its scope. Originating in a specific crisis in the life of Judah, it breaks the bounds of that situation, with a double effect: first to sustain its rhetorical

---

[32] John N. Oswalt, *The Book of Isaiah: Chapters 1–39*, NICOT (Grand Rapids: Eerdmans, 1986), 227. The interpretation goes back to B. Duhm, *Das Buch Jesaja*, HKAT 3/1: 4th ed. (Göttingen: Vandenhoeck & Ruprecht, 1922; orig. 1892). See also Hom, *Characterization of the Assyrians in Isaiah*, 34–35.

[33] G. B. Gray, *Isaiah I–XXVII*, ICC (Edinburgh: T&T Clark, 1912), 148. He cites Ruth 2:12; Pss 17:8; 36:8; 57:2; 61:5; 63:8; 91:4, and also Matt 23:37. Williamson inclines also to this view, citing the same Old Testament texts, and a range of recent scholarly literature; *Isaiah 6–12*, 255–57.

[34] So Williamson, who thinks that the line, put in place late in the development of chs. 7–8, shows that "the name [had come] to be understood exclusively in this positive sense," Williamson, *Isaiah 6–12*, 257–58.

power to call audiences to respond to the meaning of "God with us," and second, to stand finally as an affirmation of God's intent to save, now projected beyond the horizon of the Syro-Ephraimite attack, beyond even the depredations of Assyria, on to an international canvas, and into an unfinished future.

It is in this way that the Immanuel sign becomes "messianic." It is important that it is read, not just in its first appearance at 7:14, but in its full development. That development takes place against the background of the question-mark that Ahaz's refusal of the sign sets against the commitment of Yahweh to Israel as expressed through the Davidic covenant. The Immanuel sign amounts to a reassertion of Yahweh's promises in spite of the present failure of the promise-bearing dynasty. Williamson, finding the sign "more messianic than many recent commentators have allowed," thinks that the hope it engenders "is through God's adherence to his age-old promises to his people in the Zion tradition…, no matter how sharply he has to diverge from his previous path of implementation." And again, "The arrival of Immanuel bespeaks the replacement of the present line of kings."[35]

The story of Yahweh's re-commitment to his promises does not run to a conclusion within Isaiah. The book does not, in the end, simply describe a movement through judgment to salvation, the "old" passed away and the "new thing" at hand, despite the word of comfort to those whose time of punishment is past, announced in Isa 40:1–2. In fact there is a good deal of dis-comfort after this comfort, not only within 40–55 (42:18–25), but especially in 56–66, with its signs of division within the redeemed community (63:15–19; 65:13–16), and its disruptive final word (66:24). In this way, the book leaves open the question of what reality readers will recognize as true. Correspondingly, the sign of Immanuel remains open for its reception in the New Testament. Richard Hays, in showing how Matthew demonstrates the fulfillment of "Immanuel" in Christ, takes his cue from both Isa 7 and Isa 8:8, 10. Together, these show that "God with us" hits an ironic note, "a reminder that all human counsel and opposition is futile against God."[36] Matthew's use of the sign is in line with Isaiah's.

---

[35] Williamson, *Isaiah 6–12*, 161–62.

[36] Richard B. Hays, *Echoes of Scripture in the Gospels* (Waco, TX: Baylor University Press,

As in the prophet's time, Israel was under threat from domination by foreign powers, so was it also in the time of Jesus.

Matthew's identification of Jesus as Immanuel signifies that his birth is a sign: those in Israel who trust in God's salvation will see in Jesus a harbinger of salvation (the heir who will restore the Davidic line), but those who reject the divine presence in Jesus will suffer the consequences.[37]

6. Conclusion

I have considered the nature of the book of Isaiah's rhetoric from different angles. It was highlighted especially in the controversy between Yahweh and the King of Assyria in Isa 10; 36–37, where we found that language was used to not simply to convey, but to create a practical reality. Language was inseparable from the apprehension of truth. The book of Isaiah enshrines a "war of words," in which Yahweh seeks to persuade hearers of the truth of the divine word over against others. At stake is not something merely intellectual, but existential.

This worked on several levels. The account of the conflict between Yahweh and Assyria stages an event in the world of the narrative, in which the protagonists are the Assyrians and the people of Judah, who are contesting versions of the truth as advocated by Isaiah and King Hezekiah on one hand and the Rabshakeh on the other. In this narrative world, the audiences are the same as the participants in the events narrated. The loud claims of the Assyrian commander to the besieged citizens of Jerusalem function to persuade them of his truth.

The rhetoric reaches audiences beyond this world, however. As a careful literary composition, it is aimed at generations of readers, many of whom may be far removed from the narrated situation. The story of the siege finishes with the deliverance of Jerusalem from Sennacherib's forces (Isa 37:36–38), and also, in the flow of the book, adumbrates the time of Babylonian domination (Isa 39), and

---

2016), 164.

[37] Hays, *Echoes of Scripture*, 164. It is noteworthy that Matthew not only opens his gospel with an allusion to "Immanuel" (1:23), but also in effect closes it with such an allusion (28:20).

ultimately the deliverance of Judean exiles from that tyranny. One can imagine various Judean audiences for this. It could have been heard as an encouragement to believe the word of Yahweh while in the grip of other oppressive truth claims, such as the Babylonian. And it could serve to foster hope of further deliverances of Jerusalem into an indefinite future.

In the end, the rhetoric of Isaiah is at home in the canonical book of Isaiah. Turning from the account of the conflict with Assyria, we considered further instances of the rhetorical power of the book in its poetic language, namely the image of the battered body in ch. 1, and the case of Immanuel. There were indications in these also of different audience levels, and not least an expectation that the parts of the book should be read, as it were, from the end. This served to qualify two potential mistakes: first that the prophetic word had its significance only within the world of the people to whom it first came, and second, that the book tells a linear story that progresses to a definite end. There is an element of linear advance in the progression through the Syro-Ephraimite and Assyrian crises, to the deliverance of exiles from Babylonian captivity. This last is certainly a major turning-point in the book. However, in another sense, the language of Isaiah does not reach an end-point. It is not a univocal tale of those who were "blind" coming eventually to "see." Rather, it retains the power of its many parts both to reprove and encourage readers in every generation. On this, Martin O'Kane,'s comment on Isaiah, citing J.-P. Sonnet, is to the point: "the motif of the ability to see, especially from chapter 40 onwards, is presented, not as a subsequent, successive or final state that reverses or brings to full circle the enigmatic commission of 6.9-10, but should be seen rather as an expression of how the two states, sight and blindness, are maintained in an unresolved tension."[38] It is this very condition that may still be recognized in the Gospels' narratives of the recognition and non-recognition of Jesus. Immanuel, comprehended as a messianic sign, brings with it the prophetic question of whom to believe, and where to place one's trust.

---

[38] Martin O'Kane, *Painting the Text: The Artist as Biblical Interpreter* (Sheffield: Sheffield Phoenix, 2007), 22, citing J.-P. Sonnet, "Le motif de l'endurcissement (Isa. 6,9-10) et la lecture d' 'Isaïe'," *Bib* 73 (1992): 208–39 (233).

KINGS AND KINGDOM IN THE BOOK OF ISAIAH

—*John N. Oswalt*

1. Introduction

The book of Isaiah takes the idea of king and kingdom as a given in the cosmos. It does not envision some day in the future where there will be no king. For those of us raised to think of democracy as the ideal form of government, this comes as something of a surprise. Should we think of this as an indication that the writer(s) only reflects an early stage of development in political thinking, or that they indeed reflect cosmic reality? I suggest that the latter is the case. In the Bible as a whole, but especially in Isaiah, we are confronted with the understanding that Yahweh is absolutely transcendent and is the sole creator of the cosmos. As such, all authority in the universe, indeed, existence itself, extends from him. The idea that authority for governance is extended from the creature to the Creator is simply unthinkable. Yahweh is king, and that is all there is to it.[1]

At the same time, it has to be said that the book of Isaiah is very ambivalent about the subject. Broadly speaking, it is generally negative toward ordinary human kingship, while it is positive toward the Messiah's kingship, and entirely positive toward divine kingship.[2] An early, and somewhat definitive expression of this ambivalence between divine and human kingship is seen in Isa 6. It is certainly not accidental that Isaiah dates his vision "in the year that king Uzziah died" (6:1).[3] So long as king Uzziah lived, it seemed there was some hope of stemming the Assyrian

---

[1] For a treatment of the kingdom of God in Isaiah, see Andrew T. Abernethy, *The Book of Isaiah and the Kingdom of God: A Thematic-Theological Approach* (Downers Grove; IVP Academic, 2016).

[2] Robert C. Gnuse, *No Tolerance for Tyrants: The Biblical Assault on Kings and Kingship* (Collegeville: Liturgical Press, 2011) sees this same ambivalence throughout the Bible.

[3] Unless otherwise specified, biblical quotations are from NIV (2011).

tide, but with him gone, what hope was there? Jotham, a good man, seemed to be under the thumb of the pro-Assyrian party, who were possibly already promoting their tool Ahaz for co-regency. Again, it is hardly accidental that it was in this atmosphere that Isaiah cried out, "My eyes have seen the king!" Judah's hope, if there was any, was not in any human king, mortal and fallible as they were. It could lie only in the King of the Universe.

However, it is important to note that Isaiah's vision of the divine King did not result in a flood of happy feelings. This king did not exist to promote Judah's political and economic well-being. He is the King and does not exist for anyone. Thus, Isaiah's vision was cause for despair. What human individual or institution could live in the presence of purity like this? Yahweh's kingship calls all of us to account. If his appearance was cause for hope, it was only a hope that could come through a radical cleansing, ultimately one of fire.

2. The Davidic Kings: Bad and Good

This ambivalence is especially seen in the book's treatment of the Davidic kingdom: there is not much good said about Davidic kings in the present, whereas the ideal Davidic king of the future is treated very positively. This skepticism about present kings is apparent not only in regard to a relatively bad king, such as Ahaz, but also for a relatively good king, such as Hezekiah. In the case of Ahaz, we are told that the "house of David" was shaking like leaves on a tree in a windstorm at the onslaught of Pekah and Rezin (7:2). Probably a part of the reason for this shaking was the promise that the two northern kings would depose the Davidide and put the son of Tabeel, not a son of David, on the throne (7:6). Here Ahaz displayed no confidence in King Yahweh and his promises to David. Rather, he was ruled by his dread of the "two kings" (7:16).

When Isaiah gave Ahaz a direct challenge to put his trust in Yahweh, the king artfully dodged with an appearance of piety, suggesting that to ask God for some sign might have the appearance of testing him (7:12). Isaiah, seeing through the subterfuge, indicted not merely Ahaz, but the entire "house of David" (7:13) for faithlessness. In this regard, it is tempting to wonder whether the identification of the true king as coming from the "stump of Jesse" (11:1) was a way of pushing the lineage of the coming Davidic king back behind the current "house of David" as it was then manifesting itself.

But this judgment upon present Davidides was not limited to the "bad" representatives. It is also apparent that the author(s) are not seeing the "good" examples as paragons, either. On the one hand, compared to Ahaz, Hezekiah comes off rather well. His plea to God of having "walked before you faithfully and with whole-hearted devotion [doing] good in your eyes" (38:3) is clearly accepted by Yahweh at face value. Likewise, his faith in God, even if it was a last resort, was rewarded with deliverance from the Assyrian hordes. Finally, and far from least, his prayer for deliverance for the sake of Yahweh's name is certainly praiseworthy.

However, all that having been said, it is hard to avoid the sense that the book is much more ambivalent toward Hezekiah than is Kings, or even more, Chronicles. While the "you" of Isa 22:8–11 is not identified and could plausibly be referring to Shebna (22:15), it is hard to avoid the more likely identification of Hezekiah. He was the one responsible for the water system (22:11) and the strengthening of the fortifications (22:10). Thus, he is the one of whom Isaiah says that in all that work he did not really "look to the One who made it" (22:11). As king, he must be certain of the defenses of his city, but he forgot that there was a King to whom he ought to be turning first and always.

Similarly, in Isa 28–31 Hezekiah is never identified as one of the "scoffers who rule this people in Jerusalem" who "have entered into a covenant with death [Egypt?] (28:14–15). Yet it is hard to separate him from the Judean policy of going "down to Egypt for help ... but [not looking] to the Holy One of Israel, or [seeking] help from the LORD" (31:1). It is hard to imagine that Hezekiah did not endorse this policy which Isaiah so fulsomely rejected. If he allowed his officials to pursue it while not really approving it, that makes him a weaker monarch than the other texts make him out to be.

Finally, we have the very ambivalent way in which the final accounts of

Hezekiah in the book represent him. These are found in Isa 38 and 39. As mentioned above, Yahweh indicated his acceptance of Hezekiah's account of his manner of living by giving him an additional 15 years of life. But Hezekiah's hymn that follows this gift is very odd. One would expect a hymn of praise, or a song of thanksgiving, but we do not find either one of these. What we do find, although it incorporates certain expressions of gratitude, is more of a lament over mortality. Although Hezekiah has escaped death for now, he has been made very conscious that he cannot escape it finally, and as a result, says that he will live very humbly (38:15).

Then there is the incident reported in Isa 39. However we treat it, Hezekiah does not come off well. As a result of the news of his miraculous recovery an embassy from Babylon, which was currently (and perennially) in revolt against Assyria, came to Jerusalem to find out if this Judean monarch might have access to some unusual divine power. Here was an opportunity reminiscent of what Isa 2 was speaking of. Here are representatives of the nations coming to Jerusalem to learn about her God. This was a God-given opportunity for Hezekiah to give evidence that Yahweh is the only God (37:20). Instead, he showed off his armaments and his wealth—to envoys from Babylon, one of the wealthiest and most powerful cities in the world! Isaiah's sardonic comment about this behavior is that it was well that Hezekiah had displayed all these things since the Babylonians would possess them all one day (39:6)! But Isaiah's following statement was even more foreboding: some of Hezekiah's descendants, David's descendants, would be eunuchs in the Babylonian court. What of the dynasty of David?

What is going on here? We can understand why Ahaz would be denigrated as a bad example of what godly kingship ought to look like. He was a man who would trust Assyria, his worst enemy, before he would trust God. But Hezekiah? Why depict him in a less than favorable light? In contrast to king Ahaz he represented the trust in Yahweh that Isa 7–35 had been calling for. I suggest the answer is this: at their best, human kings fall short. We tend to idolize them, to look to them for that order without which we cannot live, to depend on them for the promotion of good and the punishment of evil, in short, for salvation. But it will not be. At their worst, human kings fall prey to arrogance, believing themselves to be gods, capable of doing whatever they want, caring for themselves instead of caring for those entrusted to their care, creating policies that are designed above all to secure themselves in power. And even at their best, human kings who may be able to look beyond themselves to the good of their people, and who may recognize that they rule by heavenly permission and not because of some semi-divine capacities of their own, still are fallible, and more than that, mortal.

This is what is taking place in the present structure of the book of Isaiah. Using the examples of Ahaz and Hezekiah, the author(s) show(s) us the necessity of absolute trust in Yahweh, and that if we will trust in him he will deliver us from *all* the threats of life, including death itself. But there is more to Yahweh's trustworthiness than that. Ahaz failed the test (Isa 7–8). Faced with the threat of Israel and Syria, he chose to trust the greater enemy, Assyria, rather than Yahweh (2 Kgs 16:7–9). It was then Isaiah's duty to inform Ahaz that the day would soon come when Assyria would flood Judah up to the neck (Isa 8:6–8). The result would be a darkness of despair in which the people would curse both their king and their God (8:21). The fact is: whatever we trust in place of God will turn on us and destroy us.

We might expect destruction because of failure to trust to be the end of the story: having reaped the results of their failure to trust, king and people are left to the inevitable. But that is not the case; Isa 9:1–7 depicts another king reigning "on David's throne," a child who will not rule in arrogance and pomp, but in simplicity and righteousness. There follows a statement (9:8–10:4) establishing that it is not the Assyrias of this world with which we must come to terms but the standards of Yahweh. If we will do so, we have nothing to fear from the Assyrias (10:5–31). Then follows a fuller description of this coming one, this child, who will sit on David's throne (11:1–16). In short, when we have failed to trust, and reaped the inevitable results, Yahweh comes not with curses, but with promises, promises of a king who will indeed fulfill all our hopes. Should we trust a God like that? Oh, yes!

So, who is this king? Is he to be found in the good king Hezekiah's of this world? No, he is not. To be sure, the Hezekiah's who will trust God can prove that

Yahweh is capable of being trusted, and that if he is trusted he will deliver, but what they cannot do is to replace him. No human king can solve the ultimate human problems. At his best Hezekiah is mortal and fallible; he is not the child of 9:1–7 nor humble king of 11:1–16. Human kings will always fall short of what kingship must be. This is why the book of Isaiah cannot end with Isa 39. If we are to seek the fulfillment of the promises of 9:1–7, 11:1–16, 16:5, and 32:1 we must look beyond Hezekiah, or any other human king. Even the best will fail us.

3. The Qualities of Human Kingship

Before we turn to an exploration of the true king as depicted in Isaiah, we should consider further the qualities of human kingship as described in the book. In the first place, as the Apostle Paul says in Rom 13:3–5, kingship is designed to enforce that order without which human life cannot exist. Thus, when describing the chaos that would envelop the world where we trust humanity instead of God, the prophet says simply that there will be "nothing there to be called a kingdom" (34:12). However fallible human kings may be, they have been instituted by God for the purpose of maintaining order.

However, in our thirst for order, we humans often idolize our kings (our leaders), expecting of them qualities and capacities far beyond their abilities, thus dooming them to certain failure. This situation is described particularly in Isa 28–33, which section can be titled: "Woe to Those Who Will Not Wait." In this section there is a most interesting shift in emphasis from the failed human leaders to the coming divine leader. In the earlier chapters almost the entire emphasis is on the former, whereas by the final chapter the attention has shifted almost completely on the latter. As mentioned above, the point seems to be clearly that our hope cannot be in any human kings but must be in the King of heaven alone.

Isaiah 28:1 begins with a complex figure of speech. Samaria is referred to as a "wreath," which calls to mind the crenelated walls of the city circling the top of the hill on which it was built. But it also speaks of the headdress of drunken party-goers, and finally it refers to the crown on the head of the king. This latter is confirmed by the reference to Yahweh being a "crown" or a "wreath" in v. 5. Thus, the whole complex of a kingship which is rooted in self-indulgent power is called to mind. The prophets and priests were caught up in this pattern as well (7–8) with the result that the people are left without guidance (9–13). Having used what appears to be an earlier oracle to Samaria to set the stage, the prophet turns to his primary audience, the rulers of Jerusalem in 28:14. These rulers are not physically drunk but are equally senseless in their cynical attitudes and their mocking spirits (28:22). They are not open to simple and obvious truths, as is a farmer (28:24–29). This is one of the results of the corrupting influence of power, a cynical mockery of basic values, and an attitude of superiority toward all who are "beneath" them.

The theme of senselessness continues in Isa 29 where a love of rituals (29:1, 13) takes the place of understanding and perception (29:11–12). Then the picture darkens by degrees as we see the leaders making secret plans while denying accountability. They have an eye for evil (29:20) and have no more sense of justice than to make the innocent guilty "with a word" (29:21). As mentioned above, these are people who are idolized as earthly messiahs and who thereby think that they have power to do anything.

Isaiah 30 makes plain what the secret plans of chapter 29 were, namely, to enter into an alliance with Egypt. From this remove, we can see how foolish such a move was. As the Assyrian officer was to say, Egypt was no substantial walking stick, but only a reed that would split and give way the moment any weight was put on it (36:6). We know in hindsight that such a judgment was correct, but the point of this passage is that God knew it in foresight and was making the information available through his prophet. But rulers who see themselves as all-powerful and accountable only to themselves are not interested in counsel outside of themselves (30:11). The result would be that all the expensive hardware they had purchased from Egypt would only be useful for running away (30:15–18). The irony in all of this was that all of this political machination was unnecessary. Yahweh had already decreed the defeat of the Assyrian army (31:8–9) with no help at all from Egypt. "In quietness and trust is your strength, but you would have none of it" (30:15c). This is royal power run amok.

Fundamental to this abuse of royal power is the deepest of all human sins: pride. Pride is a problem for all humans; from earliest days we have a built-in instinct to make ourselves the center of our universe. But most of us are not in a position to make very much of that. However, for those who have the absolute power of kingship there is often no effective rein upon that instinct. Isaiah depicts this characteristic of human kingship in a variety of powerful ways. The first expression of it is found in Isa 10 where the Assyrian emperor insists that he is so exalted that even his underlings are kings (10:8). Furthermore, he has seized the "kingdoms of the idols" (10:10). He is even greater than the gods and has thus been able to wrench their holdings out of their hands. It is a significant fact that throughout the book the Assyrian emperors are never made to say that their god is greater than the gods of the nations. No, they, as human kings, are greater than the gods of the nations! To such towering pride as this the thought that he might be the tool of the God of tiny Judah would not be merely offensive, it would be laughable. This confident self-centeredness is apparent in 10:13–14 where first person pronouns appear fully nine times in two verses. This king is self-motivated, self-empowered, and self-directed. As Babylon is later quoted as saying, so he might say, "I am, and there is no other" (47:8, 10). This is of course the crowning blasphemy, for only the Transcendent One is self-existent, and for any mere creature to assert such a thing is both foolish and deadly. There can be only one result: "I will punish the king of Assyria for the willful pride of his heart and the haughty look of his eyes" (10:12).

What causes kings to imagine that "I am, and there is no other" when the very tenuousness of breath (2:22) mocks such a vain idea? Isaiah 47 identifies two chief features that undergird royal arrogance. The first is the lack of accountability: "no one sees me" (47:10) says the Queen, so she can do whatever she likes, and "wickedness" is usually more attractive than goodness. The second is a false conviction of superior wisdom. The king has access to all sorts of wisdom, in this case occult wisdom, which makes him able to accomplish things, supposedly, that "mere mortals" cannot. But Isaiah says that such things only lead one "astray" (47:10). The simple farmer (28:24–29) knows that there are immutable principles in the world that no one is exempt from, not even a king or queen.

A particular expression of this royal pride is found in the speech of the Rabshakeh reported in Isa 36. Here, in a very studied way, the Assyrian sets out to exalt his master at the expense of the upstart, Hezekiah. He has come on behalf of "the great king, the king of Assyria" (36:4, 13) ostensibly to deliver a message to Hezekiah, whom he never deigns to refer to as king, and in fact only speaks of in the third person. His real intent seems to have been to bypass Hezekiah completely, and put pressure on him by appealing to the people directly. While he never refers to Hezekiah as king, he always refers to his master as "the king of Assyria." Hezekiah is a deceiver, of no more consequence than the so-called "kings" of all those other little nations whose gods "the great king" has so summarily disposed of.

But such royal pride is groundless. The most powerful indictment of it in the book, or perhaps even in western literature, is found in 14:4b–20b. This beautifully crafted poem is framed with the language and cadences of a lament for a fallen king, but in its content it is anything but a lament. It is not an expression of sorrow over the passing of the king, but an expression of delight. The towering ego that once pretended to stand astride the world is gone, and the whole world rejoices.

The poem is structured in four symmetrical stanzas, with each having a different location. The first is the earth, the second the underworld, the third heaven, and the fourth returns to earth. In each case the folly of human pride is made clear. The first stanza (14:4b–8) delineates two proud claims that that the king had made, and that now have ceased, giving cause for joy. The two claims are nicely inter-related. The Assyrian kings delighted to boast how they had arrived in a certain kingdom with their great army and with a series of mighty blows beaten that kingdom to the ground. Along with this they regularly boasted how they had cut down great forests, leaving the trees to rot, or in some cases using them to beautify their palaces. Now both the nations and the trees rejoice, because the aggressor himself has been cut down. There are limits to human pride.

The second stanza goes to the underworld (14:9–11). The great man arrives covered with a blanket of worms, and all the kings he sent there get up off their thrones and crowd around to see this one who made such great boasts but is just as weak as they. Death is the great leveler. No matter what our earthly pretensions may have been, death snickers at them all. In this sense, death is a great relief. We may think of the great tyrant-kings of an earlier day: Hitler, Mussolini, Lenin, Stalin, Pol Pot; death has delivered us from them all.

The third stanza goes to heaven (14:12–15) and speaks of the foolish imaginations of this man who is now in the Pit. He thought he would be God. In the end, that is what pride is about. We will be self-existent, self-authenticating, self-gratifying, and it is all a silly fiction. We are, and can be, none of these. We came from a womb and return to a grave, and will we believe that we have any significance in ourselves? If there is any significance for any of us in this world, it will have to be a gift of love given to us by the One who is indeed self-existent, self-authenticating and self-gratifying.

The fourth stanza (14:16–20b) comes back to earth and pictures the mighty monarch as a dead body on a heap of corpses. There is some reason to believe that this may be a reference to the Assyrian emperor Sargon II whom it seems possible was the only Assyrian emperor who was killed on the battle-field. The data are not clear, but it seems a possibility. At any rate the picture here is quite clear: after all his great claims, the mighty king is brought down to the most abject humiliation: just a bloodied corpse among a host of other corpses on the field. He does not even receive a pompous funeral but goes into a mass grave with all his nameless foot-soldiers. This, Isaiah says, is the fixed end of all royal pride.

4. Divine Kingship

When we look for a positive treatment of king and kingdom in the book of Isaiah we find that it is restricted to Yahweh and to the promised Davidic king, the Messiah. Although it is never stated as such, it seems clear that the reader is intended to recognize the contrast: kingship as a human expression is deeply flawed, even at its best. Such power can only finally be entrusted to God and to his Messiah. This point is clearly implied in Isaiah's call narrative, Isa 6. As powerful and effective as Uzziah might have been, he had died, and his power died with him. Furthermore, it was because Uzziah had tried to infringe on the holiness of Yahweh, that he had spent his last years stricken with a contagious skin disease (2 Chr 26:16–21). Only Yahweh is holy, and it is his glory alone that fills the earth. Human kingship offers no hope for the human condition, only divine kingship.

The contrast is further stated in 24:21–23: all that would pretend to absolute power, whether "the powers in the heavens above" or "the kings on the earth below" will be thrown into prison, while Yahweh of heaven's armies "will reign on Mount Zion and Jerusalem … with great glory." No created thing can stand before the Creator in the pride of its own position or accomplishments.[4]

Yet further development of the contrast is found in Isa 28–33. As noted above, there is a progressive change of emphasis in these chapters with the failure of human leadership slowly replaced by the revelation of the King whose reign would be one of blessing. The point is introduced in capsule form in the opening verses of chapter twenty-eight, where judgment on the drunken revelry of Samaria's kings in verses 1–4 is followed by this statement: "In that day Yahweh of heaven's armies will be a glorious crown, a beautiful wreath for the remnant of his people. He will be a breath of justice to the one who sits in judgment, and strength to those who turn back the battle in the gate" (28:5–6, my trans.). The failure of the human leaders to perceive reality as it is found in Yahweh is the central theme of the succeeding chapters until finally by chapter 33 the focus has shifted completely to the kingdom of Yahweh. "Your eyes will see the king in his beauty and view a land that stretches afar" (33:17). "For the LORD is our judge; the LORD is our lawgiver, the LORD is our king; it is he who will save us" (33:22). Yahweh had called on the Judeans to trust him in the face of the Assyrian threat; instead, they had preferred to trust Egypt. But the day would

---

[4] See Wilson de Angelo Cunha, "'Kingship' and 'Kingdom': A Discussion of Isaiah 24:21–23 and 27:12--13," in *Formation and Intertextuality in Isaiah 24–27;* eds. J. Todd Hibbard, and Hyun Chul Paul Kim (Atlanta: SBL Press, 2013), 61–75; also William D. Barker, *Isaiah's Kingship Polemic: An Exegetical Study of Isaiah 24–27* (Tübingen: Mohr Siebeck, 2014); I. D. Wilson, "The Seat of Kingship: (Re)constructing the City in Isaiah 24–27," *Mnemosyne Supplementum* 375 (Leiden: Brill, 2015), 395–412.

come when they would realize that the only kingdom worthy of trust is Yahweh's: "LORD, be gracious to us; we long [Heb. wait] for you. Be our strength every morning, our salvation in the time of distress" (33:3).

A similar point is made in the second part of the book (Isa 40–66).[5] It is Yahweh who subdues kings before Cyrus (41:2; see also 45:1). As much as Assyria was the tool in Yahweh's hand (10:5), so is Cyrus. Both exercise the degree of rule they do only because it is granted to them by the Supreme Ruler of all. Furthermore, it is "Jacob's King" (41:21) who calls all the idols of Babylon to account. Think of it; the king of the captive land of Jacob has the authority to command the gods who supposedly secure Babylon's power! But that is exactly what the text asserts. It is further underlined in 43:14–15. There Yahweh announces that he will make the Babylonians fugitives. How is he able to do such a thing? Because "I am the LORD, your Holy One, Israel's Creator, your King."

Notice that the text does not say "the Holy One, the Creator, the King." Just as the repeated epithet "the Holy One of Israel" insists upon joining both the transcendence and the immanence of Yahweh, so do these phrases. Yahweh's kingship is not an abstract thing but is exercised in the concrete context of committed relationships. Of course, he is the King of the Universe, but his rule is actualized in relation to a people to whom he has committed himself. It is when people own him as King that the meaning of genuine kingship begins to emerge. This is not a despotic kingdom in which the subjects exist for the king. Rather, the rule of the king serves one purpose only: the blessing of his creatures so that they may grow into all they were meant to be.[6] When his people stop asserting their own autonomy and recognize that their will was meant to be subject to his, then they find their true selves and are fully free to realize their purpose in living.

---

[5] See Ulrich Berges, "Zion and the Kingship of YHWH in Isaiah 40–55," in *"Enlarge the Site of Your Tent": The City as Unifying Theme in Isaiah,* eds. Annemarieka van der Woude and A. van Wieringen (Leiden: Brill, 2011), 95–119.

[6] To translate Gen 17:1 as "Walk before me and be blameless" is to miss much of the flavor of the term תָּמִים. "Walk before me and be unblemished, be whole" would capture the sense better. What is Yahweh's goal for us? It is for us to be all we were meant to be.

In Isa 44:6, another appellation is added to the constellation just discussed. Yahweh is "Israel's King and Redeemer." He is the king who delivers his people from their bondage, a bondage that was fully self-imposed. Refusing to grant him the sole rule of their lives that their covenant with him required, fearing they he would not supply their needs as they perceived them to be, they had "sold themselves" (cf. 2 Kgs 17:17) into bondage to the gods of the nations and thus to the nations themselves. They had done this over and over for a thousand years. A king concerned only for his own rights and prestige might have delivered them from the consequences of their actions and reclaimed them a few times, but in the end it seems likely he would have simply wiped them out. Not so with this king. This king would do whatever it might take to restore his creatures, his holy ones, to himself. He could not bear to see them falling short of what he had made them to be; he would buy them back.

5. The Messianic King

This is where the Messiah, the anointed son of David, enters the picture. As mentioned above, ideal kingship for Isaiah is not merely found in Yahweh himself, but in the ideal Davidic monarch. Yahweh would delegate his kingly authority to a human. To understand this, we need to recall the promises to Abraham. They were three-fold: progeny, land, and blessing for the nations. Abraham received the first promise during his own lifetime, although he had to take the full implications of it on faith (Isa 41:8; 51:2). In the time of Joshua, Abraham's descendants received the second promise: the land. At that point, as recounted in the book of Judges, they lost their forward focus. They were a numerous people, living in their own land; there was nothing more for them to believe for. But there was more to believe for, in fact, it was the point of the whole process. How were Abraham's progeny to bless the world, a world laboring under the curse of sin? This is where the covenant of David comes into play. It is also where the peculiar nature of the kingdom of God begins to take shape. It is by means of the royal dynasty of David that Yahweh's kingship of his people, his creation, can be realized. There is something entirely fitting about this. Yahweh entrusts the realization of his rightful role to another. And this delegate is content to be an agent through whom Yahweh's purposes, not his own, can be realized. (Cf. Ps 2.)

This quality of self-effacement in the anointed king is seen immediately in Isa 7–11.[7] In these chapters Yahweh's solution to the terrific dilemmas facing Judah is embodied in, of all things, children. There are Shear-Jashub (7:3), Maher-shalal-hash-baz (8:1), and Immanuel (7:14; 8:8, 10). Surely, what Judah needed, and indeed, what the world needs, was a great Warrior, one who could smash our enemies.[8] Yet God couches his promised deliverance in the imagery of children, making the point explicit in 9:1–7: the deliverer, the king, is a child.[9] What is the point of such imagery? Surely it is the very point Jesus made when he said that we must enter the kingdom as children (Matt 18:4; Mark 10:15). What did he have in mind? The innocence of children? But children are far from innocent, as any parent knows! Then what? Surely it is the child's nearly-complete freedom from that neurotic self-consciousness that is consumed with image and position. Human kings, as represented in the book, are consumed with these matters, but not this king. Who is he, and why is he not like all the rest?

This unusual character, in contrast with the human kings portrayed elsewhere in the book, is continued in the description of the Davidic messiah and his kingdom that is found in Isa 11.[10] Here the dominant impression is of someone who does not rule in the typical manner. His judgments do not reflect those shaped by the fallen human spirit, but rather by the Spirit of Yahweh (Isa 11:2). Furthermore, his judgments are shaped by that consciousness of responsibility to the Creator that is expressed in the phrase "the fear of the LORD." Nor is this consciousness burdensome; rather, it is a "delight" (11:3). As a result, his rule will not be shaped by superficial impressions or whims, as is so often the case with those who believe themselves to be above

---

[7] See Paul D. Wegner, *An Examination of Kingship and Messianic Expectation in Isaiah 1–35* (Lewiston, NY: Mellen Biblical Press, 1992) for a detailed discussion of probable Messianic references.

[8] There is such a warrior described in 59:15b–21 and in the chiastic duplicate in 63:1–7. However, in the context of 56:1–66:17, it is the enemy of their own sin before which the people lie prostrate, and the Warrior comes with all his power to defeat that sin and enable them to become the clean lantern through which the light of God can shine upon the nations.

[9] For an argument that this is not a reference to an actual king see Michael E. W. Thompson, "Isaiah's Ideal King," *JSOT* 24 (1982): 79–88.

[10] Gregory R. Goswell, "Messianic Expectation in Isaiah 11," *WTJ* 79 (2017): 123–35.

accountability. Instead, he will rule with those qualities that are characteristics of Yahweh: righteousness, justice, and truth (faithfulness) (11:3–5). Thus, his kingdom will not be characterized by the violent conflict that is the characteristic of most human kingdoms, but rather by a harmony reflective of an experiential knowledge of Yahweh (11:6–9).

In the remainder of Isa 11:10–16, we see the intended outcome of the Davidic covenant:[11] all the nations of the world, including the remnant of his chosen people, will rally to the banner of this child king, the One who does not need to assert his rights, who is not concerned with his image, who rules by the Word and not the sword, who gladly acknowledges his responsibility to Yahweh, who is more concerned for his people's well-being than for his own. Through this king the vision of 2:1–5 will be realized: all the nations will flow to Jerusalem to learn from God's *torah*, his instructions, how to walk in his light. Later in the book, at 55:3–5, this purpose of the Davidic covenant is reiterated, and applied to the people as a whole. Through the same Davidic covenant they will call the nations, even nations they do not know, to come to Jerusalem, the Messiah's seat, where he will be the "witness," "ruler and commander of the peoples."

One example of this coming of the nations to the Davidic messiah is found in 16:4–5, where the refugees from Moab are depicted as coming as suppliants to the one from the house of David who sits on the throne. All oppression, destruction, and aggression will have been brought to an end, and "love" (חֶסֶד), "faithfulness" (אֱמֶת), "righteousness" (צֶדֶק), and "justice" (מִשְׁפָּט), the central features of the character of Yahweh, will characterize the person's rule. In short, the only one to whom can be entrusted the absolute power of kingship is the one who fully shares the qualities of the King of the Universe. Again, we ask who this person is?

---

[11] The fact that this person is twice referred to as "the Root of Jesse" rather than "the son of David" (11:1, 10) might possibly be accounted for in the context of Ahaz's kingship where the house of David was badly besmirched. The connotations were still clear: David was the root of Jesse, but the immediate associations were avoided.

In Isa 32, there is predicted the coming of a king who "will reign in righteousness and rulers who will rule with justice" (32:1). The succeeding verses (32:2–8) describe a kingdom that exists in order to bless its subjects with provisions and protection, where fools who prey on those they rule (32:6–7) will no longer receive the accolades of nobility (32:5, 8). Instead, the character of that kingdom will be such that the blind will see, the deaf will hear, the fearful will understand, and the stammerer will be able to speak clearly. In short, this kingdom will be one in which the disabled will be enabled. Although the language used is different, the similarities in content with Isa 11 argues that this promised king is the Messiah in particular, and not Yahweh, in a more general sense (as in, e.g., 33:21–22).

It is sometimes argued that one of the features that distinguishes Isa 40–66 from Isa 1–39 is the absence of a Messianic figure in the former.[12] However, I suggest that when we consider the character of the Messiah in 1–39 and compare that character with that of the so-called suffering servant in 41–53, it is clear that we are talking about the same person.[13] Notice particularly the initial presentation of the servant in 42:1–9. It is specifically said that the Spirit of Yahweh is upon him and that he will bring "justice" (מִשְׁפָּט, Yahweh's blessed order for life) to the world (42:1, 3, 4). That thought is expanded when Yahweh says that he "will make you a covenant to the people and a light to the nations" (42:6). It is further expanded in verse seven which describes his activity as opening blind eyes and freeing captives. This is the same thing that is said of the Messiah in Isa 11, that his rule will be for the sake of the nations, and for the restoration of the remnant (so also 61:1–3; see below). Finally, the same description is given of the demeanor of this Servant as is found in Isa 7–11: he will be self-effacing, not asserting his power and position, but making his authority felt through his Word.

---

[12] Ulrich Berges, "Kingship and Servanthood in the Book of Isaiah," in *The Book of Isaiah: Enduring Questions Answered Anew*, eds. Richard J. Bautch and J. Todd Hibbard (Grand Rapids: Eerdmans, 2014), 159–78.

[13] For a contrary opinion, see Gregory R. Goswell, "A Royal Isaianic Servant of Yahweh?," *SJOT* 31 (2017): 185–201.

The same points are made in different, yet similar language in 49:1–12. Once again, the Servant is entirely dependent on Yahweh, and responsible to him (49:3–4). Again, he asserts no authority except that which is expressed in his word (49:2). The purpose of his rule is to restore God's people to him, in fulfillment of the covenant (49:5, 8), but it is also to be a light to the nations, so that his salvation might reach the ends of the earth (49:6).

The remaining two presentations of the Servant, in 50:4–10, and 52:13–53:12, focus more directly on certain details of this Servant-King's rule, with the former stressing his complete subservience to, and faith in, Yahweh, and the latter the means by which his saving function will be achieved, namely, his own obedient self-sacrifice. This is all capped in the passage that Jesus used to announce his Messiahship: 61:1–3. The connection with the so-called Servant Songs is sealed by 61:1, "to bind up the broken-hearted, to proclaim freedom for the captives, and release from darkness for the prisoners," which is a very explicit allusion to 42:7. The further connection is found in the reference to the Spirit of Yahweh that is upon him. Thus, 11:1, 42:1, and 61:1 leave little doubt that we are to understand the Messiah as the Servant, and the Servant as the Messiah. Here is kingship as it is found in Yahweh: self-giving, self-denying love.[14]

The final references to kingship in the book are those found in Isa 60–62. Here the contrasts between human and divine kingship are registered most graphically. The kings of the earth who oppressed God's people, who threatened by their aggressions to wipe his people from the face of the earth, come in caravans to Jerusalem. Not only do they bring their resources to beautify the palace of the King, the temple, but they also come carrying Judah's children in their arms (60:3, 9; 62:2). They come to join in worship of the only true King, but they who once made Israel bow to them and serve them, also come to be the servants of Israel (60:10–12) in order that Israel may carry

---

[14] For a similar conclusion, although based on somewhat different grounds, see Hedy Hung, "The Kingship Motif in Isaiah 61:1–3," in *Torah and Tradition*, eds. Klaas Spronk and Hans Barstad (Leiden: Brill, 2017), 135–49.

out her role of ministers of the King (61:5–6) whose throne is heaven (66:1).[15] This final contrast between the King and the kings underlines the theme of the book as regards kingship: the only place where absolute power can safely reside is in the Triune God, where it is always subservient to love. The radical difference in the characters of King and kings also drives home another point, namely that the concept of a divine King is not derived from human kingship. Rather, it is the other way around, with the human kings being only deficient expressions of the prototype. Why do I say this? I say it because given the universal character of human kingship: acquisition of power for the benefit of the rulers, there is no way that we can extrapolate from their example and arrive at the idea of a King who rules only for the sake of those being ruled. Such an idea must, of necessity, be revealed, and equally of necessity, must be the norm for kingship as the Creator, heaven's King, intended it.

6. Conclusion

The sub-theme of this volume, Sufferings and Glory of the Messiah, is amply demonstrated in the book of Isaiah, in particular as this book addresses the idea of kingship. The theme is most pointedly addressed in the book's picture of the divine King. As noted above, many scholars deny that the so-called suffering servant of chapters 42, 49, 50, and 52–53 has any relation to the Messiah depicted in chapters 11, 16, and 32. However, that is not the case. This is particularly evident when chapter 11 is understood in its literary context of chapters seven through twelve. In those chapters, children are featured, from Shear-jashub and Immanuel in chapter seven, to Maher-shalal-hash-baz in chapter eight, to the Child in chapter nine, to the child who leads and the one who plays over the hole of the asp in chapter eleven. What is the point being made, especially in the context of the Syro-Ephraimite and Assyrian threats? Surely it is that God's promised deliverer, his Messiah, will not be a mighty man, brandishing the weapons of the world. God's power is not to found in the power of this world.

---

[15] For a discussion of these apparently contradictory ideas, see my "The Nations in Isaiah," in *The Holy One of Israel: Studies in Isaiah* (Eugene, OR: Wipf and Stock, 2014), 94–105.

That point is confirmed in the opening verses of chapter eleven. The Messiah will not rule in the typical manner and bravado of human kings. His power will be that of the Holy Spirit, his understanding will be conditioned by the fear of Yahweh, and his rod will be the Word. The glory of this King will not be the glory of this world. Rather, on that paradoxical pattern that is familiar to all students of the Bible, his power will be in what the world calls weakness.

In that light, the depiction of the sufferer in chapters forty-two through fifty-three becomes perfectly consistent, with the opening and closing notes in 52:13 and 53:12 making perfect sense. Because the servant has given himself away in suffering, he is highly exalted and divides spoil with the strong. The way to true glory is not through self-aggrandizement and self-promotion, but through suffering and self-denial.

But is this sufferer the glorious King? The answer to this question lies first of all in the congruence between this sufferer and the Messiah of chapter eleven, etc. Just as the Messiah is Spirit-motivated and empowered, so is the Sufferer (42:1), and just as the Messiah does not rule with earthly power, neither does the Sufferer perform his work through such power (42:2–4). But even more to the point, the task of the Sufferer is to restore Jacob/Israel (42:6; 49:5–6) and bring מִשְׁפָּט to the earth (42:1, 3). In particular, the latter is the work of the King. Across the ancient world, kings boasted of having established order in their lands as they "judged" (governed) their people. But this King, this Sufferer, would not merely boast about it; he would truly do it, and do it without what this world calls power.

Thus, we see in Isaiah the true King, in whose suffering the Creation's truest glory is achieved. Human kings seek glory by avoiding anything that smacks of suffering. As a result, their glory is but tinsel and chaff. It is when we lay aside such glory and suffer the loss of rights, position and power, that the Divine King can pour genuine glory on his own, just as he has done for his Son.[16]

---

[16] I am deeply grateful for the opportunity of writing the foregoing in tribute to T. Desmond Alexander, whose work has been a treasure for the church across the years. He has been a model of scholarship that is both responsible and godly.

THE MESSIAH IN THE BOOK OF THE TWELVE: GLORY THROUGH SUFFERING

—Anthony R. Petterson

1. Introduction

"Did not the Messiah have to suffer these things and then enter his glory?" (Luke 24:26; cf. Acts 26:22–23).[1]

"Concerning this salvation, the prophets who spoke of the grace that was to come to you, searched intently and with the greatest care, trying to find out the time and circumstances to which the Spirit of Christ in them was pointing when he predicted the sufferings of the Messiah and the glories that would follow" (1 Pet 1:10–11).

This study traces the theme of kingship across the Book of the Twelve and explores how the concept of a suffering Messiah develops.[2] Apart from Hab 3:13 (arguably), the technical use of the term "Messiah" is not found in the Twelve. However, the term provides a useful short-hand to express the hope seen across the collection for an ideal royal descendant of David through whom God will establish his

---

* It was my tremendous privilege to do PhD studies under T. D. (Desi) Alexander's supervision at the Queen's University of Belfast. As well as being a consummate gentleman, Desi is a wonderful model of serious scholarship that seeks to serve the church.

[1] Scripture quotations taken from NIV 2011.

[2] Since the 1990s, scholars have observed that the books of "the Twelve" do not seem to have been randomly collected, rather, there are chronological, literary, and thematic elements that indicate an intelligent design behind the ordering of the component parts. This has important implications for how the individual books of the collection are read, as argued by Christopher R. Seitz, *The Goodly Fellowship of the Prophets: The Achievement of Association in Canon Formation* (Grand Rapids: Baker Academic, 2009). He states: "An older approach that only recasts them in an alleged historical order and then reads them as individual works in an alleged historical context fails to grapple with the achievement of the whole in its present form" (42).

eternal kingdom, in keeping with his covenant with David in 2 Sam 7:1–17.[3] While the Hebrew and Greek traditions order the first six books of the Twelve differently, this does not impact this study, since the order of the books that deal with kingship remains the same.[4] Six books have superscriptions that locate their prophet with respect to various kings of Israel, Judah, and/or Persia (Hosea, Amos, Micah, Zephaniah, Haggai, and Zechariah). In these books, kings of Israel and Judah are often condemned by the prophets for their self-serving abuse of power. Yet the prophets also express hope for the Messiah, who will reunify the nation, bring justice and righteousness to the land, subjugate the nations, and establish God's glorious kingdom and its blessings. Each of these books, apart from Zephaniah, express aspects of this hope.[5] In addition, this study examines the book of Habakkuk's contribution to the theme with its reference to "your anointed one" (3:13).

In early books of the Twelve (Hosea, Amos), the suffering of the king is only implicit insofar as the king is one of God's people who will suffer exile as the punishment of God. In Micah the suffering of the king as part of the experience of exile is explicit, but it is not apparent that the Messiah will suffer. However, after the exilic experience and return to the land, it is evident that this has not refined the remnant that earlier prophets spoke of. At the end of the Twelve, the postexilic prophets speak of a future day of battle and another attack on Jerusalem and exile. In this battle the Messiah suffers death with the result that a remnant is cleansed, refined, forgiven, and inherits God's glorious kingdom.

---

[3] See David G. Firth, "Messiah," in *DOT:Pr*, 538. T. Desmond Alexander argues that behind the Davidic covenant is the expectation for a royal deliverer that goes back to Genesis ("Royal Expectations in Genesis to Kings: Their Importance for Biblical Theology," *TynBul* 49 [1998]: 204).

[4] English Bibles follow the masoretic tradition, beginning with: Hosea, Joel, Amos, Obadiah, Jonah, Micah. The order of these books in the Greek tradition is: Hosea, Amos, Micah, Joel, Obadiah, Jonah. See Rainer Kessler, "The Twelve: Structure, Themes, and Contested Issues," in *The Oxford Handbook of the Prophets*, ed. Carolyn J. Sharp (New York: Oxford University Press, 2016), 209.

[5] Zephaniah mentions king Josiah in 1:1, and God is called "the King of Israel" in 3:15. Zephaniah 3:14, where Daughter Zion/Daughter Jerusalem is called to sing, shout aloud, rejoice, and exalt in God and his salvation is reused in Zech 9:9 in association with the coming Davidic king.

2. Hosea

The book of Hosea is dated in 1:1 with reference to kings of Judah (Uzziah, Jotham, Ahaz, Hezekiah) and Israel (Jeroboam). While the prophet's ministry is set in the northern kingdom, reference to southern kings indicates the book's importance to Judah, where it was preserved.[6] In addition, listing the kings of Judah before Jeroboam of Israel reveals the prophet's concern for the house of David.[7] This concern becomes explicit in the opening chapters of the book.

In the symbolism of Hosea's marriage to Gomer and the names of her children, God explains that after the punishment of the northern kingdom of Israel, he will gather the Judeans and the Israelites together, and "they will appoint one leader ["head"] and will come up out of the land" (1:11 [MT 2:2]). Elsewhere, the term "head" (ראש) is used synonymously with "king" (e.g., 2 Sam 22:44; Isa 7:1, 8, 9, 16; Mic 2:13; Ps 18:43 [MT 18:44]).[8] Saying they will "appoint" (שׂים) one head need not be understood as the people choosing their own king. Rather, it is better understood as the tribes recognizing God's chosen king—with the emphasis falling on the *one* head over a reunited nation. Indeed, Deut 17:15 speaks of the people appointing (שׂים) the king God chooses. Reunited with their common head they "will come up out of the land" (1:11 [MT 2:2]), a phrase that has second exodus motifs (cf. Isa 11:16; Hos 2:15 [MT 2:17]). The implication is that the "head" has undergone the same suffering as

---

[6] J. Gordon McConville explains the omission of six of the northern kings during the same period as the four kings of Judah as indicating the book's later significance for Judah ("Hosea, Book of," in *DOT:Pr*, 339). See also Gregory Goswell, "'David their king': Kingship in the Prophecy of Hosea," *JSOT* 42 (2017): 216–17.

[7] While some see references to Judah in the book as later additions (e.g., Wolff), others argue that they were original to Hosea (e.g., Andersen and Freedman). Reconstructing the history of the composition of prophetic books is notoriously subjective involving great speculation about the points of view of the prophet and his redactors. It is best to proceed with the final form of the book assuming that, as McConville says: "It remains probable that the book preserves a record of the prophet's life and ministry" ("Hosea," 341).

[8] Herbert W. Bateman IV, Gordon H. Johnston and Darrell L. Bock, *Jesus the Messiah: Tracing the Promises, Expectations, and Coming of Israel's King* (Grand Rapids: Kregel, 2012), 116. See also Goswell, "David their king." He notes Jephthah is called "head," which seems to connote his pan-tribal leadership (Judg 10:18; 11:8, 9, 11; cf. Num 14:4). He concludes that the use of "head" in Hosea "does not rule out a Davidic candidate" (220).

the people of Judah and the people of Israel before he is appointed.

Hosea 3:5 makes it clear that this "head" is "David their king," whom the Israelites will seek along with the LORD after they have repented in exile.[9] The designation "David their king" recalls the ideal David with whom God made an eternal covenant promising that he would establish the throne of his offspring's kingdom forever (2 Sam 7:14–16). Hosea describes this kingdom as a return "to the LORD and to his blessings in the last days" (3:5).

Throughout the rest of the book, Hosea evaluates kingship in the northern kingdom negatively. There are at least three reasons for this.[10] The first is the quick succession of revolutions and assassinations in Hosea's time. This is reflected in the "oven" metaphor in Hos 7:7 which conveys the political intrigue and violence that led to kings and rulers being consumed (cf. 2 Kgs 15:10, 14, 23, 25). Second is the corrupt ways of the northern kings and their officials, indicated in Hos 5:1, 7:3, and probably also in 10:4 where there is injustice because kings fail to keep their word.[11] The questions in 13:10–11 about the (non) presence of kings and rulers who might save Israel might indicate a time when Israel was without a king,[12] or it may be ironic since the contemporary king was impotent and ineffective.[13] A third and more fundamental

---

[9] See Douglas K. Stuart, *Hosea–Jonah*, WBC 31 (Waco, TX: Word, 1987). He says: "It is another way of speaking of the 'one leader' predicted in 2:2 [1:11]; i.e., a member of the Davidic line" (68). Grace I. Emmerson notes there is "evidence of a strong desire on part of at least some northerners to affirm their allegiance to David, and a jealous assertion of their right to claim him as their king (2 Sam. 19:41ff.)" (*Hosea: An Israelite Prophet in Judean Perspective*, JSOTSup 28 [Sheffield: JSOT Press, 1984], 105).

[10] See A. Gelston, "Kingship in the Book of Hosea," in *OtSt 19*, ed. A. S. Van der Woude (Leiden: Brill, 1974), 71.

[11] While some understand Hos 10:4 to refer to the people, it is better to see it referring to the king of Israel. Stuart states: "The king does not by himself produce all the injustice. His neglect, rather, allows the sinful human nature of the people (cf. 4:12) to seek its natural end: a society that is corrupt" (*Hosea–Jonah*, 161).

[12] J. Andrew Dearman suggests it is just after king Hoshea was captured by the Assyrians (2 Kgs 17:1–4) (*The Book of Hosea*, NICOT [Grand Rapids: Eerdmans, 2010], 324).

[13] The NIV translates Hos 13:11 in the past tense: "So in my anger I gave you a king, and in my wrath I took him away." Most interpret this as referring to king Saul, whom God took away in his wrath on account of Saul's disobedience. However, the verbs more usually refer to future or incomplete action: "I will give you a king in my anger and will take away a king in my wrath." In this case, it refers

reason is the belief that only kings from the house of David in Jerusalem are legitimate and those of the northern kingdom are apostate. This seems to be reflected in Hos 8, which recalls the northern kingdom setting up their own rival kingship to the house of David under Jeroboam (8:4; cf. 2 Kgs 13). These kings were set up without God's authorization ("without my consent"). This is also contrary to Deut 17:15, where the LORD is the one to choose the king that the people appoint (cf. 1 Chr 22:9). At the same time, contemporary rulers in Judah do not escape Hosea's criticism (5:8–10).[14]

In summary, Hosea consistently critiques kingship in the northern kingdom from its inception under Jeroboam to what it had become in Hosea's day.[15] The consequence is that God will bring an end to kingship in Israel. Yet Hosea does not condemn kingship as an institution.[16] Indeed, after God has brought on the people the covenant curses, which will culminate in exile, he will restore the nation to himself, and reunite them under a king from the house of David. In Hosea, the suffering of the Messiah is only implicit insofar as the people and the princes of Judah will suffer exile for their sin (5:10, 14; 6:11; 8:14; 12:2) and the Messiah is appointed in the aftermath of this suffering (1:11 [MT 2:2]).

---

to the king of Assyria as the agent of God's punishment, whom God will also remove in time (cf. 5:13; 10:6). See Duane A. Garrett, *Hosea, Joel*, NAC 19A (Nashville: Broadman & Holman, 1997), 261; Marvin A. Sweeney, *The Twelve Prophets, Volume 1: Hosea, Joel, Amos, Obadiah, Jonah*, Berit Olam: Studies in Hebrew Narrative & Poetry (Collegeville: The Liturgical Press, 2000), 133.

[14] The term "prince" (שׂר) in 5:10 can refer to a wide range of leaders in the OT, such as the leaders of tribes (e.g., Judg 5:15), and the leaders of foreign nations (Gen 12:15; 1 Sam 29:3; Isa 10:8; Jer 48:7; Amos 1:15). It can refer to various officials in the royal court such as the prison keeper, chief butler, and chief baker (Gen 39:1; Gen 40:2). Sometimes it refers to a military leader (Judg 4:2; 1 Sam 17:55; 22:2), including the head of the LORD's heavenly army (Josh 5:14–15; cf. Dan 10:13, 20, 21; 12:1). In Isa 9:6 [MT 9:5], the Messiah has the title "Prince of Peace". Jeremiah 26:10 speaks of the "princes of Judah" (*NAB* 2010) and the context indicates they have judicial power within the "king's palace" (cf. 2 Chr 21:9; 2 Chr 31:8). In the postexilic period, the term refers to heads of the priests (Ezra 8:24) as well as tribal leaders (1 Chr 27:2). Princes are also seen as corrupt and under judgment elsewhere in Hosea (7:3, 5, 16; 9:15; 13:10).

[15] Emmerson writes: "Thus the prophet objects not only to what Israel's kingship was in practice, but to its very existence" (*Hosea*, 108).

[16] Emmerson states: "We have found no evidence to support the view that Hosea condemns kingship as an institution." (*Hosea*, 108). Similarly, Goswell says: "nor is it clear that he [Hosea] disapproved in principle of the institution of kingship as a form of government" ("David their king," 219).

3. Amos

Like Hosea, Amos' ministry is set in the northern kingdom of Israel in the eighth century; however, his book is dated not only with reference to Jeroboam king of Israel, but also king Uzziah of Judah (1:1). Amos begins where Joel ends, with God roaring from Zion and from Jerusalem against foreign nations for their "sins" (compare Joel 4:16 with Amos 1:2). The association of the LORD with Zion/Jerusalem is itself a critique of the northern kingdom. The chief sins Amos identifies are religious hypocrisy and violating the terms of the national covenant, particularly by abusing the poor and needy. Like Hosea, Amos announces God will punish the Israelites for their sin by sending them into exile.[17]

The critique of northern kings is not as prominent in Amos as Hosea, but it is present. In Amos 7, the partisan priest Amaziah summarizes the message of Amos as announcing the military defeat of king Jeroboam and the exile of Israel (7:11). Amaziah does not mention that Amos first and foremost decries Israel's sin (this would be an implicit criticism of him and Jeroboam for failing to address it). Amaziah simply restates the punishment Amos had announced on the house of Jeroboam in terms that sound seditious (cf. 7:9). Though Amaziah attempts to silence Amos (7:12–13), he finds himself under personal sentence of punishment along with his family (7:17).

While exile seems at first to bring complete destruction of the nation (9:4), the second half of Amos 9 reveals that God will not totally destroy Jacob's descendants (9:8). For the first time in the Twelve, exile is associated explicitly with the idea of purifying the nation, here using the image of sifting grain (9:9).[18] Since sinners will

---

[17] The first explicit mention of exile is in Amos 5:5, where Gilgal will surely go into exile (גלה), and Bethel will become trouble (5:5). This first use of גלה in the Twelve refers to a punishment on the city of Gilgal. Yet by the end of Amos 5, the punishment of exile is extended to Israel for its idolatry and injustice (5:27), and then in Amos 6, to the leadership in Zion and Samaria for their luxurious self-indulgence (6:1–7). For a sketch that outlines the theme of exile in Amos, see David L. Petersen, "Prophetic Rhetoric and Exile," in *The Prophets Speak on Forced Migration*, ed. Mark J. Boda, et al. (Atlanta: SBL Press, 2015), 14.

[18] Mark J. Boda argues, "[Amos 9] reveals that ultimately it will take a total destruction and exile to purge sinners from among the people" (*A Severe Mercy: Sin and Its Remedy in the Old Testament* [Winona Lake, IL: Eisenbrauns, 2009], 314). Cf. Rainer Albertz, "Exile as Purification. Reconstructing the 'Book of the Four'," in *Thematic Threads in the Book of the Twelve*, ed. Paul L.

in this respect seems to use "anointed one" anachronistically,[51] in terms of the rhetoric of Habakkuk's prayer, it looks forward to another "anointed one."[52] Similarly, Habakkuk recalls how the head of the house of the wicked was crushed, and his head was pierced with his own spear (3:13–14). Though the Hebrew is difficult to translate, several scholars argue that this picture reflects God conquering the forces of chaos by breaking the heads of the dragons and crushing the heads of Leviathan, such as in Ps 74:13–14 (cf. Ps 89:9–12 [MT 89:10–13]).[53] In Habakkuk's prayer it looks back to the exodus (cf. Exod 15) and forward to the defeat of the king of Babylon and his armies, and beyond this to the ultimate conquest of evil. Early readers of Habakkuk may have connected the "anointed one" with Cyrus (cf. Isa 45:1).[54] However, those who compiled the Twelve still experienced subjugation by the nations even after the downfall of Babylon and the return from exile decreed by Cyrus. In the overall context of the Twelve, this prophecy must bring to mind the future Davidic king anticipated by Hosea, Amos, and Micah since the term "anointed one" is elsewhere in the OT often associated with kingship, particularly Davidic kingship.[55]

Brill, 1992], 98). See also Richard D. Patterson, *Nahum, Habakkuk, Zephaniah: An Exegetical Commentary* (Texas: Biblical Studies Press, 2013), 228; Martin Pakula, *Nahum, Habakkuk, & Zephaniah: The End of Evil* (Sydney South: Aquila, 2014), 128.

[51] Andersen, *Habakkuk*, 335.

[52] Daniel I. Block asserts it "refers to Israel as a whole" ("My Servant David: Ancient Israel's Vision of the Messiah," in *Israel's Messiah in the Bible and the Dead Sea Scrolls*, Richard S. Hess and M. Daniel Carroll R. [Grand Rapids: Baker Academic, 2003], 24–25). This connection would be unique and is therefore unlikely. Compare O. Palmer Robertson, *The Books of Nahum, Habakkuk, and Zephaniah*, NICOT (Grand Rapids: Eerdmans, 1990), 237.

[53] F. F. Bruce, "Habakkuk," in *The Minor Prophets: An Exegetical and Expository Commentary*, 3 vols., ed. Thomas Edward McComiskey (Grand Rapids: Baker, 1993), 2:890; Andersen, *Habakkuk*, 336–337. See also James Hamilton, "The Skull Crushing Seed of the Woman: Inner-Biblical Interpretation of Genesis 3:15," *SBJT* 10 (2006): 37.

[54] So Robertson, *Nahum, Habakkuk, Zephaniah*, 237–38.

[55] Block, "Servant," 36–49. Commentators who interpret this passage to ultimately point forward to Israel's Messiah include: Patterson, *Commentary*, 224–225; Robertson, *Nahum, Habakkuk, Zephaniah*, 238; Carl Edwin Amerding, "Habakkuk," in *Jonah, Nahum, Habakkuk, Zephaniah: The Expositor's Bible Commentary*, Revised edit., ed. Tremper Longman III and David E. Garland (Grand Rapids: Zondervan, 2008), 645.

To summarize, Habakkuk is told of the coming Babylonian crisis and prays that just as God judged and saved in the past with his anointed, he will do so again. Habakkuk's prayer anticipates a battle when the LORD and his anointed one will conquer the forces of wickedness. If the "anointed one" is the object of God's salvation, then the suffering of the Messiah is certain (since suffering is the context of Habakkuk's prayer). If he is the agent of God's salvation, which the Hebrew suggests, then like Hosea, Amos, and Micah, his suffering is only implicit. The theme of a future battle involving the Messiah is developed in Haggai and Zechariah.

6. Haggai

The book of Haggai is set after the people of Judah have experienced the destruction of Jerusalem and exile. The "remnant" are the survivors who have returned to dwell in the land (1:12, 14). Yet they live under Persian rule and mark their history not with reference to a Judean king, but Darius, the king of Persia (1:1). As the book progresses, the significance of Darius reduces. In 1:1 and 1:15 he is "King Darius," in 2:10 he is just "Darius," and in the dating formula which introduces the final oracle in 2:20 he is not mentioned at all. This reflects the movement of the book from judgment to hope, and the content of the final oracle which concerns the future Davidic king.

Haggai calls the people to rebuild the temple and their community life in view of the coming day of the LORD —a day when he will shake the heavens and the earth, filling his house with glory (2:6–9), overthrowing foreign kingdoms, and restoring his king (2:20–23). Given the expectation raised earlier in the Twelve that exile will sift and refine God's people, it is reasonable to expect that the remnant will exhibit obedience to the LORD. Indeed, the people are reported as obeying the message of Haggai as the LORD stirs up their spirit (1:12–14). However, much of the book demonstrates that the experience of exile has not changed the hearts of the people. Their failure to prioritize the building of the temple is a cause of displeasure to the LORD and they have consequently suffered drought and adversity (1:6, 9–11). Their continued defilement from this disobedience has brought the curses of the covenant on them (2:17). Hence there is some ambiguity in Haggai about the heart of the people and whether exile has truly refined a righteous remnant. Yet the book holds out hope that since the foundation of the temple is laid, and the people seem to have returned to the LORD, their circumstances will soon change, and curse will be replaced by blessing (2:18–19).

Haggai's fourth and final prophecy is addressed to Zerubbabel and concerns the house of David (cf. 2 Sam 7:11–16).[56] God promises to shake the cosmos (cf. v. 6) and devastate the power of non-Israelite kingdoms, shattering their military might (v. 22). God also promises to make Zerubbabel his signet ring. This must be understood against the background of God's punishment of King Jehoiachin in Jer 22:24–30, the punishment which included the removal of the Davidic king from the throne, the destruction of Jerusalem, and the exile of many of the city's inhabitants. Haggai promises Zerubbabel that in addition to his oversight of the temple's reconstruction, he will re-establish the Davidic line in Jerusalem from which the promised Messiah will come.[57] While some scholars argue that Haggai announced that Zerubbabel was the Messiah, this interpretation goes beyond what the oracle says and certainly cannot stand when read as part of the Twelve since the expectations associated with the Messiah are not realized with Zerubbabel.[58]

In summary, Haggai's prophecy that the LORD will make Zerubbabel like his signet ring engenders hope that with the rebuilding of the temple, God will send the Davidic king promised by earlier prophets. While the suffering of the Messiah is not explicit, since his coming is accompanied by a future day of battle against non-Israelite nations (in a similar way to Habakkuk), it opens the way for the expansion of these themes in Zechariah.

---

[56] Boda identifies the vocabulary used elsewhere as that of Davidic appointment ("Figuring the Future: The Prophets and the Messiah," in *The Messiah in the Old and New Testaments*, ed. Stanley E. Porter [Grand Rapids: Eerdmans, 2007], 53).

[57] See the detailed assessment of the relevant scholarly literature by William T. Koopmans, *Haggai*, HCOT (Leuven: Peeters, 2017), 283–94.

[58] See further, Anthony R. Petterson, *Behold Your King: The Hope for the House of David in the Book of Zechariah*, LHBOTS 513 (New York: T&T Clark, 2009), 63–65.

7. Zechariah

Like Haggai, Zechariah is dated with reference to Darius, indicating the shadow of exile still hangs over God's people (cf. 1:1, 7; 7:1). The book has three main parts. The first comprises eight night-visions that, taken together, present hope for the return of the LORD to Jerusalem, the rebuilding of the temple, the eradication of covenantal unfaithfulness from God's people, and the subjugation of hostile nations (chs. 1–6).[59] The second part deals with a question about the need for fasting in view of the near completion of the temple (chs. 7–8). The third part comprises two oracles that envision a future attack on Jerusalem by hostile nations, whereupon God comes and delivers his people and establishes his reign over all the earth (chs. 9–11; 12–14). Passages from this final part of Zechariah are quoted more often than any other prophet in the passion narratives of the Gospels. Among the Twelve, Zechariah has the most to contribute to the theme of the suffering of the Messiah before he enters his glory.

In the center of the night visions and in the sign-action that follows them, Zechariah restates the hope for a future Davidic king. In Zechariah's fourth vision, the high priest Joshua is cleansed and commissioned to serve, along with his priestly associates, in the reconstructed temple (3:1–7). Being reinstated, the priesthood serves as a symbol of God's promise to bring "my servant, the Branch" (3:8; cf. 6:12). The term "the Branch" (צֶמַח) is better translated "Shoot."[60] It refers to a future Davidic king (beyond Zerubbabel), who will sprout forth from the stump of the fallen house of David. The terminology comes from Jeremiah (23:5; 33:15), but Isaiah (11:1) and Ezekiel (17:22–24) use the image of a shoot in a similar way. As a metaphor, it highlights the failure of the house of David in history and that any future it might have lies with the LORD (in Zech 3:8 the LORD will "bring" Shoot). While the great tree of the Davidic monarchy was cut down in the judgment of the exile, God would cause a future king to shoot up from this stump. With his coming, God will "remove the sin of this land in a single day" (3:9), and usher in a day of peace and prosperity (3:10).

---

[59] As well as eight night-visions (1:7–6:8), this broader section also contains an introduction (1:1–6) and a symbolic action (6:9–15).

[60] See further Petterson, *Behold Your King*, 87–92.

In Zechariah's fifth vision of a lampstand, Zerubbabel is given the key task of completing the temple in which the priesthood will serve (4:1–10). Zerubbabel was the Persian appointed governor and was of Davidic ancestry (cf. 1 Chr 3:17–19). The two olive trees that supply the lampstand with oil are often interpreted as Joshua and Zerubbabel, who are "the two who are anointed" (4:14).[61] However, there are many problems with this interpretation. The phrase is more accurately translated "the two sons of oil" and in the vision they do not receive oil but supply it. Hence, the two olive trees are better understood as the prophets Haggai and Zechariah.[62] While this vision does not directly promise the Messiah, the promised completion of the Jerusalem temple would naturally raise the hope of a king to be reinstated on the throne of David based on the covenant with David in 2 Sam 7 and the close connection between the temple and the throne (i.e. the house of Yahweh and house of David).

After the night vision reports, Zechariah is told to fashion a crown and to set it on the head of the high priest Joshua (6:11). Space does not permit an examination of the details of this complex passage here, something I have done elsewhere.[63] Suffice to say, this symbolic action prepares a crown for and anticipates the coming of Shoot, who will build the eschatological temple promised by the earlier prophets (6:12–13; cf. Isa 2:2–3; Jer 3:16–18; Ezek 40–41; Mic 4:1–2; Hag 2:7–9). When the future Davidic king comes, he will be clothed with majesty and will rule as the LORD's co-regent and priest, which shall issue forth in a reign of peace (6:13; cf. Ps 110).

Before turning to the third part of Zechariah, it is important to note that throughout the first two parts it becomes clear that the destruction of Jerusalem and the experience of exile has not refined the righteous remnant of which earlier prophets spoke. From the beginning, the call to "return to me" (1:3) implies that exiles who

---

[61] E.g., Carol L. Meyers and Eric M. Meyers, *Haggai, Zechariah 1–8: A New Translation with Introduction and Commentary*, AB (New York: Doubleday, 1987), 258–59, 275.

[62] Mark J. Boda, *The Book of Zechariah*, NICOT (Grand Rapids: Eerdmans, 2015), 315–16.

[63] Anthony R. Petterson, "A New Form-Critical Approach to Zechariah's Crowning of the High Priest Joshua and the Identity of "Shoot" (Zechariah 6:9–15)," in *The Book of the Twelve and the New Form Criticism*, ed. Mark J. Boda, M. H. Floyd and C. M. Toffelmire (Atlanta: SBL, 2015), 285–304; Anthony R. Petterson, *Haggai, Zechariah & Malachi*, ApOTC 25 (Nottingham: Apollos, 2015), 181–91; Petterson, *Behold Your King*, 100–114.

have returned to Jerusalem are not living in full obedience to the LORD. While the people initially respond positively to the preaching of Zechariah (1:6; cf. Hag 1:12–15), several passages indicate that sin is still an issue. For instance, the fifth vision identifies some in the community who "despise the day of small things" (4:10). The sixth vision shows that theft and swearing falsely continue to be a problem, and that there is a failure of justice since those who commit these crimes are wrongly acquitted (5:3–4).[64] The seventh vision of a flying ephah anticipates the removal of iniquity, wickedness, and idolatry from the land of God's people (5:6–7). These features of the visions indicate that God's glorious kingdom promised by the earlier prophets has not fully arrived, and that the same sins that led to Jerusalem's earlier destruction and exile persist. This is also evident in chapters 7–8 where Zechariah challenges the community about their obedience to the terms of the national covenant. This problem seems to be one of the issues that the final section of the book addresses.

Zechariah 9–14 comprises two oracles that are generally considered to come from a time after the temple has been completed (cf. 11:3). These oracles present and explore different perspectives on a great battle at Jerusalem that will usher in the restored kingdom of God. Zechariah 9 establishes the broad outline of this program. Chapters 10–14 then telescope different aspects of the battle to focus on various themes. One of the features of these chapters is the way that the prophet draws on earlier biblical material to portray the future.[65]

Zechariah 9 begins by proclaiming that God is coming to re-establish the kingdom promised to David, with the cities mentioned in this section marking the extent of the kingdom at the time of David (9:1–8).[66] In 9:9–10, the coming king is presented as "the lynchpin of the restored land and people."[67] There is a fourfold

---

[64] See further, Anthony R. Petterson, "The Flying Scroll That Will Not Acquit the Guilty: Exodus 34.7 in Zechariah 5.3," *JSOT* 38 (2014): 347–61.

[65] Konrad R. Schaefer, "Zechariah 14: A Study in Allusion," *CBQ* 57 (1995): 72.

[66] For this and other proposals for why the cities are mentioned, see Petterson, *Haggai, Zechariah & Malachi*, 216.

[67] Carol L. Meyers and Eric M. Meyers, *Zechariah 9–14: A New Translation with Introduction and Commentary* (New York: Doubleday, 1993), 169.

description of the king. Unlike kings of the past, who often used their position to serve themselves, this future king will be "righteous" (cf. Jer 23:5). The NIV translates the next two descriptions as "victorious" and "lowly," but these words are better translated with their more usual meanings of "saved" (cf. Ps 33:16–17) and "afflicted" (cf. Isa 53:4, 7).[68] This indicates that that coming king will suffer some kind of ordeal before being saved by God. This ordeal is the subject of chapters 12–13. The final description of the king coming to Jerusalem "riding on a donkey" is best understood against the backdrop of the return of king David to Jerusalem after suffering exile at the hands of Absalom, an exile in which donkeys also feature (2 Sam 16:2).[69] God saved David in battle and delivered him back to Jerusalem as king. There may also be an echo of the promise of kingship to Judah in Gen 49:8–12, since it contains the only other instance of the phrase "the foal of a donkey" in the OT.[70] With these descriptions, for the first time in the Twelve, the suffering of the Messiah is clearly stated. Unlike kings of Israel's past who so often used their power in self-service, the future king trusts in the LORD, who delivers him. This king will rule over a reunited Israel, over all the nations, and over a kingdom that extends to the end of the earth (9:10; cf. Ps 72:8). The LORD will then use his people to defeat their enemies and establish them in the land under the heir of David's throne (9:11–17). In this way, chapter 9 presents the broad outline of God's plan to restore his kingdom.

Zechariah 10–11 draws on the Davidic dynasty tradition and the shepherd imagery of the earlier prophets to explain the present circumstances of the people and to offer hope for the future. The pattern of Zech 9 is reflected in chapter 10, where the king is probably to be understood as one of the leaders in 10:4 (cornerstone, tent peg, battle bow). God will use this group of leaders to defeat the enemies of his people and re-establish his people in the land, reuniting Judah and Ephraim as he had done in the

---

[68] See further Petterson, *Haggai, Zechariah & Malachi*, 221–22.

[69] Pamela J. Scalise, "Zechariah, Malachi," *Minor Prophets II* (Peabody: Hendrickson, 2009), 177–366 (274); Michael R. Stead, *Zechariah: The Lord Returns*, Reading the Bible Today (Sydney South: Aquila Press, 2015), 145.

[70] Richard C. Steiner, "Genesis 49:10: On the Lexical and Syntactic Ambiguities of עַד as Reflected in the Prophecies of Nathan, Ahijah, Ezekiel, and Zechariah," *JBL 132* (2013): 51–53.

days of David (10:6–9).

Zechariah 11 contains two sign actions.[71] The first (11:4–14) is best understood as a dramatic representation of Israel's history to the exile. It places the responsibility for the division of the kingdom and the exilic experience on self-serving and self-aggrandizing leaders (including past kings of Israel and Judah) and on the people who failed to value the LORD as their shepherd. The second sign-action (11:15–17) shows that the people have received what they deserve for their rejection of God as shepherd. A foreign shepherd who has no concern for their welfare is presently ruling them. However, the emphatic note of woe on the worthless shepherd and his allies (11:17; cf. 11:3) serves to raise the expectation of a shepherd king to come; a shepherd who will save the flock, bring them home, and deal with them righteously.

The phrase "on that day" occurs 17 times through Zech 12–14 and serves to link the events described in these chapters. Zechariah 12 portrays a future attack by the nations against Jerusalem (to which ch. 14 returns).[72] While it is reminiscent of the Babylonian attack in 587 BC, this time the LORD will intervene to strengthen his people in order to repel their attackers (12:2–9). There is no reason given for the attack, but since it follows directly from the account of Israel's rejection of God in chapter 11, and since the outcome of the battle is the opening of a fountain for the house of David and the inhabitants for sin and for impurity (13:1), it suggests that this future battle will in some way finally deal with the sin that remained in the postexilic community and its continuing defilement of the land. On the day of victory and deliverance for the inhabitants of Jerusalem and Judah, the house of David is said to be like God (12:8). That is, the house of David will once again lead and protect God's

---

[71] Elsewhere I have surveyed and assessed several different approaches to the interpretation of the sign actions. See Petterson, *Behold Your King*, 168–194; Petterson, *Haggai, Zechariah & Malachi*, 241–52.

[72] Ch. 14 is essentially a replay of the battle in ch. 12, with more detail and a greater emphasis on the agency of God who strikes the warriors with plague and panic (14:12–13). Language elsewhere associated with the Babylonian campaign against Jerusalem in 587 BC is employed in v. 2 to speak of Jerusalem being "captured" (לכד) (cf. Jer 32:3, 24, 28; 34:22; 37:8; 38:3, 28), "ransacked" (or "looted" (שסס) (cf. Ps 89:41 [MT 89:40]; Jer 30:16), and explicit reference to exile: "half the city will go into exile (בגולה)."

people like God himself, presumably through the agency of the Messiah.

In the battle's aftermath, an individual is reported to have been pierced (Zech 12:10). There are several elements that support identifying this figure as the Messiah. These include the abrupt shift from the first to third persons in referring to the one who is pierced (12:10); the allusions to the death of king Josiah at Megiddo when he was pierced by an arrow that results in a national outpouring of grief (12:11; cf. 2 Chr 36:23–25);[73] the nature and extent of the mourning that highlights the priestly and Davidic lines (12:12–14); and the cleansing that comes to the community as a result of this event through the fountain that it opens for cleansing from sin and uncleanness (13:1; cf. 3:9).

Finally, Zech 13:7–9 is a short oracle that speaks of a future refining judgment for God's people that will result in a new covenant relationship. Returning to the shepherd metaphor of chapters 9–11, the LORD commands that an individual leader called "my shepherd ... the man who is close to me" be struck with a sword so that the sheep "will be scattered" (פּוּץ), language often associated with exile (e.g., Gen 11:8–9; Deut 28:64; 30:3; Neh 1:8; Jer 9:16; Ezek 34:5). In further language reminiscent of exile (cf. Ezek 5:2–4), "two-thirds will be struck down and perish" and a third part will be refined further, like silver and gold (13:8–9).[74] While the identity of "my shepherd" is not explicit, there are several features of the immediate and wider contexts that support interpreting it as another portrait of the Messiah.[75] The suffering of the Messiah is integral to the purification of a remnant who enjoy a fully restored relationship with God (Zech 13:9; cf. 2:11 [MT 2:15]; 8:8; 9:16).

Zechariah 9–14 therefore marks a significant development in the Twelve. Because the Babylonian exile failed to bring about the purified remnant anticipated by

---

[73] Antti Laato, *Josiah and David Redivivus: The Historical Josiah and the Messianic Expectations of Exilic and Postexilic Times*, ConBOT 33 (Stockholm: Almqvist & Wiksell, 1992), 293.

[74] Boda notes: "it is possible that the two parts include those who are cut off from the community and sent into exile ... as opposed to those who perish" ("Scat! Exilic Motifs in the Book of Zechariah," in *The Prophets Speak on Forced Migration*, ed. Mark J. Boda, et al. [Atlanta: SBL Press, 2015], 174–75).

[75] See further, Petterson, *Haggai, Zechariah & Malachi*, 276–278; Stead, *Zechariah: The Lord Returns*, 197–99.

earlier prophets, Zechariah draws on the past to speak of another exile-like experience that will purify Jerusalem from sin and impurity. Then God's kingship over the whole earth will be established in all its glory (14:9).[76] Like Isaiah's presentation of the suffering servant, Zechariah prophesies the death of the Messiah. The result is a new covenant relationship between God and his people (cf. Zech 13:9).[77] While the vicarious nature of the king's death is not as explicit as it is with Isaiah's suffering servant, the fact that it results in cleansing suggests it has a sacrificial function, since in the Torah sacrifice is normally required for purification from sin. In this way the Messiah will function as a priest (cf. Zech 6:13; like David cf. 2 Sam 24:18–25), bringing cleansing.[78]

8. Conclusion

In tracing the theme of kingship across the Twelve, what comes to the fore is the problem of Israel's sin, which both the kings of Israel and Judah are caught up in. Hosea, Amos, and Micah announce God's coming judgment for sin in which the kings of Israel and Judah will inevitably suffer and the people will experience the ultimate covenant curse—attack at the hands of non-Israelite nations and exile. God will raise up the Messiah in the aftermath of this national suffering, but the suffering of the Messiah is not explicit in these books. Habakkuk looks back to Israel's past and forwards to an "anointed one" who will conquer the forces of wickedness in a battle. If he is the agent of God's salvation, which the Hebrew suggests, then his suffering is only hinted at. After the people of Judah have experienced exile and returned to the

---

[76] Boda comments: "In a final phase Yahweh threatens to return from exile, but this time to bring judgment on Jerusalem, which would experience exile again, even as Yahweh unilaterally purifies the community" ("Scat!," 180). Contrast C. & E. Meyers, who argue that "the notion of another destruction and exile that would accompany the ruler's demise does not seem warranted by prophetic evaluations of postexilic society" (*Zechariah 9–14*, 388). Yet even in 13:1–6 it is clear that idolatry, false prophecy, and impurity are present in the postexilic community.

[77] See Michael R. Stead, "Suffering Servant, Suffering David, and Stricken Shepherd," in *Christ Died for Our Sins: Essays on the Atonement*, ed. Michael R. Stead (Canberra: Barton Books, 2013), 62–83. He demonstrates that Zechariah's portrait draws on the experience of David in 2 Samuel and the Psalms, along with the suffering servant of Isaiah.

[78] See further, Petterson, *Behold Your King*, 237–45.

land, the books of Haggai and Zechariah are clear that it has not refined the righteous remnant of earlier prophetic expectation. At the same time, these prophets confirm that the earlier promises about a future Messiah still stand. Zechariah reveals most fully in the book of the Twelve the concept of a suffering Messiah. Chapters 9–14 lay out God's plan for Jerusalem to go through yet another attack and exile-like experience. Drawing on earlier biblical material, Zechariah presents a portrait of a Messiah who is afflicted and saved (Zech 9:9). As this portrait is developed, Zechariah speaks of the Messiah being pierced in battle by his own people (12:10) and struck with a sword by God's own intent (13:7). As a result, Jerusalem will be cleansed of sin and impurity (13:1), made holy (14:20–21), and God's kingship will be established over the whole earth (14:9). The New Testament richly mines Zechariah to explain the significance of Jesus and why he had to suffer death before entering his glory.[79]

---

[79] See, for instance, Craig A. Evans, "Jesus and Zechariah's Messianic Hope," in Bruce Chilton and Craig A. Evans, eds., *Authenticating the Activities of Jesus* (Leiden: Brill, 1999), 373–88; Clay Alan Ham, *The Coming King and the Rejected Shepherd: Matthew's Reading of Zechariah's Messianic Hope*, New Testament Monographs, 4 (Sheffield: Sheffield Phoenix Press, 2005).

THE SUFFERINGS AND GLORY OF MESSIAH IN THE GOSPEL OF MARK: REFLECTIONS ON THE TRANSFIGURATION (MARK 9:1–13)

—Dane C. Ortlund

1. Introduction

It is a pleasure to offer this chapter in honor of Desi Alexander, who has made such a vital contribution to the discipline of biblical theology in our time. The task at hand is to explore the Gospel of Mark's contribution to the sufferings and glory of the Messiah, as anticipated in Gen 3:15: "I will put enmity between you and the woman, and between your offspring and her offspring; he shall bruise your head, and you shall bruise his heel."[1]

Of all the books of the Bible, Mark is arguably the most explicitly centered on the sufferings and glory of the Messiah. Indeed, this chapter will begin by exploring how the entire Gospel of Mark is framed around the two macro-themes of suffering and glory: the first half of Mark highlighting the glory of the Messiah, and the second half the sufferings of the Messiah. It will then zero in specifically on the transfiguration account in Mark 9, as a microcosm of Mark's Gospel as a whole. There we see Jesus in glory (9:2–8) and also hear of his sufferings (9:9–13). This study will seek to shed light on this easily under-appreciated pericope in Mark.

My specific aim is to explore one of the more mystifying episodes in the Gospels in a carefully biblical-theological or redemptive-historical way. Most theological reflection on the transfiguration pertains to its Christological significance (who is Jesus?) and less on its redemptive-historical or (more specifically) eschatological significance (what time in history is it?). It is the latter that holds our attention in this chapter, and especially what import the transfiguration might have for

---

[1] Quotations of the Bible are from the ESV unless otherwise noted.

understanding Jesus as the bringer of the new age and new creation, in climactic fulfillment of the ancient promise of Gen 3:15.

2. Glory and Suffering as a Macro-Structure to Mark

Before moving to the focus of this study and looking at Mark's transfiguration account, where Christ's suffering and glory coalesce in a single episode, we would do well to consider these two themes as the overarching categories of thought for Mark's Gospel as a whole. This is because seeing the point at which Mark shifts from focusing on the glories of the Messiah to his sufferings (in Mark 8) will inform our treatment of the transfiguration (in Mark 9).

The key to understanding the big picture to Mark's Gospel is seeing that he frames his account of Christ in two halves. In the first half (1:1–8:30), Jesus is almost entirely welcomed and lauded. Consider the net impact of just the first chapter of the Gospel:

- John anticipates the arrival of one "who is mightier than I, the strap of whose sandals I am not worthy to stoop down and untie" (1:7).
- Christ is proclaimed God's "beloved Son," with whom he is "well pleased" (1:11).
- Those who hear Jesus' teaching are "astonished at his teaching, for he taught as one who had authority, and not as the scribes" (1:22).
- Jesus frees a man from an unclean spirit, "and they were all amazed" (1:27) and "his fame spread everywhere" (1:28).
- Later that day "the whole city was gathered together" to seek healing (1:33), and before long "Jesus could no longer openly enter a town" due to his rising popularity (1:45).

The Gospel continues similarly for another seven chapters. Jesus heals a paralytic and forgives his sins and "they were all amazed and glorified God, saying, 'We never saw anything like this!'" (2:12). He performs healings and exorcisms and we are regularly given details evincing lauding support from the populace such as "a great crowd followed" (3:7) or "he went home, and the crowd gathered again, so that he could not even eat" (3:20) or "a very large crowd followed" (4:1) or "wherever he came ... they laid the sick in the marketplaces and implored him that they might touch even the fringe of his garment" (6:56) or "they were astonished beyond measure, saying, 'He has done all things well'" (7:37). All this culminates in Peter's climactic confession, "You are the Christ" (8:29).

And yet at this point the Gospel swivels around and moves almost entirely in a different direction. In the second half of Mark (8:31–16:8), the miracles and adulation slow way down. Instead, in what must have been a stupefying about-face to the disciples, Christ's sufferings come to the fore. As is well documented, Jesus begins to repeatedly speak of his impending suffering and death, with greater specificity each time (8:31–32; 9:30–32; 10:32–34).[2] He speaks of the need for others, like him, to endure an instrument of torture if they would truly be his disciples (8:34). He announces that he did not come to be served but to serve and to offer his life on behalf of others (10:44–45). And, indeed, right here in the account of the transfiguration, Jesus speaks of the Old Testament prophecy that the Son of Man would "suffer many things and be treated with contempt" (9:12)—to which we will return below.

The pivot point is 8:22–33. Jesus heals a blind man in two stages in order to reveal to the disciples that they too see only partially: They see and receive Jesus' *glory*, as evident in Peter's ascription, "You are the Christ," in 8:29. But they have not yet understood and received the need for his *suffering*, as evident in Peter's response to Christ's announcement of his impending sufferings in 8:33. The second half of Mark fills out the disciples' understanding of who Jesus is—and by extrapolation, generations of readers ever since.

While Jesus does perform a few healings in this second half of Mark, the primary emphasis carries a clear sense of foreboding that is absent from the first half of Mark. After the series of predictions of his suffering throughout chapters 8–10, Jesus curses the fig tree as an enacted parable reflecting the curse resting on fruitless

---

[2] E.g., James R. Edwards, *Mark,* PilNTC (Grand Rapids: Eerdmans, 2002), 318–20.

Israel (ch. 11), the religious elite present a series of challenging questions to Jesus (ch. 12), and Jesus outlines the looming destruction of the temple and of coming judgment (ch. 13)—and with that, the reader is on the verge of Christ's betrayal, arrest, arraignment, and crucifixion (chs. 15–16).

This is not to say that Mark wishes to present suffering and doom as the last word concerning Jesus. While the basic structure of the Gospel does move from glory to suffering, Christ is raised at the end of Mark. Glory prevails. Viewed comprehensively, then, Mark's Gospel presents in long-form narrative what Phil 2:6–11 presents in short-form hymnody: Christ was high in glory (chs. 1–8), but came down into suffering (chs. 8–15), and was raised once again in glory (ch. 16). But Mark's central concern is to drive home the surprising element of suffering in the Messiah's glorious ministry.

3. The Transfiguration

We move now to consider the transfiguration account of Mark 9, which is the pericope that launches the second half of Mark, the half that focuses on Christ's sufferings.

3.1. Literary Placement

We come to Mark 9:1–13 mindful of this broad literary structure to Mark. The first thing we notice is that the transfiguration takes place immediately after the central pivot point of the Gospel. We are now in the "suffering" half of Mark. Indeed, given the two-part literary structure of Mark, the transfiguration functions as *the inaugural episode for the second half of Mark.*

But the transfiguration is more than this. Consider the lead-up to it. Immediately following the hinge passage (8:22–30), Jesus has predicted his imminent suffering and rising for the first time (8:31–38) as Mark shifts from the glory of the Messiah to his suffering. This section closes with Jesus speaking of the coming of the Son of Man "in the glory of his Father with the holy angels" (8:38). This clearly refers to Christ's second coming. The very next verse, however, then speaks of those present seeing "the kingdom of God after it has come with power" (9:1). Mark thus zooms out into the future in 8:38 and then promptly zooms back into the immediate present in 9:1, which anticipates the transfiguration a week later. The "some standing here" in 9:1 is most naturally taken to refer to "Peter and James and John" in 9:2.

What is Mark doing? He is communicating that *the transfiguration is the present inaugurating of that future glory*. While the coming kingdom awaits the death and especially the resurrection of Christ as its supreme validating event, the transfiguration is Mark's decisive if proleptic signal that in Christ the new age has dawned. In Mark 1:15 Jesus announced that the kingdom of God "is at hand," using the perfect tense of the verb ἐγγίζω: the kingdom is imminently upon us, right around the corner, about to break forth into the world.[3] The transfiguration stands at the central crossroads of Mark's Gospel, looking back to the announcement at the Gospel's beginning of the imminently arriving kingdom and forward to the death and resurrection at the Gospel's end. And it is here in the transfiguration that both suffering and glory come together in a way that cannot be separated if Christ is to execute his office truly.[4]

3.2. Old Testament Background to the Transfiguration

Most reflection on the transfiguration focuses on its Christological significance, asking a "who" question.[5] But how does the text itself encourage us to understand it? This is the presenting issue in 9:1, as Jesus frames the coming of the kingdom in terms of time: "There are some standing here who will not taste death until they see the kingdom of God after it has come with power." As the disciples and Jesus

---

[3] BDAG, 270.

[4] Cuvillier finds the transfiguration so out of place that he concludes it must be a freestanding pericope that was integrated into Mark's Gospel (Elian Cuvillier, *L'évangile de Marc*, Bible en face [Bayard: Labor et Fides, 2002], 178). How, he wonders, could Mark speak of Christ's suffering in 8:31–38 and then immediately relate an episode of such glory? But for Mark, suffering and glory are not in tension—it is precisely through suffering that Jesus will enter into glory. Christ will be raised into glory at the end of Mark, and here in chapter 9 we see an early glimpse of that glory—but to get from Mark 9 to Mark 16 he will go through the suffering of the cross.

[5] E.g., R. T. France, *The Gospel of Mark*, NIGTC (Grand Rapids: Eerdmans, 2002), 346–49, who otherwise is strong on OT backgrounds and eschatological undercurrents throughout Mark's Gospel.

come down from the mountain, it is "when" questions that are in play. "Why do the scribes say that first Elijah must come?" (v. 11). "Elijah does come first…" (v. 12). "Elijah has come…" (v. 13). Accordingly, we will focus here not on the Christological but the redemptive-historical and specifically eschatological significance of the transfiguration. That is, how does the transfiguration fit in to Mark's and the NT's broader portrait of Jesus as the launcher of the eschaton, the last days?

The way to draw out the eschatological significance of the transfiguration is to consider the Old Testament background to the text. Several specific details of the narrative merit reflection against the background of the Old Testament. The fact that Mark's literary style is so curt and pared back makes it all the more important that we ponder any subtle OT significance to otherwise innocuous narratival details.

3.2.1. "After six days…" (v. 2)

The transfiguration pericope begins: "After six days…" Six days after what? Six days after Jesus had given his intriguing comment in 9:1 about "some standing here who will not taste death until they see the kingdom of God after it has come in power." We have already noted that the precise time marker here likely is meant to communicate that 9:2–13 is the event anticipated in 9:1.[6] The connection between Jesus saying some present will "see" the kingdom coming and the concluding comment in 9:8 that "looking around, they no longer *saw* anyone with them but Jesus only" reinforces the events of 9:2–7 as the fulfillment of 9:1.[7]

But is there something more that Mark may wish us to detect? Why *six* days? A moment's reflection reminds us that six days is a pregnant biblical time period. While some wish to downplay any intracanonical significance to the time period of six days here,[8] and others simply ignore any OT background to this time marker,[9] the use of this designation combined with other details of the narrative in Mark 9 (see below)

---

[6] So C. E. B. Cranfield, *Mark*, CGTC (Cambridge: Cambridge University Press, 1972), 287–89.
[7] Both instances are forms of ὁράω.
[8] E.g., Robert Stein, *Mark*, BECNT (Grand Rapids: Baker, 2008), 415–16.
[9] E.g., Robert H. Gundry, *Mark: A Commentary on His Apology for the Cross* (Grand Rapids: Eerdmans, 1993), 457.

suggest otherwise. It is Genesis and especially Exodus that contain references to "six days" at pivotal points in those early stages of redemptive history. The world was created in six days (Gen 1:31); the wandering Israelites gathered bread in six days (Exod 16:6, 22, 26); and the people of God were to work only six days (Exod 20:9), a reality itself grounded in God's six-day work of creation (Exod 20:11; 31:17). Most intriguingly vis-à-vis Mark 9, the glory of the LORD dwelt on Mount Sinai for six days, after which God spoke to Moses out of the cloud (Exod 24:16).[10] In light of the presence of Moses in the transfiguration event (Mark 9:4) and the voice from the cloud (Mark 9:7) all while on a mountain (9:2), Mark's reference to six days in verse 2 is likely meant to be heard against a backdrop of Moses' ministry with its climax on Sinai.[11] Mark is thus subtly alerting the reader that another pivotal moment in redemptive history is upon us as Mark 9 opens, a moment of divine revelation to his people, uniquely accelerating the unfolding progress of redemption.

3.2.2. "led them up a high mountain." (v. 2)

Three times in Mark we are told of an event taking place on a single mountain. In Mark 3, Jesus calls the twelve to him after "he went up a high mountain" (3:13), reconstituting the people of God around the disciples as God had originally established his people via twelve tribes (Mark 3:13–19). In Mark 11:3, Jesus speaks of casting "this mountain" into the sea as a way of communicating the setting aside of the entire temple construct and sacrificial system for the forgiveness of sins.[12] Both of these are thus eschatologically charged occurrences of "mountain" language.

The third is here in Mark 9:2, as Jesus leads the disciples up a "high [also 3:13] mountain." While a mountain may seem a fairly bland geographical marker, the

---

[10] See Larry W. Hurtado, *Mark*, NIBC (Peabody: Hendrickson, 1983), 144; Cuvillier, *L'évangile de Marc*, 178–79.

[11] Edwards points in this direction (*Mark*, 262); similarly, A. Y. Collins, *Mark: A Commentary*, Hermeneia (Minneapolis: Fortress, 2007), 420–21. Most satisfying on this point among the commentators is Joel Marcus, *Mark 8–16: New Translation with Introduction and Commentary*, AB 27A (New Haven: Yale University Press, 2009), 631.

[12] Dane C. Ortlund, "What Does It Mean to Cast a Mountain into the Sea? Another Look at Mark 11:23," *BBR* 28 (2018): 218–39.

significance of mountain language in the OT requires that we consider any subsurface significance here in Mark 9.[13] We remember that the most famous mountain episode in the Bible is Moses on Sinai, just mentioned above. Mountain language is then used throughout the prophets in connection with the latter day coming of the LORD in judgment and salvation. Specifically, it is from Mount Zion that God's latter day redemption will flow (Isa 2:2–4; 51:3, 11; Jer 31:12; Joel 3:16–21; Mic 4:1–3; Zech 8:3).[14]

Given the OT use of mountain language, combined with other uses of mountain language in Mark, we should be open to the mountain in Mark 9:2 as signifying something about the coming latter day era promised in the OT and thus possessing eschatological significance. The precise identification of which mountain is left open and thus should not distract the modern interpreter. Indeed, the lack of a precise identification of which mountain makes a link to the OT eschatological mountain all the more natural.[15]

3.2.3. "his clothes became radiant, intensely white..." (v. 3)

In the OT white clothes can refer in a non-theologically charged way to uprightness of character and divine blessing (e.g., Eccl 9:8, "Let your garments be always white. Let not oil be lacking on your head.") But in this theologically and eschatologically charged event in Mark 9, might there be a deeper OT significance?

Particularly intriguing are two OT texts, one from Exodus and one from Daniel. First, in Exod 34 Moses is, so to speak, "transfigured" as he speaks with God and his face reflects the radiant glory of God (Exod 34:29). Given that Moses is mentioned in

---

[13] Other apostolic testimony likewise viewed the transfiguration mountain as more than a mere geographical happenstance; cf. Peter's reference to the transfiguration as taking place "on the holy mountain" (2 Pet 1:18).

[14] See W. Osborne, "Mountains," in *NDBT*, ed. T. Desmond Alexander and Brian S. Rosner (Downers Grove, IL: InterVarsity, 2000), 673–74.

[15] Terence L. Donaldson, *Jesus on the Mountain: A Study in Matthew Theology* (Sheffield: JSOT Press, 1985), explores the mountain motif for Matthew's Gospel, identifying six mountain contexts framing Matthew: the mountain of temptation, the mountain of teaching, the mountain of feeding, the mountain of transfiguration, the Mount of Olives and the Olivet Discourse, and the mountain of commissioning. Some (but not all) of Donaldson's study is also pertinent for the mountain motif in Mark.

the very next verse in Mark 9:4, and the other Mosaic elements mentioned above, Mark almost certainly intends his readers to see a connection between Moses' ministry and that of Jesus.

Second, there is only one OT text that speaks of white clothing in the context of heaven and earth colliding:[16]

> As I looked, thrones were placed, and the Ancient of Days took his seat; his clothing was white as snow, and the hair of his head like pure wool; his throne was fiery flames…. I saw in the night visions, and behold, with the clouds of heaven there came one like a son of man, and he came to the Ancient of Days and was presented before him. And to him was given dominion and glory and a kingdom… (Dan 7:9, 13–14).

In Daniel it is only the "Ancient of Days" who is depicted as having white clothing— the creator, the judge, the ruler of all. Yet it is Jesus who is said to possess white clothes in Mark 9. That Jesus refers to himself as the "Son of Man" in Mark 9:13 is likely a further link to Dan 7, since it is "one like a son of man" who approaches the Ancient of Days in Dan 7:13 (Dan 7:13 is unambiguously behind a later Markan text, Mark 14:62). Apparently, then, the two Danielic figures of the Ancient of Days and the son of man are brought together in a common identity in Mark 9—an observation naturally fitting to orthodox Trinitarian theology as Jesus Christ is included in the divine identity.[17]

It is entirely appropriate, therefore, for Markan commentators to discern a glimpse of Jesus' deity in the transfiguration. He was "transfigured" not in the sense of fundamental change, but in the sense that his three disciples were given a window in to his truest identity, viewing him from heaven's perspective. But there is more than a Christological point to be made. This is also an event of eschatological import, for Jesus is being presented as a new and final Moses, a figure through whom God is

---

[16] See Sigurd Grindheim, "Sirach and Mark 8:27–9:13: Elijah and the Eschaton," in *Reading Mark in Context: Jesus and Second Temple Judaism*, ed. Ben C. Blackwell, John K. Goodrich, and Jason Maston (Grand Rapids: Zondervan, 2018), 134.

[17] I use the language of "included in the divine identity" with acknowledgement to Richard Bauckham, who articulates the Gospels' identification of Christ in this way in several of his books.

bringing about the decisive culmination to all redemptive history.

3.2.4. "Elijah with Moses" (v. 4)

A common interpretation of the presence of Moses and Elijah is that Moses represents the Law and Elijah the prophets, and thus the two together represent the whole OT.[18] That Jesus would appear with them is clearly of redemptive-historical significance—Mark is giving us Jesus as the third and final prophet from God. But it is unlikely that Moses and Elijah represent the OT writings. Elijah was not a writing prophet; Isaiah or Jeremiah (so 2 Macc 2:1) would have been more sensible partners to Moses if the Hebrew Scripture was meant to be comprehensively encapsulated by two prophets.

Rather, Moses and Elijah—or rather, Elijah and Moses, to stick to the non-chronological order Mark gives us—are unique in that they are the two historical figures in the OT with the greatest forward-leaning tilt. They are the two whose ministry was expected by first-century Jews to be recapitulated in the future at a time when the latter days dawned. In other words, they are the most richly eschatological figures of the OT prophets. According to Deut 18 a prophet like Moses would appear, which Acts 3 identifies as Jesus. And a prophet like Elijah was expected to come in order to usher in the day of the LORD (Mal 4:5). Indeed, in this very text which anticipates the coming of Elijah, Moses' experience at Sinai is also expressly mentioned (Mal 4:4).

It is vital to bear in mind that Mal 4 does not identify the returning Elijah to be a forerunner to the coming Messiah. Rather Elijah would return to usher in the day of the LORD.[19] And this is precisely what the transfiguration, along with Mark's Gospel more broadly,[20] is telling us—in the coming of the Messiah, the great day of the LORD has come. The End has dawned.

---

[18] E.g., C. E. B. Cranfield, *The Gospel according to St Mark*, CGTC (Cambridge: Cambridge University Press, 1959), 295.

[19] Noted by Edwards, *Mark*, 264.

[20] E.g., Dane C. Ortlund, "History's Dawning Light: 'Morning' and 'Evening' in Mark's Gospel and their Eschatological Significance," *JETS* 61 (2018): 493–512.

The point of Elijah and Moses appearing with Jesus is thus preeminently an eschatological one. [21] If the point of the transfiguration was only to make a Christological statement about Jesus, surely Jesus would have appeared not with Moses and Elijah but with angels and archangels or with the heavenly host or some such accompaniment. But with the appearance of Moses and Elijah, Mark's Gospel is pointing readers to the eschatological fulfilment of Old Testament expectations—the reader is drawn back in time, not up in space.

3.2.5. *"three tents" (v. 5)*

Peter proposes the construction of three tents: one for Moses, one for Elijah, and one for Jesus. It is a puzzling proposal on first reading. If a supernatural phenomenon appeared in my front yard, would I, in my terror (cf. v. 6), suggest the prompt erection of a temporary dwelling for each person present?

But of course, the word used here for tent (σκηνή) plugs into a whole-Bible motif for God dwelling with his people. The intracanonical significance of tents is not primarily that they exist for people to inhabit while in the presence of God but for God to inhabit while in the presence of people. To be sure, the text tells us that Peter was frightened and not sure what to say (v. 6). But that is not to say his suggestion in verse 5 is simply meaningless nonsense. Rather, Peter is reflecting partial knowledge. Just as in 8:22–33 Peter understood that Jesus was the Messiah (8:29) but did not yet understand that this Messiah must suffer (8:31–32)—recapitulating the way the blind man saw things only partially (8:22–26)—so here in chapter 9, Peter understands that the transfiguration represents a high point in the history of divine revelation, but he does not understand that it represents *the* high point. Peter apparently takes the transfiguration to be a continuation of the Feast of Booths, in which the Jews would all make a booth or tent (σκηνή LXX) for themselves and live in it for seven days as a commemoration of God's care for them in the wilderness following the exodus (Lev 23:33–43; and note σκηνή in vv. 42, 43).[22]

---

[21] William L. Lane, *The Gospel of Mark*, NICNT (Grand Rapids: Eerdmans, 1974), 319; France, *Mark*, 351.

[22] This tent-building commemoration is then recovered in Nehemiah's day (Neh 8:13–18; and

But the humanly built σκηνή, to the Jewish mind, represented a deeper and more wonderful reality: the dwelling of God in the σκηνή, the tabernacle and then the temple. Peter wants to commemorate the Feast of Booths on the mountain in Mark 9. But it was not people dwelling in tents that was called for; God himself, in Jesus, was tabernacling with his people.[23] Peter had it backwards. Peter's call for the construction of tents is one more window into the eschatological culmination reflected in the transfiguration.

A new-creational element may be further present in Peter's apparently dazed remark, "Rabbi, it is good that we are here" (v. 5) as he goes on to propose the tents. Given the immediate content and the eschatologically rich motifs throughout, it is not unreasonable to interpret this as an echo of the creation account, in which the same word (καλός) is used to speak of God's creation time and again as "good" (Gen 1:4, 10, 12, 18, 21, 25, 31).[24] The first creation was good; the transfiguration is "good" because it is revealing the dawning new creation. Peter himself may not have been fully aware of what he was saying, but Mark likely wishes the reader of his Gospel to be more discerning.

3.2.6. "a cloud overshadowed them." (v. 7)

The redemptive-historical significance of the transfiguration comes into further light with the reference to a cloud. Why a cloud? Did it happen to be a rainy day? No, the cloud uniquely represents the presence and glory of God. The cloud shows up at important points throughout the Bible, especially in the book of Exodus. The LORD leads his people by a pillar of cloud (Exod 13:21–22; cf. 1 Cor 10:1–2), speaks to his people by appearing in a cloud (Exod 16:9–10), gives his people the ten commandments amid a cloud (Exod 19:9, 16; 24:15–18), descends in a cloud when Moses enters the tent to speak with him (Exod 33:9; 40:34–38), and proclaims his name in a cloud (Exod 34:5).

---

note σκηνή in vv. 15, 16, 17 [2x]).

[23] G. K. Beale, *The Temple and the Church's Mission: A Biblical Theology of the Dwelling Place of God*, NSBT 17 (Downers Grove, IL: InterVarsity Press, 2004), *passim*.

[24] Marcus, *Mark 1–8*, 631.

What is particularly striking is that Mark doesn't simply mention a cloud but says that "a cloud overshadowed [νεφέλη ἐπισκιάζουσα]" the men on the mountain. This is the same verb used at the end of Exodus to speak of Moses unable to enter the tabernacle (σκηνή [Exod 40:34, 35, 36, 38 LXX]) because the LORD's glory had "settled on" (Exod 40:35 LXX, using ἐπισκιάζω; also 1 Kgs 8:10–11) and filled the tabernacle.[25] God's visible glory-presence rested on the tabernacle made of wood and stone in Exodus; his visible glory-presence rested on the tabernacle made of flesh and blood in Mark 9. The hovering cloud is encouraging us to understand Jesus as the climactic summation of the glory and presence of God.

3.2.7. "a voice came out of the cloud." (v. 7)

That the cloud is a matter of unique divine revelation is further corroborated by the voice that comes from the cloud. As on Mount Sinai in Exodus, the cloud and the voice together signal the glorious presence of God revealing himself to his people in a new way. Together with the other intracanonical elements of this passage, the voice from the cloud signifies a decisive turn in redemptive history—indeed, *the* decisive turn, as God's voice from the cloud not only speaks about Jesus but is embodied in him (cf. John 1:1, 14; Heb 1:1–3). Lane associates the cloud with the tabernacle: "The cloud is God's tabernacle, the pavilion which both conceals and reveals his glory."[26] Yet he then goes on to interpret the significance of the cloud in Christological rather than eschatological terms: "The presence of the cloud and the solemn declaration of the voice affirm the same truth: Jesus is the unique Son of God who enjoys the unbroken presence and approval of the Father."[27] The present study suggests that while Christological and systematic-theological conclusions can surely be legitimately drawn from the transfiguration account, its primary interpretive significance is biblical-theological and specifically the way it proleptically inaugurates the eschatological new creation.

---

[25] Joachim Gnilka, *Das Evangelium nach Markus, 2. Teilband: Mk 8.27–16,20*, 5th ed. (Neukirchen: Neukirchener Verlag, 1999), 35.

[26] Lane, *Mark*, 320.

[27] Ibid., 321.

3.2.8. The Son of God (v. 7)

What does the voice say? "This is my beloved Son; listen to him" (9:7). In popular terms, Jesus can be understood to be both "Son of God" and "Son of Man" in that he is both divine and human, respectively. In biblical-theological terms, however, the two titles mean virtually the opposite—the "son of God" is the royal king in the line of David who will come and rule in accord with ancient promise, supremely 2 Samuel 7; whereas the "son of man" refers to the figure who receives the kind of superlative glory and laud and rule that is reserved for God himself (Dan 7:13–14). Graeme Goldsworthy has recently treated the "Son of God" theme in biblical-theological terms and made the argument that through Jesus the Son of God the new creation has been launched.[28]

We do not have the exact phrase "son of God" in Mark 9:7, though the notion is implied in the words spoken from heaven, "This is my beloved Son."[29] Though we cannot launch in to a whole-Bible reflection on the concept of "Son of God," we do pause to draw attention to the redemptive-historical significance of the notion of God's son. While systematic theology rightly draws Trinitarian significance from language such as this—after all, it is a voice from heaven identifying Jesus as "my" Son— biblical theology first recognizes the Davidic significance of the appellation "son of God."[30] The son of God is the royal heir, the Messiah, the anointed one, the coming king who would establish God's house and kingdom forever (2 Sam 7:12–16). That the voice from heaven identifies Christ as "my *beloved* Son" perhaps links up with the promise never to take away God's steadfast love from the Davidic heir (2 Sam 7:15). But as we consider the Davidic/royal significance to the "son of God," we should not forget that Israel herself was referred to as God's "son" (Exod 4:22–23), a point especially noteworthy given the other allusions to Exodus throughout Mark 9.

---

[28] Graeme Goldsworthy, *The Son of God and the New Creation*, Short Studies in Biblical Theology (Wheaton, IL: Crossway, 2015).

[29] Cf. the link between "You are my beloved Son" in Luke 3:22 and "the Son of God" in Luke 3:38 (Goldsworthy, *Son of God*, 20).

[30] We remember that the decision of a translation to occasionally capitalize "Son" does not reflect the original text.

Above we spoke of the transfiguration as a "crossroads" event, standing at the center of Mark's Gospel, looking back to the beginning and looking ahead to the end. One piece of evidence for this is the use of "Son of God" in Mark, which, aside from demonic interaction (3:11), is a title appearing only at the very beginning (1:1, 11), at the transfiguration (9:7), and at the very end (15:39).[31]

3.2.9. "Listen to him." (v. 7)

The voice from heaven not only identifies Jesus as "my Beloved son" but also tells Peter, James, and John to "listen to him [ἀκούετε αὐτοῦ]." Here we immediately remember that God had promised one day to send a final prophet to whom the people must listen:

> The LORD your God will raise up for you a prophet like me from among you, from your brothers—*it is to him you shall listen* [αὐτοῦ ἀκούσεσθε]—just as you desired of the LORD your God at Horeb on the day of the assembly, when you said, "Let me not hear again the voice of the LORD my God or see this great fire any more, lest I die." And the LORD said to me, "They are right in what they have spoken. I will raise up for them a prophet like you from among their brothers. And I will put my words in his mouth, and he shall speak to them all that I command him. And *whoever will not listen* [ἀκούσῃ] *to my words that he shall speak in my name*, I myself will require it of him. But the prophet who presumes to speak a word in my name that I have not commanded him to speak, or who speaks in the name of other gods, that same prophet shall die." (Deut 18:15–20)

Peter quotes this text in Acts 3 and explicitly transposes it onto Jesus as its deepest fulfillment. But it is apparent even within Mark's Gospel that Jesus is being quietly

---

[31] Étienne Trocmé (*L'évangile selon Saint Marc*, CNT 2 [Geneva: Labor et Fides, 2000], 234) sees the link between 9:7 and 1:11 as further evidence for a later literary compilation involving additions to a "proto-Mark," but such appeals to redaction criticism cloud one's ability to see the theological significance of the literary care with which Mark wrote.

presented as the true and final prophet à la Deut 18, given the particular emphasis on Jesus' teaching (e.g., 1:22; 6:34; 10:1)—despite reproducing less *of* that teaching—in his account. We read the injunction to "listen to" Jesus accordingly, as informed by its OT antecedent in Deut 18 and as thus presenting him as the Moses to come.[32]

Evans believes the text is emphasizing the need to hear Jesus rather than to listen to Elijah or Moses, which Stein disagrees with on the basis that elsewhere in Mark Moses is spoken of as worthy of heeding.[33] But both sides of this disagreement miss the deeper point of the transfiguration, that Jesus should be listened to because he is the ultimate end-point of the prophetic trajectory on which both Moses and Elijah were non-climactic, albeit important, players. Yes, one should listen to Jesus more fundamentally than any other figure; yet to listen to Moses truly, Jesus says in the Fourth Gospel, *is* to listen to Jesus—"for he wrote of me" (John 6:46).

3.2.10. Resurrection (vv. 9–10)

Elijah and Moses disappear (v. 8), and the second half of the pericope begins as Jesus and the three disciples descend the mountain (v. 9). This innocuous element of the passage may itself subtly hint at the events of Exodus, with the tense expectation of the people for Moses to come down from the mountain (Exod 32:1, 7; both Mark 9:7 and Exod 32:1, 7 LXX use καταβαίνω).[34]

---

[32] So *Lane, Mark*, 321; Simon Légasse, *L'évangile de Marc*, LD 5 (Paris: Cerf, 1997), 531; Edwards, *Mark*, 268; contra Stein, who interprets the injunction to listen to Jesus as a rebuke of Peter's failure to receive Jesus' teaching about his impending suffering in 8:32–33 (*Mark*, 419). It is unnecessary to choose between the two, however; and while some sense of rebuke may be present, the pervasiveness of OT imagery throughout the transfiguration account should lead us to see Deut 18 as transparently informing the call to listen to Jesus in Mark 9:7.

[33] Craig A. Evans, *Mark 8:27–16:20*, WBC 34B (Nashville: Thomas Nelson, 2001), 38; Stein, *Mark*, 419.

[34] Peter Williams has demonstrated how even such seemingly bland OT narratival details as ascending and descending can at times carry subsurface literary import ("The Value of Literal Bible Translation," in *Scripture and the People of God: Essays in Honor of Wayne Grudem*, ed. John DelHousaye, Jeff D. Purswell and John J. Hughes [Wheaton, IL: Crossway, 2018], 223–28). Légasse (*L'évangile de Marc*, 522) intriguingly refers to 9:2–13 as a diptych, the two halves being formed by ascent up the mountain (9:2–8) and descent down the mountain (9:9–13).

But it is the latter part of verse 9 that is especially worth pausing over. Here Jesus tells the three disciples not to reveal what they have seen until a certain event has transpired—his own resurrection. However obvious such a reference to resurrection might seem to us today, the disciples are understandably mystified (v. 10).

Much could be said here on the significance of resurrection for the whole Bible, but we can only briefly summarize things with a reminder that resurrection was not simply one future hope among many; according to the teaching of the New Testament, resurrection gathered up all the hopes and promises that had been hurtling down the halls of redemptive history. For resurrection meant the end of death, legal vindication, bodily restoration, and permanence in the land. To be raised—not as Lazarus, resuscitated into mortal life once more, but truly raised, raised into the life of the Age-to-Come[35]—was to step into the fullness of the promised new creation.[36]

To be sure, resurrection is not as pervasive in the OT as some other intracanonical themes in terms of explicit anticipation. Daniel 12:2 is generally taken to be the most obvious, and by some the only, explicit OT testimony to a future resurrection. But the promise of new life is pervasive (e.g., Pss 16:10; 49:15; 71:20; Isa 26:19). While at times resurrection hope is given parabolic or visionary form (Ezek 37:1–14), the point is clear: "I will open your graves and raise you from your graves, O my people" (Ezek 37:12). Even if this resurrection hope would have been understood in Ezekiel's day as restoration from exile, this restoration is conveyed through the category of resurrection from the dead. More deeply, a final resurrection is built into the very structure of biblical history given the bodily creation of Adam and Eve and the curse that brought about death—naturally anticipating a final rescue

---

[35] "There is nothing comparable to the resurrection of Jesus anywhere in Jewish literature. Certainly there are mentions of raisings from the dead, but these are always resuscitations, a return to earthly life. Nowhere in Jewish literature do we have a resurrection to *doxa* as an event of history. Rather, resurrection to *doxa* always and without exception means the dawn of God's new creation. Therefore the disciples must have experienced the appearances of the Risen Lord as an eschatological event, as a dawning of the turning point of the worlds" (Joachim Jeremias, *New Testament Theology: The Proclamation of Jesus*, trans. J. Bowden [New York: Scribner's, 1971], 309).

[36] See esp. G. K. Beale, *A New Testament Biblical Theology: The Unfolding of the Old Testament in the New* (Grand Rapids: Eerdmans, 2011), 227–354.

involving new life.[37]

The new creation materially dawned with the resurrection of Christ. He was the firstfruits, the first instance, physically and literally, of the immortal existence of the Age to Come. And Jesus tells the three disciples not to speak of what they had seen in the transfiguration *until he had been raised*. Why? Because once he has been finally raised, the disciples will be able to see what was anticipated in the transfiguration. Christ's resurrection in Mark 16 was the fulfillment of what proleptically appeared in Mark 9. Perhaps the white (λευκός) figure in 16:5 at Christ's resurrection is a link to the white (λευκός) appearance of Jesus at the transfiguration in 9:3.[38] Without Christ's resurrection, the significance of the transfiguration remains opaque, for the transfiguration is an early visible glimpse of the new-creational age that Christ's resurrection would decisively launch.

3.2.11. Elijah's return (vv. 11–13)

As we consider the Markan references to Elijah we bear in mind what the Old Testament says about Elijah. He is not only the greatest of the Former Prophets but also one whom the Latter Prophets anticipate coming again. As the New Testament opens, in other words, Elijah is not only a figure of the past but also of the future. This is clearest at the very close of the Christian Old Testament, in Mal 4.[39] After an injunction to remember "the law of my servant Moses, the statutes and rules that I commanded him" (Mal 4:4) we read: "Behold, I will send you Elijah the prophet before the great and awesome day of the LORD comes. And he will turn the hearts of fathers to their children and the hearts of children to their fathers, lest I come and strike the land with a decree of utter desolation" (Mal 4:5–6). And with that Malachi's prophecy ends.

---

[37] On the OT anticipation of final resurrection see Mitchell L. Chase, "The Genesis of Resurrection Hope: Exploring Its Early Presence and Deep Roots," *JETS* 57 (2014): 467–80.

[38] Cf. C. S. Mann, *Mark: A New Translation with Introduction and Commentary*, AB27 (Garden City: Doubleday, 1986), 360; Gnilka, *Das Evangelium nach Markus*, 33.

[39] The Jewish Scripture concludes differently, of course, but one should not downplay the reasons for which early Christians arranged the Old Testament the way they did. (Elijah also appears in the final book of the Hebrew Scriptures, though not in the final few sentences but rather at 2 Chr 21:12.)

In Mark this is exactly what we find: repeated references to Elijah leading up to the great day of judgment, the cross, the day of the Lord, the "utter desolation."[40] Jesus is thought by some to be Elijah himself in two passages before the transfiguration (6:15; 8:28), and then after five references in the transfiguration account Elijah figures notably in the crucifixion account (15:35, 36). Why does Elijah receive such attention in Mark's Gospel? To be sure, Jesus is not Elijah *redivivus*, crassly conceived;[41] but Jesus does sum up and fulfill the hope for an Elijah to come, to teach the people and to turn the hearts of the children and of the fathers.[42] At an immediate historical level Mark's Gospel presents John the Baptist as an Elijah figure, as seen for instance in the leather belt that both wear (2 Kgs 1:8; Mark 1:6; cf. Matt 11:14). Yet from a broader perspective Jesus could perhaps even more deeply be seen as Elijah who was to come, as evidenced here in the merging of Elijah with the Son of Man. John the Baptist did not "restore all things"; as we have already seen above in reflecting on Acts 3, Jesus is the restorer of all things ($\dot{\alpha}\pi o\kappa\alpha\vartheta\iota\sigma\tau\dot{\alpha}\nu\omega$ is used in Mark 9:12; $\dot{\alpha}\pi o\kappa\alpha\tau\dot{\alpha}\sigma\tau\alpha\sigma\iota\varsigma$ in Acts 3:21). The Baptist came to prepare the way for the one who would restore all things. Elijah was an important prophet, a mouthpiece of God; John too was an important herald of the times; but Jesus should perhaps be seen as the final Elijah-Prophet, the final mouthpiece of God. We see Jesus wrestling into his disciples' consciousness the combination of two apparently conflicting realities: the coming of

---

[40] Richard Hays speaks of "the day of the Lord" as a matter of judgment on Israel's enemies but not a matter of the end of the world (*Echoes of Scripture in the Gospels* [Waco, TX: Baylor University Press, 2016], 90–91), but these are not mutually exclusive; the day of the LORD in the prophetic literature is a matter of judgment but also of the end of the present world order and the ushering in of God's reign. Jesus' crucifixion accomplishes both.

[41] This is one of the key problems of Suhl's work (Alfred Suhl, *Die Funktion der alttestamentliche Zitate und Anspielungen im Markusevangelium* [Gütersloh: Mohn, 1965]). He views the notion of promise-fulfillment in Mark only in terms of one-to-one correspondence, whereas Mark's understanding of Jesus' fulfillment role is richer and more multi-dimensional, seeing Jesus as the recapitulation of a figure such as Elijah. That is, Jesus does not only repeat a specific action or role of Elijah's, but sums up Elijah's entire ministry in an escalated and climactic way. Note the way a text such as Mark 14:49 speaks of Jesus' arrest fulfilling the Scriptures yet without citing a particular OT text (Trocmé, *Saint Marc*, 350).

[42] Edwards, *Mark*, 247–48; Craig S. Keener, *The Historical Jesus of the Gospels* (Grand Rapids: Eerdmans, 2009), 41.

the final Elijah, on the one hand, and on the other hand the suffering of the Son of Man, the glorious Danielic figure of Dan 7. Elijah has come—but not in the way the disciples expect. He has come to suffer. This reading fits fluidly with Mark 8–10 as a whole, as these three chapters form the hinge on which the entire Gospel swivels from widely adulated ministry by Jesus to the announcement that he will suffer and die (8:31; 9:31; 10:33–34).[43]

What is most striking about Jesus' answer to the disciples' question about Elijah, however, is that he injects a strong element of suffering. This is evident in the likely allusion to Isa 53. While the exact phrase "suffer many things and be treated with contempt [πολλὰ πάθη καὶ ἐξουδενηθῇ]" does not appear in Isa 52:13–53:12, it is difficult to escape the conclusion that a deliberate association is intended given the strong conceptual overlap between Isa 53 and Mark 9:12. What we find then, is that Jesus is probably identifying himself as both the coming Son of Man and the coming final Elijah, but—contrary to expectation—he is a suffering Son of Man and a suffering final Elijah. Sirach 48 recounts Elijah among its lauded heroes:

> [9] You were taken up by a whirlwind of fire,
>
> > in a chariot with horses of fire.
>
> [10] At the appointed time, it is written, you are destined
>
> > to calm the wrath of God before it breaks out in fury,
> >
> > to turn the hearts of parents to their children,
> >
> > and to restore the tribes of Jacob.
>
> [11] Happy are those who saw you
>
> > and were adorned with your love!
> >
> > For we also shall surely live. (Sir 48:9–11 NRSV)[44]

---

[43] Parts of the preceding two paragraphs adapts portions of Dane C. Ortlund, "Mark's Emphasis on Jesus' Teaching, Part 2: Eschatological Significance," *BSac* 174:696 (Sept–Dec, 2017): 412–23.

[44] A text from the Dead Sea Scrolls (4Q558) mentions Elijah in apparent connection with Mal 4:5–6, but the text is too fragmentary to read beyond a reference to God sending Elijah once more (4Q558 1.2.4; see Alex P. Jassen, *Mediating the Divine: Prophecy and Revelation in the Dead Sea Scrolls and Second Temple Judaism*, STDJ 68 [Leiden: Brill, 2007], 143–44).

The triumphalistic tone of such an ascription is turned upside down by Jesus as he speaks of the final coming of Elijah as a matter of rejection and "contempt."

4. Synthesis and Conclusions

Several related conclusions can be drawn from this brief walk through the transfiguration event.

First, this event undoubtedly holds Christological implications, but its primary significance is not Christological but redemptive-historical. This is evident in the robust constellation of Old Testament categories and terms that surface as Mark tells of what happened on the mountain. Mark is drawing on the Old Testament to make sense of Jesus as the Messiah who will both suffer and be raised. The transfiguration event, in other words, when read against its OT background, tells us *what time in history it is*. Grindheim helpfully locates the Markan account of the transfiguration against the backdrop of Second Temple Jewish sources on Moses and Elijah, concluding that the transfiguration is communicating that "Jesus is the ultimate spokesperson for God, God's final messenger who brings God's revelation to its climax."[45] This is true, but we can go further—the transfiguration is a mid-Gospel glimpse of the momentous turn in redemptive history that is about to be realized in human history through the resurrection of Christ from the dead. With the transfiguration we are seeing the beginning of something new, not just the climax of something old.

Second, we have seen that it is primarily Moses and the book of Exodus that inform our understanding of the transfiguration.[46] The visit from Moses, Christ's radiant appearance, the mountain as the location, the cloud overshadowing, the voice from the cloud, the suggestion of building tents/tabernacles, the reference to God's son—all of these details in Mark 9 map cleanly on to events from Exodus. The conclusion to which we are pushed, then, is that Mark is presenting Jesus as a new

---

[45] Grindheim, "Sirach and Mark 8:27–9:13," 134.

[46] Marcus is especially strong on this point (Joel Marcus, *The Way of the Lord: Christological Exegesis of the Old Testament in the Gospel of Mark* [Louisville: Westminster/John Knox, 1992], 80–93); also Gnilka, *Das Evangelium nach Markus*, 32.

Moses, the true and final Moses who will lead God's people through suffering and into freedom and glory.

Third, the latter days and the glory they anticipate are launched, surprisingly, through suffering—this scandalized the disciples, and it remains counterintuitive to us down to the present day. Suffering and glory mingle in Mark 9, as they do throughout Mark's Gospel as a whole. To use the language of Gen 3:15, the way in which Christ bruised the head of the serpent was *by* the serpent bruising his heel.

Fourth, all this funnels into the final conclusion that the transfiguration is the proleptic inauguration of the coming kingdom, the new creation.[47] In Christ's resurrection the future glory at the end of history reached back into the middle of history; in a similar way, in Christ's transfiguration the future glory of his resurrection at the end of Mark reaches back into the middle of Mark. Standing at the crossroads of the Gospel as well as launching the second half of the Gospel, the transfiguration shows us the unbridled eagerness with which all of human history was anticipating the revealing of the coming Messiah who would encapsulate all the promises of the Old Testament. History sits, tense, waiting on the edge of its seat, for the revealing of the Son of God. So tension-laden is the anticipation that the resurrection and all that it represents cannot help but begin to burst onto the scene in the transfiguration. Or, as Jesus put it, some of his disciples did indeed get a glimpse here of "the kingdom of God after it has come with power" (9:1).

---

[47] Cranfield comments, "We take it that the Transfiguration was an anticipation or prolepsis of the Resurrection and of the Parousia" (*St Mark*, 295), but he then takes this comment in a Christological rather than eschatological direction.

The Cosmic Drama and the Seed of the Serpent: An Exploration of the Connection Between Gen 3:15 and Johannine Theology

—*Andreas J. Köstenberger*

1. Introduction

The place of Gen 3:15 in Johannine theology is strategic and undeniable, yet widely overlooked in the scholarly literature. A study of the intentional grounding of Johannine theology in Gen 3:15 yields fascinating results and provides a compelling case study of the value and contribution of Biblical Theology. With its reference to the serpent's and the woman's *seed* or descendants, Gen 3:15 provides the initial passage which then segues into the messianic promise of the seed of Abraham and David. The five Johannine uses of *seed* (σπέρμα)—three in John's Gospel and one each in 1 John and Revelation—each contribute significantly to the connection between Gen 3:15 and Johannine theology. [1] John's Gospel features (indirect) references to Jesus as Abraham's and David's "seed" (chs. 7, 8) which are further developed in 1 John with reference to God's "seed" in believers in a clear Gen 3–4 context and an unmistakable allusion to Gen 3:15 in the book of Revelation referring to the eschatological war between the dragon and the woman, symbolizing Satan and the new messianic community (Rev 12:17). In this way, Johannine theology makes a critical contribution to the biblical trajectory linking the *protoevangelium* in Gen 3:15 with the coming of the Messiah. [2]

---

[1] I believe a reasonable case can be made for the apostle John's authorship of the Gospel, letters, and Revelation, but little in the argument below rests on this identification (though the theological unity among these writings should be evident in the trajectory related to Gen 3:15 demonstrated below).

[2] A full-fledged Christological reading of Gen 3:15 is first attested in Irenaeus, *Adv. Haer.* 5.21.1 (*c.* AD 180); cf. 1.6.4: "elect seed." Gordon J. Wenham, *Genesis 1–15*, WBC 1 (Grand Rapids: Zondervan, 1987), 80–81, also mentions Justin (*c.* AD 160), as well as the Septuagint and the Palestinian

2. The "Seed" of Gen 3:15

The temptation narrative in the book of Genesis depicts Satan's struggle with humanity as a tale of deception, death, and doom. At the inception of the narrative, we find the serpent lying about dying:

> He said to the woman, "Did God actually say, 'You shall not eat of any tree in the garden?'" And the woman said to the serpent, "We may eat of the fruit of the trees in the garden, but God said, 'You shall not eat of the fruit of the tree that is in the midst of the garden, neither shall you touch it, lest you die.'" But the serpent said to the woman, "You will not surely die." (Gen 3:2–4)[3]

God said that the man and the woman would die if they were to break the commandment; the serpent flatly contradicted God's word, asserting they would "not surely die." Following the fall, God pronounces the man's judgment:

> By the sweat of your face
>   you shall eat bread,
> till you return to the ground,
>   for out of it you were taken;
> for you are dust,
>   and to dust you shall return. (3:19)

Later in the narrative we read, "Thus all the days that Adam lived were 930 years, *and he died*" (Gen 5:5; emphasis added). God spoke the truth, and the serpent lied; the man died. At the very heart, then, Genesis depicts Satan as a murderer of the human race, as well as a deceiver and a liar.

---

targums (*Ps.-Jonathan, Neofiti*, and possibly *Onqelos*). Wenham notes, however, that the narrator probably "just looked for mankind eventually to defeat the serpent's seed, the powers of evil."

[3] Scripture references in this essay are for the most part from the ESV, with occasional modifications which are indicated as appropriate below.

Even before God pronounces judgment on the woman and the man, however, he tells the serpent,

> I will put enmity between you and the woman,
>> and between your offspring [עֶרַ; *seed*] and her offspring [*seed*];
> he shall bruise your head,
>> and you shall bruise his heel. (3:15)

As John Sailhamer notes, the Hebrew pronoun "he" (הוא) in the phrase "he shall bruise your head" initially could be read as "he" or "they." Yet when one traces the identity of the promised "seed" in the remainder of Genesis, "he" turns out to refer "to the singular 'seed of Abraham,' who is the 'king from the tribe of Judah' (Gen 49:9–12) and the one who will reign over Israel and the nations 'in the last days' (Num 24; Deut 33)."[4]

The narrative strategy in Gen 11, for its part, depicts a battle to the death. As Sailhamer sketches the story, "With the entry of sin into the world, the whole of humanity was divided into two peoples (seed), each locked in mortal combat with the other in an intense struggle of good and evil." Yet "[t]he battle will result in a decisive victory of one 'seed' over the other (Gen 3:15). God and the forces of good (the 'seed' of the woman) will mount a victorious campaign against the forces of evil and those aligned with them (the 'seed' of the serpent)."[5]

In view of the above mentioned ambiguity regarding the identity of the "seed" (whether singular or plural), "the 'seed' is both a select *individual* and a *line* from

---

[4] John H. Sailhamer, *The Meaning of the Pentateuch: Revelation, Composition, and Interpretation* (Downers Grove, IL: IVP, 2009), 321. Cf. Jack Collins, "A Syntactical Note (Genesis 3:15): Is the Woman's Seed Singular or Plural?," *TynBul* 48 (1997): 139–48; T. Desmond Alexander, "Further Observations on the Term 'Seed' in Genesis," *TynBul* 48 (1997): 363–67 (esp. 363), who writes that on the basis of Collins' argument, "the 'seed of the woman' in Genesis 3:15 must be understood as referring to a single individual and not numerous descendants." See also Bruce K. Waltke, *Genesis: A Commentary* (Grand Rapids: Zondervan, 2001), 93–94, who notes that "*zera*ʿ can refer to an immediate descendant (Gen. 4:24; 15:3), a distant offspring, or a large group of descendants." He adds, "The immediate seed is Abel (in contrast to Cain), then Seth. The collective seed is the holy offspring of the patriarchs (Gen. 15:8; 22:17)." Later OT references include 2 Sam 7:12; NT references include Gal 3:16, 29; and Rom 16:20.

[5] *Meaning of the Pentateuch*, 587.

which that individual will come." Standing in the line of Noah, Shem, and Abraham (cf. e.g., Gen 12:7), "the 'seed' is identified as a future king who will arise from the house of Judah (Gen 49:8-12)."[6] Later in the Hebrew Scriptures, the "seed" will be identified further as the future king descended from David (Ps 72:17; Jer 4:2).

With this contextual understanding of the "seed" references in Gen 3:15 as a proper interpretive framework, the stage is set for our exploration of this vital and foundational salvation historical passage in Johannine theology.

3. John's Writings and the "Seed"

3.1. John's Gospel

The Fourth Evangelist presents the story of Jesus as a cosmic drama against a creation backdrop in which Jesus, the Son of God, is pitted against Satan, the "ruler of this world" (12:31; 16:11).[7] While the other canonical Gospels focus on Jesus' proclamation of the "kingdom of God," John has transposed the Synoptic major tune from "kingdom" to "life," at least in part in order to underscore the universal significance of Jesus' coming which transcends ethnic boundaries.[8] In his signature passage, the Fourth Evangelist writes, "For God so loved the world that he gave his only Son, that whoever believes in him should not perish but have eternal life" (3:16).[9] Later, he

---

[6] *Meaning of the Pentateuch*, 587. Emphasis added.

[7] Intriguingly, John features no demon exorcisms, in contrast to the Synoptics, most likely so as to focus attention on Satan as the chief antagonist. On John as a cosmic drama, see Andreas J. Köstenberger, *A Theology of John's Gospel: The Word, the Christ, the Son of God*, BTNT (Grand Rapids: Zondervan, 2009), ch. 6, esp. 12.2: "The Cosmic Conflict between God and His Messiah vs. Satan and the World." See also Köstenberger, "The Cosmic Trial Motif in John's Letters," in *Communities in Dispute: Current Scholarship on the Johannine Epistles*, ECL 13; ed. R. Alan Culpepper and Paul N. Anderson (Atlanta: Society of Biblical Literature, 2014), 157–78.

[8] Andreas J. Köstenberger, "John's Transposition Theology: Retelling the Story of Jesus in a Different Key," in *Earliest Christian History: History, Literature, and Theology. Essays from the Tyndale Fellowship in Honor of Martin Hengel*, ed. Michael F. Bird and Jason Maston, WUNT 2/320 (Tübingen: Mohr Siebeck, 2012), 191–226.

[9] For an exploration of this passage, see Andreas J. Köstenberger, "Lifting Up the Son of Man and God's Love for the World: John 3:16 in Its Historical, Literary, and Theological Contexts," in *Understanding the Times: New Testament Studies in the 21st Century: Essays in Honor of D. A. Carson on the Occasion of His 65th Birthday*, ed. Andreas J. Köstenberger and Robert W. Yarbrough (Wheaton, IL: Crossway, 2011), 141–59.

represents Jesus as saying, "Truly, truly, I say to you, whoever hears my word and believes him who sent me has eternal life. He does not come into judgment, but has passed from death to life" (5:24). These representative passages demonstrate that John essentially depicts Jesus' coming and the human condition as hanging in the balance between death and life, with God and Jesus as protagonists and Satan as chief antagonist.

Not only does the Fourth Evangelist present the story of Jesus as a struggle with Satan for humanity resulting in people receiving (eternal) life or remaining in death, he also, even more importantly for the purposes of this present essay, depicts Jesus' coming and mission in terms of two competing, warring "seeds." Already in the prologue, the Evangelist writes, "He came to his own, and his own people did not receive him. But to all who did receive him, who believed in his name, he gave the right to become children [τέκνα] of God, who were born, not of blood nor of the will of the flesh nor of the will of man, but of God" (1:11–13). Later, Jesus is shown to impress the importance of a new, spiritual birth on Nicodemus, representing non-messianic Israel: "Truly, truly, I say to you, unless one is born again [or: from above] he cannot see the kingdom of God" (3:3), which is shortly identified as a birth "of water and spirit" (i.e., as a spiritual birth involving cleansing and renewal; cf. Ezek 36:25–27).[10]

The three references to "seed" (σπέρμα) in the Fourth Gospel are all found in chapters 7–8, which recount Jesus' visit to Jerusalem at the Feast of Tabernacles. In a possible Johannine transposition of the Synoptics, Jesus is identified as both the "seed" of David and the "seed" of Abraham (John 7:42; 8:33, 37; cf. esp. Matt. 1:1, 2, 6, 17), though in both cases this is done indirectly by way of Johannine irony. In the first passage, featuring representative characters, the Fourth Evangelist narrates the supposition of some who say regarding Jesus, "This is the Christ," while others are objecting, "Is the Christ to come from Galilee? Has not the Scripture said that the Christ comes from the offspring [seed] of David, and comes from Bethlehem, the village where David was?" (John 7:41–42; cf. 1 Sam 16:1, 4; Mic 5:2). John's readers,

---

[10] Contra the ESV rendering, "born of water and the Spirit."

of course, realize (possibly implying his expectation that they are familiar with the Matthean or Lukan birth narrative) that Jesus was indeed born in Bethlehem and thus truly the "seed" of David (not to mention his adoptive father Joseph's Davidic lineage, cf. Matt 1:20; see also Ps 132:11; Isa 11:1, 10; Jer 23:5).

The struggle pertaining to the "seed" comes to a head in Jesus' interchange with the Jewish leaders in chapter 8. Ironically, the narrative starts with the statement, "As he was saying these things, many believed in him" (v. 30). Jesus, however, pointedly replies "to the Jews who had believed him, '*If you abide in my word*, you are truly my disciples, and you will know the truth, and the truth will set you free'" (8:31–32; emphasis added). At this, those who had "believed" in Jesus take exception to his implicit claim that they have need to be *set free*: "We are offspring (σπέρμα) of Abraham and have never been enslaved to anyone. How is it that you say, 'You will become free?'" (8:33).[11] Jesus clarifies that he is referring to spiritual slavery to sin: "So if the Son sets you free, you will be free indeed," while conceding, "I know that you are offspring (σπέρμα) of Abraham; yet you seek to kill me because my word finds no place in you" (vv. 36–37). By referring to the plot to "kill" him Jesus shifts the interchange from the question of "seed" to the subject of murder, which moves the conversation toward the Genesis fall narrative. He adds, "I speak of what I have seen with my Father, yet you do what you have heard from your father" (v. 38).[12] In this way, Jesus posits two distinct, opposite sides, one aligned with God's purposes (Jesus' "Father"), the other with an opposing force, which he will shortly identify more explicitly.

In response, the Jews reiterate, in exasperation and possibly incredulity that Jesus dared to question their Abrahamic lineage, "Abraham is our father" (v. 39). While Jesus has just conceded their *physical* Abrahamic descent, however, he now challenges their true *spiritual* Abrahamic lineage: "If you were Abraham's children [τέκνα], you would be doing the works Abraham did, but now you seek to kill me, a

---

[11] The Jews considered themselves "sons of the kingdom" (cf. Matt 8:12); Rabbi Akiba was credited with saying that all Israelites were sons of the king as descendants of Abraham, Isaac, and Jacob (*m. Shab.* 128a). Cited in D. A. Carson, *The Gospel according to John*, PilNTC (Grand Rapids: Eerdmans, 1991), 349.

[12] I have slightly emended the ESV translation here to reflect the adversative καί ("yet") in v. 38.

man who has told you the truth that I heard from God. This is not what Abraham did" (vv. 39–40; cf. v. 37). In this way, Jesus moved from Abraham's *nature* to his *works*. Abraham was not a murderer; he killed no one. To the contrary, he was prepared even to sacrifice his "only" son, Isaac, an event the Fourth Evangelist likely alluded in 3:16 ("God … gave his one and only Son").[13] Jesus adds, "You are doing the works your father did," moving even further to drive a wedge between the Jews' overt identification as the "seed" of Abraham and their true spiritual lineage.

Now the gloves come off completely. The Jews reply, "*We* were not born of sexual immorality. We have one Father – even God" (v. 41; emphasis added), arguably implying: But we're not so sure about you (likely alluding to the alleged scandal surrounding the virgin birth)! While Jesus' paternity was in doubt (was Joseph his father or perhaps someone else?), theirs, they asserted confidently, was not. No DNA testing needed here! Absorbing the blow with ease, Jesus retorts, "If God were your Father, you would love me, for I came from God … he sent me" (v. 42). The Jews' murderous designs on Jesus' life, however, show that Jesus' message does not resonate with them as it should. Rather, Jesus now draws the inexorable conclusion to which he has been building up all along: "You are of your father *the devil*, and your will is to do your father's desires. He was a murderer from the beginning…. When he lies, he speaks his native language,[14] for he is a liar and the father of lies" (v. 44; emphasis added). Can it be that those who are the physical "seed" of *Abraham* are the spiritual seed of *Satan*? In this way, even Jews are subsumed under the power of sin and the effects of the fall on humanity, contrary to their own belief that only Gentile were "sinners."[15]

---

[13] In the way in which Jesus confronts the murderous plot of the Jewish leaders leading up to the crucifixion, the present interchange resembles the Synoptic parable of the Wicked Tenants (Matt 21:33–46; Mark 12:1–12; Luke 20:9–19). John, however, features no parables; he rather recounts actual interchanges, noting various instances of misunderstanding and irony. On the absence of parables in John's Gospel, see Köstenberger, *Theology of John's Gospel and Letters*, 161.

[14] I am following the NIV here. Cf. ESV: "he speaks out of his own character."

[15] Note that John, unlike the Synoptics, does not use the Jewish designation of Gentiles as "sinners." See Adolf Schlatter, *Der Evangelist Johannes: Wie er spricht, denkt und glaubt*. Second edition (Stuttgart: Calwer, 1948), 49.

Thus, the battle lines are clearly drawn. On the one side are Jesus and God the Father, and with them those who believe that Jesus is the Messiah and Son of God and who therefore can become children of God (cf. 1:12). Jews, however, being sinners along with all of humanity, need to be reborn spiritually. What in the case of Nicodemus manifested itself in ignorance and incredulity has now degenerated into denial, hostility, and even outright hatred. Jesus' Jewish opponents deny that they are sinners and thus reject their need for a Messiah to save them from their sin. All they want is a national champion who leads their troops into battle against the godless heathen. Yet John makes clear that, by denying their own sinfulness and need for salvation, Jesus' Jewish opponents have forfeited their salvation historical privilege and are now subsumed under the hostile and sinful world that lies in darkness and under the dominion of the devil. They are neither better than the world nor are they worse; they must believe in Jesus in order to receive eternal life. Yet because they insist that they are better than the Gentiles and thus should be held to a different standard, they are under God's judgment.

Thus, the entire discourse ultimately revolves around confronting the Jews' erroneous assertion of ethnic privilege, insisting that they can come to the Messiah on different terms than non-Jews.[16] No, Jesus asserts, they must recognize that they are in bondage to sin just like everyone else. Only if they do so can they be set free from their bondage to sin, and the only one who can set them free is Jesus, the very one in whom they refuse to believe and whom they are planning to kill. Thus, ironically and tragically, they are intent on killing the very one who is their sole potential source of salvation. In a further irony, of course, in God's sovereignty, it is precisely Jesus' cross-death that makes salvation possible.[17] In this way, John masterfully explores the deep spiritual irony and misunderstanding underlying the cross in the context of Jewish obduracy. He will address this matter further in Isaianic terms at the conclusion of the "Book of Signs" (cf. John 12:38–41, citing both Isa 53:1 and 6:9–10).

---

[16] Cf. Carson, *John*, 349: "Jesus thus finds himself in the place where he must … disabuse his interlocutors of any sense of privilege that depends on merely physical lineage to Abraham."

[17] Cf. John 11:49–52.

In sharp retaliation, the Jews proceed to accuse Jesus of demon possession. While John does not feature the Beelzebub controversy, including the question of blasphemy of the Holy Spirit, the present passage is similar in nature.[18] In the process, the Jews manage not only to accuse Jesus of demon possession but to offend Samaritans as well (to whom Jesus has ministered earlier in John's Gospel): "Are we not right in saying that you are a Samaritan and have a demon?" (v. 48; cf. 4:1–42) By alleging that Jesus is "a Samaritan," they most likely are not literally implying he is ethnically a Samaritan; rather, they are again suggesting that he is a half-breed, not wholly a Jew, perhaps because the true identity of his father (echoes of the virgin birth?) is in doubt. Jesus coolly replies, "I do not have a demon, but I honor my Father, and you dishonor me" (v. 49).

At this, Jesus returns to the question of death and frames his coming as being a matter of life or death: "Truly, truly, I say to you, if anyone keeps my word, he will never see death" (v. 51). With heightened antagonism and glaring disrespect, the Jews respond, "Now we know that you have a demon! Abraham died, as did the prophets, yet you say, 'If anyone keeps my word, he will never taste death.' Are you greater than our father Abraham, who died?[19] And the prophets died! *Who do you think you are?*" (vv. 52–53).[20] In response, Jesus makes plain that the Jews do not truly know God or else they would recognize him. Acknowledging their physical descent from Abraham for a second time, he states, "Your father Abraham rejoiced that he would see my day. He saw it and was glad" (v. 56). When the Jews object that Jesus is barely fifty years old, so how could he have seen Abraham, Jesus asserts his preexistence and preeminence over Abraham: "Truly, truly, I say to you, before Abraham was, I am," using the divine name with reference to himself (v. 58). The Jews pick up stones, convinced that Jesus has just committed blasphemy, but he withdraws from the temple in an ominous sign of impending divine judgment (v. 59).

---

[18] Cf. Matt 12:22–32; Mark 3:22–30; Luke 11:14–23.

[19] Notice that the Jews here ignore Jesus' earlier pronouncement that Abraham was not their real, spiritual father.

[20] ESV translates the final sentence (italicized words) as: "Who do you make yourself out to be?"

In this seminal (pun intended) passage, then, Jesus asserts his descent from Abraham—and what is more, his superiority over Abraham and existence prior to Abraham—which extends not merely to his physical lineage but carries clear spiritual and messianic connotations. In this way, Jesus stakes an unmistakable claim to being the "seed" of the woman who would crush the serpent's head in Gen 3:15. What is more, in a striking reversal, it pushes the Jews who deny his messianic claims into the "seed of the serpent" column rather than aligning them with the messianic line. What is implicit is that being Abraham's "seed" is not merely a matter of biology, genetics, and ethnicity; it has an inevitable and overriding spiritual dimension as well. Consequently, those who are Abraham's true "seed" will spiritually discern that Jesus is the "seed" of Abraham through whom God's promise in Gen 3:15 is being fulfilled.

3.2. 1 John

Yet there is more. While Jesus' remarks in John 7 and 8 form the basis for John's further reflection, John takes the "seed" motif in relation to Gen 3:15 a decisive step further in his first letter in what is arguably the passage with the strongest connection to Gen 3:15 anywhere in the Johannine corpus.[21] In 1 John 3:8–10, John writes,

> Whoever makes a practice of sinning is of the devil, for the devil has been sinning from the beginning. The reason the Son of God appeared was to destroy the works of the devil. No one born of God makes a practice of sinning, for God's seed [σπέρμα] abides in him, and he cannot keep on sinning because he has been born of God. By this it is evident who are the children of

---

[21] See esp. Judith Lieu, *I, II & III John: A Commentary* (Louisville: Westminster John Knox, 2008), 137–40, esp. 138 n.76, who notes that "the Gospel's development of the birth image follows different lines from that of 1 John." Remarkably, the grounding of 1 John 3:9 in Gen 3:15 is almost universally overlooked. Scholars who do not discuss Gen 3:15 include Daniel L. Akin, *1, 2, 3 John*, NAC 38 (Nashville: B&H, 2001); Raymond E. Brown, *The Epistles of John*, AB 30 (New York: Doubleday, 1982); Martin M. Culy, *I, II, III John* (Waco, TX: Baylor University Press, 2004); Karen H. Jobes, *1, 2 & 3 John*, ZECNT (Grand Rapids: Zondervan, 2014); I. Howard Marshall, *The Epistles of John*, NICNT (Grand Rapids: Eerdmans, 1978); John Painter, *1, 2, and 3 John*, SacPag 18 (Collegeville, MN: Liturgical Press, 2002); Stephen S. Smalley, *1, 2, 3 John*, WBC 51 (Waco, TX: Word, 1984); and Robert W. Yarbrough, *1–3 John*, BECNT (Grand Rapids: Baker, 2008).

God, and who are the children of the devil: whoever does not practice righteousness is not of God, nor is the one who does not love his brother.

A close parallel is found in 1 Pet 1:23–25, where Peter writes,

> since you have been born again, not of perishable seed [σπορᾶς] but of imperishable, though the living and abiding word of God; for
>
> "All flesh is like grass
>
> and all its glory like the flower of grass.
>
> The grass withers,
>
> and the flower falls,
>
> But the word of the Lord remains forever."
>
> And this word is the good news that was preached to you.[22]

Clearly, in this passage, Peter links the spiritual new birth ("born again") with the "living and abiding word of God" as the agent of regeneration, citing Isa 40:6, 8. In 1 John 3:9, however, a reference to the Holy Spirit as "God's seed" appears more likely due to structural, contextual, and theological factors.[23] With regard to the structure of the passage, Colin Kruse presents the reference to "God's seed" in verse 9 as the center of a chiasm as follows:

a No one born of God

    b makes a practice of sinning,

        c *for God's seed abides in him*;

    b´ and he cannot keep on sinning,

a´ because he has been born of God.[24]

---

[22] See the discussion in Rudolf Schnackenburg, *The Johannine Epistles: A Commentary* (New York: Crossroad, 1992), 175. Neither Jobes, *1, 2 & 3 John*, nor Yarbrough, *1-3 John*, mention 1 Pet 1:23–25. Cf. Jas 1:18 ("He brought us forth by the word of truth") and 21 ("the implanted word").

[23] Cf. Brown, *Epistles of John*, 411; Schnackenburg, *Johannine Epistles*, 175 (adducing 2:20, 27); and Colin Kruse, *The Letters of John*, PilNTC (Grand Rapids: Eerdmans, 2000), 124–25, esp. 125 n.123 (see further discussion below). Judith M. Lieu, "What Was from the Beginning: Scripture and Tradition in the Johannine Epistles," *NTS* 39 (1993): 458–77 (cf. Lieu, *I, II & III John*, 137–40) argues for an allusion to Seth (cf. Gen 4:25).

[24] Kruse, *Letters of John*, 125.

Structurally and contextually, then, the reference to God's seed abiding in believers is framed by references to being "born of God" enabling believers to overcome the bondage to sin which was introduced at the fall narrated in Gen 3. Theologically, in Johannine thought it is the Spirit who serves as the agent of the spiritual new birth (cf. 1:12–13; 3:3, 5).[25] As Kruse rightly notes, "The author seems to be saying, within the wider context of a metaphor of God begetting, that the reason why those born of God cannot continue in sin is that God's 'sperm' remains in them; a most daring metaphor indeed."[26] Canvassing the interpretive options as follows, Kruse makes a compelling case for the "seed of God" referred to in 1 John 3:9 being the Spirit:

> Within 1 John believers are said to have remaining in them (be indwelt by) the gospel message they heard from the beginning (2:24), the anointing/Holy Spirit (2:27), and God himself (3:24; 4:12, 15, 16). Of these three, the Holy Spirit is the most satisfactory option, in the light of the fact that the new birth is effected by God through the Spirit, and it is the Spirit who in Johannine theology remains with and in believers.[27]

Thus, people can be grafted into the line of the "seed" of the woman culminating in Jesus the Messiah by receiving God's "seed", the Holy Spirit, in them.[28] In case there

---

[25] Lieu, *I, II & III John*, 138, rightly notes that in the Parable of the Sower and the Soil the seed metaphorically refers to the word of God, with God being the sower (cf. Mark 4:3–20). However, in the present context "seed" more likely "evokes not grain but (human/male) generative power." She adds, "Perhaps the most that can be said is that although the metaphor of birth is becoming stretched – properly, the seed implanted in the woman is the source of conception – the language serves to emphasize that God's relationship to those born from God is not simply one of generation and origin but continues ... to be effective. God's seed is not to be identified with any particular agent of continuing energizing, but merely asserts its potency. Being born from God means to continue to be vivified by God's creative power; such birth cannot be lost or abrogated." However, there is no reason why "seed" within the purview of Johannine theology cannot or should not refer to God's Spirit.

[26] Kruse, *Letters of John*, 125.

[27] Kruse, *Letters of John*, 125. Kruse (n.122) further cites J. du Preez, "'Sperma autou' in 1 John 3:9," *Neot* 9 (1975): 105–6, who discusses six different interpretations: (1) children of God; (2) the proclaimed word of God; (3) Christ; (4) the Holy Spirit; (5) new life from God; and (6) the new nature, himself opting for (5).

[28] This may represent yet another instance of Johannine transposition of a Synoptic pattern or

is any question whether John has the Genesis narrative in mind, the next verse removes all doubt. John continues,

> For this is the message that you have heard from the beginning, that we should love one another. We should not be like Cain, who was of the evil one and murdered his brother. And why did he murder him? Because his own deeds were evil and his brother's righteous.... Everyone who hates his brother is a murderer, and you know that no murderer has eternal life abiding in him. (vv. 11–15)

The answer to the world's hatred is love: "By this we know love, that he laid down his life for us, and we ought to lay down our lives for the brothers" (v. 16). In this way, John establishes a direct connection between the hatred and murder introduced by Satan, the quintessential "murderer from the beginning" who brought death to the human race, and the love of Jesus making salvation possible. Notably, Jesus, the Messiah and Son of God, overcame Satan's and the world's hatred by dying on the cross for the sins of the world as God's Passover lamb (cf. John 1:29, 36). Thus, the cosmic conflict motif is placed in the larger orbit of the Johannine love ethic.[29]

3.3. Revelation

We have seen that the references to Jesus as Abraham's and David's "seed" in John's Gospel have established a direct connection between the promise of Gen 3:15 and Jesus as the Messiah and Son of God. We have also seen that John, in his first letter, places believers' new birth squarely within a Gen 3:15 context by aligning believers with the messianic "seed" of the woman by way of the Spirit as the agent of regeneration. This, indeed, is a striking further development of the messianic "seed" promise, extending it to the Spirit as the spiritual seed of God abiding in born-again believers.

---

motif, in the present case, the virgin birth. While the Holy Spirit conceived Jesus in Mary's womb, and thus he, the God-man, came to earth, all believers, likewise, need to be conceived spiritually by receiving the "seed" of the Holy Spirit within them. For the notion that the elect or those who are 'spiritual' are possessed of a divine "seed," see Irenaeus, *Adv. Haer.* 1.6.1–2 (cited by Lieu, *I, II & III John*, 139 n.78).

[29] See Köstenberger, *Theology of John's Gospel and Letters*, ch. 13.

But there is even more. In Rev 12:17, John directly alludes to Gen 3:15 in an eschatological context which depicts the struggle between Satan and the followers of the Messiah: "Then the dragon became furious with the woman and went off to make war on the rest of her offspring [or 'seed', σπέρμα], on those who keep the commandments of God and hold to the testimony of Jesus." Here, John aligns believers with Jesus as the woman's "seed" or offspring in clear allusion to Gen 3:15, depicting the climactic cosmic conflict between Jesus and God's people on the one hand and Satan, "the dragon," on the other.[30] Ever since the fall, Satan's deception and humanity's fall have triggered a giant cosmic drama of spiritual warfare and redemption, fulfilled in Jesus' first coming and consummated in his second coming, and effectually realized in the Spirit's regenerating work in believers.

In this way, the "seed" motif spans from Gen 3:15 to the development of the messianic promise in the OT and the depiction of its fulfilment in the NT. This NT depiction is found in the Synoptic Gospels as well as the NT letters (esp. Galatians) and finds a more central and strategic expression in John's writings—his Gospel, letters, and the Apocalypse.

4. Johannine Theology and the "Seed" of Gen 3:15

In the interchange between Jesus and the Jews in chapter 8 of his Gospel, not to mention the sequel in 1 John 3, John teases out the implications of Gen 3:15:

> I will put enmity between you and the woman,
>> and between your offspring [lit., "seed"] and her offspring;
> he shall bruise your head,
>> and you shall bruise his heel.

---

[30] See the discussion and interpretive options given in Grant R. Osborne, *Revelation*, BECNT (Grand Rapids: Baker, 2002), 484–86, esp. 485, who notes the allusion to Gen 3:15, also citing J. Ramsey Michaels, *Revelation*, IVPNTC (Downers Grove, IL: InterVarsity, 1997), 153, note on 12:17; and David E. Aune, *Revelation 6–16*, WBC 52B (Nashville: Thomas Nelson, 1998), 708. See also G. K. Beale, *The Book of Revelation*, NIGTC (Grand Rapids: Eerdmans, 1999), 279, who says Rev 12:17 depicts "a partial fulfillment of the promise in Gen. 3:15, where God prophesies that the individual (messianic) and corporate seed of the woman will bruise fatally the head of the serpent."

Shockingly, however, John shows that while Jesus, the Messiah, is the woman's "seed" who (in the singular) will bruise Satan's head through his cross-death followed by the resurrection, Jesus' Jewish opponents have aligned themselves with Satan. Spiritually speaking, they are Satan's "seed," his spiritual offspring.[31] Like Satan, who was a murderer, liar, and deceiver from the beginning, so the Jewish leaders are bent on death—the death of the Messiah, the one who has life in himself (1:4) and is the Giver of life (5:26). Tragically, therefore, their opposition to Jesus will keep them in spiritual death and prevent them from receiving eternal life, which is now open to "whoever" believes that Jesus is the Messiah and Son of God (cf. 3:16).

In this way, the Fourth Evangelist, in his Gospel as well as in his first letter and in the Apocalypse, conceives of Jesus' coming as part of a cosmic drama which represents a spiritual struggle between Jesus the Messiah and Satan, the ruler of this world. Shockingly, the Jewish leaders have chosen to align themselves with Satan while opposing and even rejecting the God-sent Messiah, the seed of Abraham and David.[32] In this way, John draws a straight line from the *protoevangelium* in Gen 3:15 to Jesus' coming and shows that Jesus is the seed who stands in the lineage of Abraham and his royal offspring, as the remainder of the book of Genesis develops.[33] What is more, descent from Abraham is redefined not merely in ethnic but spiritual terms. In this, Jesus is shown in many ways to anticipate Paul's treatment in Gal 3 (or, conversely, Paul is shown to ground his theology in Gal 3 in Jesus' teaching).

Thematically, the Genesis backdrop of John's dramatic presentation of the story of Jesus signifies several things. First, John presents Jesus' coming within the

---

[31] On the potential relevance of the *Palestinian Targums* on Gen 3, see Stephen Motyer, *Your Father the Devil? A New Approach to John and the Jews*, Paternoster Biblical and Theological Monographs (Carlisle: Paternoster, 1997), 188–89, citing Frederic Manns, *"La Verité vous fera libres"*: *Etude exégétique de Jean 8,31–59*, SBFA 11 (Jerusalem: Franciscan Printing Press, 1976), 152–76. Motyer notes that *Tg. Ps.-J.* Gen 3:6 calls the serpent "the angel of death" and that "seed" (זֶרַע) in Gen 3:15 is translated with "son" (both Heb. בֵּן and Aram. בַּר). Cf. Matt 13:36–43: "sons of the kingdom", "sons of the evil one."

[32] See esp. Margaret Daly-Denton, *David in the Fourth Gospel: The Johannine Reception of the Psalms*, AGJU 47 (Leiden: Brill, 1999).

[33] See the introduction above.

matrix of a polarity between life and death, light and darkness. These cosmic, universal categories flow directly from the Genesis creation narrative, which John invokes in the very first verse of his Gospel ("In the beginning," 1:1) and continues to develop in the following verses in the prologue. This is part of John's distinctive worldview which sets him apart from the Synoptics.[34] Second, at the same time, starting with the prologue, John, in his Gospel, puts front and center the question of the identity of the true children of God as heirs of the promised messianic "seed". R. Alan Culpepper is likely correct when he identifies the pivot of the Johannine prologue as John's statement in 1:12 that "to all who did receive him, who believed in his name, he gave the right to become children of God."[35]

As shown above, this theme that is strategically sounded in the prologue is developed further in Jesus' interchange with Nicodemus, the "teacher of Israel," and reaches a climax in Jesus' interaction with the Jews in chapter 8. In this way, John presents a penetrating discussion and analysis of why it is that the Jewish people rejected Jesus as Messiah, as part of the "Book of Signs" that ends on a note of Jewish obduracy and rejection (12:38–41).[36] Translated into Synoptic parlance, John, in effect, tells his readers, "Someone greater than Abraham is here" (cf. 8:58), and, "Someone greater than David is here" (cf. 7:41–42).[37] In this way, John provides a spiritual analysis of the nature of Jewish opposition to Jesus, which, he shows, is rooted ultimately in the Jews' sinfulness and their alignment with Satan's rather than God's "seed" through the woman, Jesus the Messiah.

What is more, in this way the Fourth Evangelist also provides a profound analysis of the spiritual dynamics underlying the cross. Humanly speaking, the cross would never have occurred, had not the Jews aligned themselves with the "seed" of

---

[34] On John's worldview, see Köstenberger, *Theology of John's Gospel and Letters*, chap. 6.

[35] R. Alan Culpepper, "The Pivot of John's Prologue," *NTS* 27 (1980–81): 1–31.

[36] See Craig A. Evans, "*Obduracy* and the *Lord's Servant*: Some Observations on the Use of the Old Testament in the Fourth Gospel," in *Early Jewish and Christian Exegesis: Studies in Memory of William Hugh Brownlee*, ed. Craig A. Evans and William F. Stinespring; Homage 10 (Atlanta: Scholars Press, 1987), 221–36.

[37] Cf. Matt 12:41: "Now something greater than Jonah is here"; 12:42: "Now something greater than Solomon is here."

Satan. And yet, in God's sovereign providence, as mentioned, it was that very cross that became the source of salvation for everyone who believes.

In this context, it is necessary to touch briefly upon the alleged "anti-Semitism" of John's Gospel. Contrary to any such notion, and the surface plausibility of such a charge, John does not in fact present all Jews as "children of the devil" in a negative light, reflecting ethnic prejudice. Jesus himself is a Jew (4:9). He tells the Samaritan woman, "Salvation is from the Jews" (4:22). The twelve are all Jews, including the Fourth Evangelist himself. Nicodemus is shown to progress as a character, defending Jesus at the Sanhedrin (7:50–51) and burying Jesus along with Joseph of Arimathea, another Sanhedrin member (19:38–42). Other Jews are presented in a positive or neutral light (e.g., in the Lazarus narrative: 11:1–44). What John opposes, rather, is Jewish opposition to Jesus the Messiah that is grounded in Satanic lies, deception, and even hateful murder. This, John opposes, because it runs counter to God's salvation purposes.

Thus, John argues that Jewishness does not necessarily entail or require rejection of Jesus as Messiah. To the contrary, those who truly love God and claim physical descent from Abraham, those who read what Moses wrote about the Messiah, should be open to Jesus' claims and embrace him as the one whom God sent (cf. 5:45–47). In this way, John deals squarely with the nature and roots of Jewish opposition to Jesus' messianic claims and shows that any such opposition is ultimately unfounded, and even sinful. What is more, by opposing Jesus, the Jews in fact align themselves with Satan. This, to be sure, is an explosive charge, but for John, it is also an inexorable reality. There is ultimately no middle ground. People—including Jews—must decide and declare if they are for Jesus or against him. What is more, opposition to Jesus is ultimately rejection of God and tantamount to rejection of his salvation-historical purposes. If Jesus is the only way to the Father, for Jews as well as non-Jews, and no one comes to the Father except through him (14:6), then there is no other way. Tragically, they chose to reject Jesus and put him on the cross.[38]

---

[38] Interestingly, Jesus' death is also described in terms of a "seed" falling into the ground and dying, and thus producing "many seeds", as part of an agricultural metaphor, though a different word for "seed" is used there (ὁ κόκκος τοῦ σίτου ... πολὺν καρπὸν [12:24]).

Yet the story does not end there. In the second act of John's cosmic drama, "The Book of Exaltation" (chs. 13–21), Jesus is shown to equip his new messianic community—a Jewish remnant—for their mission subsequent to his exaltation with God the Father. He celebrates the Passover with the twelve, exposes Judas the betrayer, and talks to the eleven about the coming παράκλητος—the "Spirit of truth", the Holy Spirit—who will be *in* them just as he was *with* them (14:18). They will be his representatives, sent on a Trinitarian mission: "As the *Father* sent *me*, even so *I* am sending you.... Receive *the Holy Spirit*" (20:21–22).[39] Thus, the twelve are now Jesus' "own" (13:1; cf. 1:11). They are in the messianic vine—Jesus, the true Israel (15:1–10). They worship the true temple, Jesus (2:19–22; cf. 4:21–24).[40] They are in the trajectory of the "seed" of the woman through their faith in Jesus the Messiah and Son of God, commissioned to represent him and his message of the forgiveness of sins.

This message, importantly, still goes out to Jews as well as non-Jews. Even their rejection of Jesus the Messiah is not the unpardonable sin. As can be seen in the book of Acts, the mission of the twelve takes its point of departure in Jerusalem, and even Paul, the apostle to the Gentiles, still abides by the maxim, "To the Jew first, and then also to the Greeks" (Rom 1:16; cf. Acts, *passim*). In presenting the story of Jesus in the trajectory of the "seed" of the woman in Gen 3:15, John truly projects Jesus' coming onto a broad canvass of universal, cosmic, and global proportions. The playing field has been leveled. Jesus came for all, and all must receive him on identical terms. A half-century after Jesus' coming, and close to a half-century after the launch of the Gentile mission, John presents a compelling account of Jesus' messianic identity and mission that is both historically faithful and yet characteristically reflects theological hindsight in teasing out the deeper spiritual implications of Jesus' coming for Jews

---

[39] See Andreas J. Köstenberger, "John's trinitarian mission theology", in *Father, Son and Spirit: The Trinity and John's Gospel*, ed. Andreas J. Köstenberger and Scott R. Swain, NSBT 24 (Downers Grove, IL: IVP, 2008). See also Andreas J. Köstenberger, *The Missions of Jesus and of the Disciples according to the Fourth Gospel* (Grand Rapids: Eerdmans, 1998).

[40] See Andreas J. Köstenberger, "The Destruction of the Second Temple and the Composition of the Fourth Gospel," in *Challenging Perspectives on the Gospel of John*, ed. John Lierman, WUNT 2/219 (Tübingen: Mohr Siebeck, 2006), 69–108.

and non-Jews alike.

Indeed, John's is the "spiritual gospel," and in many ways the New Testament equivalent of the book of Genesis, the book of origins and creation realities. As a result, in vintage Johannine fashion, the Fourth Evangelist moves from a *physical* to a *spiritual* understanding of the word "seed" and what the term implies. The (implicit) grounding of John's presentation of Jesus as the "seed of Abraham" and the "seed of David," the alignment of believers in him with the woman's "seed," and the alignment of the Jewish leaders who oppose him with the "seed" of Satan provide a compelling framework for conceiving of Jesus' messianic mission, including the rejection of Jesus resulting in his saving death on the cross.

In this way, John penetrates to the very heart of the matter, providing a powerful, compelling explanation to the question, "Why did Jesus die on the cross?" Not only this, he also provides a cogent answer to the question, "Why should Jews (and non-Jews) believe in a crucified Messiah?"

5. The Fulfillment of Gen 3:15 in Jesus and Believers in Johannine Theology

The above discussion provides strong evidence that Jesus thought of himself as fulfilling Gen 3:15 as the "seed" of the woman (Eve) and as the "seed" and rightful heir of Abraham and David. The above discussion also provides strong evidence that John considered Jesus to have fulfilled Gen 3:15 and that he expressed this conviction in all three of his writings: (1) his Gospel (see esp. ch. 8); (2) his first letter (3:8–10); and (3) the book of Revelation (12:17). Not only does the trajectory of the woman's "seed" culminate and find fulfilment in Jesus, the son of Abraham and David, the trajectory of the serpent's (Satan's) "seed" is fulfilled in the Jewish leaders who opposed Jesus and ultimately put him on the cross.

In this matter of life and death, the Jewish leaders acted out the designs of their spiritual "father," Satan, who was a murderer from the beginning and introduced death into humanity. The trajectory of the woman's seed is also fulfilled in believers in the Messiah who have God's "seed," the Holy Spirit, in them, as the agent of the new birth. While Satan sowed the seeds of discord, doom, and destruction, God implanted his Spirit in believers' hearts, reversing the effects of the fall in them.

In this way, we see that Genesis was exceedingly important and foundational for Johannine theology, not only the creation (cf. John 1:1–11) but also the fall narrative (see esp. John 8:44; 1 John 3:8–12). Not only does John espouse a new creation theology, he also places Jesus' cosmic conflict with Satan within the framework of the Genesis fall narrative, and here particularly Gen 3:15. In this context, Jesus' breathing on his new messianic community at the final commissioning in allusion to Gen 2:7 signifies the commissioning of the twelve as representatives of a new humanity who have God's Spirit in them as they serve as Jesus' representatives and proclaim forgiveness of sins and eternal life in the Messiah.

What is more, in extending the "seed" trajectory from the messianic line spanning from Gen 3:15 over Abraham and David to Jesus to the Holy Spirit indwelling believers (1 John 3:8–10), John, remarkably, in his first letter extends the trajectory even beyond the Gospel. It is by the Spirit that believers are set free from their bondage to sin and the stranglehold of Satan is broken in their lives. The new messianic community is therefore a community of believers who have been set free from Satan and the effects of the fall, believers who are sent by Jesus on a mission to proclaim that in Jesus, the "seed of the woman", Satan's head has been crushed. Nevertheless, Satan has bruised the Messiah's heel. Now, his followers bear the brunt of Satan's rage which will last only for a limited time until Jesus crushes the old serpent once and for all at his return and the final judgment.

6. Conclusion

It is not that with the fulfilment of Gen 3:15 in Jesus, the Messiah, the application of the *protoevangelium* has been concluded. Rather, believers today continue to operate within the matrix of the two warring "seeds"—the seed of Satan and the seed of the woman. This is the clear implication from the reference to Gen 3:15 in both 1 John 3:9 and Rev 12:17. Believers are incorporated into the messianic seed by having received the "seed of God" in them—the indwelling Holy Spirit—and as members of the new messianic community are part of the cosmic drama and conflict pitting God, Jesus the Messiah, and the believing community against Satan and his minions. In this way, our biblical theological exploration of the trajectory taking its point of departure in Gen 3:15 and, in Johannine theology, spanning to John's Gospel, letters, and Apocalypse has proven to be extremely relevant for the church and believers today as it helps them grasp their identity and understand the nature of their God-given mission within this messianic trajectory that does not come to an end in the crucifixion and Jesus' first coming but continues throughout the church age with a view toward its culmination at Jesus' second coming.

This has been a fascinating case study in biblical theology, in the context of the entire present volume. There are many other strands of motifs I could have teased out, such as John's reference to Isa 53:1 at the end of the "Book of Signs," where Jesus is cast implicitly as the suffering servant of Isaiah (cf. 52:13–53:12). Yet for now, I must conclude. What I hope to have provided is a suggestive study of the connection between Johannine theology and Gen 3:15, in honor of one of the foremost biblical theologians of our day, T. Desmond Alexander, to whom I respectfully dedicate this essay. *Soli Deo gloria.*

THE SUFFERINGS AND GLORY OF JESUS THE MESSIAH IN ACTS 2–3

—*Rita F. Cefalu*

1. Introduction

While the postexilic period witnessed Israel's return to the land, the first century opens with several prophetic promises unfulfilled. The faithful remnant waited in anticipation for a messianic deliverer who would establish the everlasting promises made to David and thereby usher in the Abrahamic blessing to the nations. The writers of the New Testament attest to the historical reality that Jesus the Messiah has indeed inaugurated the latter-day restoration of Israel by suffering before entering into glory (cf. Luke 24:25–27, 44–49; 1 Pet 1:10–12). This essay will explore the redemptive-historical[1] significance of Peter's speeches as recorded by Luke in Acts 2–3 in light of the death, resurrection, and exaltation of the Messiah—with particular attention being given to the surprising fulfillment of prophecy relating to the Davidic and Abrahamic covenants.

2. Peter's Speeches in Acts 2–3 in Historical, Literary, and Redemptive Contexts

The book of Acts describes the redemptive-historical period which narrates the first thirty years of the early church.[2] Canonically situated between the Gospel of John and Paul's Epistle to the Romans, Acts serves as a bridge document linking the

---

[1] This term is used broadly to express God's words and deeds in history in order to accomplish salvation for his people.

[2] The constraints of this essay do not permit a lengthy discussion on introductory issues pertaining to Luke–Acts. The reigning consensus is that one author is responsible for both volumes. Luke, the beloved Physician mentioned in Col 4:14, is the likely candidate based upon the "we" sections in Acts and the strong patristic evidence in support of his authorship. Cf. F. F. Bruce, *The Book of the Acts*, NICNT (Grand Rapids: Eerdmans, 1988), 7. Ben Witherington, *The Acts of the Apostles: A Socio-Rhetorical Commentary* (Grand Rapids: Eerdmans, 1998), 54–58. For a full discussion on introductory matters, see David G. Peterson, *The Acts of the Apostles,* PilNTC (Grand Rapids: Eerdmans; Nottingham: Apollos, 2009), 1–97.

Gospels with the Epistles and the book of Revelation, while also providing the historical background for many of the letters found in the New Testament.

Scholars have rightly observed that Acts 1:8 provides the general outline for the book with its thematic focus on the Spirit-empowered apostolic witness from Jerusalem to the ends of the earth.[3] As Blomberg observes, Luke understands "the Acts as what Jesus *continues* to do and teach, through his Spirit, in the lives of his closest followers."[4] Peter's speeches in Acts 2–3 appear in the first section of the book and concern the apostolic witness that begins in Jerusalem (Acts 1–7).

The redemptive-historical setting for Acts 2 is the Feast of Pentecost which occurred on the fiftieth day after the Sabbath Passover (cf. Lev 23:15–16). However, this was no ordinary festival. Luke records it as the fulfillment of Joel's latter-day prophecy regarding the promised Spirit of the new covenant (Joel 2:28–32). This spectacular event occurred fifty days after Jesus' death, resurrection, and ascension into heaven, thus remarkably linking the Passover with his sufferings, and Pentecost with his exaltation to glory and the subsequent gift of the eschatological Spirit (cf. Acts 1:3–5). If under the old economy Pentecost celebrated the first fruits of an agrarian harvest (cf. Exod 23:16; Num 28:26), something greater has now arrived: the first fruits of a spiritual harvest, commensurate upon the Messiah's resurrection and ascension to God's right hand.

3. Peter's First Speech (Acts 2:22–36)

After interpreting the dramatic events related to Pentecost in fulfillment of Joel's latter-day prophecy (Acts 2:14–21), Peter turns to focus on the significance of Jesus' sufferings and glory in light of the dawn of the eschatological age and its soteriological benefits (Acts 2:22–47). His Christology centers on the humanity of

---

[3] Acts 1–7 centers on the apostolic witness beginning in Jerusalem, while chapters 8–9 narrate the growth of the gospel into Judea and Samaria, with chs. 10–28 recording its spread to the ends of the earth. Cf. Lewis Foster, "Luke-Acts," in *Zondervan New American Standard Study Bible*, ed. Kenneth L. Barker, et al. (Grand Rapids: Zondervan, 1999), 1572.

[4] Craig L. Blomberg, *The Historical Reliability of the New Testament*, ed. Robert B. Stewart, B & H Studies in Christian Apologetics (Nashville: B & H Academic, 2016), 234.

Jesus of Nazareth, a man attested to by God through various signs and wonders which "God performed through him" in the midst of the Jewish nation (Acts 2:22).[5] This Jesus was "delivered over by the predetermined plan and foreknowledge of God" into the hands of sinful men who were responsible for his crucifixion and death (Acts 2:23). Nevertheless, "God raised him up again, putting an end to the agony of death, since it was impossible for him to be held in its power" (Acts 2:24). Peter then quotes from Ps 16:8–11, as scriptural evidence in support of the messianic implications of Jesus' resurrection from the dead.

3.1. Peter's Use of Ps 16:8–11 [15:8–11 LXX][6]

He begins by stating that David wrote this psalm about Jesus (Acts 2:25). Thus, Jesus, not David, is its main subject. As such, the psalm expresses the subject's complete confidence that because God is at his right hand he will not be shaken (Acts 2:25; cf. Ps 16:8). For this reason, his heart is glad and his tongue rejoices. Moreover, his flesh will also live in hope because God will not abandon his soul to Hades nor allow his holy one to see corruption (Acts 2:26–27; Ps 16:9–10). God has made known to him the ways of life and will make him full of gladness with his presence (Acts 2:28; Ps 16:11).

The main emphasis of Ps 16:8–11 falls on verses 9–10; namely, that the subject will live in hope because God will not abandon his soul to Hades. This is also Peter's main point: he confidently asserts that this psalm could not have been written about David, because David died and was buried, and his tomb was still present in their midst (Acts 2:29). And so, because David was *a prophet*, who knew that God had sworn an oath to put one of his descendants on his throne (Acts 2:30; Ps 132:11; 2 Sam 7:12–16; cf. Ps 89:3–4), looked ahead and spoke of the resurrection of Jesus from the dead (Acts 2:31; Ps 16:10). It is this resurrection of Jesus to which the apostles bear witness (Acts 2:32).

Peter then moves from the death and resurrection of Jesus to his exaltation by

---

[5] All translations *NASB* (1999), unless otherwise indicated.

[6] Peter follows the LXX with the exception of the last clause of verse 11, i.e., "Pleasures in your right hand forevermore," which is omitted in Acts 2:25–28 (my trans.).

linking Pentecost with the new covenant gift of the Spirit (Acts 2:33). He grounds this event in yet another Psalm of David, making the same claim as above: David could not have been talking about himself when he wrote: "The LORD says to my Lord, 'Sit at My right hand, Until I make Your enemies a footstool for Your feet'" (Ps 110:1; Acts 2:34–35). Peter concludes confidently by stating, "Therefore let all the house of Israel know for certain that God has made Him both Lord and Christ—this Jesus whom you crucified" (Acts 2:36).

In sum, we have seen Peter's use of Pss 16:8–11 and 110:1 in light of their prophetic reference to the sufferings and glory of Jesus the Messiah. However, more needs to be said regarding Peter's allusion to the Davidic covenant in Acts 2:30 (i.e., the statement concerning God's oath to sit one of David's descendants on his throne). This allusion to 2 Sam 7:12–13 forms the basis for Peter's statements about the sufferings and glory of the Messiah in relation to the prophecies of Pss 16 and 110 as having found their fulfillment in the death, resurrection, and exaltation of Jesus. Thus, we turn now to consider the prophetic implications associated with the Davidic covenant within the context of Peter's overall argument.

3.2. Peter's Allusion to 2 Samuel 7:12–13 and the Surprising Fulfillment of the Davidic Covenant

After explaining that Ps 16:8–11 could not have been written about David because his body is still in the grave, Peter asserts the following:

> Being therefore a prophet and having known that God had sworn to him
> an oath to seat the fruit of his loins on his throne, he looked ahead and
> spoke of the resurrection of the Messiah that he was neither abandoned to
> Hades, nor did his flesh see corruption. (Acts 2:30–31, my trans.)

The general scholarly consensus supports the view that the primary source for Peter's allusion to the Davidic covenant (above) is taken from Ps 132:11 [131:11 LXX].[7]

---

[7] I. Howard Marshall, "Acts," in *Commentary on the New Testament Use of the Old Testament*, ed. G. K. Beale and D. A. Carson (Grand Rapids: Baker Academic, 2007), 539–40.

However, there are good reasons to prefer the original oath found in 2 Sam 7 over Ps 132. The most significant reason is that when Peter alludes to the Davidic covenant, he draws attention to David's own experience. He writes: "because he [David] was a prophet and knew that God had *sworn to him with an oath* to seat one of his descendants on his throne, he looked ahead and spoke of the resurrection of the Christ" (Acts 2:30–31a, emphasis added). According to Peter, it is on the basis of the original covenant sworn to David in 2 Sam 7 that he (David) was inspired to write the prophecies concerning the Messiah's sufferings and glory in Pss 16 and 110. This personal element of David's own experience is what makes Ps 132 the less likely choice for Peter's allusion to the covenant.

Conversely, Ps 132 is written by an unidentified third party who simply looks back on the mutual oaths that were made between David and God in his (the psalmist's) request of divine favor for the Davidic kingship: "Remember, O LORD, on David's behalf, all his affliction; How he swore to the LORD …. For the sake of David Your servant, do not turn away the face of Your anointed," Ps 132:1–2, 10). Moreover, in addition to envisioning a series of Davidic sons who would rule on David's throne, Ps 132:11–12 makes the oath's fulfillment contingent upon the sons' continuing obedience to the Mosaic covenant (see below):

> The LORD swore to David a truth which he will not do away with: from the fruit of your lower belly I will place on your throne; If your sons keep my covenant and my testimonies that I will teach them, their sons also shall sit on your throne forever. (Ps 131:11–12 LXX, my trans.)

In contrast, 2 Sam 7:12–13 envisions an individual son ("seed") with whom God covenants unconditionally to establish an everlasting kingdom (see below):

> And when your days are fulfilled and you sleep with your fathers, I will raise up your <u>seed</u> after you <u>who will come</u> from your lower belly, and I will establish <u>his </u>kingdom. <u>He shall build</u> a house for my name and I will restore the throne of <u>his</u> kingdom forever. (2 Sam 7:12–13 LXX, my trans.)

Regarding the term "seed," Collins has persuasively argued that certain syntactical features enable us to determine whether a text is speaking about an individual or a corporate entity. He maintains that when referring to "a specific descendant ... it appears with singular verb inflections, adjectives, and pronouns."[8]

Applying the insights of Collins to 2 Sam 7:12–13, it may be confidently stated that the Davidic oath is indeed made to an <u>individual seed</u> whom God promises to raise up (ἀναστήσω)[9] in the future and with whom God promises to establish an everlasting kingdom (see underlining in 2 Sam 7:12–13 above).

Now, it is true that the Greek verb ἀνίστημι may simply refer to the raising up of a future seed of David to sit on his throne—which is likely how it was understood within the immediate historical context of 2 Sam 7; however, the verb may also be used with reference to the resurrection from the dead, which is clearly the way Peter uses ἀνίστημι in Acts 2:31.

It is also true that Peter does not make explicit reference to 2 Sam 7:12–13 in connection with the resurrection of Jesus from the dead as he does with respect to Pss 132 and 110. Nevertheless, it is quite possible that he had this very thing in mind. I say this because this train of thought falls in line with Peter's own redemptive-historical understanding of how OT prophets and prophecy functioned (cf. 1 Pet 1:1–10).[10] Moreover, in Peter's second speech, he does make explicit reference to Samuel and his successors regarding the messianic age in direct connection with the sufferings and glory of Jesus (Acts 3:24; cf. v. 17). This is intriguing because, when considering prophets like Samuel and Nathan, one would not immediately associate either of their ministries with prophesies relating to the sufferings and glory of the future Messiah. However, Peter does. Therefore, I think it is reasonable to conclude that Peter had this

---

[8] Jack Collins, "A Syntactical Note (Genesis 3:15): Is the Woman's Seed Singular or Plural?," *TynBul* 48.1 (1997): 144.

[9] Ἀναστήσω (future form of ἀνίστημι) in the LXX of 2 Sam 7:12, appears four times in the aorist form (past event) in Acts 2:24, 32; 3:22, 26 to speak of Jesus' resurrection from the dead.

[10] I am aware of the scholarly challenges to the Petrine authorship of 1 and 2 Peter, and hold to the view that Peter was the author of both, although he may have made use of an amanuensis which was a common practice in his day (cf. 1 Pet 5:12).

very thing in mind when he alluded to 2 Sam 7:12–13 as the ground for David's resurrection hope. Thus I suggest that, from a redemptive-historical perspective, even the oath that was made to David looks beyond the raising up of successive sons of David on the stage of world history (e.g., Solomon, Hezekiah, Josiah) with a focus on one particular son who is to come; namely, Jesus of Nazareth.

This suggestion is based, firstly, on the language and syntax of 2 Sam 7:12–13; and secondly, on the observation that none of David's sons lived to see the oath fulfilled during their tenure. At best, all the sons of David—from Solomon to Jesus—were under God's discipline (cf. 2 Sam 7:14–15), and only Jesus was able to secure the oath made to David because only Jesus was the completely obedient Son.

It is my conviction, therefore, that 2 Sam 7:12–13 is a prophetic announcement concerning the resurrection and exaltation of Jesus the Messiah! And this prophetic word is the ground for which David's resurrection hope is given expression in Pss 132 and 110. Moreover, this understanding of an individual seed who bears the restoration promises of God is extremely important for understanding God's overall redemptive plans for the world. Within the Davidic hope in the resurrection of Jesus from the dead lies the future hope for Israel and the nations—a living hope that has its antecedents in the Abrahamic covenant which stems from the seed promise of Gen 3:15.

In sum, Peter's allusion to the Davidic covenant of 2 Sam 7:12–13 in Acts 2:30 forms the basis for his exegesis of Pss 16:8–11 and 110:1. Neither the Psalms nor the oath were speaking about David or his immediate successors. Rather, these texts witness prophetically to the sufferings and glory of Jesus the Messiah, who, through his life, death, resurrection and exaltation has secured the everlasting promises made to David, and whose end-time kingdom has begun (2 Sam. 7:12–13; cf. Luke 24:25–27, 44–46). In our next section will take a look at Peter's second speech with a particular focus on how Jesus fulfills the Abrahamic covenant.

4. Peter's Second Speech (Acts 3:11–26)

Peter's second speech comes within the context of healing a lame man, which the crowd had mistakenly thought was due to the apostles' piety and power (Acts 3:1–

11). Peter instead draws attention to the death of Jesus—whom the Jews, in ignorance, were responsible for crucifying; nevertheless, God raised him from the dead. Peter makes it clear that it is on the basis of faith in the name of Jesus that the lame man received healing (Acts 3:15–17), and points further to the prophetic fulfillment of Scripture concerning the sufferings and glory of the Messiah in announcing the Jewish crowd's need for repentance so that God "may send Jesus ... whom heaven must receive until the *period of restoration* of all things about which God spoke [through the prophets]" (Acts 3:18–21, emphasis added).

Peter then proclaims the death and resurrection of Jesus as the fulfillment of latter day prophecies (cf. Acts 3:22–24): He draws attention to Moses who had prophesied that God would raise up a prophet like himself (Deut 18:15–19),[11] and to Nathan who prophesied concerning the Davidic oath (2 Sam 7:12–13), and concludes by reminding the crowd that they are the "sons of the prophets" and of the covenant in which God swore to Abraham that his seed would become the blessing to the nations (Acts 3:25).

4.1. Peter's Use of the Abrahamic Blessing to the Nations

While it is difficult to determine the exact referent for Peter's scriptural citation in Acts 3:25 (i.e., Gen 12:3, 18:18, 22:18, 26:4, or 28:14),[12] it is clear that he has the Abrahamic covenant in mind, and in particular, that aspect of the covenant which speaks of God's promise to bless the nations through Abraham's seed.[13] It is equally clear that Peter sees Jesus as that *particular seed* through whom the Abrahamic blessing to the nations has begun to be fulfilled. Intriguingly, he refers to Jesus, the seed of Abraham, as God's "servant" (Acts 3:26), a somewhat ambiguous figure in Isaiah, yet, extremely important for Peter's overall argument concerning the prophetic

---

[11] It is also possible that from a redemptive-historical perspective something more than Jesus' earthly prophetic ministry is in view. It may be likely that his resurrection and ascension are also hinted at here.

[12] Marshall, 548.

[13] Note Peter's reference to "the covenant which God made with [their] fathers," followed by a direct reference to Abraham and the quote concerning the blessing to all the families of the earth (Acts 3:25).

witness to Jesus' sufferings and glory. More will be said about the servant figure in the next section, but for now, our focus is on Peter's interpretation of the Abrahamic blessing to the nations as having begun to be fulfilled in the resurrection and exaltation of Jesus (Acts 3:25–26). Thus, a quick overview of the main components of the covenant is in order.

In Gen 12:1–3 the main components of the Abrahamic covenant are laid out in the form of three specific promises: "great nationhood," "a great name," and "blessing to the nations."[14] In Gen 15, God cuts a covenant with Abram, promising him numerous seed and land. While this picks up on the promise of nationhood in Gen 12, it says nothing about the great name or blessing to the nations. Abram believes God and it is credited to him as righteousness (Gen 15:6). Interestingly, the land promise made to Abram and his seed comes within the prediction that they will first become strangers in a land not their own, where they will be enslaved and oppressed for 400 years, but God will judge that nation and bring them out with many possessions (Gen 15:13–14). Contemporaneous to this situation is the judgement on the nations of Canaan. God will dispossess those nations because of their sin and give the land to Abram and his offspring (Gen 15:17–21).

In Gen 17 God makes an "everlasting covenant" with Abram, wherein he is promised to become "the father of a multitude of nations," provided he walks before God and is blameless (Gen 17:1–5). With this covenant, both Abram and Sarai's names are changed to reflect their new status (Gen 17:5, 15). Together they will become the father and mother of a "multitude of nations" from which kingship shall emerge (Gen 17:6, 16). This particular notion of fatherhood seems to point beyond mere physical offspring. As Alexander observes, the term "father" may be used in a variety of ways that take us beyond a simple biological understanding. He writes, "By taking the word in this non-biological sense, we may understand Genesis 17:4-5 as stating that Abraham will be the 'father of many nations' not because these nations are his physical descendants but because he will be for them a channel of divine

---

[14] Scott W. Hahn, *Kinship by Covenant: A Canonical Approach to the Fulfillment of God's Saving Promises* (New Haven & London: Yale University Press, 2009), 103.

blessing."[15]

This covenant is also conditioned upon Abraham's obedient faith, an obedience that will later be tested when God asks him to sacrifice his beloved son, Isaac (Gen 22). What God is asking Abraham to do is to give up the very child through whom the covenant promises are to be advanced (Gen 17:19, 21). As von Rad observes, "In him every saving thing that God has promised to do is invested and guaranteed."[16]

In Gen 22 Abraham successfully passes this extreme test of faith. Having seen that Abraham was willing to sacrifice Isaac, the Angel of the LORD stopped him from doing so. Abraham then saw a ram caught in the thicket, and offered it up in the place of his son. He called the name of that place, "the LORD will provide" (Gen 22:14). There also, on the basis of Abraham's willingness to sacrifice his one and only son, God swore an unconditional oath to bless the seed of Abraham, promising that Abraham's seed would become a blessing to the nations (Gen 22:17–18). Significantly, this oath is both particular and universal. As Alexander points out, "the first half affirms that Abraham's 'seed' will become very numerous, the second half asserts that Abraham's 'seed' will defeat his enemies and mediate blessing to the nations of the earth."[17] Summarizing the significance of Gen 22 in relationship to chapters 12, 15, and 17, Hahn concludes: "In Genesis 22:15–18, the last and climactic promise of Gen 12:2–3—blessing for all nations—is finally given covenant form, and the previous covenants of chs. 15 and 17 are ratified and confirmed."[18]

This brief overview is important for understanding the significance of the Abrahamic covenant as a whole, and more particularly with respect to how Peter understands its last component as having begun to be fulfilled in the resurrection and exaltation of Jesus. We have seen that Peter proclaims to his Jewish audience that they "are the sons of the prophets and of the covenant which God made with [their] fathers, saying to Abraham: 'And in your seed all the families of the earth shall be blessed'"

---

[15] T. Desmond Alexander, "Royal Expectations in Genesis to Kings," *TynBul* 49 (1998): 201.

[16] G. von Rad, *Genesis: A Commentary*, OTL (Philadelphia: Westminster, 1972), 244.

[17] Alexander, 202.

[18] Hahn, 111.

(Acts 3:25–26). In quoting from his scriptural source, he emphasizes the one through whom all the families of the earth shall be blessed, using the neuter singular dative of σπέρμα (i.e., ἐν τῷ σπέρματί σου) along with [ἐν]ευλογηθήσονται. This exact same verbal form and phrase occur in the LXX translation of Gen 22:18; 26:4; 28:14. When examining the potential references for Peter's use of Scripture (i.e., Gen 22:18, 26:4, or 28:14), it appears that Gen 22:18 is the most likely candidate, since, as we have seen, this is the initial place where God swears an unconditional oath that an individual seed will emerge through whom the blessing to the nations is destined to flow. The MT also confirms this reading:

> And I will surely bless you and I will greatly multiply your seed like the stars of the heavens and the sand which is on the seashore (Gen 22:17a); and your <u>seed shall possess</u> the gate of <u>his</u> enemies (Gen 22:17b). And in your <u>seed</u>[19] all the nations of the earth will be blessed, because you obeyed my voice. (Gen 22:18a, my trans.)

In analyzing the syntax of the MT (above), Alexander concludes that while the first clause of Gen 22:17(a) "obviously refers to a very large number of descendants, the second [Gen 22:17b] would, following Collins' approach, denote a single individual who is victorious over his enemies."[20] He continues:

> This latter reading of 22:17[b] has implications also for 22:18a which states … 'and all the nations of the earth will be blessed through your offspring'. If the immediately preceding reference to 'seed' in 22:17[b] denotes an individual, this must also be the case in 22:18a, for there is nothing here to indicate a change in number. The blessing of 'all the nations of the earth' is thus associated with a particular descendant of Abraham, rather than with all those descended from him.[21]

---

[19] This individual is the one through whom the nations shall be blessed.

[20] T.D. Alexander, "Further Observations on the Term 'Seed' in Genesis," *TynBul* 48 (1997): 365.

[21] Ibid.

While the immediate individual in view may appear to be Isaac, the Abrahamic oath is later reiterated to Jacob (cf. Gen 28:10–22; 35:9–21), and at the close of Genesis the promise remains unfulfilled, as was also the case with the Davidic oath. Thus, it continues to point to an individual yet to come, whom Peter understands to be Jesus of Nazareth (Acts 3:25).[22]

4.3. Peter's Use of the "Servant" Motif and the Surprising Fulfillment of the Abrahamic Covenant

Peter asserts that the last component of the Abrahamic covenant (i.e., the blessing to the nations), must be applied (surprisingly) first to the nation Israel before going out to the Gentile nations: "For you first, God having raised up his servant, sent him to bless you by turning every one of you from your wickedness" (Acts 3:26).

In keeping with Peter's pattern that focuses on the resurrection of the Messiah from the dead, the key figure here is the "servant." Thus, the servant's resurrection is the means by which God brings blessing: first to Israel, and then to the nations.

While Peter's use of the term "servant" is somewhat obscure, since many biblical characters have been referred to as such (e.g., Abraham, Moses, David, Israel, etc.), the most likely candidate appears to be the Isaianic Servant of Yahweh, who is also the Messiah (cf. Isa 42:1–9; 49:1–13; 50:4–11; 52:13–53:12; cf. the language of Isa 9:6–7; 11:1–3).[23] The reason that the Isaianic Servant is the best candidate for Peter's use of the term "servant" is because the servant's unique mission entails both suffering and glory (see esp. Isa 52:13–53:12).

---

[22] It is no coincidence that the original oath sworn to Abraham in Gen 22:17–18, concerning his seed who would become a blessing to the nations, takes place within the context of the near sacrifice of Isaac, the seed of promise and Abraham's only begotten son (at this stage in redemptive-history). Nor is it a coincidence that God provides a substitute in Isaac's place, a substitute pointing to the only beloved Son of God, seed of Abraham, and seed of the woman (cf. Gen 3:15), who, by laying down his life will become the means by which the Abrahamic blessing to the nations finally comes to fruition!

[23] David Pao has persuasively argued for Isaiah's influence in providing the theological framework for Luke-Acts, particularly in relation to what he calls the "Isaianic New Exodus" (*Acts and the Isaianic New Exodus* [Grand Rapids: Baker, 2002]). According to Pao, Luke sees three stages to the Isaianic program as outlined in Acts 1:8: the dawn of redemptive-history, beginning in Jerusalem, the restoration of Israel, and the larger mission to the nations (cf. Isa 49:6).

As stated earlier, from a redemptive-historical perspective, none of Abraham's descendants lived to see the last component of the Abrahamic blessing to the nations come to fruition—at least not in its fullest sense. Likewise, they did not live to see Abraham's seed possess the gates of his enemies, nor did they witness the multiplication and expansion of Abraham's spiritual descendants to the four corners of the earth (cf. the promise of the multiplication of Zion's offspring [Isa 54] in light of the Servant's work [Isa 52:13–53:12]).

The reason that none of these prophecies were fulfilled during Israel's long history is because, once again, they were pointing to an individual seed who was yet to come; namely, Jesus, the Messiah. Thus, in speaking to his Jewish audience, Peter applies the Abrahamic blessing to the nations in light of the Isaianic Servant's work, surprisingly, first, with an application to Israel, before the results of the Servant's work may be extended to the nations (Acts 3:26). In other words, in order for the seed of Abraham, who is also the Isaianic Servant of Yahweh, to become a blessing to the nations, *he must first become a blessing to Israel* by enabling them to find forgiveness and restoration in Jesus' name (Acts 2:37–39; Cf. Isa 49:5–6; Rom 1:16–17).

This interpretation also fits well with the overall structure of the book of Acts in which the Spirit-filled apostolic proclamation of the gospel that occurs in Peter's first two speeches begins with the Jewish nation in Jerusalem (Acts 1:1–7) before extending out to the Gentile world (Acts 8–28).

5. Conclusion

We have focused on the redemptive-historical significance of Peter's speeches in Acts 2–3 with particular attention being given to the surprising fulfillment of prophecy in relation to the Davidic and Abrahamic covenants.

In regards to the former, it was argued that Peter's allusion to the Davidic covenant of 2 Sam 7:12–13 forms the basis for his exegesis of Pss 16:8–11 and 110:1, and that neither the Psalms nor the oath were speaking about David or his immediate successors. Rather, these texts witness prophetically to the sufferings and glory of Jesus, the son of David, who, by virtue of his life, death, resurrection and exaltation has secured the everlasting promises that were spoken about him (Acts 2:22–36).

With regard to the latter, we have seen that before the last component of the Abrahamic covenant could be fulfilled (i.e., the blessing to the nations), the Isaianic Servant of Yahweh, who, is both Abraham's and David's seed, must first become a blessing to repentant and believing Israel:

> And now says the LORD, who formed Me from the womb to be His Servant, to bring Jacob back to Him, so that Israel might be gathered to Him.... He says, 'It is too small a thing that You should be My Servant to raise up the tribes of Jacob and to restore the preserved ones of Israel; I will also make You a light to the nations so that My salvation may reach to the end of the earth.' (Isa 49:5–6)

Thus, the faithful remnant of Israel must first be regathered and restored before the Abrahamic blessing to the nations can go forth (cf. Isa 49:6). As the result of the Servant's work (Isa 53), the seed of eschatological Israel will be multiplied and spread abroad (Isa 54), through the Spirit-empowered apostolic witness that begins in Jerusalem and extends to the uttermost ends of the earth (Acts 1:8). This is good news indeed, pointing us to the wonderfully surprising way in which God has fulfilled his promise concerning "the seed of the woman" (Gen 3:15) through the royal seed of Abraham and David who is also their Lord (cf. John 8:56; Matt 22:45)!

ROMANS 16:20 AS A SUMMARY OF CENTRAL THEMES OF ROMANS

—Brian S. Rosner

1. Introduction

There is just one allusion to Gen 3:15 in Paul's letters, namely Rom 16:20a: "The God of peace will soon crush Satan under your feet." While it has been widely noticed, it has escaped close scrutiny, appearing as it does at the end of Paul's most majestic letter; so many more pressing issues in Romans exhaust the attention of commentators and theologians. Yet a closer look reveals some surprising twists in Paul's appropriation of the Genesis text and opens a window to central themes surrounding his understanding of the sufferings and glory of Messiah Jesus. These include the description of "the God of peace" as the one who brings victory over Satan, the fact that it will happen "soon," the language of "crushing" the enemy, and the easily-missed detail that it is under the feet of believers that it will occur.[1]

As it turns out, a veritable thicket of text-critical, literary, exegetical and theological issues awaits the curious interpreter: Did Paul write the words in question with his own hand? What is the relationship between Rom 16:20a and what immediately precedes it and what follows it? How does the text relate to Gen 3:15? (At least one scholar disputes any connection).[2] Does the victory in view entail the imminent demise of the false teachers mentioned in the warning of Rom 16:17–19? Or does Paul have an eschatological triumph in mind? How soon is "soon"? How does Rom 16:20a relate to the purpose(s) of Romans?

Three questions in particular drive the present study, which focus attention on its connection to Gen 3:15: (1) What is the function of Rom 16:20a in the letter

---

[1] It is a pleasure to dedicate this essay to Desmond Alexander with thanks for his encouraging and instructive example of faithful Christian biblical scholarship.

[2] See note 26 below.

closing? (2) How does Rom 16:20a relate to the rest of Romans? And (3) What does Rom 16:20a teach about the sufferings and glory of the Messiah? The following sections of this essay address these questions in order.

2. The Place of Romans 16:20a in the Letter Closing of Romans

Jeffrey Weima contends that "the Pauline letter closings are carefully constructed units, shaped and adapted in such a way that they relate directly to— sometimes, in fact, even summarize—the major concerns and themes previously addressed in the body sections of their respective letters."[3] The contention that the final section of Paul's letters distills many of the big ideas of the letters which they close is uncontroversial in New Testament scholarship. Indeed, those who find affinities to the structure and argument of Paul's letters in Greco-Roman rhetorical theory make a similar point, arguing that the final part of many discourses in the ancient world serves "the function of recapitulating or summarizing the main points previously raised in the oration."[4] A related point in the opposite direction is often made with respect to the Pauline introductory thanksgivings; rather than reiterate, they pre-empt major themes of the letters they introduce. For that reason, it is always worth comparing letter openings and closings, the epistolary frame, to notice common features.

In more general terms, a recapping and summarizing function for Paul's letter closings makes sense in the light of basic literary theory about the experience of reading. Reading is by nature a process of retrospection and prospection, looking back and looking forward across a book and making connections. Influential phenomenologist Wolfgang Iser asserts:

> Whenever we read past segments must be retained in each present moment. The new moment is not isolated, but stands out against the old,

---

[3] Jeffrey A. D. Weima, "The Pauline Letter Closings: Analysis and Hermeneutical Significance," *BBR* 5 (1995): 182–83. See further Weima, *Neglected Endings: The Significance of the Pauline Letter Closings* (Sheffield: Sheffield Academic, 1999); and *Paul the Ancient Letter Writer: An Introduction to Epistolary Analysis* (Grand Rapids: Baker, 2016).

[4] Weima, "The Pauline Letter Closings," 182–83.

and so the past will remain as a background to the present, exerting influence on it and, at the same time, itself being modified by the present.... Reading does not merely flow forward, but recalled segments also have a retroactive effect, with the present transforming the past.[5]

The letter closing of Romans is the longest final section of any of his letters, running from 15:33 to 16:27.[6] According to Weima, in terms of its structure, it opens with a peace benediction (15:33), contains a letter of commendation (16:1–2), two greeting lists (16:3–16 and 16:21–23), a hortatory section (16:17–20a; the Autograph section), a grace benediction (16:20b) and closes with a doxology (16:24–27).[7]

The decision to place Rom 16:20a, the focus of our attention, in the hortatory section is supported by most modern English versions. The KJV, ASV, NRSV, ESV, NET, NLT, Lexham English Bible, all take Rom 16:17–20 as a unit.[8] Not dissimilarly, TEB and NKJV regard 16:17–20a as one section, marking off the grace benediction (16:20b) as a separate unit of thought. Such decisions color the interpretation of 16:20a in terms of Paul's warnings about false teachers. That God would soon crush Satan under the feet of the faithful in Rome is an encouragement to stand against those who cause divisions and oppose Paul's teaching.

This interpretation goes back at least as far as John Chrysostom: "For since he [Paul] had spoken of those who 'caused divisions and offences among them,' he has mentioned 'the God of peace' also, that they might feel hopeful about the riddance of these evils."[9]

---

[5] Wolfgang Iser, *The Act of Reading: A Theory of Aesthetic Response* (Baltimore: John Hopkins University Press, 1978), 114, 116.

[6] It is also the messiest in terms of its textual history. For example, the grace benediction is found in different positions in various Greek manuscripts (15:20b, 16:24, 16:28) and the authenticity of 16:25–27 is disputed. In my judgment there are good reasons to accept the text as presented in NA 28.

[7] Jeffrey A. D. Weima, *Neglected Endings: The Significance of the Pauline Letter Closings* (Sheffield: Sheffield Academic, 1999), 222.

[8] Likewise the German versions Luther Bibel 2017, Schlachter 2000, Zürcher Bibel, and Gute Nachricht Bibel.

[9] John Chrysostom, "Homilies of St. John Chrysostom, Archbishop of Constantinople, on the Epistle of St. Paul to the Romans" in *Saint Chrysostom: Homilies on the Acts of the Apostles and the*

Many modern commentators from a range of traditions concur with this reading:

> "It is the 'God of peace' who will overthrow Satan, because the effect of these divisions [mentioned in Rom 16:17–19] is to break up the peace of the Church."[10]

> "*[T]he God of peace will soon crush Satan:* the false teachers are not merely mistaken; they are the missionaries of the Devil."[11]

> "Paul probably means that if the Roman believers watch out for and keep away from those who cause divisions (16:17), then God will crush Satan under their feet, that is, confound Satan's designs to lead them astray."[12]

> "This verse [Rom 16:20a] thus indicates that God will deal with the problem that is troubling the weak in Rome, and will do so with dispatch."[13]

> "The God of peace (cf. 15:33) will soon 'crush under your feet' the snake, that is, Satan, who is at work in the deceptive words of the false teachers."[14]

> "In verse 20[a] Paul adds an assurance to his warning. He has written about good and evil; he wants the Roman Christians to know that there is no doubt about the ultimate outcome, the triumph of good over evil. He detects the strategy of Satan behind the activity of the false teachers, and he is confident that the devil is going to be overthrown."[15]

Epistle to the Romans, ed. J. B. Schaff; trans. J. B. Morris, W. H. Simcox, & G. B. Stevens (New York: Christian Literature Company, 1989), Vol. 11, 560–61.

[10] William Sanday and Arthur C. Headlam, *A Critical and Exegetical Commentary on the Epistle to the Romans* (Edinburgh: T&T Clark, 1902), 431.

[11] J. A. Ziesler, *Paul's Letter to the Romans*, TPINTC (London: SCM, 1989), 355.

[12] Colin G. Kruse, *Paul's Letter to the Romans*, Pilllar New Testament Commentary (Nottingham, Apollos; Grand Rapids: Eerdmans, 2012), 575–81.

[13] Ben Witherington and Diane Hyatt, *Paul's letter to the Romans: A Socio-rhetorical Commentary* (Grand Rapids: Eerdmans, 2004), 398–99.

[14] Peter Stuhlmacher, *Paul's Letter to the Romans: A Commentary*, trans Scott J. Hafemann (Louisville, Kentucky: Westminster John Knox, 1994), 253–54.

[15] John Stott, *The Message of Romans,* BST (Nottingham: Inter-Varsity Press, 1994), 400.

As to the timing of the promise, Leon Morris, noting the language of Satan's imminent downfall, argues that it is best to "see the promise of a victory over Satan in the here and now."[16] In favor of this interpretation is the appeal to the immediately preceding context of Romans 16:17–18, in which Paul warns the Roman Christians to watch out for false teachers, and 16:19, which calls for them to continue their obedience and to be innocent with regard to evil.

However, there are good reasons to doubt the consensus view. The NIV and NCV take 16:20, the peace and grace benedictions together, as a new and discrete paragraph; and HCSB, CSB and the Message take 16:19–20 as a unit. Both placements of 16:20a suggest a different understanding of its function and meaning. Instead of reading 16:20a in the light of the warning about false teaching, the God of peace soon crushing Satan under the feet of the Christian believers in Rome turns out to be, in Cranfield's words, "a promise of much more far-reaching significance."[17]

With reference to the majority of modern commentators and most English Bible versions Cranfield asserts:

> It is very often assumed both by those who think that the reference [to crushing Satan in Rom 16:20a] is to a deliverance in the ordinary course of history and those who think the reference is to the final eschatological defeat of evil that Paul must have in mind the rout of the people mentioned

---

[16] Leon L. Morris, *The Epistle to the Romans* (Grand Rapids: Eerdmans; Leicester: Inter-Varsity Press, 1988), 541.

[17] C. E. B. Cranfield, *A Critical and Exegetical Commentary on the Epistle to the Romans, vol. 2* (London: T&T Clark, 1979), 803. R. G. Gruenler, "Romans," in *Evangelical Commentary on the Bible*, ed. Walter A. Elwell (Grand Rapids: Baker, 1995), vol. 3, 957, sees the attraction of both views: "This last prophecy likely goes beyond the immediate threat of false teachers, however, as Paul envisions the full and final defeat of Satan in God's good time (soon = swiftly, surely). Accordingly, verse 20 could stand by itself (so NIV), though it is probably better to take it as a prophecy that flows confidently out of the previous warning [against false teachers in 16:17-19]." David G. Peterson allows for both interpretations: "This eschatological vision [in Rom 16:20a] may be applied to the defeat of false teachers in their immediate situation.... But the complete end to Satan's power and the universal peace that will flow from that victory is the broader meaning of the imagery" (*Commentary on Romans*, BTCP [Nashville: Broadman & Holman, 2017], 547).

in v. 17f regarded as the servants of Satan. But this is by no means clear.[18]

Four lines of evidence suggest that a more independent and broader interpretation of Rom 16:20a is correct.

First, the related case can be made that the verses immediately preceding and following Rom 16:20a (16:19 and 25–26 respectively) are meant to remind readers of important themes from Romans. Paul's intimation that "everyone has heard about your *obedience*" in verse 19 (cf. "the obedience of faith"; v. 26) recalls a major theme of Romans. Roy E. Ciampa notes that:

> Romans begins and ends with the theme of 'the obedience of faith' (1.5; 16.26). Within the letter Paul speaks of what God has accomplished through Christ "to bring the Gentiles to obedience' (15.18). In 6.16 he speaks of 'obedience leading to righteousness' (or possibly to 'justification'). Paul's message has to do with obedience from the heart (6.17) to the truth (Rom. 2.8; Gal. 5.7), the gospel (Rom. 10.16; 2 Thess. 1.8), or Christ (2 Cor. 10.5-6). It is Christ's own obedience which provides the righteousness (and obedience) of his people (5.19; cf. Phil. 2.8).[19]

With reference to verses following Rom 16:20a I argue in *Paul and the Law* that Rom 16:25–26 recalls Rom 1:1–3, forging a striking *inclusio* enveloping the entire letter.[20] In 1:2 Paul affirms that the gospel was promised in advance in the holy scriptures "through his prophets" (διὰ τῶν προφητῶν αὐτοῦ); and in 16:26 this gospel is disclosed "through the prophetic scriptures" (διά τε γραφῶν προφητικῶν).[21]

---

[18] Cranfield, *Romans*, 803.

[19] Roy E. Ciampa, "Deuteronomy in Galatians and Romans," in *Deuteronomy in the New Testament*, ed. M. J. J. Menken and Steve Moyise (London: T&T Clark, 2007), 109.

[20] See Brian S. Rosner, *Paul and the Law: Keeping the Commandments of God* (Downers Grove, IL: InterVarsity Press, 2013), 148–55.

[21] For a full defense of the idea that the letter closing in Romans revisits themes introduced in the Romans letter opening see J. A. D. Weima, "The Reason for Romans: The Evidence of Its Epistolary Framework (1:1-15; 15:14–16:27)," *RevExp* 100 (2003): 17–33.

Secondly, the study of letter closings suggests a reason for the placement of 16:20a as an independent element. The final section of Romans begins in 15:33 with a peace benediction: "The God of peace be with you all." Such peace benedictions "typically occupy the first position in a closing section."[22] Normally, following this component Paul offers other standard elements to close his letters, all of which appear in Rom 16: a hortatory section, a list of greetings, an autograph formula and a grace benediction (see above). The problem for Paul in writing Romans is that his closing greeting is so long, and in two parts. This means that by the time he is ready to sign off the letter, so to speak, his peace benediction in 15:33 is all but forgotten. In this light, it is likely that he offers the second peace benediction in 16:20a, as a reprisal of the first, to signal that he is indeed now closing out the letter. In that case 16:20a is a separate element in the letter closing, not closely tied to the warning about false teachers in 16:17–19.

Thirdly, the content of this second peace benediction, with its focus on the defeat of evil, is apocalyptic in tone, suggesting an eschatological focus rather than the more mundane meaning of thwarting false teachers.[23] Several features of the promise point in this direction. Witherington notes that "the hope of Satan being crushed under foot is common in apocalyptic Jewish and Christian contexts (*Jubilees* 5.6; 10.7–11; 23.29; *1 Enoch* 10.4, 11–12; 13.1–2; 1QM 17.5–6; 18.1; Rev. 20:10)."[24] With reference to the verb "to crush" (συντρίβω) Jewett notes that "[t]he word is used in connection with mistreating people, beating them severely, bruising them, or annihilating them" and that "[t]here are numerous parallels to this usage of the verb in the context of holy war."[25] The suitability of the idea of crushing someone under your feet to a setting in Jewish eschatology that includes the participation of the faithful can be seen in T. Levi 18:12 where, after the apocalyptic battle, the LORD "shall grant to his children the authority to

---

[22] Weima, *Neglected Endings*, 216.

[23] Cf. Michael F. Bird, *Romans*, SGBC (Grand Rapids: Zondervan, 2016), 533: "The hope for Satan to be crushed underfoot is extant in several Jewish apocalypses."

[24] Witherington and Hyatt, *Paul's Letter to the Romans*, 399.

[25] Robert Jewett, *Romans: A Commentary*, Hermeneia (Minneapolis: Fortress, 2007), 994.

trample on wicked spirits."[26] Taken together, these features suggest a broader meaning than simply resisting the false teachers is probably meant in Rom 16:20a.

A fourth point leads us into the next section of this essay. Since Paul's letter closings typically perform the function of distilling the major themes of their respective letters, it is worth asking whether Rom 16:20a is an apt concluding summary of some key themes of Romans. I will argue that this is precisely the case. The proper context for the interpretation of Rom 16:20a is not 16:17–19 but rather the whole letter!

3. Romans 16:20a and the Rest of Romans

Does Rom 16:20a summarize and distill key themes from Romans? There are two ways to answer this question and both are needed. The first is to consider some of the details of Paul's promise, such as: (1) God as the agent of the action; (2) the epithet of "peace" attached to "God;" (3) the allusion to Gen 3:15;[27] and (4) the reference to human feet. A second broader consideration concerns whether the basic assertion of the defeat of evil recalls any specific texts in Romans.

3.1. The Details of Paul's Promise

With so many intriguing features of Paul's closing peace benediction vying for attention it is easy to miss the first element of Paul's pithy composition, namely, that God is the subject of the action. Does the fact that *God* will soon crush Satan summarize anything significant from Romans?

---

[26] Cited in Jewett, *Romans*, 994.

[27] Derek R. Brown, "'The God of peace will shortly crush Satan under your feet': Paul's Eschatological Reminder in Romans 16:20a,' *Neot* 44.1 (2010): 1–14, while admitting that an allusion to Gen 3:15 in Rom 16:20a cannot be ruled out, argues against seeing such a link between the two texts. Instead, he sees Paul drawing on the early Christian tradition of interpreting Ps 110:1 "as speaking of the subjugation of Christ's enemies 'under his feet'" (13). While Brown makes a reasonable case for the possible influence of Ps 110:1 on Rom 16:20a he does not consider the more likely possibility that Ps 110:1 is a general witness to a broad biblical theme and is developed in the NT specifically in connection with Jesus Christ. The focus on the defeat of *Satan* in Rom 16:20a points to a link to Gen 3:15.

The theme of Romans has exercised commentators for centuries. Whereas doctrinal proposals (e.g., salvation or justification) were once in vogue, the pendulum of late has swung towards a more occasional purpose, emphasizing the need to bring unity to a divided church in Rome. In either case, the 1970 contribution of Leon Morris is relevant to our purposes. Morris points out that "God comes more prominently before us in Romans than in any other part of the New Testament (with the possible exception of 1 John)."[28] In Romans the word "God" occurs as often as once every 46 words.[29]

Thinking in terms of the epistolary frame of Romans: God appears three times in the final eight verses of the letter, with the epithets "God of peace" (16:20a), "the eternal God" (16:26), and "the only wise God" (16:27); and five times in the letter opening (1:1–10), including references to "the gospel of God" (1:1) and "God's will" (1:10). Most pertinently for our purposes, Paul opens his letter by wishing all believers in Rome "peace" from God (1:7) and closes it by reassuring them that "the God of peace" would soon crush Satan under their feet (16:20a). As far as the theme of God in Romans goes, Morris rightly points out that "sometimes Paul gives information about the kind of God God is, but mostly he is concerned with what God does,"[30] and we might add, what he "soon" will do.

Other occurrences of "peace" in Romans fill out the theme of "the God of peace" with implications for the Roman Christians. Whereas unredeemed humanity does not by nature know "the way of peace" (3:13), the story of redemption that Romans narrates includes the blessing of a status of peace with God (5:1), a kingdom characterized by peace (14:17), a call to do "whatever leads to peace" with other believers (14:19) and peace with hostile outsiders (12:18), and a wish that God will fill believers with "all joy and peace" (15:13).

---

[28] Leon Morris, "The Theme of Romans," in *Apostolic History and the Gospel: Biblical and Historical Essays Presented to F.F. Bruce on his 60th birthday*, ed. W. Ward Gasque & Ralph P. Martin (Exeter: Paternoster, 1970), 263.

[29] The next book that focuses most directly on God in the NT is Acts with "God" appearing once every 110 words.

[30] Morris, "The Theme of Romans," 263.

The allusion to Gen 3:15 in Rom 16:20a is not an unexpected and isolated reference but rather serves to climax Paul's use of Gen 1–3 in his exposition of the gospel. The idyllic creation narratives of Gen 1 and 2 are infamously interrupted by the transgressions of Adam and Eve in Gen 3. Apart from God making Adam and Eve items of clothing in Gen 3:21, the only note of hope that is struck in these opening chapters of Scripture is Gen 3:15, however it is interpreted.

For our purposes it is significant that the fall of humanity and of creation in Gen 3 looms large in Paul's multi-faceted teaching about sin and salvation in Rom 5, 7, and 8:

- The description of sin and death entering the world through one man's sin in Rom 5:12 is a clear allusion to Gen 2:17 ("you must not eat from the tree of knowledge of good and evil, for when you eat it you will certainly die") and Gen 3:6 ("When the woman saw that the fruit of the tree was good for food and pleasing to the eye, and also desirable for gaining wisdom, she took some and ate it. She also gave some to her husband").[31]

- Paul's description of his own struggle with sin in Rom 7 recalls a verse in Gen 3. In Rom 7:11 Paul writes: "For sin, seizing the opportunity afforded by the commandment, *deceived* (ἐξαπατάω) me, and through the commandment put me to death." In Gen 3:13 Eve describes her own succumbing to temptation in similar terms: "Then the LORD God said to the woman, 'What is this you have done?' The woman said, 'The serpent *deceived* (LXX: ἀπατάω) me, and I ate.'"

- In Rom 8:20 Paul notes that "the creation was subjected to frustration," echoing the cursing of the ground, producing thorns and thistles resulting in sweaty brows and painful toil in Gen 3:17–19.

In this light the allusion to Gen 3:15 in Rom 16:20a brings a sense of fitting relief to these bleak Genesis intertexts. If temptation and sin has led to death, a tragedy of

---

[31] Cf. Gen 3:19: "dust you are and to dust you will return."

cosmic proportions, the final defeat of evil is a succinct and welcome reminder of the good news of the gospel. Paul is certainly not obliged to take his readers (with ears to hear) back to the Garden of Eden. However, the striking recollection of Gen 3:15 in Rom 16:20a certainly offers hope in pointing to the denouement to the story of redemption that has occupied much of his attention in the letter.

Finally, does a reference to "feet" in the promise of Rom 16:20a call anything to mind from Romans? Human feet are mentioned three times in the letter, all in connection with Old Testament texts.[32] In Rom 3:15, in the catena of condemnation, "*feet* swift to shed blood" (cf. Isa 59:7) appear as the essence of human sin. To deal with this dire condition, in Rom 10:15 (cf. Isa 52:7) beautiful *feet* bring the good news of the gospel. And then in Rom 16:20a, believers participate in God's victory in crushing Satan under their own *feet*.

3.2. Two Key Texts in Romans

The basic message of Rom 16:20a, the promise of the victory of believers over evil, picks up and draws together ideas from two specific texts in Rom 12 and 13.

In Rom 12:17–21 Paul instructs the Christians in Rome on how to respond to those who wish to do them harm. Quoting two Old Testament passages, Deut 32:15 in Rom 12:19 and Prov 25:21–22 in Rom 12:20, Paul urges that believers take the difficult path of non-retaliation in the hope of turning their enemies into friends. He closes his advice in v. 21 with a pithy and poignant saying: "Do not be overcome by evil, but overcome evil with good."[33]

Morris notes that in Rom 12:21 "it is possible to take τοῦ κακοῦ as masculine, 'the evil one;'"[34] however, the neuter sense of an abstract noun, "evil," comports better with the use of the term in 12:17a. The reference to "evil" in v. 21 picks up on two occurrences of the same word in Rom 12:17a ("Do not repay anyone evil for evil")

---

[32] Rom 1:23 mentions τετραπόδων "animals," literally, "four-footeds."

[33] Cf. Newman and Nida who comment: "This verse is best taken as a summary statement of what Paul has said in verse 17–20." B. M. Newman & E. A. Nida. *A handbook on Paul's letter to the Romans* (New York: United Bible Societies, 1973), 243.

[34] Leon Morris, *The Epistle to the Romans*, 455.

and demarcates the unit with an effective *inclusio*. Nonetheless, given the widespread association of Satan with evil across the New Testament and the use of "the evil one" as a moniker for Satan (e.g., Matt 5:37; 6:13; Luke 11:4; John 17:15; Eph 6:16; 2 Thess 3:3; 5x in 1 John), it is significant that in Rom 12:21 it is believers who triumph over evil. Indeed, the first group of glosses for νικάω (typically translated "overcome" in Rom 12:21) in BDAG is "win in the face of obstacles, be victor, conquer, overcome, prevail,"[35] and the word is regularly used in battle contexts not dissimilar to the image of vanquishing an enemy deployed in Rom 16:20a.

If in Rom 12:17–21 Paul promises God's decisive eschatological action against evil (v. 19: "leave room for God's wrath") and holds out the prospect of believers having a part in overcoming evil themselves, the promise of God defeating evil in connection with the activity of believers in Rom 16:20a brings to mind the earlier text in Romans and is a fitting further encouragement for believers to do good in the present.

A similar link can also be seen between Rom 16:20a and 13:11–14. In Rom 13:11–14 Paul supports his previous call to love (Rom 13:8–10) by telling the Roman Christians what time it is: "do this, understanding the present time" (Rom 13:11a). They live in the last days when "the night is nearly over [and] the day is almost here" (Rom 13:12). In that dawning light they are to avoid the sins of the night (drunkenness, sexual immorality, dissention and jealousy), resisting the desires of the flesh; instead they must put on the new humanity of the Lord Jesus Christ (Rom 13:14) and behave in ways appropriate to those living in the "daytime" (Rom 13:13). In addition, Paul mixes military imagery with this 'enlightening' metaphor: in Rom 13:12 he calls on believers to "put on the armor of light."

The connections with Paul's promise in Rom 16:20a are noteworthy. If in Rom 13:11–14 Paul calls on Christians to behave well in the light of the coming eschaton (13:11b: "because our salvation is nearer now than when we first believed"), doing

---

[35] W. Bauer, W. F. Arndt, F. W. Gingrich & F. W. Danker. *A Greek-English lexicon of the New Testament and other early Christian literature.* Third edition (Chicago: University of Chicago Press, 2001), 673.

battle with the evils of self-indulgence and social strife, in Rom 16:20a he repeats that the final victory will occur "soon" and the end of all evil is in sight. When the Roman Christians heard Paul's sure promise of this future victory in the letter closing they would have taken it as further encouragement to live in ways (mentioned in Rom 13:11–14) that are in keeping with that coming day.

4. Romans 16:20a and the Sufferings and Glory of the Messiah's People

To this point I have argued that argued that Rom 16:20a, Paul's second peace benediction in the Romans letter closing, is a promise of far-reaching significance and that it summarizes major themes of Romans and recalls key texts in the letter. We are now in a position to consider the theme of this volume of essays directly: What does Rom 16:20a teach about the sufferings and glory of the Messiah?

Romans 16:20a recalls and reinforces three big themes from Romans: (1) sin as a power; (2) the victory of the cross over evil; and (3) the suffering of believers in union with Christ. As it turns out, while regularly noticed, all three themes are relatively neglected in treatments of the theology of Romans. For example, in the *New Dictionary of Biblical Theology* article on Romans, Doug Moo summarizes the main themes of the letter as salvation history, the human predicament, the "righteousness of God" and justification, the law, Israel, and the Christian life.[36] Yet, arguably, all three are of critical pastoral significance to the daily life of the church in Rome (whatever specific purpose for the letter one assumes).

Broadly speaking, Romans offers a two-pronged diagnosis of human sin in terms of sin as guilt, in chapters 1–4, and *sin as a power,* in chapters 5–7. As Beverley Gaventa contends: "Paul's letter to the Romans depicts Sin as one of the anti-God powers whose final defeat the death and resurrection of Jesus Christ guarantees. The framework of cosmic battle is essential for reading and interpreting this letter in the life of the church."[37] According to Paul, all people are sinners (3:23) and as such are

---

[36] D. J. Moo, "Romans" in *New Dictionary of Biblical Theology.* Electronic edition, ed. T. Desmond Alexander and Brian S. Rosner (Downers Grove, IL: InterVarsity Press, 2000), 296.

37 Beverly R. Gaventa, "The Cosmic Power of Sin in Paul's Letter to the Romans: Toward a Widescreen Edition," *Int* 58.3 (2004): 229–40.

slaves of sin (6:17, 20) and sold under sin (7:14; cf. 7:25). And death, sin's ally, reigns over the entire human race thanks to Adam's sin (5:14, 21). As Leon Morris puts it: "The theme of sin as an alien, potent and active power recurs in Romans 5–7."[38] When Paul closes the letter with the good news of Satan's downfall in 16:20a, "Satan" stands as a comprehensive metonymy for the power of all evil,[39] and the Roman Christians would be reminded of the apostle's dire and realistic description of the human condition and plight and our need for deliverance.

Whereas the vast bulk of scholarly reflection on what the cross achieves in Romans is taken up with issues of righteousness and justification, the letter also includes clear teaching on *the cross as a victory over evil*. With respect to the theme of the triumph of God through the death and resurrection of Christ in the New Testament Gary Millar writes: "In one sense this victory is achieved over God's personal adversary, the devil; in another the impersonal enemies of sin and death, resulting from human rebellion, are the defeated foes."[40] According to Romans this victory is demonstrated in the resurrection of Christ from the dead in 1:4 ("[Jesus Christ] appointed the Son of God in power"), 4:25 ("raised to life for our justification") and most explicitly in the final verses of chapter 8 ("[Jesus Christ] raised to life – is at the right hand of God interceding for us;" 8:34). As Rom 8:37 states: "we are more than conquerors through him who loved us." This verse would be ringing in the ears of the Roman Christians when they heard Paul's bold assertion in 16:20a that God of peace would soon complete his victory over Satan through them.

Yet Romans 16:20a is not entirely good news, even if it includes believers in God's ultimate triumph over Satan and evil. For in God's crushing of Satan under the feet of believers lurks the suspicion that the battle will not be without some cost. Indeed, Gen 3:15a sets the tone for the verse as one of mutual hostility between the serpent and Eve's offspring: "I will put enmity between you and the woman, and

---

[38] Cf. Leon L. Morris, "Sin, Guilt" in *Dictionary of Paul and his Letters*, ed. G. F. Hawthorne, R. P. Martin, & D. G. Reid (Downers Grove, IL: InterVarsity Press, 1993), 878.

[39] This is the case whether or not the referent of "Satan" is taken to be a personal being.

[40] J. G. Millar, "Victory" in *New Dictionary of Biblical Theology*. Electronic edition, ed. T. Desmond Alexander and Brian S. Rosner (Downers Grove, IL: InterVarsity Press, 2000), 831–32.

between your offspring and hers."

When read in the light of Gen 3:15, where the serpent bruises the heal of Adam's seed, Rom 16:20a can be seen to include the sobering implication that the victory of believers over such a formidable adversary will involve some personal distress. However, Paul has prepared the Roman Christians well for dealing with this reality with his profound teaching about *the suffering of believers in union with Christ*. Extensive treatments of the beneficial purpose of such suffering occurs in Rom 5:3–5 and 8:12–39, where such suffering is seen to be "the divinely orchestrated means by which God strengthens their faithful endurance and hope by pouring out his own love and Spirit to sustain or deliver them in their distress."[41] And Rom 8:17 makes clear that all Christians should expect to suffer as a result of their identification with Christ: "if we are children, then we are heirs—heirs of God and co-heirs with Christ, if indeed we share in his sufferings in order that we may also share in his glory." If Rom 16:20a reminds the Christians in Rome of the travails of their lives as those in union with Christ in waiting for God's imminent victory, the recollection of Rom 8 would comfort them that their suffering is the pathway to sharing in Christ's glory: "Who shall separate us from the love of Christ? Shall trouble or hardship or persecution or famine or nakedness or danger or sword" (Rom 8:25)? Romans 16:20a tell us something about the sufferings and glory of the Messiah, but it also speaks about the sufferings and glory of the Messiah's people.

To end on a positive note, we must not miss the point that given Gen 3:15 is primarily about enmity and hostility, in Paul's gospel promise of Rom 16:20a it is the God of peace who resolves the conflict and brings ultimate victory to the offspring of Eve.[42]

---

[41] S. J. Hafemann, "Suffering" in *Dictionary of Paul and his Letters*, ed. G. F. Hawthorne, R. P. Martin, & D. G. Reid (Downers Grove, IL: InterVarsity Press, 1993), 920.

[42] By way of clarification, the major interpretive issue of Gen 3:15 in its original context in Genesis is the identity of the woman's offspring who will crush the serpent's head: Does "your offspring" refer to all of the woman's descendants or is only one descendant in view? In one sense it makes no difference to Paul's appropriation of the text, for in applying it to the Roman believers he does so either in accordance with its original intent or via the union of believers in Christ. I am in agreement with Desmond Alexander who takes Gen 3:15 to refer to an individual of royal status. See

5. Conclusion

"The God of peace will soon crush Satan under your feet" (Rom 16:20a).

Armed with Weima's work on letter closings, Iser's insights into the experience of reading as retrospection and prospection, and Cranfield's insistence that Rom 16:20a is a promise of far-reaching significance, and paying due attention to Paul's allusion to the promise of Gen 3:15, this essay has explored the manifold connections that Paul's words forge across his most majestic letter.

Paul's words in Rom 16:20a, his second peace benediction in the Romans letter closing, strike the notes of joy and hope, recalling key texts in Romans that summarize several major themes in the letter. Paul reminds the Roman Christians of their deliverance by God from the power of sin as those in union with Christ, urging them to understand the present time by overcoming evil and doing good, so as to be comforted in their suffering—all in light of the reassurance that the night is almost over and the day will soon be here.

T. Desmond Alexander, "Messianic Ideology in the Book of Genesis," in *The Lord's Anointed: Interpretation of Old Testament Messianic Texts*, ed. P. E. Satterthwaite, R. S. Hess and G. J. Wenham (Grand Rapids: Baker, 1995), 27–32.

HEBREWS, MELCHIZEDEK, AND BIBLICAL THEOLOGY

—Stephen Motyer

1. Introduction

The great focus of Desi Alexander's scholarly work—feeding into his popular writing, also—has been his commitment to biblical theology: that is, to tracing the lines of development between the Testaments, especially the ways in which Jesus Christ, and the church of Jesus Christ, stand at the climax of a story-line embracing the whole of Scripture. Interestingly, whereas others seek to identify a single key theme as the focus of the biblical story-line, Desi's approach is multi-thematic, as he weaves together the presence of God, Temple, Cult, City, Kingship and covenant People as interlocking strands in the developing narrative.[1]

Another feature of his work has been the way in which he stays close to the text. He does not allow his concern for the over-arching narrative to pull him away from the actual data of the biblical texts. At every level he has been concerned to let the Bible speak for itself, so that he first discerns local plot-lines (for instance, within Genesis and the Pentateuch) which then feed into wider OT and biblical narratives.

---

[1] I am thinking particularly of his recent study *The City of God and the Goal of Creation* (Wheaton, IL: Crossway, 2018); also, *From Eden to the New Jerusalem. Exploring God's Plan for Life on Earth* (Nottingham: Inter-Varsity Press, 2008), and *The Servant King. The Bible's Portrait of the Messiah* (Leicester: Inter-Varsity Press, 1998). In his major scholarly work *From Paradise to the Promised Land. An Introduction to the Pentateuch* (Grand Rapids: Baker Academic, 3rd ed. 2012) he concludes each thematic chapter with a section entitled "New Testament Connections," in which he draws lines across to the related thematic development in the New Testament. His commitment to the task of biblical theology is of course particularly shown by his editorship of the *New Dictionary of Biblical Theology*, ed. T. Desmond Alexander and Brian S. Rosner (Nottingham: Inter-Varsity Press; Downers Grove, IL: InterVarsity Press, 2000), to which he also contributes the article on "Genesis to Kings" (115–20).

His is an approach which essentially draws out the continuities between the Testaments, albeit with development *en route*. One might have thought that Hebrews, with its focus on the way in which Old Testament priesthood and cult functions as "a shadow of the good things coming" (10:1), would exemplify this approach *par excellence* within the New Testament itself. But Hebrews' approach is interestingly different, and this paper—in homage to Desi Alexander—explores that difference, not in order to argue for a better approach, but simply in order to explore some of the issues involved in the teasingly difficult task of understanding the unity of the Bible as the Word of the *one* God who has now revealed himself as the God and Father of our Lord Jesus Christ. We adopt Hebrews' use of Melchizedek (Heb 7) as a focus for our discussion.

2. Hebrews and Biblical Theology

Hebrews' interest in "biblical theology" arises, I believe, directly from the author's pastoral and rhetorical purpose in writing. The question of the purpose of Hebrews has not been settled, but a widely-held view (which I support) is that the author wants to persuade a group of Jewish believers in Christ *not* to give up their faith in Jesus as Messiah and relapse into Jewish-only faith. So he[2] needs to convince them that salvation is no longer to be had through the synagogue, but only through Christ. But *at the same time* he needs to build his case on the conviction, shared with his readers, that God spoke through Moses, that the covenant with Israel was true and valid, and that atonement for sin was fully available to the people he calls "the elders" (11:2). So in Hebrews it is not the *continuity*—the single, developing, and coherent biblical narrative—which is the focus, but the *discontinuity* between old and new: and the author must make the case that the old covenant is ineffective for salvation *from within the Scriptures themselves*, because the Scriptures are the shared authoritative "word of God" on which he and his readers rest.

It is an extraordinary task! He cannot simply reject the "old" covenant (or the

---

[2] We do not know his identity, but his gender is almost certainly settled by the masculine participle which he uses in passing in 11:32!

"first," 8:13) as no longer valid, because his readers will simply disagree and carry on seeking salvation through synagogue faith and practice. He has to show that the Scriptures themselves teach their own inadequacy, so that God's new word through his Son (1:1–2) is the only way of salvation.

So, for Hebrews the task is not to trace a positive story-line and to show that Jesus is the glorious topping on the cake, bringing the baking process to a triumphant conclusion. That would leave his readers able to say, "Well, we are sad to have to give up the icing, but at least we still have the cake!"[3] No—the task for Hebrews is to show that apart from Christ *there is no cake,* no nourishment for salvation, and that the Old Testament Scriptures themselves teach this.

3. Melchizedek within Hebrews' Hermeneutic

Let us then consider Melchizedek—so central to the argument in Hebrews, but actually marginal in Desi Alexander's writings on biblical theology thus far. This is not surprising, because Melchizedek is marginal in the Old Testament! A biblical theology starting from within the Old Testament would hardly base itself on a figure who appears once, briefly, in Genesis (14:18–20) and then in a single reference in one Psalm (110:4). However, a good case can be made that the presentation of Melchizedek in Heb 7 is the very heart of the author's argument—anticipated in 5:5–10, and giving scriptural substance to his claim that Jesus is a *different kind* of high priest, one unlike every other occupant of that office, who offers a *different kind* of atoning sacrifice (one that like King John's wished-for pocket-knife "really cuts"[4]). Hebrews 7's explanation of Jesus as "high priest according to the order of

---

[3] A good case can be made that the Jewish-Christians addressed in Hebrews were a *charismatic* messianic group, still part of the synagogue but meeting separately to worship and to enjoy the gifts of the Spirit ("the powers of the age to come," 6:5). Possibly under pressure from persecution (10:32–39), they are tempted to give up these separate meetings and carry on with synagogue membership and worship—because they were holding an "icing on the cake" view of Jesus as the Christ. The author must, therefore, adopt a different approach. See further Steve Motyer, "The Spirit in Hebrews: No Longer Forgotten?," in *The Spirit and Christ in the New Testament and Christian Theology. Essays in Honor of Max Turner*, ed. I. Howard Marshall, Volker Rabens, and Cornelis Bennema (Grand Rapids: Eerdmans, 2012), 213–27.

[4] I am alluding to A. A. Milne's lovely poem "King John's Christmas."

Melchizedek" (6:20) lays the foundation for the explanation of his atoning death in chapters 8–10, albeit in a very surprising way as we shall see further below.[5] The author exploits both the Old Testament references to Melchizedek, employing one of Hillel's seven rules of exegesis (*gezera shawa:* in which two verses employing the same words in different parts of Scripture are interpreted together),[6] and first expounding the Gen 14 story in 7:1–10 before unpacking the strange allusion to a "priest forever according to the order of Melchizedek" (Ps 110:4) in 7:11–25.

This use of Melchizedek, I suggest, is a master-stroke which takes us to the heart of the hermeneutic underlying Hebrews' approach to biblical theology. We see this hermeneutic also in the catena of Psalm quotations in Heb 1, and in the use of Ps 8 in Heb 2:5–9,[7] and it is summarized in the poignant 7:11, the verse in which the author shifts his attention from Gen 14 to Ps 110:

> I'm sure you'll agree: if the Levitical priesthood offered a route to perfection (for Israel's whole legal framework rested on this priesthood), then we must ask why there was a need for another priest to rise up "according to the order of Melchizedek" and to be listed as not according to the order of Aaron?[8]

This makes the basic shape of his argument clear: *the Old Testament undermines itself* by including this positive affirmation of another "order" of priesthood alongside the

---

[5] I part company from Paul Ellingworth, who writes of "the awkwardness of the introduction of Melchizedek into the argument ... he constitutes an unnecessary complication in the comparison and contrast between priesthood in the old and new dispensations." (*The Epistle to the Hebrews*, NIGTC [Grand Rapids: Eerdmans; Carlisle: Paternoster, 1993], 351). I think that Ellingworth fundamentally misconstrues Hebrews' hermeneutic and the role of Melchizedek in the argument.

[6] See Richard N. Longenecker, *Biblical Exegesis in the Apostolic Period* (Grand Rapids: Eerdmans, 1975), 33–35.

[7] See S. Motyer, "The Psalm-Quotations of Hebrews 1: A Hermeneutic-free Zone?," *TynBul* 50 (1999): 3–22.

[8] Heb 7:11, my trans. "I'm sure you'll agree" is an attempt to bring out the force of the double conjunction μὲν οὖν. "Offered a route to" attempts to capture the verbal quality of τελείωσις (only here in Hebrews—the *process* of reaching perfection). "According to the order of Melchizedek" is the language of Ps 110:4. And of course "rise up" (ἀνίστασθαι) is a quiet allusion to the resurrection and the Son's "indestructible life" (7:16).

Levitical. The author hears the very presence of Melchizedek as the Old Testament's question-mark against the effectiveness of its own central cultic provisions for atonement—just as Ps 40:7–9 (quoted in Heb 10:5–10) expresses God's extraordinary back-pedaling towards his own requirement of animal sacrifices.

This is the hermeneutic: to exploit these puzzles, tensions, inconsistencies, even contradictions within the Scriptures in order to develop the need for Jesus as the one who rescues the Scriptures as Word of God—who allows them to be true, not just in spite of the tensions and puzzles but *because of* them.[9] For the author of Hebrews, Melchizedek's presence in the Old Testament questions the sufficiency of the cult and of the whole legal and religious structure founded on it—and thus sets up the need for one who truly provides atonement and who thus makes sense of Temple and sacrifice as *foreshadowings* of the great Day of Atonement that this high priest conducts.[10]

But how much sense does this make? I have no doubt that the first readers of Hebrews were skeptical. They would not want to question the whole edifice of legal obedience and the cult that sustains it[11] on the basis of two marginal references to Melchizedek. Even dignified by the respectable *gezera shawa*, how could such a flimsy connection undermine the whole law and Aaronic priesthood? We must ask this question for ourselves, as well as (in imagination) for the first readers of Hebrews.

To answer it, we need to follow Desi Alexander's excellent example and get

---

[9] The quotation of Ps 8:5–7 in Heb 2:6–8, interpreted in 2:8–9, provides a brilliant example of this technique. In itself, Ps 8 says things about humankind which have never been true (in particular, "crowned with glory and honor" and "all things under [their] feet"): Hebrews concedes, "*in fact,* we do not yet see everything subjected to [them]" (2:8). But we do not have to dispute the truth of the Psalm, because "we see Jesus ... crowned with glory and honor." Hebrews is not reading the Psalm as *about* Jesus. It's about humankind, but only the man Jesus makes it true.

[10] On this, see further the chapter on Hebrews in Stephen Motyer, *Come Lord Jesus! A Biblical Theology of the Second Coming of Christ* (London: Apollos, 2016), 270–92.

[11] There's another open question here. I take the view that Hebrews is best dated before AD 70, so that the Jerusalem Temple is still standing and the readers are therefore involved—wherever they may live (yet another open question)—in supporting its priesthood and cult by paying the Temple tax. Even if they have never been there, their world-view as Jews is oriented around it and its theology of place and holiness—something Desi Alexander has well explored. See S. Motyer, "The Temple in Hebrews: Is It There?," in *Heaven on Earth. The Temple in Biblical Theology,* ed. T. Desmond Alexander and Simon Gathercole (Carlisle: Paternoster, 2004), 177–89.

close to the relevant texts, both in Hebrews and in the Old Testament. Can we follow more closely the thought-processes of this amazing biblical theologian, who wrestled so deeply with the challenge of relating the "new" word of God in Christ with his "old" word through the prophets? We will follow his line of thought through the chapter, starting first with his reflection on Gen 14:18–24 in 7:1–10, then considering how he expounds Ps 110 in 7:11–28.

4. Heb 7:1–10: Melchizedek like the Son of God

Who is this "priest of God Most High" to whom Abraham gives a tithe of his spoils from the war with the four kings—and whose name is then given to a whole "order" of priesthood, according to Ps 110? Chapter 7 begins with a brilliant re-casting of the narrative language of Gen 14:17–20 so as to create a single powerful sentence which extends the descriptive and interpretative material on Melchizedek until it reaches a climax in the delayed main verb and clause at the end of 7:3, "remains a priest forever." By the time we get there, we have not only heard the story in outline, but we have heard interpretations of Melchizedek's name and kingdom ("king of righteousness," and "king of peace"), and have also been treated to a string of descriptions not drawn from Gen 14: "without father, without mother, without genealogy, having neither beginning of days nor end of life, in appearance like the Son of God" (7:3, my trans.).

Where do these extraordinary descriptions come from? There are three possible answers, not mutually exclusive: (a) the author may think that they are legitimate deductions from the Genesis story, perhaps particularly because Melchizedek's parentage is not named; (b) the author may be responding to contemporary speculations about Melchizedek, especially to beliefs which name him as a powerful angelic figure, maybe even as "an angelic (high) priest of the celestial temple," exercising judgment and dispensing a final Day of Atonement;[12] (c) the author may be

---

[12] The description is Jody Barnard's. He provides a succinct survey and evaluation of this possible background to Hebrews in *The Mysticism of Hebrews. Exploring the Role of Jewish Apocalyptic Mysticism in the Epistle to the Hebrews*, WUNT 2/331 (Tübingen: Mohr Siebeck, 2012), 128–30 (esp. 128).

allowing his language to be influenced by his destination, i.e. his comparison with Jesus the Son of God.

Option (b) depends particularly on the appearance of Melchizedek in 11QMelch, a fragmentary 1st century AD Qumran document in which Melchizedek is presented in terms drawn from Isa 61:1–2, bringing in an eschatological Jubilee involving both judgment and deliverance.[13] The relevance of this for Hebrews is very differently evaluated in contemporary scholarly discussion—from enthusiastic approval as significant background to Hebrews' understanding of Christ by, e.g., Attridge,[14] to cautious affirmation by Barnard ("precedents to, and possible influences on, the author of Hebrews"),[15] to firm denial by Cockerill, who argues that "Melchizedek" in 11QMelch is not a name but a title ("king of righteousness" applied to the archangel Michael who is the real agent in mind), so that 11QMelch is irrelevant to Hebrews.[16] Our judgment here has to take account of an unknown: that is, how widespread might a Qumran tradition be, beyond the bounds of the Qumran community? Even if the author of Hebrews was aware of it, there is nothing in 11QMelch which might prompt or influence his "without mother, without father, without genealogy, having neither beginning of days nor end of life, made like the Son of God" (7:3), or his later language about Jesus' heavenly intercession for us (7:25–26). The best we can say is that Hebrews' presentation of Christ would *be heard to speak* to this heavenly, angelic view of Melchizedek (or of Michael with this title), if readers were aware of it; but we cannot presume that the author of Hebrews is influenced by it. He presents his argument as based on Scripture.

But that simply compounds our difficulty! Option (a) above (he gets it all from Genesis) seems impossible. He might derive "without mother, without father, without

---

[13] See Geza Vermes, *The Complete Dead Sea Scrolls in English* (London: Penguin, 1998), 500–02; Florentino García Martínez and Eibert J. C. Tigchelaar (eds.), *The Dead Sea Scrolls. Study Edition*, 2 vols (Leiden: Brill; Grand Rapids: Eerdmans, 1997, 1998), 2:1206–09.

[14] H. W. Attridge, *The Epistle to the Hebrews*, Hermeneia (Philadelphia: Fortress, 1989), 191–95.

[15] Barnard, *Mysticism,* 129.

[16] Gareth Lee Cockerill, "Melchizedek without Speculation: Hebrews 7:1-25 and Genesis 14:17-24," in *A Cloud of Witnesses. The Theology of Hebrews in its Ancient Contexts*, ed. Richard Bauckham et al.; LNTS 387 (London: T&T Clark, 2008), 128–44.

genealogy" simply from the lack of mention of these in Genesis, but it seems as though for him this *implies* a life without prospect of death, "made like the Son of God". How does this follow—and how convinced would his readers be? They would certainly not be convinced if he is simply smuggling in descriptions that are actually derived from Jesus Christ (option [c]), and passing these off as derived from Genesis. We must remember his strategy—to show that Scripture undermines itself and in so doing to create the need, the *necessity,* for Jesus.

We need to dig deeper here, noticing that Hebrews presents Melchizedek as a *priest-king*. He uses the word βασιλεύς (king) four times of Melchizedek in 7:1–2, within the presentation of him as a priest (ἱερεύς) which forms an *inclusio* around 7:1–3. Let's ask: with what theology of *royal priesthood* would the author have approached the interpretation of Melchizedek in Gen 14? We are into the realm of speculation here, but there are certain basic observations about Old Testament "royal priesthood" to be made, and we can be fairly sure that at least some of this will be part of the "presupposition pool" shared by the author of Hebrews and his audience. We can certainly say that in the ancient Near East kings often performed sacerdotal roles, and years ago Aubrey Johnson made a case that this kind of "sacral kingship" was a strong tradition in Jerusalem long before it became Israel's capital.[17] We meet it Gen 14, where "Salem" would be identified with "Jerusalem," and also in Josh 10 where the king of Jerusalem is called "Adonizedek," a closely cognate name ("*Lord* of righteousness").

Johnson suggested that "king [or 'lord'] of righteousness" was a kind of dynastic name for the occupiers of this priestly throne in Jerusalem, and that this is the origin of the notion of the "order" of Melchizedek which we meet in Ps 110:4. He suggested further that when David took over Jerusalem as his capital, he adopted this royal priesthood for himself.[18] This explains why we then meet David dancing before the Ark of the Covenant in a linen ephod (priestly garb) in leading the procession to Jerusalem (2 Sam 6:14). Later both he and Solomon offer sacrifices and preside at the

---

[17] A. R. Johnson, *Sacral Kingship in Ancient Israel* (Cardiff: University of Wales Press, 1955).

[18] Johnson, *Sacral Kingship,* 46. Cf. also Artur Weiser, *The Psalms. A Commentary* (London: SCM, 1962), 695.

altar without any apparent question.[19] The tradition persists through to postexilic times, appearing in Zechariah's vision of the royal status given to Joshua the high priest, who is to stand alongside the throne (Zech 6:11–13).

So, when the author comments that the Lord Jesus arose from the tribe of Judah, "a tribe in relation to which Moses said nothing about priests" (7:14, my trans.), the emphasis needs to fall on "Moses." No provision is made *in the law* for royal priests—something pointed out forcefully to king Uzziah by the high priest Azariah and eighty other priests, according to 2 Chr 26:16–20. This "royal priest" tradition is disputed within the Old Testament itself—but it is present nonetheless, *outside* the law. That is the author's point!

So, when he describes Melchizedek as immortal, and as "in appearance like the Son of God" (7:3), is he viewing him through the lens of Jesus Christ? To some extent, it must be so. His perception of Jesus as "son of God" enables him to see Melchizedek more clearly. But there is more to be said from Genesis: in fact, a closer look at 7:3 against the background of Gen 14:18–22 within its wider Genesis context suggests that its language it not inappropriate, even without a reading of Melchizedek through the lens of Jesus Christ.

"See how great he is!" is the author's comment (7:4), deducing this from Abraham's gift of the tithe to Melchizedek. It is easy to overlook the fact that tithing was an act of worship. The tithe was given later, as the author notes, to the Levites or to the priests, but always within the context of an act of worship, and often in association with the offering of the firstfruits.[20] So Abraham's gift of the tithe to Melchizedek is an act of worship of the God for whom Melchizedek is priest, "God Most High" (אֵל עֶלְיוֹן)—explained then in Abraham's words to the king of Sodom (Gen 14:22–24): Abraham recognizes that this God has given him his victory (cf. 14:20), and he has taken an oath to this God that he will renounce all the spoils from the defeat of the four kings. As priest of אֵל עֶלְיוֹן, Melchizedek is able to dispense the blessing of אֵל עֶלְיוֹן, which he does (14:19). Hence the author's conclusion that he is "greater" than

---

[19] See 2 Sam 6:13, 17–19; 24:25; 1 Kgs 3:15; 8:22, 62; 9:25; 10:5.
[20] See H. H. Guthrie, "Tithe," *IDB* 4:654–55.

Abraham (7:7), and that Abraham recognizes this greatness in giving the tithe. *Melchizedek is therefore Abraham's priest,* able to dispense God's blessing to the one in whom all the nations will be blessed (Gen 12:1–3). He is the vehicle of the blessing God promises to Abraham in Gen 12:2.

And we can say more. One of the distinctive things about Desi Alexander's presentation of the biblical theology of the Pentateuch is his emphasis on the twin roles of priesthood and kingship. He traces a royal lineage through Genesis, starting with Adam and leading through the narrative to the choice of Ephraim, Joseph's son, as the recipient of the blessing[21]—and of course beyond Genesis to the house of David and the Davidic Messiah. Alongside this royal lineage, and in concert with others like J. R. Middleton and G. J. Wenham, Alexander understands the Garden of Eden in "Temple" terms, and sees Adam not merely as a gardener but as a priest of this sacred space where God meets with humankind. This sets the scene for his fundamental understanding of biblical theology, which gathers around the idea that underlying the creation of the earth is God's desire to make a dwelling place for himself. In the light of this aspiration, the opening two chapters of Genesis reveal that humans are created with the intention that they should participate in transforming the earth into a divine dwelling. To this end they are given a holy or priestly status that enables them to be in God's presence and serve in his sanctuary.[22]

Back to Melchizedek. In a significant footnote, commenting on the development of the "royal" line in Genesis, Alexander writes:

> Gen. 1:28 indicates that humans were created by God to rule over the earth. This being the case, Adam is to be viewed as the first member of this royal line. However, not only was Adam a king, but he was also a priest.... In the light of this, the concept of priest-king takes on a special significance. In Gen. 14 we encounter this unusual status in the figure of Melchizedek. *Clearly it is implied that anyone who enjoys this particular status*

---

[21] Alexander, *From Paradise to Promised Land,* 134–45.
[22] Alexander, *From Paradise to Promised Land,* 126.

resembles Adam before he was expelled from the Garden of Eden. Later
the Israelites are called by the LORD to be a royal priesthood.[23]

Is something like this in the mind of the author of Hebrews as he reflects on
Melchizedek? In the exercise of this unique kingly and priestly role, dispensing
righteousness, peace and blessing in the world, Melchizedek is like a breath of re-
creation, a token of things as they should be—as they once were, in Eden, before Adam
and Eve sinned. In this relationship to the Creator, he is, like Adam, "without father,
without mother, and without genealogy." Stepping before Abraham as the priest-king
of God Most High to give God's blessing, he stands whole in himself. He is no one's
son, no one's father. In becoming such a priest, he is "in appearance like the Son of
God," because his appointment to such an office is like the creation of Adam himself,
called into being to prepare a sanctuary where God may dwell.

Adam is not called "son of God" directly in Gen 1–3, but this relationship is
implied, as we can see in Gen 5:1–3: "When God created Adam, he made him in the
likeness of God ... When Adam had lived for one hundred and thirty years, he became
the father of a son in his likeness, according to his image, and named him Seth."[24]
Fulfilling the same priestly and royal (image-bearing) relationship with God,
Melchizedek could also be called "Son of God." As with Adam in the Garden, death
cannot strike him down. The life that animates this priest-king has no beginning or
end, is "indestructible"—as indeed also is the life of the new Priest-King in
Melchizedek's "order," who is born into a new indestructible life after the suffering
that qualified him for appointment to this office (Heb 5:7–10).

Of course, the background to this encounter also lies in Gen 3 and the "fall"
narrative. Adam and Eve lost their royal and priestly status as they were banished from
the Temple-Garden. But they left with God's promise to the serpent ringing in their
ears, "I will put enmity between you and the woman, and between your offspring and

---

[23] Alexander, *From Paradise to Promised Land,* 142–43 n.9, my emphasis.

[24] We remember how Luke completes his genealogy of Christ by calling Adam "the son of
God" (Luke 3:38).

hers; he will strike your head, and you will strike his heel" (Gen 3:15). There will be comeback!—an "offspring" ("seed") who will defeat the serpent and redeem the damage. Who, and how, is this to be? This question carries us forward not just into the ongoing Genesis narrative, but beyond into the history of Israel and into whole-biblical theology. The Sethite "sons of God" in Gen 6:2, 4 are one of the first staging-posts: descended from Seth, Adam's new "seed" (Gen 4:25), they are in the line of promise (in contrast to the line of Cain), but they mess up, recapitulating Eve's sin.[25] But in that line of promise others come—most notably Noah, who receives the same commission as Adam in a re-constituted earth (Gen 9:1–6), and Abraham, who receives the promise of blessing for "all the families of the earth"—including the family of rebellious Cain (Gen 12:3). Where will the story go next?

Ultimately, we know the answer—forward into the election of Israel and the establishment of a special people, covenant, cult and kingship, and thence on to the New Testament where Jesus Christ is the "Son of God" who exercises this Royal Priesthood for God's people and all the earth. But here at the beginning of that long story appears Melchizedek "like the Son of God," picking up the status and calling of Adam and the Sethites (albeit forfeited).[26] "Without father, without mother, without genealogy" points, I suggest, not to *no birth* but to *new birth*. Appointed to this office, Melchizedek is drawn into a relationship with God like that of the Davidic Priest-King to whom Ps 2:7 is addressed: "You are my Son; today I have begotten you" (NRSV): a new-birth relationship in which all others no longer "count." And, of course, these are the words which the New Testament then adopts in application to the resurrection of Jesus Christ (Acts 13:33)—not to mention the author to the Hebrews (1:5, 5:5)! The "oath" which appoints Jesus to be a priest in Melchizedek's order makes him into "a

---

[25] See the fascinating article by Rita Cefalu, "Royal Priestly Heirs to the Restoration Promise of Genesis 3:15: A Biblical Theological Perspective on the Sons of God in Genesis 6," *WTJ* 76 (2014): 351–70. She compellingly identifies the "sons of God" as the heirs of Seth's line of the "seed" who "see" that something is "good" and then "take" what they see, just as Eve did (Gen 6:2 parallel to Gen 3:8).

[26] So far as I can see, not a single commentary on Hebrews makes any connection between Hebrews' description of Melchizedek as "like the Son of God" and either Adam or the Sethite "sons of God" in Gen 6.

Son made perfect forever" (7:28).

This is the point also of the genealogical reflection in Heb 7:4–10. The later requirement of the tithe enabled the Levites to be a lasting priesthood, but the tithe was levied "according to the law" (7:5), and they could only levy it based on their own descent from Abraham through Levi. But Abraham's tithe-giving response to Melchizedek was not framed by any legal requirement, but simply by the power and significance of "God Most High" and of Melchizedek as his priest-king. Hence the rather strange comment in 7:7, "beyond all contradiction, the lesser is blessed by the greater."[27] The author does not intend this as a statement of principle which, applied here, must mean that Melchizedek (the blesser) is greater than Abraham, the blessee. It is easy to point to instances that violate this, as a principle.[28] Indeed, Melchizedek blesses not only Abraham but also "God Most High, who has delivered your enemies into your hand!" (Gen 14:20, NRSV). The point is that *in this story* Abraham recognizes Melchizedek as "the greater" and himself as "the lesser," because Melchizedek has this unique and priceless relationship with "God Most High" as his Priest, ruling on his behalf, and Abraham submits to him and worships his God as he receives his blessing.

5. Heb 7:11–28: The High Priest "forever"

And then along comes Ps 110:4, revealing that Melchizedek is an "order," and not just a one-off. We now turn to look at the author's handling of this Psalm in 7:11–28. Psalm 110 is a deeply mysterious text. If we take seriously the ascription to David—as the author to the Hebrews certainly would have done, like Jesus himself (Mark 12:36) and Peter (Acts 2:34–35)—it seems inescapable that David is celebrating a coming one whom he addresses as "my Lord." This "Lord" is addressed first as King (Ps 110:1–3) and then as Priest (Ps 110:4–7). Verse 4 is a kind of appointment text, installing the King of verses 1–3 to a permanent priesthood in Melchizedek's order,

---

[27] My translation.

[28] There are, as several commentators point out (e.g., Attridge, *Hebrews,* 196): "numerous biblical examples of inferiors blessing their superiors."

and thus forms a pivot between the two halves of the Psalm, which both celebrate the victory of this warrior King-Priest over his enemies.

For the author of Hebrews, this is an absolute gift: a Psalm which celebrates a coming Priest-King who will ensure the victory of Zion over all her enemies, and who apparently achieves this entirely without reference to the "normal" cultic provisions for salvation: and—to boot—the Psalm envisages that this Priest-King will remain in office "forever." The author's creative theological juices are in full spate as he reflects on this "forever." Very possibly "forever" in Ps 110:4 refers to the *priesthood* rather than to the *priest*—on the analogy of 2 Sam 7:13 where the promise for David's "seed" is "I will establish the throne of his kingdom forever."[29] But on the other hand the promise is expressed personally in Ps 110:4, and so it is open for the author of Hebrews—as indeed for several commentators—to read it as promising personal immortality, and *therefore* an everlasting priesthood, to the figure addressed.[30] This is important for our reading of 7:15–17:

> The appearance of this new priesthood is even more clear, since another priest has risen up, in the likeness of Melchizedek. He occupies his priesthood not on the basis of a law requiring a physical qualification, but by the power of his indestructible life. For Scripture's testimony is "You are a priest forever, according to the order of Melchizedek."[31]

On the one hand, the phrase "by the power of his indestructible life" is a deduction from Ps 110:4, as the immediately appended quotation makes clear. But on the other, the actual wording (especially the word "power") references the

---

[29] So Weiser, *Psalms,* 695.

[30] So, e.g., F. Delitzsch, *Biblical Commentary on the Psalms, Vol 3,* 2nd ed. (Edinburgh: T&T Clark, 1881), 194: Delitzsch interprets it alongside Zech 6:12–13 as messianic expectation of the coming royal priest; also D. Kidner, *Psalms 73–150,* TOTC (London: Inter-Varsity Press, 1975), 395.

[31] My trans. The phrase "in the likeness of Melchizedek" (κατὰ τὴν ὁμοιότητα Μελχισέδεκ) is really an alternative translation of the Hebrew phrase rendered κατὰ τὴν τάξιν Μελχισέδεκ in the Septuagint. The Hebrew דִּבְרָה means "cause, reason, manner" (BDB 184a), which Delitzsch renders "after the manner, measure of" Melchizedek (*Psalms,* 193). ὁμοιότης would be an equally suitable translation.

resurrection, as indeed does the use of the word "rise up" (ἀνίστασθαι) in 7:15, which likewise has a double meaning: Christ rises onto the scene as another Melchizedek priest by rising from the dead.

The author draws his surprising conclusion from this "rising" in 7:18–19: "What this means is that, on the one hand, the pre-existing command is set aside because of its weakness and uselessness (for the law made nothing perfect), and on the other hand a better hope is brought in, through which we draw close to God" (my translation). This is the point which his readers would most resist. Even if we see Christ as a priest of a different "order" from Aaron, does that require the setting aside of the law? This depends on the presupposition expressed in that aside in the key verse, 7:11, "for Israel's whole legal framework rested on this priesthood"—referring there, of course, to the Levitical priesthood. This expresses not only the central role of the priesthood within Israel's social and religious life, but also the role of the priests as teachers and interpreters of the law to Israel. It seems as though the author's argument has three elements to it: (a) the very existence of the Melchizedekian priesthood points to the insufficiency ("weak and useless", 7:18) of the Levitical priesthood, and therefore (b) of the law which the Levitical priesthood administered and on which it rested. Neither can bring "perfection". But this uselessness does not matter, because (c) we do in fact now "draw near to God" with greater confidence because of the new Melchizedekian "priest forever" who has risen onto the scene.

This is one of those typical Hebrews statements which anticipates later arguments, for point (b) awaits further elaboration in chapters 8–10. Point (c) is the basic one—the *experience* of free access to God through Christ, and of the "greater hope" which he has brought, the greater confidence and certainty in their relationship with God which the author and his readers have experienced because of Jesus.[32]

---

[32] Barnabas Lindars famously argued that the readers of Hebrews were feeling a lack of confidence and assurance in their new Christian faith because they missed the solidity of the synagogue and festival rituals, and the assurance of forgiveness which these gave (*The Theology of the Letter to the Hebrews* [Cambridge: Cambridge University Press, 1991]). Actually 7:19, with its appeal to the "greater hope" which "we" now experience in worship, seems to suggest the opposite—even if the readers need to be reminded of it.

Fundamentally, the author is reading the Old Testament material through the lens of Jesus Christ. But the Old Testament, through the tension generated by the *unexplained* presence of this alternative priesthood alongside the Aaronic, gives him the space within which to see Jesus not just as its "fulfilment," but as something "better," or "greater," which allows the word through the Son to be greater than the word through the prophets (1:1–4).

The phrase εἰς τὸν αἰῶνα ("forever") runs through the last section of the chapter (7:20–28), used with four distinct connotations in reference to the priesthood of Jesus Christ. Firstly, it expresses the *certainty* of his appointment, because it is spoken as an oath uttered by God (7:20–22). Secondly, it underlines his *permanence* in office: unlike the Aaronic priests who were prevented by death from continuing, he "holds his priesthood permanently" (7:24, NRSV). Thirdly, it underscores his *effectiveness* (7:25): his permanence means that he never fails to be available for all who approach God through him, and is never unequal to their needs. And finally it emphasizes his *personal fitness* for this role: he is "a son made perfect forever" (7:28),[33] totally fit to exercise his priesthood because he is "holy, blameless, undefiled, separated from sinners" (7:26) and therefore not needing to make sacrifice for his own sin like the Levitical priests (7:27).

6. Conclusions

The readers of Hebrews would probably not have been surprised by this messianic interpretation of Ps 110:4. The expectation of a priestly Messiah was well established in first century Judaism. But they would surely have been surprised and puzzled by the way in which the author of Hebrews has interpreted the Melchizedekian priesthood as so distinct from the Aaronic, and indeed as *undermining* the Aaronic priesthood. After all, the Priest-King in Zechariah is the *Levitical* high priest, Joshua, being offered a royal crown (Zech 6:11). Their response might well have paralleled

---

[33] υἱόν εἰς τὸν αἰῶνα τετελειωμένον. We must remember that part of the background to the use of the important verb τελειοῦν in Hebrews is its use in the Pentateuch in connection with the ordination of Aaron and his sons: e.g., Exod 29:9, 29; Lev 4:5, 8:33; Num 3:3.

that of Azariah the high priest who denounced King Uzziah, "It is not for you, Uzziah, to make offering to the LORD, but for the priests the descendants of Aaron, who are consecrated to make offering. Go out of the sanctuary; for you have done wrong" (2 Chr 26:18). And they might well remind our author that the LORD then struck Uzziah down with leprosy for his presumption in insisting that his kingship, in the line of David, was a *priestly* one.

But I think that our author's reply would be clear. We must recognize, he would say, that there is a clear tension between David's exercise of a royal priesthood and the denial of this to Uzziah in 2 Chronicles: a tension to which the Old Testament supplies no resolution. As far as the law is concerned, Azariah was right to banish Uzziah from the altar. Were it not for Jesus Christ, this tension would be a straight contradiction—but he resolves it: for his Royal Priesthood in the line of Melchizedek also perfects the Aaronic, and thus releases the Scriptures to be truly what they are, the Word of God. Christ the Melchizedekian high priest has now entered the holy of holies in the performance of a single, cosmic, Day of Atonement sacrifice, and we await his reappearance from the Sanctuary just as the crowds waited for the high priest to emerge at the climax of that great annual festival (Heb 9:23–28).[34] But the purpose of the "shadow" passes when the reality comes. As the new Melchizedek, Christ has become the reality towards which Aaron pointed, ministering in the heavenly sanctuary of which the earthly was only ever a "copy and shadow" (8:5).

This is an incredibly creative piece of biblical theology which *both* takes all the texts concerned seriously and exactly, *and* reads them retrospectively in the light of what God has now done in Christ—and all in the service of discerning the voice of the *one* God who spoke through the prophets and now also "in these last days has spoken to us in his Son" (Heb 1:2). I am grateful that the church of Jesus Christ has in its service scholars and pastors like Desi Alexander who seek to do this still!

---

[34] On this amazing paragraph and its distinctive understanding of the second coming, see further Motyer, *Come, Lord Jesus,* 270–92.

SNAKES AND DRAGONS: A NEGLECTED THEOLOGICAL TRAJECTORY OF GENESIS 3:15 IN SCRIPTURE?

—Paul R. Williamson

1. Introduction

While there is significant debate over the interpretation of the snake in Gen 3,[1] the full identity of this "crafty" creature is arguably unmasked in the NT. Paul's allusion in Rom 16:20 implicitly equates this extraordinary נָחָשׁ with Satan:[2] "The God of peace will soon crush Satan under your feet."[3] Much more explicitly, Revelation associates this "ancient serpent" with "the devil, or Satan, who leads the whole world astray" (Rev 12:9; cf. 20:2).[4] Accordingly, it is easy to see why—even apart from its a-typical acumen and abilities—a figurative interpretation of this wily snake in Gen 3 has obvious hermeneutical appeal. However, while the NT unquestionably provides the canonical key to this interpretative crux, it would be exegetically naive to read these later texts back into Genesis or to assume that Genesis is simply employing figurative language for the devil. Rather, we must consider more carefully the biblical-theological rationale for the hermeneutic we see reflected in the NT; that is to say, in terms of the text itself, and its unfolding trajectory in Scripture, how can the

---

[1] For a concise discussion, see John Day, "The Serpent in the Garden of Eden and its Background" in http://www.bibleinterp.com/articles/2015/04/day398028.shtml.

[2] See Rosner's discussion in ch. 15 above. Rather than Gen 3:15, some understand the allusion in Rom 16:20 to be to Ps 110:1. For a defense of the latter, see Derek R. Brown, *The God of This Age: Satan in the Churches and Letters of the Apostle Paul*, WUNT 2.409 (Tübingen: Mohr Siebeck, 2015), 102–10. For other arguments against seeing the allusion being to Gen 3:15, see John H. Walton, and J. Harvey Walton, *Demons and Spirits in Biblical Theology: Reading the Biblical Text in its Cultural and Literary Context* (Eugene: Wipf & Stock, 2019), 141–43. On the concept of such a nefarious being as *Satan* in the OT, see section 3 below.

[3] Unless otherwise stated, biblical citations in this chapter are from the NIV (2011).

[4] Such an interpretation (of the serpent as Satan) can be traced as far back as the first century BC, where it is reflected in *Wisdom of Solomon* (Wis 2:24).

duplicitous snake of Gen 3 be understood to "morph" into the fearsome dragon who wages war against the seed of the woman (Rev 12:17)?

To answer this question, we must obviously begin with Gen 3 and examine the snake's depiction there, as well as the anticipated conflict between it, the woman, and their respective "seed." We must then consider how this conflict is elevated to one of cosmic proportions in the rest of the OT and beyond. Of particular concern will be the recurring motif of fearsome serpents and/or dragons, creatures which—like the snake of Gen 3—have often been interpreted exclusively in either naturalistic or mythical terms. However, while in some instances this may appear a valid or reasonable interpretation, in most cases these extraordinary creatures are much better understood in the OT as *symbols* of chaos, ultimately alluding to the spiritual and supernatural power(s) that the woman's "seed" will finally vanquish. Thus understood, the NT— and Rev 12 in particular—is not necessarily foisting a foreign or idiosyncratic meaning upon Gen 3:15; rather, informed by subsequent biblical theology, NT interpreters are highlighting the eschatological and cosmic significance of the perennial enmity enunciated in this programmatic OT text.[5]

2. The Cunning Creature of Genesis 3: A talking snake, or something more?

The portrayal of the serpent in Gen 3 is admittedly enigmatic. Following the naming of all the wild animals in Gen 2:19–20, the snake's description as "more crafty than any of the wild animals the LORD God had made" (3:1) undeniably implies that it was numbered among such wildlife. Indeed, this is further underscored by the curse that Yahweh subsequently pronounces on it: "Cursed are you above all livestock and all wild animals" (3:14). When we also note that it will crawl on its belly (3:14) and strike the *heel* of the woman's seed (3:15d), it's easy to see why many understand the author to be depicting an actual snake, rather than just employing a figurative character or some kind of symbolic image.[6]

---

[5] *Pace* Walton (*Demons and Spirits*, 130–31), in the context of Genesis *as a whole*, with its significant emphasis on "seed," Gen 3:15 seems to be about much more than the conflict that unfolds in the rest of this 'toledot' pericope (Gen 2:4–4:26).

[6] Understood only in a figurative sense, Gen 3 paradigmatically recounts the story of

However, even when one acknowledges that the author is referring here to a genuine serpent, it is clearly a most unusual example, possessing some extraordinary characteristics.[7] The most striking such feature is its communicative ability—this creature can verbalize its thoughts and converse rationally with human beings.[8] Moreover, it has astonishing knowledge—as well as being aware of God's prohibition concerning the tree in the center of the garden, this snake knows what will happen when its forbidden fruit is consumed.[9] The uncanny intelligence of this serpent, along with the fact that both God and the woman speak to it,[10] thus suggests that—as with Balaam's talking donkey—something extraordinary and unnatural is depicted here. Moreover, as the narrative progresses, the snake's "cleverness" (ערום) is portrayed in

---

Everyman, so specific details—such as the serpent—are not pressed literally. However, there are some aspects which suggest that Gen 3 is recounting a unique, historical event, "not merely a paradigmatic one"; so Gordon J. Wenham, *Rethinking Genesis 1–11: Gateway to the Bible*, The Didsbury Lecture Series (Eugene, OR: Cascade, 2015), 32. As a symbol, the snake has been variously understood. For a concise review and critique of some such interpretations, again see Day, who tentatively suggests that the Gen 3 account is a radical reworking of analogous elements of the Gilgamesh Epic (particularly, the serpent that snatches and consumes the rejuvenating plant of life, thus depriving Gilgamesh of immortality).

[7] One of the serpent's extraordinary features that has traditionally been inferred from God's curse in v. 14 (cf. Josephus, *Antiquities* 1.1.4; Targum Pseudo-Jonathan on Gen 3:14; Midrash Genesis Rabbah 20:5) is the presence of limbs, an inference drawn also by some modern scholars (e.g., James Charlesworth, *The Good and Evil Serpent*, AYBRL [New Haven: Yale University Press, 2010], 87–88). However, as Day ("The Serpent in the Garden," n.p.) more cautiously observes, "since nothing explicitly is said of the serpent's having feet and legs and being deprived of them here it is perhaps preferable to think of the serpent as originally having a good sense of balance so that it could move upright without legs."

[8] The fact that the woman expresses no shock or surprise does not imply that talking animals were considered normal by her; such is clear from Balaam's equally unstartled response to his speaking donkey—which the biblical narrator clearly attributes to supernatural intervention (Num 23:28a). As Collins insightfully points out, "This is why the notion that we have here a 'mythological world' in which animals talk … misses the point badly." C. John Collins, *Genesis 1–4: A Linguistic, Literary, and Theological Commentary* (Phillipsburg: Presbyterian & Reformed, 2006), 171.

[9] It is clear from vv. 7 and 22 that the snake's claim—that their eyes would be opened, and that they would become like God, knowing good and evil—was not entirely inaccurate. Rather, it was his positive spin on this—along with maligning God's motivations and denying that they would die—that was deceptive, as the woman subsequently recognizes (v. 13).

[10] Significantly, in the case of Balaam's donkey, with which this account is often compared, it is only after Balaam is addressed by his donkey that he actually speaks to it. Conversing with dumb animals was evidently not considered normal in either biblical account.

an unambiguously sinister and negative light: not only does this creature impugn Yahweh's motives and trustworthiness (3:5); he flatly contradicts what God has said, intentionally "deceives" (Hiphil נשׁא) the woman (3:13),[11] and is consequently cursed by God (3:14).

Accordingly, many interpreters reasonably conclude that the author is describing more than an encounter between the woman and an ordinary creature—even though a natural wild animal is undeniably involved.[12] For example, Delitzsch infers that "An animal is intended, but an animal not speaking of its own accord, but as made the instrument of itself by the evil principle ... subsequently spoken of as Satan and his angels."[13] Others likewise conclude that some "Dark Power,"[14] operating "behind the scene," is manipulating each of the other characters (i.e., the woman, the man, and the snake) for its own malevolent purposes. Thus understood, "the Father of lies" (John 8:44) is here communicating with humans through the agency of a physical serpent, much as God subsequently communicated with Balaam through the mouth of the seer's donkey. Admittedly, no such identification of the serpent with the devil is expressly made either here or elsewhere in Genesis, nor is this snake associated or equated with Satan anywhere else in the Hebrew Bible. Therefore, such explicit identification of the serpent with an evil power seems to transcend the boundaries of OT exegesis. Nevertheless, as already noted, there are several exegetical grounds for deducing that there is more to this creature than a naturalistic reading permits. The snake is not only surprisingly articulate, but also vilifies God and is deceitful with respect to the woman. Rather than simply explaining these extraordinary aspects in terms of ancient Near Eastern mythology,[15] we should arguably find in them a

---

[11] God does not disregard the woman's excuse, but immediately responds by cursing the snake.

[12] I.e., rather than a figurative depiction of a supernatural being who may or may not have appeared to the woman in serpentine form, a real snake is involved.

[13] Franz Delitzsch, *A New Commentary on Genesis* (Minneapolis: Klock & Klock 1978 [orig. T&T Clark, 1888]), 1:149. Such an interpretation can be traced back as far as the intertestamental era (see below).

[14] Collins, *Genesis 1–4*, 171.

[15] For the possible echoes of such ancient Near Eastern thought in Gen 3, see John H. Walton, *The Lost World of Adam and Eve: Genesis 2–3 and the Human Origins Debate* (Downers Grove, IL:

legitimate basis for subsequent Jewish and Christian interpretation. That is to say, while ancient readers might initially have thought in terms of a physical or even a mythological snake, by its deviant behavior the biblical author is at least implicitly portraying it as something quite sinister. Thus, however much we should avoid reading the later, more developed understanding of Satan back into the text of Genesis, we must nevertheless pick up the textual cues that direct us beyond a naturalistic interpretation. Accordingly, while it is correct to understand the strange creature depicted here in terms of a genuine, physical serpent, it is apparently one that is being manipulated or controlled by an unidentified supernatural intelligence.

Thus understood, the ensuing enmity referred to in v. 15 almost certainly alludes to something more significant than the mutual dread or animosity that exists between humans and snakes. While such a concept is undeniably present in the text, it arguably serves as a metaphor or symbol for something less mundane: the conflict between the woman and the serpent's diabolical "puppet-master" that would evolve and reach its climax in their respective "seed." Such a *climactic* understanding of verse 15b is indisputably controversial, but "it must be remembered that this is a curse on the serpent, not on mankind, and something less than a draw would be expected."[16] Construing the reference to the woman's "seed" here as nothing more than a collective noun, many fail to discern any hint of a *Protoevangelium* in this text. However, the use of singular pronouns in association with זרע ("seed") in Genesis arguably alludes to a single descendant.[17] Moreover, the fact that this singular "seed" of the woman will

InterVarsity, 2015), 128–39; idem, *Demons and Spirits*, 128–29.

[16] Gordon J. Wenham, *Genesis 1–15*, WBC 1 (Waco, TX: Word, 1987), 80. Wenham further notes that "the serpent is in a tactically weaker situation, being able only to strike at man's heel, while man can crush its head." Moreover, while the same root (שוף "batter, crush, bruise") is probably used in each line, "[o]nce admitted that the serpent symbolizes sin, death, and the power of evil, it becomes much more likely that the curse [on the serpent] envisages … mankind eventually triumphing" (Wenham, *Genesis 1–15*, 80).

[17] So Jack Collins, "A Syntactical Note on Genesis 3:15: Is the Woman's Seed Singular or Plural?," *TynBul* 48.1 (1997):141–48. See also T. Desmond Alexander, "Further Observations on the Term 'Seed' in Genesis," *TynBul* 48.2 (1997): 363–67, and James M. Hamilton, ch. 1 above (a slightly revised version of "The Skull Crushing Seed of the Woman: Inner-Biblical Interpretation of Genesis 3:15," *The Southern Baptist Journal of Theology* 10:2 [2006]: 30–54 [32]).

crush the head of *the serpent* (הוא ישופך ראש)—rather than the heads of the serpent's *seed*—may be a further indication that a climactic engagement is in view.[18] Once again, it would be exegetically mistaken to infer from this more than the text of Genesis specifically suggests, but even here there seems to be at least some hint of the climactic battle that is subsequently and most graphically recounted in Rev 12.

But to find more explicit connections between the serpent and the great dragon we must look beyond the book of Genesis to the rest of the OT, especially its portrayal of Rahab, Leviathan, and other examples of what are often dubbed "chaos creatures" that either have been or will yet be subdued by God.

3. Other such "fantastic beasts" in the OT

While the OT nowhere reflects the more developed doctrine of Satan (as the personal embodiment and chief orchestrator of evil) that we find in the NT or in intertestamental literature, it is not without its own conceptual imagery for referring to the quintessence of such moral evil. Significantly, chief among such motifs are the likes of Rahab and Leviathan, fearsome creatures that threaten the divine order, instill dread in humans, but are ruled over and subdued by God. Of particular interest for the present study is the fact that such creatures are closely associated with both serpentine *and* draconic imagery.

3.1. Rahab

In terms of direct or indirect reference to a chaos-creature, "Rahab" appears six times in the OT: twice in Job (9:13; 26:12), twice in Psalms (87:4; 89:10 [MT 89:11]), and twice in Isaiah (30:7; 51:9). While at least two of these texts employ it primarily as a metaphorical reference to the nation of Egypt (Ps 87:4; Isa 30:7),[19] all six are apparently alluding to the concept of a "primeval monster of mythic proportions" that typifies the opposition with which Israel must contend but which is powerless against

---

[18] If the reference was to the serpent's *collective* "seed," the second person pronominal suffix on the verb here is arguably confusing and unnecessary (cf. Gen 49:10).

[19] Possibly a dual referent is intended in Ps 89:10, as in Isa 51:9, where Rahab arguably refers to *both* the chaos monster *and* to Egypt who is being likened to such.

God.[20]

Rahab's "helpers" are mentioned only in Job 9:13, but undoubtedly these allude to other forces of chaos that God has subdued and continues to hold in check (cf. Job 7:12).[21] Such forces are particularly associated with the sea—the archetypal symbol of chaos—as is further attested in Job 26:12, where cutting up Rahab and piercing the "fleeing serpent" demonstrates God's sovereign control over all such tumultuous powers. Similar imagery is reflected in Ps 89:9–10 [MT 89:10–11], where the crushing of Rahab attests to God's rule over the surging sea and its mounting waves, as possibly demonstrated at creation.[22] Yahweh's ongoing sovereignty over such chaotic forces is supremely demonstrated, however, in his defeat of Egypt, God's key saving act in terms of OT theology. Accordingly, Yahweh's climactic victory over Egypt is aptly depicted as a decisive subjugation of Rahab.

Rahab's associations with Leviathan (see below) suggest that these two should at least be thought of as close allies, if not synonyms for the same monstrosity. Moreover, the serpentine imagery associated with both (cf. Job 26:13; Isa 27:1) is at least reminiscent of the sinister snake of Gen 3, just as the explicit association of each with dragons (cf. Isa 27:1; 51:9) is arguably significant for the draconic imagery used to describe "that ancient serpent" in Rev 12. Thus, while Rahab is not explicitly identified in the OT with the crafty snake of Gen 3, some of the associations between them throw significant light on the biblical-theological connections made by John in Rev 12. And this is equally, and perhaps more obviously so, with respect to Leviathan.

---

[20] Frank Anthony Spina, "Rahab," in *NIDOTTE*, ed. Willem A. VanGemeren, 5 vols. (Carlisle: Paternoster, 1996), 4:1121–23 (1121). Such a monster is known as *Rahab* only in the OT.

[21] Interestingly, "the monster of the deep" (Heb. תַּנִּין) refers to a great sea-creature or *dragon* (cf. Gen 1:21; Ps 74:13; 148:7; Isa 27:1; 51:9; cf. Jer 51:34, where such imagery is a simile for Nebuchadnezzar), but is also clearly used with reference to serpents (Exod 7:9, 10, 12; Ps 91:13). Significantly, the psalmist speaks of the *heads* of these תַּנִּין —as well as Leviathan's—being "broken" or "crushed" (Ps 74:13–14). The latter two verbs arguably overlap *conceptually* with the "bruising" referred to in Gen 3:15.

[22] Alternatively, this language metaphorically refers to "destructive action against his enemies, [by which] Yahweh accomplished his salvation"; so David Tsumura, *Creation and Destruction: A Reappraisal of the* Chaoskampf *Theory in the Old Testament* (Winona Lake, IN: Eisenbrauns, 2005), 194.

3.2. Leviathan

Like Rahab, Leviathan appears in only Job, Psalms and Isaiah. However, unlike Rahab, Leviathan is never clearly used with reference to any specific nation such as Egypt.[23] Rather, it is primarily, if not exclusively, used of a creature—whether natural or supernatural—posing a significant threat to humans, but no menace to God. Indeed, Ps 104:26 suggests that rather than alarming or intimidating God, Leviathan is a harmless plaything—a wonderful example of God's creative power and absolute sovereignty. This less threatening portrayal of Leviathan has unfortunately prompted a naturalistic interpretation as some kind of whale.[24] But this completely overlooks the main point here, [25] as well as Leviathan's consistently terrifying portrayals elsewhere—particularly in Isaiah and Job. It is difficult to correlate the latter descriptions with any extant creature, including the huge salt-water crocodiles of Northern Australia! But any such attempt to so identify Leviathan is simply mistaken, for this sea monster, like its mythological ancient Near Eastern counterparts, [26]

---

[23] In keeping with the interpretation reflected in the Targum (which points to Egypt, Assyria and a non-specific nation), several commentators infer that the threefold reference to Leviathan in Isa 27:1 is an allusion to particular nations such as Babylon, Tyre, Assyria or Egypt. See Joel R. Soza, *Lucifer, Leviathan, Lilith, and Other Mysterious Creatures of the Bible* (Lanham, MD: Hamilton Books, 2017), 51. However, such an identification with any specific nation is unnecessary, and reads too much into what Ugaritic texts have shown to be "simply a poetic convention in the Canaanite area." So John N. Oswalt, *The Book of Isaiah Chapters 1-39*, NICOT (Grand Rapids: Eerdmans, 1986), 491. Rather, as Fyall correctly points out, "Leviathan here sums up all that is evil and opposed to God, no matter if its earthly manifestation is Assyria, Babylon, Edom or any other power." Robert S. Fyall, *Now My Eyes Have Seen You: Images of Creation and Evil in the Book of Job*, NSBT 12 (Leicester: Apollos, 2002), 171.

[24] For a concise discussion of the numerous ways that Leviathan has been interpreted, grouped under four main alternatives (i.e., naturalistic; mythological; mythological-hyperbolic; emblematic/representative), see René A. López, "The Meaning of 'Behemoth' and 'Leviathan' in Job," *BSac* 173 (2016): 401–24.

[25] As Fyall (*Now My Eyes*, 170) suggests, "Leviathan appears to have lost his fearsome qualities. However, close attention to the structure and imagery of the psalm shows this to be a superficial view ... Psalm 104, like Genesis 1, emphasizes the unapproachable transcendence of God in the heavens, on the earth, on the land and its creatures and the sea and its inhabitants. Before the awesomeness of this God the fearsome Leviathan is cut down to size and becomes merely a plaything."

[26] Note in particular, Lotan, the seven-headed sea-serpent destroyed by Baal in Ugaritic mythology, with whom Leviathan shares some obvious characteristics as well as, most significantly, the same tri-lateral root. While this overlap is hardly coincidental, Soza (*Lucifer, Leviathan, Lilith*, 51) goes too far when he concludes "that the Israelite and Ugaritic cultures cross pollinated on matters of

transcends the natural domain. Thus in Ps 74 the introduction of Leviathan elevates the pressing concern—the destruction of the temple and subsequent experience of exile—to a cosmic level. As Fyall explains:

> The exile, like the flood (cp. the imagery in Jer. 4), appears to have undone not only the exodus but creation, and returned the world to primordial chaos. Thus, faced with the cruel realities of exile, the psalmist here calls on God the king who defeated the chaos monster, Leviathan, and drove back the waters of the Red Sea. The God of creation and history is one God and the use of the words 'day and night' and 'sun and moon' underlines this for they are natural phenomena but they are also markers of time and thus belong to both spheres. Again the imagery is borrowed from Canaanite myth and is used here to evoke the atmosphere of cosmic struggle.[27]

Rather like the apocalyptic visions in the book of Daniel, the battle against the forces of chaos and disorder must be fought on two fronts: against Leviathan, the multiheaded sea-monster that God has already "defeated" (Ps 74:13–17), but who has apparently resurfaced as it were, and against his earthly counterpart—the foreign enemy responsible for defiling the temple (Ps 74:3b–8, 18–23).

Much the same idea is communicated through the Leviathan reference in Isa 27:1, which "serves as a summation of the defeat of all enemies of Israel that have been envisioned throughout the oracles against the nations and the Isaianic apocalypse."[28] Here, however, the emphasis is clearly eschatological and climactic. Rather than looking *back* to Leviathan's crushing defeat in the past, Isaiah looks *forward* to his final defeat in the future:

---

religion and myth." The Israelites clearly did adopt some of their neighbors' mythological concepts, but these were suitably adapted (and de-mythologized) in an Israelite setting where Yahweh, unlike Baal, was sole creator and reigned supreme. Significantly, the seven-headed sea monster re-surfaces as the beastly representation of evil in Rev 13.

[27] Fyall, *Now My Eyes*, 169.

[28] Soza, *Lucifer, Leviathan, Lillith*, 47.

In that day,

the LORD will punish with his sword—

his fierce, great and powerful sword—

Leviathan the gliding serpent,

Leviathan the coiling serpent;

he will slay the monster of the sea.

The threefold description of Leviathan here—"the gliding/fleeing [?] serpent" [נָחָשׁ בָּרִחַ],[29] "the coiling/writhing serpent" [נָחָשׁ עֲקַלָּתוֹן], and "the monster which is in the sea" [הַתַּנִּין אֲשֶׁר בַּיָּם]—is arguably significant, not just in terms of the utter destruction of this monster that it emphasizes (cf. the threefold description of Yahweh's sword in the previous line),[30] but also in terms of the inner-biblical allusions that it evokes. Not only does נחשׁ implicitly connect Leviathan with the same kind of wild animal that deceives the woman in Gen 3,[31] but describing it here as a תנין clearly associates Leviathan with the great sea-serpents or *dragons* that either pose a threat or are subdued elsewhere.[32] Thus here a primeval serpent and a great dragon are fused

---

[29] While the strangely pointed בָּרִחַ is a *hapax legomenon*, it is generally assumed to be some form of ברח I ("to flee"); cf. נָחָשׁ בָּרִיחַ (Job 26:13); cf. also Dead Sea Scroll's Qal ptcp. בורח, "fleeing." The Vulgate's *serpentem vectem* (*vectis* = "bolt"; cf. ברח II ("bar") makes no sense here. Albright's suggestion of "primordial" ("Are the Ephod and the Teraphim Mentioned in Ugaritic Literature?," *BASOR* 83 [1941]: 39 n.5) has not won scholarly support. Motyer's questionable inference of an "aerial power" or "the power of the air" leans much more on the parallel reference in Job 26:13 than here. J. Alec Motyer, *The Prophecy of Isaiah: An Introduction and Commentary* (Leicester: Inter-Varsity, 1993), 222. See also note 38 below.

[30] Admittedly, however, this also (see note 21 above) may be reading too much into a poetic convention that is likewise employed in analogous, mythological Ugaritic material: e.g., "When you smite Lotan, the fleeing [ברח] serpent, finish off the twisting [עקלתון] serpent, the close-coiling one with seven heads..." The BA'LU Myth (1.86), (CTA 5), tr. Dennis Pardee in William W. Hallo and K. Lawson Younger Jr. (eds), *The Context of Scripture, Volume I, Canonical Compositions from the Biblical World* (Leiden: Brill, 2003), 265. The terminological overlap between this Ugaritic text and Isa 27:1 is also striking, clearly reflecting common coinage used in relation to this monstrosity (see also Job 26:13).

[31] For Motyer (*Prophecy of Isaiah*, 222), this is a deliberate allusion to *the* snake of Gen 3. However, this could arguably have been made more obvious by attaching the definite article to נחשׁ here in Isaiah.

[32] See esp. Ps 74:13; 91:13 (cf. also Jer 51:34). In light of the NT's depictions of Satan as a

together in the eschatological smiting of Leviathan—something that is associated with the defeat of death (26:19), the punishment of sin (26:21) and (in light of the rest of ch. 27) may also be associated with a new exodus resulting in the repatriated people of God united in proper worship "on the holy mountain in Jerusalem" (Isa 27:12–13).[33] In the light of Isa 65–66, this latter scenario must be thought of in terms of new creation. Thus, while there is still no explicit link with either Satan or the devil, the slaying of Leviathan in Isa 27:1 seems to provide at least some of the biblical-theological building blocks for the connections that John will subsequently draw in Rev 12.

More such material may arguably be gleaned from Leviathan's depiction in the book of Job. Indeed here, more than anywhere else in the OT, some interpreters find implicit connections between Leviathan and Satan. As is well known, Job's heavenly "accuser" or "challenger" (lit. "the satan," השטן) plays a significant role in the opening two chapters of the book, in some sense instigating the extreme suffering of Job,[34] which in turn generates the acrimonious debate between Job and his well-intentioned friends, as well as the serious challenge to Job's faith and his ongoing relationship with God. However, after his uninvited—by Job, at least—intrusion into Job's personal affairs, this extra-terrestrial provocateur disappears from the narrative, his cynical suggestions having been disproven by Job's steadfast faith in terrible circumstances. Most commentators thus understand the satan to play little or no part in the rest of the book: Job's complaint is not with this supernatural being—of whom Job and the earthly characters remain oblivious—but with God, who has apparently assumed an adversarial stance towards his unfortunate servant. However, while the

---

lion (1 Pet 5:8), a serpent (Rev 12:9, 15; 20:2), and a seven-headed dragon (Rev 12:3), Ps 91:13 is particularly noteworthy.

[33] It is not altogether clear whether Isa 27:1 is the opening verse of a new chapter (so English versions, following MT), the concluding verse of the preceding segment or chapter, or a short transitional or independent unit. In any case, the eschatological thrust of this verse (and its context) is not in any doubt.

[34] Admittedly, much depends on precisely how the satan's activity is viewed in relation to Yahweh, who calls attention to Job (1:8; 2:3a), places Job in the satan's power (1:12; 2:6) and assumes responsibility for the disaster that befell his faithful servant (2:3b; cf. 42:11b).

satan is not mentioned explicitly again, commentators generally find subtle echoes of his suggestions in the advice of Job's wife (Job 2:9), and that of his "friends" in the ensuing dialogue. There seems to be at least some unintentional complicity with the satan, for had Job listened to their bad advice, he would actually have proved the satan's misgivings to be correct. Thus while certainly not center stage after the initial two chapters, the satan may play a more significant "cameo" role in the rest of the book than often assumed. Indeed, a few infer that he resurfaces several times—including the crucial final chapters—chiefly in the guise of Leviathan.[35]

Accordingly, to determine what role, if any, Satan or the devil plays in the book of Job, the book's depiction of Leviathan (in association with other such "chaos" creatures) warrants particular attention. While the second Yahweh speech contains the longest depiction of Leviathan in Scripture, this fantastic creature is also explicitly mentioned or alluded to (see 7:12; cf. 26:13) several times previously. The first of these earlier occurrences is in Job's opening soliloquy (ch. 3), where Leviathan is clearly an entity associated with negative, de-creative or destructive activity (3:6–10). "Day-cursers" are those perceived as putting a hex on certain days (i.e., making them ill-omened),[36] but here Job somewhat ironically wishes they had done so for the day of his birth, and associates them with those who "rouse Leviathan"—one of the figures deemed "capable of destroying light [that] are invoked to return Job's day of origin to dark oblivion."[37] The particular activity of Leviathan that might achieve this is left

---

[35] Notably, Fyall, *Now my Eyes*, and (following Fyall) Christopher Ash, *Job: The Wisdom of the Cross*, Preaching the Word (Wheaton, IL: Crossway, 2014).

[36] Given the associations between Leviathan/sea dragons (תַּנִּין) and Yam (Sea) in other biblical (cf. Isa 27:1; 51:9–10; Ps 74:13–14; 89:10–11) and ancient Near Eastern texts (such as the Ugaritic Baal Myth), it might initially seem tempting to emend יוֹם (day) here to יָם (sea), as per BHS apparatus, making the parallelism with Leviathan more explicit in this verse. However, as Habel observes, there are good reasons to conclude that יוֹ is the superior reading and should thus be retained: (i) the emphasis on 'day' and 'night' in these verses; (ii) the allusion back to the מְרִירֵי יוֹם in v. 5; (iii) the obvious wordplay (יוֹם/יָם) and irony ("day-cursers" hexing the *night* Job was conceived) in these verses. Norman C. Habel, *The Book of Job*, OTL (Philadelphia: Westminster, 1985), 101.

[37] Habel, *Book of Job*, 108. For Habel (pp.108–109), "In rousing Leviathan ... Job is calling up the powers of chaos to destroy the created order and return the night of his creation to the domain of primordial absence." Clines, however, rightly rejects this suggestion, arguing rather that the malediction relates only to one particular night, which Job wishes were so eclipsed by the realm of darkness that

unstated, but "may well be the swallowing up of the sun or moon, i.e., the causing of eclipses."[38] In any case, Leviathan is clearly understood to be a provokable creature with ominous and significant destructive power.

The same is true of Job 41, by far the most detailed portrayal of the OT chaos monster. Leviathan is a creature that can be provoked by people (v. 10 [MT 2]), but this is self-evidently inadvisable (cf. vv. 8–9 [MT 40:32–41:1]). While such a creature does not intimidate or frighten God (v.10b–11 [MT 2–3]; cf. 40:19), it clearly does and should terrify human beings, who are no match for it (vv.33–34); they are unable to catch, tame or subdue it—regardless of what equipment (vv.1–2, 7 [MT 40:26–27, 31]) or weaponry they have at their disposal (vv. 25–29 [MT 17–21]). Any hope of exercising control over, negotiating with, or overpowering this fearsome creature is simply vain (cf. vv.3–5, 13–25 [MT 40:27–29, 41:5–17]). Like Behemoth, the *Beast* par excellence (40:15–24),[39] Leviathan is emphatically portrayed as beyond human— though not divine—control.

But while certainly depicted as dangerous, there is nothing said here that might lead us to believe that Leviathan should be considered *evil*.[40] Nor, it must be said, is any explicit connection made between Leviathan (or Behemoth) and the satan character of the book's prologue. This, however, has not stopped some scholars from

---

that "conception of life would have been either impossible or ill-omened." David J. A. Clines, *Job 1– 20*, WBC 17 (Dallas: Word, 1989), 87.

[38] So Clines (*Job 1–20*, 87), who notes that the sun and Leviathan-like sea-monsters were considered enemies, drawing evidence from T. H. Gaster, *Myth, Legend, and Custom in the Old Testament* (New York: Harper and Row, 1969), 787–88, and John Day, *God's Conflict with the Dragon and the Sea*, UCOP 35 (Cambridge: Cambridge University Press, 1985), 45.

[39] Rather than being two separate beasts, some have construed Behemoth and Leviathan as *complementary* descriptions of a single monster. Wilcox, for example, argues that "Leviathan *is* Behemoth" pointing out that "Often in Hebrew poetry a general term is mentioned first and then the specific is given. So here: Behemoth is the beast (par excellence). Which beast? Answer: Leviathan". John T. Wilcox, *The Bitterness of Job: A Philosophical Reading* (Ann Arbor: University of Michigan Press, 1989), 231 n.7.

[40] However, Habel (*Book of Job*, 365) follows Cyrus Gordon's proposal that such is the nuance of בָּרִיחַ (cf. Arabic *barḥ* "evil") in the phrase נָחָשׁ בָּרִיחַ back in Job 26:13. See C. H. Gordon, "Near East Seals in Princeton and Philadelphia," *Or* 22 (1953): 242–50 (243–44); idem, "Leviathan: Symbol of Evil," in A. Altmann (ed), *Biblical Motifs* (Cambridge, MA: Harvard University Press, 1966), 1–10.

drawing such connecting dots or conclusions. Fyall, for example, has mounted such a case, concluding from suggested ancient Near Eastern parallels that "along with Behemoth, [Leviathan] is the embodiment of cosmic evil itself, that power ceaselessly opposed to God and his purposes. As Behemoth probably is to be identified with Mot, the god of death, so it appears that in Leviathan we have another guise of Satan."[41] Fyall's case—in support of such a supernaturalistic (rather than naturalistic) interpretation—can be summarized briefly as follows:

(a) A naturalistic interpretation of these creatures (e.g., in terms of a hippopotamus and a crocodile) makes "the second speech rather tedious and repetitive and Job's reaction to it difficult to explain."[42] It mistakenly dismisses the "surreal" imagery as "poetic flourish," and fails to pay sufficient attention to the cosmic tensions reflected elsewhere in the book, not least in the heavenly court of the prologue.

b) The context suggests that Behemoth and Leviathan are aspects of the problem that Job must contend with, were he to assume God's role as universal king.[43] Chapter 38 has highlighted "the mysteries inherent in creation itself."[44] The following chapter "deals with untamed nature and shows not so much that animals are evil, but that animal life is shot through with a savagery which mirrors ultimate cosmic evil."[45] The immediate context underlines Job's inability to dispatch the wicked to the underworld (40:1–14). The introductory "behold" (40:15) links the depiction of Behemoth with the aforementioned underworld.[46]

---

[41] *Now my Eyes*, 157. Following Fyall, Ash (*Job: The Wisdom of the Cross*) likewise equates "the satan" of Job 1 and 2 with Satan/the devil.

[42] *Now my Eyes*, 127. Fyall approvingly cites Bernard Shaw's cynical observation that God, when challenged about his justice and providence, really needs to do better than retort: "You can't make a hippopotamus can you?" (ibid.)

[43] Fyall, *Now my Eyes*, 130.

[44] Ibid.

[45] Ibid.

[46] Ibid. Fyall subsequently notes (*Now my Eyes*, 157) that these same two figures of cosmic

c) Comparative (Ugaritic & Egyptian) evidence suggests that the description of Behemoth in Job reflects a typical ancient Near Eastern depiction of Mot. In some of the Ugaritic material, Mot is "quite explicitly what he is elsewhere implicitly, the personification of death simpliciter, humanity's ultimate enemy, a primaeval earth monster every whit as dangerous to mankind as the primaeval sea monster Yam Nahar."[47]

d) Information and images in the earlier part of the book are crucial to a correct interpretation of both creatures. In the case of Leviathan, Job 9:24 is key: Job can see only one possible author of his calamities, but in the divine speeches at the end of the book his true adversary (introduced to readers in the prologue) is finally unmasked.[48] Moreover, Leviathan is expressly mentioned back in Job 3:8 (cf. 7:12), where a supernatural meaning is accepted by all commentators.[49]

e) Unlike his friends, Job gives due weight to other powers lurking in the cosmos: e.g., Leviathan (3:8), Rahab (9:13; 26:12), Yam and Tannin (7:12), and the slippery [i.e., elusive] serpent (נָחָשׁ בָּרִיחַ 26:13).[50] The full significance of these more sinister elements in God's creation is now being drawn out in a way that no-one in the book, including Job, has fully appreciated.

f) Other Leviathan passages in the OT (cf. Ps 74:12–17; 104:26; Isa 27:1) also depict this menacing creature as totally under the control of God.[51]

---

evil (i.e. death and the devil), are affiliated in Heb 2:14, where the focus is Christ's decisive victory over them.

[47] Fyall, *Now my Eyes*, 133, citing J. C. L. Gibson (ed.), *Canaanite Myths and Legends*, Second edition (Edinburgh: T&T Clark, 1978), 18. As Fyall recognizes (134), however, the critical theological question this raises is this: how can God be said to create "death" or "evil"? The post-OT concept of a demonic Satan figure (see below) in some measure addresses this monotheistic conundrum.

[48] Fyall, *Now my Eyes*, 141, 163, 174.

[49] Ibid., 142–43.

[50] Ibid., 168.

[51] Ibid., 168–71.

Although these are certainly stimulating arguments, Fyall's identification of Leviathan with Satan may arguably be overstated. As previously noted, with one possible exception there is little, if anything, in the book of Job to suggest that Leviathan is an intrinsically *evil* creature (it is one thing to be dangerous and another to be evil). Nor is there anything in the book of Job that indicates a clear connection between this detailed depiction of Leviathan at the end of the book and the depiction of "the satan" in the prologue. But perhaps most significantly, many would challenge Fyall's suggested correlation between "the satan" character in the book of Job, and the personal embodiment of evil, the arch-enemy of God and his people (i.e., NT's Satan or the devil).[52] However, while we must beware of simply importing a later and more developed understanding of Satan back into the text of Job, we may well have some evidence here, at least in embryonic form (as with Gen 3), of this emerging figure in Scripture. In other words, like the fantastic beasts we have just considered,[53] this is arguably another motif which the NT (and particularly, Revelation) uses to construct its conflated portrayal of the adversary which the Seed of promise has (and will)

---

[52] As well as most recent commentaries, for a fairly typical scholarly approach to "the satan" in Job—presented as a valid member of the divine council legitimately carrying out a particular task ("challenging the validity of a moral order in which the righteous unfailingly prosper"), see Peggy L. Day, *An Adversary in Heaven: śāṭān in the Hebrew Bible*, HSM 43 (Cambridge, MA: Harvard University Press, 1988), 69–106 (81). There is obviously insufficient space in the present chapter for a detailed discussion of the meaning and significance of the שטן lexeme, or a more comprehensive examination of the developing concept, personality and role of Satan/the devil in Scripture. For more on the latter, see the concise discussion in Page, *Powers of Evil*, 11–42. See further, Brown, *The God of This Age*, 21–60. For more speculative approaches, see T. J. Wray and Gregory Mobley, *The Birth of Satan: Tracing the Devil's Biblical Roots* (New York: Palgrave Macmillan, 2005), and Miguel A. De La Torre and Albert Hernández, *The Quest for the Historical Satan* (Minneapolis: Fortress, 2011).

[53] "Lilith" (Isa 34:14; Heb. לִילִית, trans. "night creatures" by NIV) might possibly warrant some attention because of its significance in ancient Near Eastern literature and much later (Talmudic and Kabbalistic) Judaism. In one such ancient Near Eastern example, the Sumerian tale of "Gilgamesh and the Huluppu Tree" (dating back to ca. 2000 BC), the coveted tree—with a bird at the top and a snake's nest at its base—is inhabited (in the middle) by Lilith, "a maid of desolation." Gilgamesh kills the snake, and forces the bird and Lilith to flee, enabling Inanna to cut down the tree and construct the furniture she prizes. In the later Jewish literature, Lilith and the serpent are combined, along with a bird-like ability to fly away. She becomes a seductive and demonic power, sometimes being conflated with both the tempting serpent of Gen 3 and "Sammael" (i.e., a synonym for the devil). For more on these post-NT Jewish Lilith legends, see Soza, *Lucifer, Leviathan, Lilith*, 85–100.

overcome. So, it is to this last piece of the biblical jigsaw that we must now briefly turn.

4. Satan(s) in the OT and Beyond

A nefarious, malevolent protagonist such as the NT Satan is seldom, if ever, explicitly mentioned in the OT. In fact, in the vast majority of its OT occurrences, the Hebrew lexeme (שטן) refers to human adversaries.[54] Of the rest, a celestial "satan" sometimes functions expressly as God's agent (cf. the Angel of the LORD in Num 22:22, 32). A "divinely-delegated" role (e.g., to spy or examine, on analogy with an ancient Near Eastern royal court) is also suggested by some interpreters in the case of the celestial satan who features in the prologue of Job.[55] However, in this case it is less clear that the satan is simply following divine orders; his refusal to accept Yahweh's initial verdict (Job 2:3–4), and the alacrity with which he afflicts Job, might possibly suggest otherwise. Even so, the text makes clear that the satan is operating on each occasion within the constraints of divine permission (Job 1:12; 2:6), and as already noted, Yahweh assumes ultimate responsibility (Job 2:3b). The identity of "the satan" figure in Zechariah may seem less ambiguous, for here Yahweh rebukes him for his accusatory stance (Zech 3:1–2).[56] However, it is possible to argue that, as in Job, this figure is simply verbalizing the apprehension of others (in this case, that of the community rather than God himself) that sin has disqualified them, an apprehension this particular vision addresses.

Thus, in each of the three cases we have considered so far, identifying a celestial OT "satan" with the NT's evil counterpart is not quite so straightforward as might first appear. This is likewise true in the case of David's adversary appearing in 1 Chr 21:1, which most interpreters (and English translations) do recognize as an OT

---

[54] 1 Sam 29:4; 2 Sam 19:23; 1 Kgs 5:4; 11:14, 23, 25; Ps 109:6; cf. also Pss 38:21; 71:13; 109:4, 20, 29.

[55] E.g., Longman, for whom the scene is not to be taken literally. Tremper Longman III, *Job*, BCOTWP (Grand Rapids: Baker, 2012), 52, 91–92.

[56] The presence of the definite article (השטן) in both Job and Zechariah suggests to some that there it must refer to a particular role—such as "prosecutor" or "challenger"—rather than to a *malevolent* spiritual being. However, such reasoning is somewhat specious since over half the NT occurrences of Satan also attract the definite article.

text employing שטן as a proper noun (i.e., Satan). Given the late dating of Chronicles, most scholars would not consider a use of Satan here as anachronistic; after all, it would simply be a harbinger of the more developed understanding of evil powers that blossoms in Second Temple Judaism.[57] However, while שטן may quite possibly refer to such a celestial being in 1 Chr 21:1, it is also possible to interpret the anarthrous noun here as a *human* adversary (cf. 1 Sam 29:4; 1 Kgs 5:4), whose hostile intent prompted David to conduct his military census.

As is clear from this brief discussion of its OT usage, the precise meaning of "satan" in the relevant OT texts must therefore be determined on contextual and exegetical grounds. But however it is understood, Page is surely correct to infer that the concept of Satan is not nearly so well developed or as significant in the OT as was the case in later Judaism and the NT.[58]

The final pieces of the puzzle, almost certainly informing the NT interpretation of Gen 3:15, are thus the conceptual developments that evidently took place within the intertestamental era. As previously mentioned,[59] it was in this period that the devil (διάβολος) was first expressly associated with action of the snake in Gen 3:

> for God created us for incorruption,
> and made us in the image of his own eternity,
> but *through the devil's envy* death entered the world,
> and those who belong to his company experience it.
> (Wis 2:23–24 NRSV, emphasis mine)[60]

---

[57] Why Satan (whether as a proper noun or even conceptually, as a nefarious fallen angel or "watcher") makes no such appearance in Daniel (allegedly dating from even later, in the second century BC), must surely be an anomaly for such scholars.

[58] Sydney H. T. Page, *Powers of Evil: A Biblical Study of Satan and Demons* (Grand Rapids: Baker, 1995), 11.

[59] See note 4 above.

[60] Though some see the allusion being to Abel's murder in Gen 4, a reference to Gen 3 (esp. v.19) is more likely, especially since LXX's διάβολος "regularly translates 'Satan', with whom the Eden serpent became equated." Day, "The Serpent in the Garden," n.p.

In a similar vein, the later Similitudes of Enoch (dated somewhere in the first or early second century AD) associates the temptation narrative with a "fallen" angel (Gadreel):

> And the third was named Gadreel: he it is who showed the children of men all the blows of death, *and he led astray Eve*, and showed [the weapons of death to the sons of men] the shield and the coat of mail, and the sword for battle, and all the weapons of death to the children of men. (1 En. 69:6, emphasis mine)[61]

Even more explicit is the Apocalypse of Moses—a first century Jewish "biography" of Adam and Eve covering the period from their expulsion from Eden to the time of their deaths. Here Eve explains her past encounter with the snake as follows: "The devil answered me through the mouth of the serpent" (Apoc. Mos. 17:4; my tr.).[62]

As this latter material clearly demonstrates, it is also during this particular era (Second Temple Judaism) that we first meet the unambiguous concept of a supernatural antagonist or displaced heavenly being who orchestrates and/or heads up opposition to God. Rather than consistently using the same nomenclature, this evil being is identified by a number of different epithets, including "Satan." For example, 1 Enoch assigns such a nefarious leadership role (i.e., over the "Watchers" or fallen angels) first to Semiaza and to Aza[z]el, and in its final chapters (37–71, the Similitudes), to Satan(s). Jubilees refers to "the ruler of the demons" (17:6) as

---

[61] Unless otherwise indicated, citations of the Pseudepigrapha are from Craig Evans, *Pseudepigrapha English*, Copyright © Oaktree Software, Inc. 2009; Version 2.7, Accordance 11.2.

[62] The *Apocalypse of Moses* is the Greek version of *the Life of Adam and Eve*. Both in the immediate context (16:1–5) and on two other occasions (cf. 28:3; 39:1–3) this book suggests that Satan/the devil operated through the serpent to deceive the woman—and subsequently through the voice of the woman to deceive the man (21:3)—to have Adam and Eve expelled from the garden. It is hard to determine if this material had any bearing on contemporary NT books, or vice versa; possibly both are reflecting some degree of what—by then—were common theological assumptions and ideas. See also 3 Bar. 9:7 (cf. 4:8), according to which "the devil being envious deceived [Adam] through his vine" (4:8) and "[the vine] was near Sammael when he *took the serpent as a garment*" (9:7, emphasis added).

Mastema ("hatred"),[63] Beliar ("without light"), and Satan.[64] Other such nomenclature includes Sammael (3 Baruch; Martyrdom of Isaiah), Belial/Beliar (Testimony of the Twelve Patriarchs; the Lives of the Prophets; Qumran's *Damascus Rule*) and Beelzebul (Testament of Solomon). However, while this demonic figure is referred to in extrabiblical material by several different names, all these undoubtedly allude to the same evil nemesis that we meet in the NT: the arch-opponent of God, the accuser of God's people, and the personal embodiment of evil. As such, it is unsurprising that there also, "the devil, or Satan," should be plainly identified with the primeval snake of Gen 3 "who leads the whole world astray" (Rev 12:9). However, this is not simply a matter of a piecemeal human *creation* and *development* of a spiritual concept.[65] Rather, as we have sought to demonstrate in our analysis above, this reflects the final stages in God's progressive *revelation* of a spiritual reality—first disclosed through a crafty snake, but subsequently revealed by means of even more fantastic beasts, and possibly also through some of the OT's more enigmatic characters—such as the celestial "satan."

5. Conclusion

The enmity envisaged in Gen 3:15 has usually been traced through the *spiritual* offspring of the snake and that of the woman, and rightly so. After all, it is through such offspring that the promise here finds its climactic fulfilment in the cross of Christ. Even that, however, was clearly a struggle of cosmic proportions (cf. Col 2:15), and thus we must avoid reducing what Gen 3:15 envisages merely to the physical realm. Rather, as Revelation so graphically suggests, the enmity between the snake and the woman, *and* their respective offspring, finds ultimate expression in the colossal conflict between Satan and God's anointed King (Rev 12:4–5, 10–11). While this

---

[63] A cognate (שׂטם) of שׂטן.

[64] *Pace* Wray and Mobley (*The Birth of Satan*, 104), references to Satan (and Mastema) appear throughout the book rather than only towards the end: cf. 10:11; 23:29; 40:9; 46:2; 50:5. Admittedly, however, 10:11 underlines that Satan has taken over from Mastema as the supreme evil spiritual being on earth.

[65] As is claimed throughout Wray and Mobley, *Birth of Satan*.

cosmic battle has its inception in Gen 3, and finds its climax in Christ's victory over sin, death and the devil (Col 2:13–15; Heb 2:14–15), one significant aspect of its trajectory in Scripture has largely been overlooked: the recurring biblical motifs of serpents and dragons—symbols of the spiritual and supernatural opposition that is finally vanquished by "the seed of the woman," just as God had promised in Gen 3.

BIBLIOGRAPHY

Abernethy, Andrew T. *The Book of Isaiah and the Kingdom of God: A Thematic-Theological Approach*. Downers Grove, IL: InterVarsity Press Academic, 2016.

Akin, Daniel L. *1, 2, 3 John*, NAC. Nashville: B&H, 2001.

Albertz, Rainer. "Exile as Purification. Reconstructing the 'Book of the Four'." Pages 232–51 in *Thematic Threads in the Book of the Twelve*. Edited by Paul L. Redditt and Aaron Schart. Berlin: de Gruyter, 2003.

Albright, W. F. "Are the Ephod and the Teraphim Mentioned in Ugaritic Literature?" *BASOR* 83 (1941): 39–42.

_____. "The Psalm of Habakkuk." Pages 1–18 in *Studies in Old Testament Prophecy*. Edited by H. H. Rowley. Edinburgh: T&T Clark, 1950.

Alexander, T. Desmond. "From Adam to Judah: The Significance of the Family Tree in Genesis." *EvQ* 61 (1989): 5–19.

_____. "Genealogies, Seed, and the Compositional Unity of Genesis." *TynBul* 44 (1993): 255–70.

_____. "Messianic Ideology in the Book of Genesis." Pages 19–39 in *The Lord's Anointed: Interpretation of Old Testament Messianic Texts*. Edited by P. E. Satterthwaite, R. S. Hess and G. J. Wenham. Grand Rapids: Baker, 1995.

_____. "Further Observations on the Term 'Seed' in Genesis." *TynBul* 48 (1997): 363–67.

_____. "Royal Expectations in Genesis to Kings: Their Importance for Biblical Theology." *TynBul* 49 (1998): 191–212.

_____. *The Servant King: The Bible's Portrait of the Messiah*. Leicester: InterVarsity Press, 1998.

_____. "Seed." Pages 769–73 in *New Dictionary of Biblical Theology: Exploring the Unity & Diversity of Scripture*. Edited by T. Desmond Alexander, *et al*. Downers Grove, IL: InterVarsity Press, 2000.

_____. "The Regal Dimension of the תלדות־יעקב: Recovering the Literary Context of Genesis 37–50." Pages 196–212 in *Reading the Law: Studies in Honour of Gordon J Wenham*. Edited by J. G. McConville and Karl Möller. LHBOT 461. Edinburgh: T&T Clark, 2007.

_____. *From Eden to the New Jerusalem. Exploring God's Plan for Life on Earth*. Nottingham: Inter-Varsity Press, 2008.

_____. *From Paradise to the Promised Land: An Introduction to the Pentateuch*. Third edition. Grand Rapids: Baker Academic, 2012.

_____. *The City of God and the Goal of Creation*. SSBT. Wheaton, IL: Crossway, 2018.

Amerding, Carl Edwin. "Habakkuk." Pages 603–48 in *Jonah, Nahum, Habakkuk, Zephaniah: The Expositor's Bible Commentary*. Edited by Tremper Longman III and David E. Garland. Revised ed. Grand Rapids: Zondervan, 2008.

Andersen, Francis I., *Habakkuk*. AB. Garden City, NY: Doubleday, 2001.

Andersen, Francis I. and David Noel Freedman. *Hosea: A New Translation with Introduction and Commentary*. AB. Garden City, NY: Doubleday, 1980.

Ash, Christopher. *Job: The Wisdom of the Cross*, Preaching the Word. Wheaton, IL: Crossway, 2014.

Attridge, H. W. *The Epistle to the Hebrews*, Hermeneia. Philadelphia: Fortress, 1989.

Aune, David E. *Revelation 6–16*, WBC 52b. Nashville: Thomas Nelson, 1998.

Bahnsen, Greg L. *Van Til's Apologetic: Readings and Analysis*. Phillipsburg, NJ: Presbyterian & Reformed, 1998.

Baker, David W "Further Examples of the *Waw Explicativum*." VT 30 (1980): 129–36.

_____. "Explicative *wāw*." Pages 890–92 in Volume 1 of *Encyclopedia of Hebrew Language and Linguistics*. Leiden: Brill, 2013.

Barker, William D. *Isaiah's Kingship Polemic: An Exegetical Study of Isaiah 24–27*. Tübingen: Mohr Siebeck, 2014.

Barnard, Jody. *The Mysticism of Hebrews. Exploring the Role of Jewish Apocalyptic Mysticism in the Epistle to the Hebrews*, WUNT 2/331. Tübingen: Mohr Siebeck, 2012.

Barr, James. *The Semantics of Biblical Language*. London: Oxford University Press, 1961.

_____. *Biblical Words for Time*. London: SCM, 1962 (2nd ed. 1969).

_____. "The Image of God in the Book of Genesis—A Study of Terminology." *BJRL* 51 (1968–1969): 11–26.

Bateman, Herbert W. IV, Gordon H. Johnston, and Darrell L. Bock. *Jesus the Messiah: Tracing the Promises, Expectations, and Coming of Israel's King*. Grand Rapids: Kregel, 2012.

Bauckham, Richard. "Reading Scripture as a Coherent Story." Pages 38–53 in *The Art of Reading Scripture*. Edited by Ellen F. Davis and Richard B. Hays. Grand Rapids: Eerdmans, 2003.

Bauer, David R. *The Structure of Matthew's Gospel*. JSNTSup 31. Sheffield: Almond, 1989.

Bauer, W., F. W. Danker, W. F. Arndt, & F. W. Gingrich. *A Greek-English Lexicon of the New Testament and Other Early Christian Literature*. Chicago: University of Chicago Press, 2001.

Beale, G. K. "Did Jesus and His Followers Preach the Right Doctrine from the Wrong Texts?" *Them* 14 (1989): 89–96.

_____. ed. *The Right Doctrine from the Wrong Texts? Essays on the Use of the Old Testament in the New*. Grand Rapids: Baker, 1994.

_____. *The Book of Revelation*, NIGTC. Grand Rapids: Eerdmans, 1999.

_____. *The Temple and the Church's Mission: A Biblical Theology of the Dwelling Place of God*. NSBT 17. Downers Grove, IL: InterVarsity Press, 2004.

_____. *A New Testament Biblical Theology: The Unfolding of the Old Testament in the New*. Grand Rapids: Eerdmans, 2011.

Becker, Joachim, *Gottesfurcht im Alten Testament,* AnBib 25. Rome: Papal Biblical Institute, 1965.

Beckwith, Roger T. *The Old Testament Canon of the New Testament Church: And Its Background in Early Judaism*. Grand Rapids: Eerdmans, 1984.

Begg, Christopher T. "The Significance of Jehoiachin's Release: A New Proposal." *JSOT* 36 (1986): 49–56.

Berges, Ulrich. "Zion and the Kingship of YHWH in Isaiah 40–55." Pages 95–119 in *"Enlarge the Site of Your Tent": The City as Unifying Theme in Isaiah*. Edited by Annemarieka van der Woude and A. van Wieringen. Leiden: Brill, 2011.

_____. "Kingship and Servanthood in the Book of Isaiah." Pages 159–78 in *The Book of Isaiah: Enduring Questions Answered Anew*. Edited by Richard J. Bautch and J. Todd Hibbard. Grand Rapids: Eerdmans, 2014.

Bernard, J. H. *A Critical and Exegetical Commentary on the Gospel according to St. John*, 2 vols. ICC. Edinburgh: T&T Clark, 1928.

Bird, Michael F. *Romans*. SGBC. Grand Rapids: Zondervan, 2016.

Blaising, Craig A. and Darrell L. Bock. *Progressive Dispensationalism*. Wheaton, IL: Bridgepoint, 1993.

Blenkinsopp, Joseph. *Isaiah 1–39*, AB. New York: Doubleday, 2000.

_____. *David Remembered: Kingship and National Identity in Ancient Israel*. Grand Rapids: Eerdmans, 2013.

Block, Daniel I. "Will the Real Gideon Please Stand Up?" *JETS* 40 (1997): 353–66.

_____. *Judges, Ruth*. NAC. Nashville: Broadman & Holman, 1999.

_____. "My Servant David: Ancient Israel's Vision of the Messiah." Pages 17–56 in *Israel's Messiah in the Bible and the Dead Sea Scrolls*. Edited by Richard S. Hess and M. Daniel Carroll R. Grand Rapids: Baker Academic, 2003.

_____. *Ruth: The King is Coming, Exegetical Commentary on the Old Testament*. Grand Rapids: Zondervan, 2015.

Blomberg, Craig L. *The Historical Reliability of the New Testament*. B&H Studies in Christian Apologetics. Nashville: B&H Academic, 2016.

Boda, Mark J. "Figuring the Future: The Prophets and the Messiah." Pages 35–74 in *The Messiah in the Old and New Testaments*. Edited by Stanley E. Porter. Grand Rapids: Eerdmans, 2007.

_____. *A Severe Mercy: Sin and Its Remedy in the Old Testament*. Winona Lake, IN: Eisenbrauns, 2009.

_____. "Scat! Exilic Motifs in the Book of Zechariah." Pages 161–80 in *The Prophets Speak on Forced Migration*. Edited by Mark J. Boda, *et al*. Atlanta: SBL Press, 2015.

_____. *The Book of Zechariah*. NICOT. Grand Rapids: Eerdmans, 2015.

Bodner, Keith. *An Ark on the Nile: Beginning of the Book of Exodus*. Oxford and New York: Oxford University Press, 2016.

Brettler, Mark. "The Structure of 1 Kings 1–11." *JSOT* 49 (1991): 87–97.

Brown, Derek R. "'The God of peace will shortly crush Satan under your feet': Paul's Eschatological Reminder in Romans 16:20a." *Neotestamentica* 44.1 (2010): 1–14.

_____. *The God of This Age: Satan in the Churches and Letters of the Apostle Paul*, WUNT 2.409. Tübingen: Mohr Siebeck, 2015.

Brown, Raymond E. *The Gospel according to John*. 2 vols. AB. New York: Doubleday, 1966, 1970.

_____. *The Epistles of John*. AB. New York: Doubleday, 1982.

Bruce, F. F. *The Book of the Acts*. NICNT. Grand Rapids: Eerdmans, 1988.

_____. "Habakkuk." Pages 831–96 in volume 2 of *The Minor Prophets: An Exegetical and Expository Commentary*. Edited by Thomas Edward McComiskey. 3 vols. Grand Rapids: Baker, 1993.

Brueggemann, Walter. *The Prophetic Imagination*. 2nd edition. Minneapolis: Fortress, 2001.

Bush, Frederic W. *Ruth, Esther*. WBC 9. Dallas: Word, 1996.

Butler, T. *Joshua*. WBC 7. Waco, TX: Word, 1983.

Carroll R., M. Daniel. "New Lenses to Establish Messiah's Identity? A Response to Daniel I. Block." Pages 71–81 in *Israel's Messiah in the Bible and the Dead Sea Scrolls*. Edited by Richard S. Hess and M. Daniel Carroll R. Grand Rapids: Baker Academic, 2003.

Carson, D. A. *The Gospel according to John*, PilNTC. Grand Rapids: Eerdmans, 1991.

Casey, Maurice. "Christology and the Legitimating Use of the Old Testament in the New Testament." Pages 42–64 in *The Old Testament in the New Testament*. Edited by Stephen Moyise. JSNTSup 189. Sheffield: Sheffield Academic, 2000.

Cefalu, Rita F. "Royal Priestly Heirs to the Restoration Promise of Genesis 3:15: A Biblical Theological Perspective on the Sons of God in Genesis 6." *WTJ* 76 (2014): 351–70.

Chan, Michael J. "Joseph and Jehoiachin: On the Edge of the Exodus." *ZAW* 125 (2013): 566–77.

Charlesworth, James H. (ed.). *The Messiah: Developments in Earliest Judaism and Christianity*. Minneapolis: Fortress, 1992.

_____. *The Good and Evil Serpent*. AYBRL. New Haven: Yale University Press, 2010.

Chase, Mitchell L. "The Genesis of Resurrection Hope: Exploring Its Early Presence and Deep Roots." *JETS* 57 (2014): 467–80.

Childs, Brevard. *Biblical Theology of the Old and New Testaments: Theological Reflection on the Christian Bible*. Minneapolis: Fortress, 1993.

Chisholm, Robert B., Jr. *From Exegesis to Exposition: A Practical Guide to Using Biblical Hebrew*. Grand Rapids: Baker, 1998.

Chrysostom, John. "Homilies of St. John Chrysostom, Archbishop of Constantinople, on the Epistle of St. Paul to the Romans." Pages 335–564 in *Saint Chrysostom: Homilies on the Acts of the Apostles and the Epistle to the Romans* (Vol. 11). Edited by P. Schaff; Trans. J. B. Morris, W. H. Simcox, & G. B. Stevens. New York: Christian Literature Company, 1889.

Ciampa, Roy E. "Deuteronomy in Galatians and Romans." Pages 99–117 in *Deuteronomy in the New Testament*. Edited by M. J. J. Menken and Steve Moyise. London: T&T Clark, 2007.

Clements, R. E. "The Messianic Hope in the Old Testament." *JSOT* 43 (1989): 3–19.

Clendenen, E. Ray. "Salvation by Faith or Faithfulness in the Book of Habakkuk?" *BBR* 24 (2014): 505–13.

Clines, David J. A. *Job 1–20*. WBC 17. Dallas: Word, 1989.

_____. "The Psalms and the King," *TSF Bulletin* 71 (1975): 1–6; reprinted in his *On the Way to the Postmodern*. Two volumes. Sheffield: Sheffield Academic, 1998, 2:687–700.

Cockerill, Gareth Lee. "Melchizedek without Speculation: Hebrews 7:1–25 and Genesis 14:17–24." Pages 128–44 in *A Cloud of Witnesses. The Theology of Hebrews in its Ancient Contexts*. Edited by Richard Bauckham et al. LNTS 387. London: T&T Clark, 2008.

Cogan, Mordechai. *Understanding Hezekiah King of Judah: Rebel King and Reformer*. Jerusalem: Carta, 2017.

Cohen, C. "The Neo-Assyrian Elements in the First Speech of the Biblical Rab-Šaqe." *IOS* 9 (1979): 32–48.

Cohick, Lynn H. *Ephesians: A New Covenant Commentary*. Cambridge: Lutterworth, 2013.

Collins, A. Y. *Mark: A Commentary*. Hermeneia. Minneapolis: Fortress, 2007.

Collins, C. John (Jack). "A Syntactical Note (Genesis 3:15): Is the Woman's Seed Singular or Plural?" *TynBul* 48 (1997): 139–48.

_____. *Genesis 1–4: A Linguistic, Literary, and Theological Commentary*. Phillipsburg: Presbyterian & Reformed, 2006.

Collins, John J. *The Scepter and the Star: The Messiahs of the Dead Sea Scrolls and Other Ancient Literature*. New York: Doubleday, 1995.

Conrad, Edgar W. *Reading Isaiah*, OBT. Minneapolis: Fortress, 1991.

Craigie, P. C. *Psalms 1–50*. WBC 19. Waco, TX: Word, 1983.

Cranfield, C. E. B. *Mark: The Cambridge Greek Testament Commentary*. Cambridge: Cambridge University Press, 1972.

_____. *A Critical and Exegetical Commentary on the Epistle to the Romans, vol. 2*. London: T&T Clark, 1979.

Critchlow, James R. *Looking Back for Jehoiachin: Yahweh's Cast-Out Signet*. Africanus Monographs. Eugene, OR: Wipf & Stock, 2013.

Cross, Frank Moore. "The Themes of the Book of Kings and the Structure of the Deuteronomistic History." Pages 274–90 in *Canaanite Myth and Hebrew Epic: Essays in the History of the Religion of Israel*. Cambridge, MA: Harvard University Press, 1997.

Cruse, D. A. *Lexical Semantics*. Cambridge: Cambridge University Press, 1986.

Cuffey, Kenneth H. *The Literary Coherence of the Book of Micah: Remnant, Restoration, and Promise*. LHBOTS 611. New York: Bloomsbury T&T Clark, 2015.

Culpepper, R. Alan. "The Pivot of John's Prologue." *NTS* 27 (1980–1981): 1–31.

Culy, Martin M. *I, II, III John*. Waco, TX: Baylor University Press, 2004.

Cunha, Wilson de Angelo. "'Kingship' and 'Kingdom': A Discussion of Isaiah 24:21–23 and 27:12–13." Pages 61–75 in *Formation and Intertextuality in Isaiah 24–27*. Edited by J. Todd Hibbard and Hyun Chul Paul Kim. Atlanta: SBL Press, 2013.

Cuvillier, Elian. *L'évangile de Marc*. Bible en face. Bayard: Labor et Fides, 2002.

Dahood, M. *Psalms 1–50*. AB 16. New York: Doubleday, 1966.

Daly-Denton, Margaret. *David in the Fourth Gospel: The Johannine Reception of the Psalms*. Arbeiten zur Geschichte des antiken Judentums und des Christentums 47. Leiden: Brill, 1999.

Davies, John A. *A Royal Priesthood: Literary and Intertextual Perspectives on an Image of Israel in Exodus 19.6*. JSOTSup 395. London; New York: Continuum International, 2004.

Davies, W. D. and Dale C. Allison. *A Critical and Exegetical Commentary on the Gospel according to Saint Matthew*. 3 vols. ICC. London; New York: T&T Clark, 1988–1997.

Day, Edward. "The Deuteronomic Judgements of the Kings of Judah." *JTS* 11 (1909): 74–83.

Day, John. *God's Conflict with the Dragon and the Sea*. UCOP 35. Cambridge: Cambridge University Press, 1985.

_____. "The Serpent in the Garden of Eden and its Background" in The Bible and Interpretation
http://www.bibleinterp.com/articles/2015/04/day398028.shtml.

Day, Peggy L. *An Adversary in Heaven: Śāṭān in the Hebrew Bible*. HSM 43. Cambridge, MA: Harvard University Press, 1988.

De La Torre, Miguel A. and Albert Hernández. *The Quest for the Historical Satan*. Minneapolis: Fortress, 2011.

Dearman, J. Andrew. *The Book of Hosea*. NICOT. Grand Rapids: Eerdmans, 2010.

deClaissé-Walford, N., R. A. Jacobson, B. L. Tanner. *The Book of Psalms*. NICOT. Grand Rapids: Eerdmans, 2014.

Delamarter, Steve. "The Death of Josiah in Scripture and Tradition: Wrestling with the Problem of Evil?" *VT* 54 (2004): 29–60.

Delitzsch, Franz. *Biblical Commentary on the Psalms, Vol 3*, 2nd ed. Edinburgh: T&T Clark, 1881.

_____. *A New Commentary on Genesis*. Minneapolis: Klock & Klock 1978; orig. T&T Clark, 1888.

Dempster, Stephen G. *Dominion and Dynasty: A Biblical Theology of the Hebrew Bible*. NSBT 15. Downers Grove, IL: InterVarsity Press; Leicester: Apollos, 2003.

_____. "Canons on the Left and Canons on the Right: Finding a Resolution in the Canon Debate." *JETS* 52:1 (2009): 47–77.

_____. "Hannah's Song, A New World Order and the Right Side of History." Pages 3–32 in *Ecclesia Semper Reformanda Est: A Festschrift on Ecclesiology in Honour of Stanley K. Fowler*. Edited by Michael A. G. Haykin, David G. Barker, and Barry H. Howson. Hamilton: Joshua Press, 2016.

_____. *Micah*. Grand Rapids: Eerdmans, 2017.

_____. "The Tripartite Canon and the Theology of the Prophetic Word." Pages 74–94 in *Interpreting the Old Testament Theologically: Essays in Honor of*

Willem A. VanGemeren. Edited by Andrew T. Abernethy. Grand Rapids: Zondervan, 2018.

Dodd, C. H. *According to the Scriptures.* London: Nisbet & Co., 1952.

Donaldson, Terence L. *Jesus on the Mountain: A Study in Matthew Theology.* Sheffield: JSOT Press, 1985.

du Preez, J. "'Sperma autou' in 1 John 3:9." *Neot* 9 (1975): 105–12.

Dubovsky, Peter. "The Assyrian Downfall through Isaiah's Eyes (2 Kings 15–23): The Historiography of Representation." *Bib* 89 (2008): 1–16.

Duhm, B. *Das Buch Jesaja.* HKAT 3/1, 4th ed. Göttingen: Vandenhoeck & Ruprecht, 1922 (German orig. 1892).

Duling, D. C. "Solomon, Exorcism, and the Son of David." *HTR* 68 (1975): 235–52.

Dumbrell, W. J. "'In those days there was no king in Israel; every man did what was right in his own eyes.' The Purpose of the Book of Judges Reconsidered." *JSOT* 25 (1983): 23–33.

Edwards, James R. *Mark.* PilNTC. Grand Rapids: Eerdmans, 2002.

Eichrodt, Walther. *Theology of the Old Testament.* Philadelphia: Westminster Press, 1961.

Ellingworth, Paul. *The Epistle to the Hebrews*, NIGTC. Grand Rapids: Eerdmans; Carlisle: Paternoster, 1993.

Ellis, E. Earle. "Jesus' Use of the Old Testament and the Genesis of New Testament Theology." *BBR* 3 (1993): 59–75.

Emmerson, Grace I., *Hosea: An Israelite Prophet in Judean Perspective.* JSOTSup 28. Sheffield: JSOT Press, 1984.

Eskenazi, Tamara C., and Tikva Frymer-Kensky. *Ruth.* Jewish Publication Society Bible Commentary. Philadelphia: Jewish Publication Society, 2011.

Eslinger, Lyle. "Inner-Biblical Exegesis and Inner-Biblical Allusion: The Question of Category." *VT* 42 (1992): 47–58.

Evans, Craig A. "*Obduracy* and the *Lord's Servant*: Some Observations on the Use of the Old Testament in the Fourth Gospel." Pages 221–36 in *Early Jewish and Christian Exegesis: Studies in Memory of William Hugh Brownlee. Edited by*

Craig A. *Evans* and William F. Stinespring. Homage 10. Atlanta: Scholars Press, 1987.

_____. "Jesus and Zechariah's Messianic Hope." Pages 373–388 in *Authenticating the Activities of Jesus*. Edited by Bruce Chilton and Craig A. Evans. Leiden: Brill, 1999.

_____. *Mark 8:27–16:20*. WBC 34B. Nashville: Thomas Nelson, 2001.

_____. "The Old Testament in the New." Pages 130–45 in *The Face of New Testament Studies*. Edited by Scot McKnight and Grant Osborne. Grand Rapids: Baker Academic, 2004.

_____. *Pseudepigrapha English*, Copyright © Oaktree Software, Inc. 2009; Version 2.7, Accordance 11.2.

Evans, Paul S. "The End of Kings as Presaging an Exodus: The Function of the Jehoiachin Epilogue (2 Kgs 25:27–30) in Light of Parallels with the Joseph Story in Genesis." *McMaster Journal of Theology and Mission* 16 (2014): 65–100.

Even-Shoshan, Avraham. *A New Concordance of the Old Testament: Thesaurus of the Language of the Bible Hebrew and Aramaic Roots, Words, Proper Names, Phrases and Synonyms*. 2nd ed. Jerusalem: Kiryat Sefer, 1997.

Exum, J. C. "The Centre Cannot Hold: Thematic and Textual Instabilities in Judges." *CBQ* 52 (1990): 410–31.

Fewell, Danna Nolan. "Sennacherib's Defeat: Words at War in 2 Kings 18:13–19:37," *JSOT* 34 (1986): 79–90.

Firth, David G. "Messiah." Pages 537–44 in *Dictionary of the Old Testament: Prophets*. Edited by M. J. Boda and J. G. McConville. Downers Grove, IL: InterVarsity Press, 2012.

Fischer, Irmtraud. "The Book of Ruth: A 'Feminist' Commentary to the Torah?" Pages 24–49 in *Ruth and Esther: A Feminist Companion to the Bible, Second Series*. Edited by Athalya Brenner. Sheffield: Sheffield Academic, 1999.

Flint, P. W. "Unrolling the Dead Sea Psalms Scrolls." Pages 229–50 in *The Oxford Handbook of the Psalms*. Edited by W. P. Brown. Oxford: Oxford University

Press, 2014.

Foster, Lewis. "Luke-Acts." Pages 1568–1630 in *Zondervan New American Standard Study Bible*. Edited by Kenneth L. Barker, et al. Grand Rapids: Zondervan, 1999.

Foulkes, Francis. *Ephesians*. TNTC. London: Tyndale Press, 1963.

France, R. T. *The Gospel of Mark*. NIGTC. Grand Rapids: Eerdmans, 2002.

Freedman, David N. "The Law and the Prophets." Pages 251–59 in *Congress Volume: Bonn, 1962*. Edited by G. W. Anderson et al. VTSup 9. Leiden: Brill, 1963.

_____. "The Earliest Bible." Pages 29–37 in *Backgrounds for the Bible*. Edited by Michael Patrick O'Connor and David N. Freedman. Winona Lake, IN: Eisenbrauns, 1987.

_____. *The Unity of the Hebrew Bible*. Ann Arbor: University of Michigan Press, 1993.

Fretheim, Terence E. *Reading Hosea-Micah: A Literary and Theological Commentary*. Macon, GA: Smyth & Helwys, 2013.

Fukuyama, Francis. *The End of History and the Last Man*. New York: Penguin, 1992. https://www.amazon.com/End-History-Last-Man/dp/0743284550.

Fyall, Robert S. *Now My Eyes Have Seen You: Images of Creation and Evil in the Book of Job*, NSBT 12. Leicester: Apollos, 2002.

Garr, Randall E. "Image and Likeness in the Tell Fakhariyeh Inscription." *IEJ* 50 (2000): 227–34.

Garrett, Duane A. *Hosea, Joel*. NAC 19A. Nashville: Broadman & Holman, 1997.

Gaster, T. H. *Myth, Legend, and Custom in the Old Testament*. New York: Harper and Row, 1969.

Gaventa, Beverly R. "The Cosmic Power of Sin in Paul's Letter to the Romans: Toward a Widescreen Edition," *Interpretation* 58 (2004): 229–240.

Gelston, A. "Kingship in the Book of Hosea." Pages 71–85 in *Oudtestamentische Studiën 19*. Edited by A. S. Van der Woude. Leiden: Brill, 1974.

Gese, Harmut. *Lehre und Wirklichkeit in der alten Weisheit: Studien zu den Sprüchen Salomos und zu dem Buche Hiob*. Tübingen: Mohr Siebeck, 1958.

Gibson, J. C. L. (ed.). *Canaanite Myths and Legends*. 2nd edition. Edinburgh: T&T Clark, 1978.

Glatt-Gilead, David A. "The Deuteronomistic Critique of Solomon: A Response to Marvin A. Sweeney." *JBL* 116 (1997): 700–703.

Gnilka, Joachim. *Das Evangelium nach Markus, 2. Teilband: Mk 8.27–16,20*. 5th ed. Neukirchen: Neukirchener, 1999.

Gnuse, Robert C. *No Tolerance for Tyrants: The Biblical Assault on Kings and Kingship*. Collegeville: Liturgical Press, 2011.

Goldingay, John. *Old Testament Theology. Volume One. Israel's Gospel*. Downers Grove, IL: InterVarsity Press, 2003.

Goldsworthy, G. "The Problem of the Accommodation of Wisdom Literature in the Writing of Old Testament Theologies," Unpublished Th.M. Research Paper, Union Theological Seminary in Virginia, 1970.

_____. "Empirical Wisdom in Relation to Salvation-History in the Psalms," Unpublished Ph.D. thesis, Union Theological Seminary in Virginia, 1973.

_____. "'THUS SAYS THE LORD!'—The Dogmatic Basis of Biblical Theology." Pages 25–40 in *God Who is Rich in Mercy: Essays Presented to Dr. D. B. Knox*. Edited by P. T. O'Brien and D. G. Peterson. Homebush West, NSW: Lancer Books, 1986.

_____. *Gospel and Wisdom: Israel's Wisdom Literature in the Christian Life*. Exeter: Paternoster, 1987 (now included in *The Goldsworthy Trilogy*. Milton Keynes: Paternoster, 2000).

_____. *The Son of God and the New Creation*. Short Studies in Biblical Theology. Wheaton, IL: Crossway, 2015.

Gordon, C. H. "Near East Seals in Princeton and Philadelphia." *Or* 22 (1953): 242–50.

_____. "Leviathan: Symbol of Evil." Pages 1–10 in *Biblical Motifs*. Edited by A. Altmann. Cambridge, MA: Harvard University Press, 1966.

Gordon, R. P. "טוב." Pages 353–57 in vol. 2 of *New International Dictionary of Old Testament Theology and Exegesis*. 5 volumes. Edited by William A.

VanGemeren. Carlisle: Paternoster, 1996.

Goswell, Gregory R. "A Royal Isaianic Servant of Yahweh?" *SJOT* 31 (2017): 185–201.

_____. "'David their king': Kingship in the Prophecy of Hosea." *JSOT* 42 (2017): 213–31

_____. "Messianic Expectation in Isaiah 11." *WTJ* 79 (2017): 123–35.

_____. "David rule in the prophecy of Micah." *JSOT* (2019): 1–13.

Gray, G. B. *Isaiah I–XXVII*, ICC. Edinburgh: T&T Clark, 1912.

Gray, John. *I & II Kings*. OTL. Philadelphia: Westminster, 1976.

Grindheim, Sigurd. "Sirach and Mark 8:27–9:13: Elijah and the Eschaton." Pages 130–36 in *Reading Mark in Context: Jesus and Second Temple Judaism*. Edited by Ben C. Blackwell, John K. Goodrich, and Jason Maston. Grand Rapids: Zondervan, 2018.

Groom, Susan Anne. *Linguistic Analysis of Biblical Hebrew*. Carlisle: Paternoster, 2003.

Gruenler, R. G. "Romans." Pages 923–57 in *Evangelical Commentary on the Bible* Vol. 3. Edited by Walter A. Elwell. Grand Rapids: Baker, 1995.

Gundry, Robert H. *Mark: A Commentary on His Apology for the Cross*. Grand Rapids: Eerdmans, 1993.

Gunkel, Hermann (and Joachim Begrich), *Introduction to Psalms: The Genres of the Religious Lyric of Israel*. Trans. James D. Nogalski. Macon, GA: Mercer University Press, 1998. (German orig. *Einleitung in die Psalmen: Die Gattungen der religiösen Lyrik Israels*. Göttingen: Vandenhoeck & Ruprecht, 1933).

Guthrie, H. H. "Tithe." *IDB* 4:654–55

Haak, Robert D. *Habakkuk*. VTSup 44. Leiden: Brill, 1992.

Habel, Norman C. *The Book of Job*, OTL. Philadelphia: Westminster, 1985.

Hafemann, S. J. "Suffering." Pages 919–21 in *Dictionary of Paul and his Letters*. Edited by G. F. Hawthorne, R. P. Martin, & D. G. Reid. Downers Grove, IL: InterVarsity Press, 1993.

Hahn, Scott W. *Kinship by Covenant: A Canonical Approach to the Fulfillment of God's Saving Promises*. New Haven: Yale University Press, 2009.

Hallo, William W. and K. Lawson Younger Jr., eds. *The Context of Scripture. Volume 2. Monumental Inscriptions from the Biblical World*. Leiden: Brill, 2000.

_____. *The Context of Scripture. Volume I. Canonical Compositions from the Biblical World*. Leiden: Brill, 2003.

Ham, Clay Alan. *The Coming King and the Rejected Shepherd: Matthew's Reading of Zechariah's Messianic Hope*. New Testament Monographs 4. Sheffield: Sheffield Phoenix, 2005.

Hamilton, James M. "The Glory of God in Salvation Through Judgment: The Centre of Biblical Theology?" *TynBul* 57 (2006): 57–84.

_____. "The Messianic Music of the Song of Songs: A Non-Allegorical Interpretation." *WTJ* 68 (2006): 331–45.

_____. "The Skull Crushing Seed of the Woman: Inner-Biblical Interpretation of Genesis 3:15." *The Southern Baptist Journal of Theology* 10:2 (2006): 30–54.

Hamilton, V. P. *Handbook on the Historical Books*. Grand Rapids: Baker, 2001.

Handy, Lowell K. *The Age of Solomon: Scholarship at the Turn of the Millennium*, Studies in the History and Culture of the Ancient Near East 11. Leiden: Brill, 1997.

Hawk, L. Daniel. "Joshua." Pages 477–80 in *Dictionary of the Old Testament: Pentateuch*. Edited by T. Desmond Alexander and David W. Baker. Leicester: Inter-Varsity Press, 2003.

_____. *Ruth*. ApOTC 7B. Nottingham: Inter-Varsity Press, 2015.

Hays, J. Daniel. "If he Looks Like a Prophet, and Talks Like a Prophet, Then he Must Be … A Response to Daniel I. Block." Pages 57–69 in *Israel's Messiah in the Bible and the Dead Sea Scrolls*. Edited by Richard S. Hess and M. Daniel Carroll R. Grand Rapids: Baker Academic, 2003.

Hays, Richard B. *Echoes of Scripture in the Gospels*. Waco, TX: Baylor University Press, 2016.

Hensley, A. D. *Covenant Relationships and the Editing of the Hebrew Psalter.* LHBOTS 666. London: T&T Clark, 2018.

Hess, Richard S. *Joshua.* TOTC. Leicester: Inter-Varsity Press, 1996.

Hess, Richard S. and M. Daniel Carroll R., eds., *Israel's Messiah in the Bible and the Dead Sea Scrolls.* Grand Rapids: Baker, 2003.

Hillers, Delbert R. *Micah.* Hermeneia. Philadelphia: Fortress, 1984.

Holmes, Stephen. "The Identity Illusion." *New York Review of Books*, January 17, 2019.

Hom, Mary Katherine. *The Characterization of the Assyrians in Isaiah: Synchronic and Diachronic Perspectives*, LHBOTS 559. London; New York: T&T Clark, 2012.

House, Paul R. *Old Testament Theology.* Downers Grove, IL: InterVarsity Press, 1998.

Höver-Johag, I. "טוב *ṭôb.*" Pages 296–317 in vol. 5 of *Theological Dictionary of the Old Testament.* 16 vols. Edited by G. Johannes Botterweck and Helmer Ringren. Trans. David E. Green. Grand Rapids: Eerdmans, 1974–2018.

Hubbard, Robert L. Jr. *The Book of Ruth*, NICOT. Grand Rapids: Eerdmans, 1988.

Hung, Hedy. "The Kingship Motif in Isaiah 61:1–3." Pages 135–49 in *Torah and Tradition.* Edited by Klaas Spronk and Hans Barstad. Leiden: Brill, 2017.

Hurtado, Larry W. *Mark.* NIBC. Peabody, MA: Hendrickson, 1983.

Iser, Wolfgang. *The Act of Reading: A Theory of Aesthetic Response.* Baltimore: John Hopkins University Press, 1978.

Jacobs, Mignon R. "The Conceptual Dynamics of Good and Evil in the Joseph Story." *JSOT* 27 (2003): 309–38.

Jang, Sehoon. "Is Hezekiah a Success or Failure? The Literary Function of Isaiah's Prediction at the End of the Royal Narratives in the Book of Isaiah." *JSOT* 42 (2017): 117–35.

Janzen, David. "An Ambiguous Ending: Dynastic Punishment in Kings and the Fate of the Davidides in 2 Kings 25.27–30." *JSOT* 33 (2008): 39–58. https://doi.org/10.1177/ 0309089208094459.

_____. "The Sins of Josiah and Hezekiah: A Synchronic Reading of the Final Chapters of Kings." *JSOT* 37 (2013): 349–70.

Jassen, Alex P. *Mediating the Divine: Prophecy and Revelation in the Dead Sea Scrolls and Second Temple Judaism.* STDJ 68. Leiden: Brill, 2007.

Jenson, Philip P. "Models of Prophetic Prediction and Matthew's Quotation of Micah 5:2." Pages 189–211 in *The Lord's Anointed: Interpretation of Old Testament Messianic Texts.* Edited by Philip E. Satterthwaite, Richard S. Hess, and Gordon J. Wenham. Carlisle: Paternoster, 1995.

_____. *Obadiah, Jonah, Micah.* LHBOTS 496. New York: T&T Clark, 2008.

Jeremias, Joachim. *New Testament Theology: The Proclamation of Jesus.* Translated by J. Bowden. New York: Scribner's, 1971.

Jewett, Robert. *Romans: A commentary.* Minneapolis: Fortress, 2007.

Jobes, Karen H. *1, 2 & 3 John*, ZECNT. Grand Rapids: Zondervan, 2014.

Johnson, R. *Sacral Kingship in Ancient Israel.* Cardiff: University of Wales Press, 1955.

Johnston, P. S. "'Left in Hell'? Psalm 16, Sheol and the Holy One." Pages 213–22 in *The Lord's Anointed: Interpretation of Old Testament Messianic Texts.* Edited by Philip E. Satterthwaite, Richard S. Hess and Gordon J. Wenham. Carlisle: Paternoster, 1995.

_____. *Shades of Sheol: Death and Afterlife in the Old Testament.* Leicester: Apollos, 2002.

_____. "Distress in the Psalms." Pages 63–84 in *Interpreting the Psalms: Issues and Approaches.* Edited by P. S. Johnston and D. G. Firth. Leicester: Apollos, 2005.

_____. "Old Testament and Christ." Pages 506–10 in *New Dictionary of Christian Apologetics.* Edited by C. Campbell-Jack and G. J. McGrath. Leicester: Inter-Varsity Press, 2006.

Jones, Gwilym H. *1 and 2 Kings.* NCB. 2 vols. Grand Rapids: Eerdmans, 1984.

Jonge, Marinus de. "Messiah." Pages 777–88 in volume 4 of *Anchor Bible Dictionary.* Edited by David Noel Freedman. 6 vols. New York: Doubleday, 1992.

Joseph, Alison L. *Portrait of the Kings: The Davidic Prototype in Deuteronomistic Poetics*. Minneapolis: Augsburg Fortress: 2015.

Joüon, P. *A Grammar of Biblical Hebrew*. 2 vols. Translated and revised by T. Muraoka. Rome: Pontifical Biblical Institute, 1993.

Juel, Donald. *Messianic Exegesis: Christological Interpretation of the Old Testament in Early Christianity*. Philadelphia: Fortress, 1988.

Kalimi, Isaac. "Love of God and Apologia for a King: Solomon as the Lord's Beloved King in Biblical and Ancient Near Eastern Contexts," *JANER* 17 (2017): 28–63.

Keener, Craig S. *The Historical Jesus of the Gospels*. Grand Rapids: Eerdmans, 2009.

Kessler, Rainer. "The Twelve: Structure, Themes, and Contested Issues." Pages 207–223 in *The Oxford Handbook of the Prophets*. Edited by Carolyn J. Sharp. New York: Oxford University Press, 2016.

Kidner, D. *Psalms 73–150*, TOTC. London: Inter-Varsity Press, 1975.

Kitchen, K. A. *On the Reliability of the Old Testament*. Grand Rapids: Eerdmans, 2003.

Kline, Meredith. "Divine Kingship and Genesis 6:1-4." *WTJ* 24 (1962): 187–204.

Knoppers, Gary N. "'There Was None Like Him': Incomparability in the Books of Kings." *CBQ* 54 (1992): 411–31.

König, Adrio. *The Eclipse of Christ in Eschatology: Toward a Christ-Centered Approach*. Grand Rapids: Eerdmans; London: Marshall Morgan and Scott, 1989.

Koopmans, William T., *Haggai*. HCOT. Leuven: Peeters, 2017.

Koorevaar, Hendrik J. "Die Chronik als intendierter Abschluss des alttestamentlichen Kanons." *Jahrbuch für Evangelikale Theologie* 11 (1997): 42–76.

Köstenberger, Andreas J. *The Missions of Jesus and of the Disciples according to the Fourth Gospel*. Grand Rapids: Eerdmans, 1998.

_____. "The Destruction of the Second Temple and the Composition of the Fourth Gospel." Pages 69–108 in *Challenging Perspectives on the Gospel of John*. Edited by John Lierman. WUNT 2/219. Tübingen: Mohr Siebeck, 2006.

_____. *A Theology of John's Gospel: The Word, the Christ, the Son of God.* BTNT. Grand Rapids: Zondervan, 2009.

_____. "Lifting Up the Son of Man and God's Love for the World: John 3:16 in Its Historical, Literary, and Theological Contexts." Pages 141–59 in *Understanding the Times: New Testament Studies in the 21st Century: Essays in Honor of D. A. Carson on the Occasion of His 65th Birthday.* Edited by Andreas J. Köstenberger and Robert W. Yarbrough. Wheaton, IL: Crossway, 2011.

_____. "John's Transposition Theology: Retelling the Story of Jesus in a Different Key." Pages 191–226 in *Earliest Christian History: History, Literature, and Theology. Essays from the Tyndale Fellowship in Honor of Martin Hengel.* Edited by Michael F. Bird and Jason Maston. WUNT 2/320. Tübingen: Mohr Siebeck, 2012.

_____. "The Cosmic Trial Motif in John's Letters." Pages 157–78 in *Communities in Dispute: Current Scholarship on the Johannine Epistles.* Early Christianity and Its Literature 13. Edited by R. Alan Culpepper and Paul N. Anderson. Atlanta: Society of Biblical Literature, 2014.

Köstenberger, Andreas J. and Scott R. Swain. *Father, Son and Spirit: The Trinity and John's Gospel.* NSBT. Downers Grove, IL: InterVarsity Press, 2008.

Kruse, Colin G. *Paul's Letter to the Romans.* PilNTC. Grand Rapids: Eerdmans, 2012.

_____. *The Letters of John,* PilNTC. Grand Rapids: Eerdmans, 2000.

König, Adrio. *The Eclipse of Christ in Eschatology: Toward a Christ-Centered Approach.* Grand Rapids: Eerdmans; London: Marshall Morgan and Scott, 1989.

Laato, Antti. *Josiah and David Redivivus: The Historical Josiah and the Messianic Expectations of Exilic and Postexilic Times.* ConBOT 33. Stockholm: Almqvist & Wiksell, 1992.

Lane, William L. *The Gospel of Mark.* NICNT. Grand Rapids: Eerdmans, 1974.

Légasse, Simon. *L'évangile de Marc.* LD 5. Paris: Cerf, 1997.

Lehrer, Adrienne. *Semantic Fields and Lexical Structure,* North-Holland Linguistic

Series 11. Amsterdam: North-Holland, 1974.

Lehrer, Adrienne and Eva Feder Kittay, eds. *Frames, Fields, and Contrasts: New Essays in Semantic and Lexical Organization.* Hillsdale, NJ: L. Erlbaum Associates, 1992.

Lemaire, André, Baruch Halpern (eds.), Matthew J. Adams (associate ed.). *The Books of Kings: Sources, Composition, Historiography and Reception,* VTSup 129. Leiden: Brill, 2010.

Levine, Étan. *The Aramaic Version of Ruth.* Rome: Biblical Institute Press, 1973.

Lieu, Judith M. "What Was from the Beginning: Scripture and Tradition in the Johannine Epistles." *NTS* 39 (1993): 458–77.

_____. *I, II & III John: A Commentary.* Louisville: Westminster John Knox, 2008.

Lindars, Barnabas. *The Theology of the Letter to the Hebrews.* Cambridge: CUP, 1991.

Long, V. Philips. "Renewing Conversations: Doing Scholarship in an Age of Skepticism, Accommodation, and Specialization." *BBR* 13 (2003): 227–49.

Longenecker, Richard N. *Biblical Exegesis in the Apostolic Period.* Grand Rapids: Eerdmans, 1975. Second edition, 1999.

Longman, Tremper III. "The Case for Spiritual Continuity." Pages 161–87 in *Show them No Mercy: 4 Views on God and Canaanite Genocide.* Counterpoints. Edited by Stanley N. Gundry. Grand Rapids: Zondervan, 2003.

_____. *Job,* BCOTWP. Grand Rapids: Baker, 2012.

López, René A. "The Meaning of 'Behemoth' and 'Leviathan' in Job." *BSac* 173 (2016): 401–24.

Machinist, Peter. "Assyria and its Image in First Isaiah." *JAOS* 103 (1983): 719–37.

Maier, Paul L. *Josephus: The Essential Writing. A New Translation.* Grand Rapids: Kregel Publications, 1988.

Malone, Fred. *The Baptism of Disciples Alone: A Covenantal Argument for Credobaptism Versus Paedobaptism.* Cape Coral, FL: Founders, 2003.

Mann, C. S. *Mark: A New Translation with Introduction and Commentary.* AB 27. Garden City, NY: Doubleday, 1986.

Manns, Frederic. *"La Verité vous fera libres"*: *Etude exégétique de Jean 8,31–59*. SBFA 11. Jerusalem: Franciscan Printing Press, 1976.

Marcus, Joel. *The Way of the Lord: Christological Exegesis of the Old Testament in the Gospel of Mark*. Louisville: Westminster John Knox, 1992.

_____. *Mark 8–16: New Translation with Introduction and Commentary*. AB 27A. New Haven: Yale University Press, 2009.

Markl, Dominik. "No Future without Moses: The Disastrous End of 2 Kings 22–25 and the Chance of the Moab Covenant (Deuteronomy 29–30)." *JBL* 133 (2014): 711–28.

Marshall, I. Howard. *The Epistles of John*, NICNT. Grand Rapids: Eerdmans, 1978.

_____. "Acts." Pages 513–606 in *Commentary on the New Testament Use of the Old Testament*. Edited by G. K. Beale and D. A. Carson. Grand Rapids: Baker Academic, 2007.

Martin, R. A. "The Earliest Messianic Interpretation of Genesis 3:15." *JBL* 84 (1965): 425–27.

Martínez, Florentino García and Eibert J. C. Tigchelaar (eds.), *The Dead Sea Scrolls. Study Edition*. 2 vols. Leiden: Brill; Grand Rapids: Eerdmans, 1997, 1998.

Mathews, K. *Genesis 11:27–50:26*. NAC. Nashville: Broadman & Holman, 2005.

Matthews, Victor H. *Judges and Ruth*. New Cambridge Bible Commentary. Cambridge: Cambridge University Press, 2004.

McConville, J. Gordon. *Deuteronomy*. ApOTC. Leicester: Apollos; Downers Grove, IL: InterVarsity Press, 2002.

_____. *The Prophets*. Exploring the Old Testament, Volume 4. London: SPCK, 2002.

_____. "Hosea, Book of." Pages 338–50 in *Dictionary of the Old Testament: Prophets*. Edited by Mark J. Boda and J. Gordon McConville. Downers Grove, IL: InterVarsity Press, 2012.

_____. "Human 'Dominion' and Being 'Like God': An Exploration of Peace, Violence and Truth in the Old Testament." Pages 194–206 in *Encountering Violence in the Bible*. Bible in the Modern World 55. Edited by Markus

Zehnder and Hallvard Hagelia. Sheffield: Sheffield Phoenix, 2013.

McKane, William. *Proverbs: A New Approach*. OTL. Philadelphia: Westminster, 1970.

Meyers, Carol L. and Eric M. Meyers. *Haggai, Zechariah 1–8: A New Translation with Introduction and Commentary*. New York: Doubleday, 1987.

Meyers, Carol L. and Eric M. Meyers. *Zechariah 9–14: A New Translation with Introduction and Commentary*. New York: Doubleday, 1993.

Michaels, J. Ramsey. *Revelation*. IVPNTC. Downers Grove, IL: InterVarsity Press, 1997.

Middleton, J. Richard. *The Liberating Image: The Imago Dei in Genesis 1*. Grand Rapids: Brazos, 2005.

Milgrom, J. *Numbers*. Philadelphia: Jewish Publication Society, 1990.

Millar, J. Gary. "Victory." Pages 831–832 in *New Dictionary of Biblical Theology*. Edited by T. Desmond Alexander and Brian S. Rosner. Downers Grove, IL: InterVarsity Press, 2000.

_____. "1 & 2 Kings." Pages 491–898 in *ESV Expository Commentary*. Volume 3. *1 Samuel–2 Chronicles*. Edited by I. M. Duguid, J. M. Hamilton Jr. and J. Sklar. Wheaton, IL: Crossway, 2019.

Minear, P. S. "Far as the Curse Is Found: The Point of Rev. 12:15–16." *NovT* 33 (1991): 71–77.

Miscall, Peter D. *Isaiah*. Sheffield: Sheffield Academic, 1993.

Mitchell, D. C. *The Message of the Psalter: An Eschatological Programme in the Book of Psalms*. JSOTSup 252. Sheffield: Sheffield Academic, 2007.

Moberly, R. W. L. *Old Testament Theology: Reading the Hebrew Bible as Christian Scripture*. Grand Rapids: Baker, 2013.

Moo, Douglas J. *The Epistle to the Romans*, NICNT. Grand Rapids: Eerdmans, 1996.

_____. "Romans." Pages 291–97 in *New Dictionary of Biblical Theology*. Edited by T. Desmond Alexander and Brian S. Rosner. Downers Grove, IL: InterVarsity Press, 2000.

Morgan, Donn F. *Wisdom in the Old Testament Traditions*. Atlanta: John Knox, 1981.

Morris, Leon L. "The Theme of Romans." Pages 249–63 in *Apostolic History and the Gospel. Biblical and Historical Essays Presented to F.F. Bruce on His 60th Birthday*. Edited by W. Ward Gasque and Ralph P. Martin. Exeter: Paternoster, 1970.

_____. *The Epistle to the Romans*. Grand Rapids: Eerdmans; Leicester: Inter-Varsity Press, 1988.

_____. "Sin, Guilt." Pages 877–881 in *Dictionary of Paul and his letters*. Edited by G. F. Hawthorne, R. P. Martin, & D. G. Reid. Downers Grove, IL: InterVarsity Press, 1993.

Motyer, J. Alec. *The Prophecy of Isaiah: An Introduction and Commentary*, TOTC. Leicester: Inter-Varsity Press, 1993.

_____. *The Prophecy of Isaiah*. Leicester: Inter-Varsity Press, 1999.

Motyer, Stephen. *Your Father the Devil? A New Approach to John and the Jews*. Paternoster Biblical and Theological Monographs. Carlisle: Paternoster, 1997.

_____. "The Psalm-Quotations of Hebrews 1: A Hermeneutic-free One?" *TynBul* 50 (1999): 3–22.

_____. "The Temple in Hebrews: Is It There?" Pages 177–89 in *Heaven on Earth. The Temple in Biblical Theology*. Edited by T. Desmond Alexander and Simon Gathercole. Carlisle: Paternoster, 2004.

_____. "The Spirit in Hebrews: No Longer Forgotten?" Pages 213–27 in *The Spirit and Christ in the New Testament and Christian Theology. Essays in Honor of Max Turner*. Edited by I. Howard Marshall, Volker Rabens and Cornelis Bennema. Grand Rapids: Eerdmans, 2012.

_____. *Come Lord Jesus! A Biblical Theology of the Second Coming of Christ*. London: Apollos, 2016.

Mowinckel, Sigmund. *He that Cometh*. Trans. G. W. Anderson. Nashville: Abingdon, 1954.

_____. *The Psalms in Israel's Worship*. Trans. D. R. Ap-Thomas. 2 vols. Oxford: Basil Blackwell, 1962.

Moyise, Steve. "Intertextuality and the Study of the Old Testament in the New

Testament." Pages 14–41 in *Old Testament in the New*. Edited by Steve Moyise. JSNTSup 189. Sheffield: Sheffield Academic, 2000.

Murphy, Roland E. *The Tree of Life, An Exploration of Biblical Wisdom Literature*, third edition. Grand Rapids: Eerdmans, 2002.

Murray, Donald F. "Of All the Years the Hopes—or Fears? Jehoiachin in Babylon (2 Kings 25:27--30)." *JBL* 120 (2001): 245–65.

Nelson, Richard D. *Joshua*. Louisville: Westminster John Knox, 1997.

_____. *First and Second Kings*. Louisville: Westminster John Knox, 2012.

Newman, B. M. & E. A. Nida. *A Handbook on Paul's Letter to the Romans*. New York: United Bible Societies, 1973.

Nogalski, James D. "The Problematic Suffixes of Amos IX 11." *VT* 43 (1993): 411–18.

Noth, Martin. *Überlieferunggeschichtliche Studien: Die sammelnden und bearbeitenden Geschichtswerke im Alten Testament*. Second Edition. Tübingen: Max Niemeyer, 1957.

O'Brien, Peter T. *Colossians, Philemon*, WBC 44. Milton Keynes: Word (UK), 1987.

_____. *The Letter to the Ephesians*, PilNTC. Grand Rapids: Eerdmans, 1999.

O'Kane, Martin. *Painting the Text: The Artist as Biblical Interpreter*. Sheffield: Sheffield Phoenix, 2007.

Ortlund, Dane C. "Mark's Emphasis on Jesus' Teaching, Part 2: Eschatological Significance," *BSac* 174:696 (Sept–Dec, 2017): 412–23.

_____. "History's Dawning Light: 'Morning' and 'Evening' in Mark's Gospel and their Eschatological Significance." *JETS* 61 (2018): 493–512.

_____. "What Does It Mean to Cast a Mountain into the Sea? Another Look at Mark 11:23." *BBR* 28 (2018): 218–39.

Ortlund, Raymond C. *Proverbs: Wisdom that Works*. Wheaton, IL: Crossway, 2012

Osborne, Grant R. *Revelation*, BECNT. Grand Rapids: Baker, 2002.

Osborne, W. "Mountains." Pages 673–74 in *New Dictionary of Biblical Theology*. Edited by T. Desmond Alexander and Brian S. Rosner. Downers Grove, IL: InterVarsity Press, 2000.

Oswalt, John N. "The Nations in Isaiah." Pages 94–105 in *The Holy One of Israel: Studies in Isaiah*. Eugene, OR: Wipf and Stock, 2014.

_____. *The Book of Isaiah Chapters 1–39*, NICOT. Grand Rapids: Eerdmans, 1986.

_____. *The Book of Isaiah: Chapters 40–66*, NICOT. Grand Rapids: Eerdmans, 1998.

Page, Sydney H. T. *Powers of Evil: A Biblical Study of Satan and Demons*. Grand Rapids: Baker; Leicester: Apollos, 1995.

Painter, John. *1, 2, and 3 John*. SacPag. Collegeville: Liturgical Press, 2002.

Pakula, Martin, *Nahum, Habakkuk, & Zephaniah: The End of Evil*. Sydney: Aquila, 2014.

Pao, David W. *Acts and the Isaianic New Exodus*. Grand Rapids: Baker, 2002.

Park, Song-Mi Suzie. *Hezekiah and the Dialogue of Memory*. Minneapolis: Augsburg Fortress, 2015.

Parker, Kim I. "Solomon as Philosopher King? The Nexus of Law and Wisdom in 1 Kings 1–11." *JSOT* 53 (1992): 75–91.

Parpola, S. *Assyrian Prophecies*. SAA 9. Helsinki: Helsinki University Press, 1997.

Patterson, Richard D., *Nahum, Habakkuk, Zephaniah: An Exegetical Commentary*. Texas: Biblical Studies Press, 2013.

Patton, Matthew H. *Hope for a Tender Sprig: Jehoiachin in Biblical Theology*. Winona Lake, IN: Eisenbrauns, 2017.

Paul, Ian. "The Use of the Old Testament in Revelation 12." Pages 256–76 in *The Old Testament in the New Testament*. Edited by Steve Moyise. JSNTSup 189. Sheffield: Sheffield Academic, 2000.

Perdue, Leo G. *Wisdom and Creation: The Theology of Wisdom Literature*. Nashville: Abingdon, 1994.

Perrin, Nicholas. "Messianism in the Narrative Frame of Ecclesiastes?" *RB* 108 (2001): 37–60.

Petersen, David L. "Prophetic Rhetoric and Exile." Pages 9–18 in *The Prophets Speak on Forced Migration*. Edited by Mark J. Boda, et al. Atlanta: SBL Press, 2015.

Peterson, David G. *The Acts of the Apostles*. PilNTC. Grand Rapids: Eerdmans; Nottingham: Apollos, 2009.

_____. *Commentary on Romans*. BTCP. Nashville: Broadman & Holman, 2017.

Petterson, Anthony R. *Behold Your King: The Hope for the House of David in the Book of Zechariah*. LHBOTS 513. New York: T&T Clark, 2009.

_____. "The Shape of the Davidic Hope Across the Book of the Twelve." *JSOT* 35 (2010): 225–46.

_____. "The Flying Scroll That Will Not Acquit the Guilty: Exodus 34.7 in Zechariah 5.3." *JSOT* 38 (2014): 347–61.

_____. "A New Form-Critical Approach to Zechariah's Crowning of the High Priest Joshua and the Identity of "Shoot" (Zechariah 6:9–15)." Pages 285–304 in *The Book of the Twelve and the New Form Criticism*. Edited by Mark J. Boda, M. H. Floyd, and C. M. Toffelmire. Atlanta: SBL, 2015.

_____. *Haggai, Zechariah & Malachi*. ApOTC 25. Nottingham: Apollos, 2015.

Provan, Iain. "The Messiah in the Book of Kings." Pages 67–85 in *The Lord's Anointed: Interpretation of Old Testament Messianic Texts*. Edited by P. E. Satterthwaite, Richard Hess and Gordon J. Wenham. Carlisle: Paternoster, 1995.

Provan, Iain, V. Philips Long, and Tremper Longman III. *A Biblical History of Israel*. Louisville: Westminster John Knox, 2003, 2nd edition, 2015.

Rad, Gerhard von. "Josephgeschichte und ältere Chokma." Pages 120–27 in *Congress Volume Copenhagen 1953*. Edited by G. W. Anderson et al. VTSup 1. Leiden: Brill, 1953.

_____. *Old Testament Theology*, 2 vols. Trans. D. M. G. Stalker. Edinburgh: Oliver and Boyd, 1962.

_____. "The Deuteronomic Theology of History in 1 and 2 Kings." Pages 205–21 in *The Problem of the Hexateuch and Other Essays*. Edinburgh; London: Oliver and Boyd, 1966.

_____. *Genesis: A Commentary*. OTL. Philadelphia: Westminster Press, 1972.

Rapaport, Uriel, and Paul L. Redditt. "Maccabeus." Page 454 in volume 4 of *Anchor Bible Dictionary*. Edited by David Noel Freedman. 6 vols. New York: Doubleday, 1992.

Richelle, Matthieu. "Un triptyque au cœur du livre de Michée (Mi 4–5)." *VT* 62 (2012): 232–47.

Roberts, J. J. M. "The Old Testament's Contribution to Messianic Expectations." Pages 39–51 in *The Messiah: Developments in Earliest Judaism and Christianity*. Edited by J. H. Charlesworth. Minneapolis: Fortress, 1992.

Robertson, O. Palmer, *The Books of Nahum, Habakkuk, and Zephaniah*. NICOT. Grand Rapids: Eerdmans, 1990.

Ron, Zvi. "The Genealogical List in Ruth." *JBQ* 38 (2010): 85–92.

Rose, W. H. "Messiah." Pages 565–68 in *Dictionary of the Old Testament: Pentateuch*. Edited by T. Desmond Alexander and David W. Baker. Downers Grove, IL: InterVarsity Press, 2003.

Rosenberg, Roy A. "The Slain Messiah in the Old Testament." *ZAW* 99 (1987): 259–61.

Rosner, Brian S. "Biblical Theology." Pages 3–11 in *New Dictionary of Biblical Theology*. Edited by T. Desmond Alexander and Brian S. Rosner. Nottingham: Inter-Varsity Press, 2000.

_____. *Paul and the Law: Keeping the Commandments of God*. Downers Grove, IL: InterVarsity Press, 2013.

Sailhamer, John H. *The Pentateuch as Narrative: A Biblical-Theological Commentary*. Grand Rapids: Zondervan, 1992.

_____. *Introduction to Old Testament Theology: A Canonical Approach*. Grand Rapids: Zondervan, 1995.

_____. "Creation, Genesis 1–11, and the Canon." *BBR* 10 (2000): 89–106.

_____. "The Messiah and the Hebrew Bible." *JETS* 44 (2001): 5–23.

_____. "Biblical Theology and the Composition of the Hebrew Bible." Pages 25–37 in *Biblical Theology: Retrospect and Prospect*. Edited by Scott J.

Hafemann. Downers Grove, IL: InterVarsity Press, 2002.

_____. *The Meaning of the Pentateuch: Revelation, Composition, and Interpretation*. Downers Grove, IL: InterVarsity Press, 2009.

Sakenfeld, Katharine Doob. *Ruth*, Interpretation. Louisville: Westminster John Knox, 1999.

Sanday, William and Arthur C. Headlam. *A critical and exegetical commentary on the Epistle to the Romans*. Edinburgh: T&T Clark, 1902.

Sanders, E. P. *Paul and Palestinian Judaism*. Minneapolis: Fortress, 1977.

Sasson, Jack M. *Ruth, A New Translation with a Philological Commentary and a Formalist-Folklorist Interpretation*. Baltimore and London: John Hopkins University Press, 1979.

Sawyer, J. F. A. *Semantics in Biblical Research: New Methods of Defining Hebrew Words for Salvation*, SBT 2, 24. London: SCM, 1972.

Scalise, Pamela J. "Zechariah, Malachi." Pages 177–366 in J. Goldingay and P. Scalise, *Minor Prophets II*. NIBC. Peabody: Hendrickson, 2009.

Schaefer, Konrad R. "Zechariah 14: A Study in Allusion." *CBQ* 57 (1995): 66–91.

Schipper, Jeremy. "'Significant Resonances' with Mephibosheth in 2 Kings 25:27–30: A Response to Donald F Murray." *JBL* 124 (2005): 521–29.

_____. *Ruth, A New Translation with Introduction, Notes and Commentary*. Anchor Yale Bible 7D. New Haven: Yale University Press, 2016.

Schlatter, Adolf. *Der Evangelist Johannes: Wie er spricht, denkt und glaubt*. Second edition. Stuttgart: Calwer, 1948.

Schmid, Hans Heinrich. *Gerechtigkeit als Weltordnung*. BHT 40. Tübingen: Mohr Siebeck, 1968.

_____. *Wesen und Geschichte der Weisheit*. Berlin: Alfred Töpelmann, 1966.

Schmid, Konrad. *Genesis and the Moses Story: Israel's Dual Origins in the Hebrew Bible*. Siphrut: Literature and Theology of the Hebrew Scriptures 3. Winona Lake, IN: Eisenbrauns, 2010.

Schnackenburg, Rudolf. *The Johannine Epistles: A Commentary*. New York: Crossroad, 1992.

Schreiner, Thomas R. "Editorial: Foundations for Faith." *SBJT* 5.3 (2001): 2–3.

_____. *Romans*, BECNT. Grand Rapids: Baker, 1998.

Schultz, Richard L. *The Search for Quotation: Verbal Parallels in the Prophets*, JSOTSup 180. Sheffield: Sheffield Academic, 1999.

Scobie, Charles H. H. *The Ways of Our God: An Approach to Biblical Theology*. Grand Rapids: Eerdmans, 2003.

Seitz, Christopher R. *The Goodly Fellowship of the Prophets: The Achievement of Association in Canon Formation*. Grand Rapids: Baker Academic, 2009.

Shepherd, Michael B. *A Commentary on the Book of the Twelve*. Grand Rapids: Kregel, 2018.

Silva, Moisés. "The New Testament Use of the Old Testament: Text Form and Authority." Pages 147–65 in *Scripture and Truth*. Edited by D. A. Carson and John D. Woodbridge. Grand Rapids: Zondervan, 1983.

_____. *Biblical Words and their Meanings: An Introduction to Lexical Semantics*, rev. ed. Grand Rapids: Zondervan, 1995.

Smalley, Stephen S. *1, 2, 3 John*. WBC 51. Waco, TX: Word, 1984.

Smith, Gary V. *Hosea, Amos, Micah*. NIVAC. Grand Rapids: Zondervan, 2001.

Smith, Ralph L. *Micah–Malachi*. WBC 32. Waco, TX: Word, 1984.

Sommer, Benjamin. *A Prophet Reads Scripture: Allusion in Isaiah 40–66*. Stanford: Stanford University Press, 1998.

Sonnet, J.-P. "Le motif de l'endurcissement (Isa. 6,9–10) et la lecture d' 'Isaïe'." *Biblica* 73 (1992): 208–39.

Soza, Joel R. *Lucifer, Leviathan, Lilith, and Other Mysterious Creatures of the Bible*. Lanham, MD: Hamilton Books, 2017.

Spina, Frank Anthony. "Rahab." Pages 1121–23 in vol. 4 of *New International Dictionary of Old Testament Theology and Exegesis*, 5 vols. Edited by Willem A. VanGemeren. Carlisle: Paternoster, 1996.

Stead, Michael R. "Suffering Servant, Suffering David, and Stricken Shepherd." Pages 62–83 in *Christ Died for Our Sins: Essays on the Atonement*. Edited by Michael R. Stead. Canberra: Barton Books, 2013.

_____. *Zechariah: The Lord Returns*. Reading the Bible Today. Sydney: Aquila, 2015.

Stein, Robert. *Mark*. BECNT. Grand Rapids: Baker, 2008.

Steiner, Richard C. "Genesis 49:10: On the Lexical and Syntactic Ambiguities of עַד as Reflected in the Prophecies of Nathan, Ahijah, Ezekiel, and Zechariah." *JBL 132* (2013): 33–60.

Stone, L. G. "Judges, Book of." Pages 592–606 in *Dictionary of the Old Testament: Historical Books*. Edited by B. T. Arnold and H. G. M. Williamson. Downers Grove, IL: InterVarsity Press, 2005.

Stott, John. *The Message of Romans*. BST. Nottingham: Inter-Varsity Press, 1994.

Stromberg, Jacob. *An Introduction to the Study of Isaiah*. London; New York: T&T Clark International, 2011.

_____. *Isaiah After Exile: The Author of Third Isaiah as Reader and Redactor of the Book*, Oxford Theological Monographs. Oxford: Oxford University Press, 2011.

Stuart, Douglas K. *Hosea–Jonah*. WBC 31. Waco, TX: Word, 1987.

Stuhlmacher, Peter. *Paul's Letter to the Romans*. Trans. Scott J. Hafemann. Louisville: Westminster John Knox, 1994.

Suhl, Alfred. *Die Funktion der alttestamentliche Zitate und Anspielungen im Markusevangelium*. Gütersloh: Mohn, 1965.

Swanson, D. "Qumran and the Psalms." Pages 247–61 in *Interpreting the Psalms: Issues and Approaches*. Edited by P. S. Johnston and D. G. Firth. Leicester: Apollos, 2005.

Sweeney, Marvin A. "Davidic Polemic in the Book of Judges." *VT* 47 (1997): 517–29.

_____. "The Critique of Solomon in the Josianic Edition of the Deuteronomistic History," *JBL* 114 (1995): 607–22.

_____. *The Twelve Prophets, Volume 1: Hosea, Joel, Amos, Obadiah, Jonah*. Berit Olam: Studies in Hebrew Narrative & Poetry. Collegeville: The Liturgical Press, 2000.

_____. *The Twelve Prophets, Volume 2: Micah, Nahum, Habakkuk,*

Zephaniah, Haggai, Zechariah, Malachi. Berit Olam: Studies in Hebrew Narrative & Poetry. Collegeville: The Liturgical Press, 2000.

Tate, M. E. *Psalms 51–100*. WBC 20. Dallas: Word, 1990.

Thomas, Benjamin D. *Hezekiah and the Compositional History of the Book of Kings*. FAT/2 63. Tübingen: Mohr Siebeck, 2014.

Thomas, David Winton, ed. *Documents from Old Testament Times*. New York: Harper & Row, 1961.

Thompson, Michael E. W. "Isaiah's Ideal King." *JSOT* 24 (1982): 79–88.

Todd, E. W. "The Reforms of Hezekiah and Josiah." *SJT* 9 (1956): 288–93.

Trocmé, Étienne. *L'évangile selon Saint Marc*. CNT 2. Geneva: Labor et Fides, 2000.

Tsumura, David. *Creation and Destruction: A Reappraisal of the* Chaoskampf *Theory in the Old Testament*. Winona Lake, IN: Eisenbrauns, 2005.

Van Groningen, W. *Messianic Revelation in the Old Testament*. Grand Rapids: Baker, 1990.

Van Seters, John. "The Creation of Man and the Creation of the King." *ZAW* 101 (1989): 333–42.

Van Til, Cornelius. "My Credo." Pages 3–21 in *Jerusalem and Athens: Critical Discussions on the Philosophy and Apologetics of Cornelius Van Til*. Edited by E. R. Geehan. Phillipsburg: Presbyterian and Reformed, 1971.

_____. *The Defense of the Faith*. Philadelphia: Presbyterian and Reformed, 1975.

Vermes, Geza. *The Complete Dead Sea Scrolls in English*. London: Penguin, 1998.

Vrolijk, Paul D. *Jacob's Wealth: An Examination into the Nature and Role of Material Possessions in the Jacob–Cycle (Gen 25:19–35:29)*. VTSup 146. Leiden: Brill, 2011.

Walsh, Jerome T. "The Characterization of Solomon in 1 Kings 1–5." *CBQ* 57 (1995): 471–93.

Waltke, Bruce K. "A Canonical Process Approach to the Psalms." Pages 3–18 in *Tradition and Testament. Essays in Honor of Charles L. Feinberg*. Edited by John S. Feinberg and Paul D. Feinberg. Chicago: Moody, 1981.

_____. *Genesis: A Commentary*. Grand Rapids: Zondervan, 2001.

_____. *A Commentary on Micah*. Grand Rapids: Eerdmans, 2007.

Walton, John H. "The Imagery of the Substitute King Ritual in Isaiah's Fourth Servant Song." *JBL* 122 (2003): 734–43.

_____. *The Lost World of Adam and Eve: Genesis 2–3 and the Human Origins Debate*. Downers Grove, IL: InterVarsity Press, 2015.

Walton, John H. and J. Harvey Walton, *Demons and Spirits in Biblical Theology: Reading the Biblical Text in its Cultural and Literary Context*. Eugene, OR: Wipf & Stock, 2019.

Webb, B. G. *The Book of the Judges: An Integrated Reading*. Sheffield: JSOT Press, 1987.

Wegner, Paul D. *An Examination of Kingship and Messianic Expectation in Isaiah 1–35*. Lewiston, NY: Mellen Biblical Press, 1992.

Weima, Jeffrey A. D. "The Pauline Letter Closings: Analysis and Hermeneutical Significance." *BBR* 5 (1995): 177–98.

_____. *Neglected Endings: The Significance of the Pauline Letter Closings*. Sheffield: Sheffield Academic, 1999.

_____. "The Reason for Romans: The Evidence of Its Epistolary Framework (1:1–15; 15:14–16:27)." *Review and Expositor* 100 (2003): 17–33.

_____. *Paul the Ancient Letter Writer: An Introduction to Epistolary Analysis*. Grand Rapids: Baker Academic, 2016.

Weiser, Artur. *The Psalms. A Commentary*. OTL. London: SCM, 1962.

Wenham, Gordon J. *Numbers*. TOTC. Leicester: Inter-Varsity Press, 1981.

_____. *Genesis 1–15*. WBC 1. Waco, TX: Word, 1987.

_____. *Genesis 16–50*. WBC 2. Waco, TX: Word, 1994.

_____. *Story as Torah: Reading the Old Testament Ethically*. Edinburgh: T&T Clark, 2003

_____. *Rethinking Genesis 1–11: Gateway to the Bible*, The Didsbury Lecture Series. Eugene, OR: Cascade, 2015.

Westermann, C. *Creation*. Trans. by John J. Scullion. Philadelphia: Fortress, 1974.

_____. *Praise and Lament in the Psalms*. Edinburgh: T&T Clark, 1981.

Whybray R. N. *Proverbs*. NCB. Grand Rapids: Eerdmans, 1994.

Wierzbicka, Anna. "Semantic Primitives." Pages 209–28 in *Frames, Fields, and Contrasts: New Essays in Semantic and Lexical Organization*. Edited by Adrienne Lehrer and Eva Feder Kittay. Hillsdale: L. Erlbaum Associates, 1992.

_____. *Semantics: Primes and Universals*. Oxford: Oxford University Press, 1996.

Wifall, Walter. "Gen 3:15—A Protevangelium?" *CBQ* 36 (1974): 361–65.

Wilcox, John T. *The Bitterness of Job: A Philosophical Reading*. Ann Arbor: University of Michigan Press, 1989.

Wilcox, Max. "The Promise of the 'Seed' in the New Testament and the Targumim." *JSNT* 5 (1979): 2–20.

Williams, James G. *Those Who Ponder Proverbs: Aphoristic Thinking and Biblical Literature*. Sheffield: The Almond Press, 1981.

Williams, Peter J. "The Value of Literal Bible Translation." Pages 216–34 in *Scripture and the People of God: Essays in Honor of Wayne Grudem*. Edited by John DelHousaye, Jeff T. Purswell, and John J. Hughes. Wheaton, IL: Crossway, 2018.

Williamson, H. G. M. "Recent Issues in the Study of Isaiah." Pages 21–39 in *Interpreting Isaiah*. Edited by David G. Firth and H. G. M. Williamson. Downers Grove, IL: InterVarsity Press Academic; Nottingham: Apollos, 2009.

_____. *Isaiah 6–12*. ICC. London; New York: T&T Clark, 2018.

Wilson, G. H. *The Editing of the Hebrew Psalter*. SPLDS 76. Chico, CA: Scholars Press, 1985.

_____. "The Use of Royal Psalms at the 'Seams' of the Hebrew Psalter." *JSOT* 35 (1986): 85–94.

Wilson, Ian Douglas. "Joseph, Jehoiachin and Cyrus: On Book Endings, Exoduses and Exiles, and Yehudite/Judean Social Remembering." *ZAW* 146 (2014): 521–34.

_____. "The Seat of Kingship: (Re)constructing the City in Isaiah 24–27."

Pages 395–412 in *Urban Dreams and Realities in Antiquity: Remains and Representations of the Ancient City*. Edited by Adam Kemezis. Mnemosyne Supplementum 375. Leiden: Brill, 2014.

Witherington III, Ben. *The Acts of the Apostles: A Socio-Rhetorical Commentary*. Grand Rapids: Eerdmans, 1998.

Witherington, B., III, and Diane Hyatt. *Paul's Letter to the Romans: A Socio-rhetorical Commentary*. Grand Rapids: Eerdmans, 2004.

Wolde, Ellen, van. "Texts in Dialogue with Texts: Intertextuality in the Ruth and Tamar Narratives." *BibInt* 5.1 (1997): 1–28.

Wolff, Hans Walter. *Amos the Prophet*. Philadelphia: Fortress, 1973.

_____. "The Kerygma of the Deuteronomic Historical Work." Pages 83–100 in *The Vitality of Old Testament Traditions*. Edited by W. Brueggemann and H.W. Wolff. Atlanta: John Knox, 1982.

Wray Beal, Lissa M. *1 & 2 Kings*, ApOTC. Nottingham: Apollos, 2014.

Wray, T. J. and Gregory Mobley. *The Birth of Satan: Tracing the Devil's Biblical Roots*. New York: Palgrave Macmillan, 2005.

Wright, G. Ernest. *God Who Acts, Biblical Theology as Recital*, SBT 8. London: SCM, 1952.

Yarbrough, Robert W. *1–3 John*. BECNT. Grand Rapids: Baker, 2008.

Young, E. J. *The Book of Isaiah*. 3 vols. Grand Rapids: Eerdmans, 1965.

Younger, K. L. Jr. "The Configuring of Judicial Preliminaries: Judges 1:1–2:5 and its Dependence on the Book of Joshua." *JSOT* 68 (1995): 75–92.

Zakovitch, Y. "Inner Biblical Interpretation." Pages 92–118 in *Reading Genesis: Ten Methods*. Edited by Ronald Hendel. New York: Cambridge University Press, 2010.

Ziesler, J. A. *Paul's Letter to the Romans*. TPINPC. London: SCM, 1989.

AUTHOR INDEX

SUBJECT INDEX

CPSIA information can be obtained
at www.ICGtesting.com
Printed in the USA
LVHW020720170723
752620LV00008B/189